ICASTES: MARSILIO FICINO'S
INTERPRETATION OF PLATO'S *SOPHIST*

Published with the cooperation of the

CENTER FOR MEDIEVAL AND RENAISSANCE STUDIES

University of California, Los Angeles

Icastes: Marsilio Ficino's Interpretation of Plato's *Sophist*

(Five Studies and a Critical Edition with Translation)

Michael J. B. Allen

UNIVERSITY OF CALIFORNIA PRESS
BERKELEY   LOS ANGELES   OXFORD

University of California Press
Berkeley and Los Angeles, California

University of California Press, Ltd.
Oxford, England

Copyright © 1989 by The Regents of the University of California

Library of Congress Cataloging-in-Publication Data

Allen, Michael J. B.
    Icastes: Marsilio Ficino's Interpretation of Plato's Sophist: five studies
and a critical edition with translation / by Michael J. B. Allen.
        p.   cm.
    Bibliography: p.
    Includes index.
    ISBN 0–520–06419–4 (alk. paper)
    1. Ficino, Marsilio, 1433–1499. Commentaria in Platonis Sophistam.
2. Plato. Sophist.   3. Ontology—History.   I. Ficino, Marsilio, 1433–1499.
Commentaria in Platonis Sophistam. English & Latin.   1989.   II. Title.
B384.F533A44   1989
184—dc19   89–4729
                                                                        CIP

Printed in the United States of America
1 2 3 4 5 6 7 8 9

The paper used in this publication meets the minimum requirements of
American National Standard for Information Sciences—Permanence of Paper for
Printed Library Materials, ANSI Z39.48–1984 ∞

Dedicated
To Peggy and Ian Reid
for
the golden days
at Wye

Contents

Acknowledgments

It is with warmth and pleasure that I again acknowledge my indebtedness to Professor Paul Oskar Kristeller of Columbia University. I have long been inspired by his extraordinary achievement in so many areas of humanistic studies and more particularly by his authoritative scholarship on every aspect of Ficino's work, philological, codicological, and interpretative. But I would like to thank him for the help he has given me personally over the years—always with his characteristic expedition, magnanimity, and scholarly passion—by letter, over the telephone, and pacing Florentine and Neapolitan paving stones and the campus diagonals of UCLA, Columbia, and SUNY Binghamton. *In nocte consilium.*

I am grateful also to Professor Charles Trinkaus of the University of Michigan for his generous support, and I am delighted to acknowledge my indebtedness to his wide-ranging, magisterial studies of Renaissance thinkers and notably of their views on the dignity of man.

At various stages of this typescript I have imposed tyrannically upon the goodwill, acuity, and learning of other friends and colleagues, and in particular of David Blank of UCLA, Jay Bregman of the University of Maine, Brian Copenhaver of the University of California at Riverside, and James Hankins of Harvard. To these four dedicated scholars I owe more than Platonic thanks.

I am also grateful to Steven Wight for setting up a computer version of the text edited in Part II and for establishing the apparatus; and, once again, to Nicholas Goodhue for his discriminating help at the copyediting stage.

Likewise I am grateful to UCLA's Academic Senate for various research grants. One of these made possible the Serenissima pleasures, among them Benjamin mesmerized by the piazzetta's seething pigeons, the Cima in a delicate morning light in the Madonna dell'Orto, and the zattere with Pier Pasinetti's Campari before the family's longest-ever vespertine vaporetto ride to Campo San Geremia—*a bono in bonum omnia diriguntur*.

Finally, I must turn in gratitude to my sweetest wife, Elena. At a nice psychological moment in this fourth Ficinian labor, she insisted that I buy a computer for Will's room, where I could gaze out at the hummingbird in the crimson bottlebrush and the pink-blown nectarine, and master the *fin de millénium* skill of word processing.

Versions of the fifth chapter were given as invited papers in the autumn of 1987 to a seminar at Yale and to a conference organized by SUNY Binghamton's Center for Medieval and Early Renaissance Studies. I wish to thank both institutions for their hospitality on those genial occasions, and in particular to acknowledge the kindness of Professor and Mrs. George Hunter and of Professor Mario Di Cesare.

Santa Monica, 13 March 1988

Introduction

The enormously influential Florentine scholar-philosopher Marsilio Ficino (1433–1499) was the architect of Renaissance Platonism and its leading theorist of the soul and of the soul's ascent to the divine by way of magic, music, philosophy, and love. Along with other Plato commentaries, his unfinished *Sophist* Commentary was first published in Florence in 1496 in a volume entitled *Commentaria in Platonem*. It is the best guide, as we might predict, to his interpretation of the *Sophist,* one of Plato's most difficult dialogues but, according to a distinguished modern interpreter, an "unusually constructive" one.[1] However, it is also a vital source, though hitherto neglected, for a full understanding of Ficino's ontology, demonology, and magic, and of his theories of art, imitation, and the imagination. As such, it offers us an intriguing perspective on the Florentine's profound and enduring impact on Renaissance thought and culture.

This book is an attempt to explore Ficino's views on the *Sophist* and to assess his *Sophist* Commentary as an independent treatise. The ancillary second part presents a critical edition and a translation of the text, based on the *editio princeps* of 1496. The first part, consisting of five studies, explores major topics that the dialogue raised for Ficino and tries to unravel his complicated responses to them.

I begin with Ficino's perspective on the dialogue and its position in the Platonic canon, and with the unexpectedly pivotal role it played in an interesting controversy in the 1490s with Pico della Mirandola, the other philosophical star in the Medicean circle who

---

1. Kenneth M. Sayre, *Plato's Analytic Method* (Chicago and London, 1969), p. 215. Throughout I shall be using the translation by Francis M. Cornford in his *Plato's Theory of Knowledge: The "Theaetetus" and "Sophist" of Plato Translated with an Introduction and Running Commentary* (London, 1935; reprint, New York, 1957); it is also available in *The Collected Dialogues of Plato Including the Letters,* ed. Edith Hamilton and Huntington Cairns (Princeton, 1961), pp. 957–1017. For the Greek text I shall be using the edition by J. Burnet in the Oxford Classical Text edition of Plato (Oxford, 1900 ff.), 1:357–442.

is traditionally regarded as Ficino's *complatonicus*. This controversy concerned the all-important question of the primacy of the One over Being, the metaphysical issue that lay at the heart of the centuries-old quarrel between the Neoplatonists, the standard-bearers of Platonism, and the radical Aristotelians, a quarrel which Pico entered, to Ficino's regret and surprise, on the Aristotelian side, albeit with the irenic aim of reconciling Plato with Aristotle.

My second chapter examines Ficino's encounter with the greatest interpreter of the *Sophist* in antiquity, the third-century Alexandrian-Roman founder of Neoplatonism, Plotinus, whose *Enneads* he translated and commented on throughout the 1480s, having been urged to do so by the exhortations of Pico himself. Plotinus he regarded as another Plato and on occasions as more profound, if that were possible, than his master, even admiring the density and difficulty of Plotinus's style. For Plotinus the *Sophist* was Plato's masterpiece of ontology and second only, in its strictly metaphysical insights, to the *Parmenides*. Ficino was deeply committed to Plotinus's vision of being and embraced it in large part as his own, though his Christian faith compelled him to make some signal modifications, many of which we can see adumbrated in the various chapters of his Commentary. Had he completed this, it would have necessarily been the most developed expression of his ontology; even in its skeletal form, it is a revealing treatise.

Another more elusive and more speculative debt is the subject of chapter 3. This is devoted to the Neoplatonists who succeeded Plotinus, and notably to Iamblichus and Proclus, thinkers who shared his ontological preoccupations with the dialogue but who turned their attention also to other questions in their attempt to define its major theme and to understand its composite structure. My primary concern here is with the scholion that Ficino found accompanying the Greek text of the dialogue in the manuscripts he consulted and that he attributed to Proclus. The scholion provided him, ironically, with a very un-Plotinian perspective, redefining the role and nature of the sophist in terms of the arcane and intricate motif of the sublunar demiurge.

The fourth chapter turns to a theme which literary scholars particularly associate with the *Sophist*: Plato's involved discussion of icastic and phantastic art and their mutual relationship. Directly or indirectly this discussion made an impact on a number of Renaissance theorists of art, particularly later in the sixteenth century, and Mazzoni and Sidney are only the most obvious figures that spring to mind. Ficino's understanding of this theme is best revealed in certain key passages from his *Platonic Theology,* his magnum opus written in 1469–1474 but first published in 1482 in Florence. There we see him also addressing the cognate issues of the hierarchy of the arts and skills, the relationship of the artist to the Creator and to Nature, and the relationship of objects to images, human and divine.

The question of images also preoccupies my fifth chapter, which focusses on a long and remarkable analysis at the end of Ficino's *Sophist* Commentary. There Ficino examines what he sees as the implications of Plato's knotty passage at 266B ff. on *eidôla,* which, like objects themselves, are the creation of "a wonderful skill" or "divine contrivance," a phrase which Ficino renders more literally as "the skill of the demons." The implications of this interpretation, particularly for an understanding of the Ficinian view of the imagination, take us far from the world of modern Plato scholarship into one reflecting characteristically Renaissance attitudes and themes and predicated on the assumption that Plato was also a theorist of magic and demonology, two areas of inquiry which Ficino predictably regarded as intrinsic to, and legitimately part of, Platonic philosophy. It enables us to glimpse a very different Ficino from the thinker whose primary allegiance was to Plotinus's austere ontological preoccupations.

Treating as they do of ontology, of the figure of the sophist in its manifold senses, of man as icastes and phantastes, of the phantastic art of the demons, and of the demons' rule over the imagination, my five studies cover the principal sources of Ficino's attraction to the *Sophist.* They also present us with a largely unfamiliar, essentially Neoplatonic interpretation that is at the same time peculiarly Ficinian. Deeply indebted to the ancient commentators, it is nevertheless the product of the Florentine Quattrocento and articulates some of the special features of its Platonism. In this independent relationship to the past, the Ficinian *Sophist* replicates the situation that obtains, as I have suggested elsewhere, with the Ficinian *Phile-bus, Phaedrus, Parmenides,* and *Timaeus,* and, it is generally ac-knowledged, with the Ficinian *Symposium.*[2] In interpreting all six dialogues Ficino turned at various times to Plotinus and to the later *Platonici* principally to seek support for, or elaboration of, his own views, which were nicely sensitive to the difficulties the *Platonici* presented for a Christian apologist. The Renaissance *Sophist* was not entirely Ficino's, as the dramatic case of Pico will demon-strate, but he put his stamp indelibly upon it. The full-scale, detailed commentary he had first intended was never written; but the sub-stance of his interpretation, together with its unexpected extensions, emerges quite clearly from the materials he mustered for the 1496 volume and from earlier, cognate passages in his *Platonic Theology* to enhance our understanding of his philosophy and of its extra-ordinary impact on the intellectual and cultural life of an entire epoch.

Ficino's interpretation thus constitutes, I shall argue, a signal mo-ment in the historical fortune of a dialogue that scholars have gen-erally regarded in the past as a rewarding but technical treatise lacking the irony, the drama, and the imaginative inventiveness of such literary masterpieces in the Platonic canon as the *Symposium,*

2. *Marsilio Ficino: The Philebus Commentary* (Berkeley, Los Angeles, London, 1975; rev. ed., 1979); "Two Commentaries on the *Phaedrus:* Ficino's Indebtedness to Hermias," *Journal of the Warburg and Courtauld Institutes* 43 (1980), 110–129; *Marsilio Ficino and the Phaedran Charioteer* (Berkeley, Los Angeles, London, 1981); *The Platonism of Marsilio Ficino* (Berkeley, Los Angeles, London, 1984); "Ficino's Theory of the Five Substances and the Neoplatonists' *Parmenides,*" *Journal of Medieval and Renaissance Studies* 12.1 (1982), 19–44; "The Second Ficino-Pico Controversy: Parmenidean Poetry, Eristic and the One," in *Marsilio Ficino e il ritorno di Platone: Studi e documenti,* ed. Gian Carlo Garfagnini, 2 vols. (Florence, 1986), pp. 417–455; "Marsilio Ficino's Interpretation of Plato's *Timaeus* and Its Myth of the Demiurge," in *Supplementum Festivum: Studies in Honor of Paul Oskar Kristel-ler,* ed. James Hankins, John Monfasani, and Frederick Purnell, Jr. (Binghamton, N.Y., 1987), pp. 399–439; and "Cosmogony and Love: The Role of Phaedrus in Ficino's *Symposium* Commentary," *Journal of Medieval and Renaissance Studies* 10.2 (1980), 131–153.

May I ask the reader's forbearance for the number of references to my own work in this study and take the opportunity to note errors in *The Platonism of Ficino* that have come to my attention: p. 18 n. 41.6 du<1>cibus [*em.*]; p. 28 n. 63.6 Cf. Seneca; p. 35 n. 83.4 (18.39); pp. 35.7 and 37.5 274C ff.; p. 37.17 text; p. 54 n. 43.3 This; p. 63.16 birth; p. 91.1up complication; p. 103.3 soul's tomb; p. 121 n. 22.1up *Heptaplus* 2.2; p. 151.18 Ficino; p. 182.9up analyses; p. 185 n. 1.3 and p. 268.25 scolastiques; p. 193 n. 25.2-4 *saturus nous* . . . and that Pico used in a letter to him (printed in Ficino's *Opera,* p. 889.4). Ficino often punned on Pico; p. 220.4 the species in the body; p. 243.1 passages as; p. 267.1 *omit* of.

the *Protagoras,* and the *Apology.*[3] For the Ficinian *Sophist* emerges
from this study as itself a luminous and sublime work in that canon
and as one of the repositories of Plato's deepest theological mysteries. As such, I believe we should henceforth set it beside other
major dialogues that Ficino reinterpreted as a revealing guide to

3. Predictably, this traditional view has been modified somewhat in recent years. For a
revealing commentary on the dialogic drama, see especially Stanley Rosen, *Plato's "Sophist" : The Drama of Original and Image* (New Haven, Conn., 1983). In the last quarter-century
the *Sophist* has become a favorite text, moreover, for analytically oriented philosophers and
for those concerned with addressing the issues they raise, particularly whether Plato had in
mind an existential or a predicative use of "being." See, for instance: John L. Ackrill,
"Symplokê Eidôn," Bulletin of the Institute of Classical Studies in the University of London 2
(1955), 31–35, reprinted in *Studies in Plato's Metaphysics,* ed. Reginald E. Allen (London
and New York, 1965), pp. 199–206, and in *Plato I, Metaphysics and Epistemology,* ed.
Gregory Vlastos (Garden City, N.Y., 1970), pp. 201–209; Reginald E. Allen, "Plato and
the Copula: *Sophist* 251–259," *Journal of Hellenic Studies* 77 (1957), 1–6, reprinted in his
Studies in Plato's Metaphysics, pp. 207–218, and in Vlastos, *Plato I,* pp. 210–222; Reginald
E. Allen, "Participation and Predication in Plato's Middle Dialogues," *Philosophical Review*
69 (1960), 147–164, reprinted in his *Studies in Plato's Metaphysics,* pp. 43–60; Seth Ben-
ardete, "Plato's *Sophist* 223b1–7," *Phronesis* 5 (1960), 129–139; idem, *The Being of the
Beautiful: Plato's Theaetetus, Sophist and Statesman, Translated with Commentary* (Chicago,
1984); Richard S. Bluck, *Plato's "Sophist" : A Commentary,* ed. Gordon C. Neal (Manches-
ter, Eng., 1975); Lambertus Marie de Rijk, *Plato's "Sophist" : A Philosophical Commentary*
(Amsterdam and New York, 1986); Wolfgang Detel, *Platons Beschreibung des falschen
Satzes in Theätet und Sophistes,* Hypomnemata: Untersuchungen zur Antike und ihrem
Nachleben, Heft 36 (Göttingen, 1972); Michael Frede, *Prädikation und Existenzaussage:
Platons Gebrauch von "ist" und "ist nicht" im Sophistes,* Hypomnemata: Untersuchungen
zur Antike und ihrem Nachleben, Heft 18 (Göttingen, 1967); W. K. C. Guthrie, *A History
of Greek Philosophy,* vol. 5 (Cambridge, 1978), pp. 122–163; R. Ketchum, "Participation
and Predication in the *Sophist* 251–260," *Phronesis* 23 (1978), 42–62; Jacob Klein, *Plato's
Trilogy: Theaetetus, the Sophist and the Statesman* (Chicago, 1977); Edward N. Lee, "Plato
on Negation and Not-Being in the *Sophist,*" *Philosophical Review* 81 (1972), 267–304;
J. Malcolm, "Plato's Analysis of *to on* and *to mê on* in the *Sophist,*" *Phronesis* 12 (1967),
130–146; Rainer Marten, *Der Logos der Dialektik: Eine Theorie zu Platons Sophistes* (Berlin,
1965); Julius M. E. Moravcsik, *"Symplokê Eidôn* and the Genesis of *Logos,*" *Archiv für
Geschichte der Philosophie* 42.2 (1960), 117–129; idem, "Being and Meaning in the *Sophist,*"
Acta Philosophica Fennica 14 (1962), 23–78; G. E. L. Owen, "Plato on Not-Being," in
Vlastos, *Plato I,* pp. 223–267; A. Chadwick Ray, *For Images: An Interpretation of Plato's
"Sophist"* (Lanham, Md., 1984); W. G. Runciman, *Plato's Later Epistemology* (Cambridge,
1962), pp. 84–98; Sayre, *Plato's Analytic Method,* pp. 138–215; Paul Seligman, *Being and
Not-Being: An Introduction to Plato's "Sophist"* (The Hague, 1974); Henry Teloh, *The
Development of Plato's Metaphysics* (University Park, Pa., 1981), pp. 189–204; Gregory
Vlastos, "An Ambiguity in the *Sophist,*" in his *Platonic Studies* (Princeton, 1973; rev. 1981),
pp. 270–322; and Attilio Zadro, *Ricerche sul linguaggio e sulla logica del Sofista,* Proagônes:
Collezioni di studi e teste, ed. Carlo Diano, Studi, vol. 5 (Padua, 1961).
    Among earlier studies, see especially Cornford's important *Plato's Theory of Knowledge;*
also Auguste Diès, *La définition de l'être et la nature des idées dans le "Sophiste" de Platon*
(Paris, 1909); and E. M. Manasse, *Platons Sophistes und Politikos: Das Problem der
Wahrheit* (Berlin, 1937).

some of the salient characteristics of Renaissance Platonism and to its complex, creative relationship to the Platonism of late antiquity from which it ultimately derived, however alien both Platonisms might seem to our current perceptions of what Plato himself had originally intended and achieved.

PART I
Five Studies

Chapter 1: The Ficinian *Sophist* and the Controversy with Pico

> "Il est, par Dieu, sophiste argut, ergoté et naif. Je guaige qu'il est marrabais. Ventre beuf, comment il se donne guarde de mesprendre en ses parolles! Il ne respond que par disjonctives: il ne peult ne dire vray, car à la vérité d'icelles suffist l'une partie estre vraye." (Rabelais, III. 22)

The Renaissance was no stranger to sophistry and sophists. Some of its greatest imaginative and intellectual triumphs call upon subtle sleights of hand, multiple illusions and disguises, false perspectives, anamorphic games, equivocations—the range of strategies we casually associate with the notion of the sophistical. Moreover, the ancient sophists and their schools were not yet properly understood by scholars and were certainly far from being appreciated as legitimate and valuable contributors to the development of both philosophy and education. Because Plato's (and Cicero's) account of them prevailed, they and their movement, and by extension that of the Second Sophistic after Augustus, were synonymous in Renaissance minds with disingenuous and venal reasoning, with thinking aimed not at the truth but at advantage, with skill at epideictic display. Only a few of the greatest sophists had escaped Plato's unequivocal or partial censure—Protagoras, Gorgias, Hippias of Elis, and Prodicus of Ceos—though before the fifth century B.C. the term "sophist" had originally referred to someone skilled in an art or craft, and thus to a wise man generally, in which sense it had been applied to the Seven Sages. Perhaps something of these pristine connotations lay behind his grudging acceptance in the *Sophist* at 230B–231B and 231E that, on particular occasions at least, a sophist did play a valid role as "purger" of men's intellectual errors, though these passages more probably refer to a sophist's ability to reduce men to confusion and thus to puncture their intellectual arrogance.

The sophists raised for Plato the particularly complex metaphysical and epistemological issue of the relationship of words to things.[1] If they were able to propound false propositions, or arrive at false conclusions by way of specious chains of reasoning, did this mean that they were prisoners merely of a false logic or, at the worst, subtle manipulators of that false logic for their own pecuniary advantage? Or did it mean instead that they were possessed of a false vision of reality and saw what did not exist or existed only partially? This question bred kindred questions: How could one think about what does not exist in the first place, or comprehend the nature and status of false or impossible propositions, let alone wield the power to persuade others to believe in them? How could the sophists predicate not-being of being and being of not-being if not-being does not exist? But such metaphysical doubts, such aporetic probings were properly and fundamentally the subject of philosophical rather than sophistical inquiry since they were centered on the abiding concerns of philosophy: the nature of being and the nature of the good. The sophists may have raised such concerns, and the greatest of the sophists may even have explored them to a degree, but only the philosophers could come to a genuine understanding of them. For the hallmarks of a sophist were less his pursuit of education as a money-making career than his refusal to enter on the arduous path of understanding the truth, the path of wonder (*Theaetetus* 155D), and his concomitant commitment to the superficially dazzling verbal world of easy persuasion and deceit. Not that Plato was an enemy of the sweet smoke of rhetoric or an innocent in the use of its armory of figures and tropes. To the contrary, he not only devoted the second half of the *Phaedrus* to a sympathetic consideration of various Greek rhetors and the role of a philosophical rhetoric but is universally recognized as one of its most brilliant practitioners. Even so,

---

1. In general, see Werner Jaeger's important chapter in *Paideia: The Ideals of Greek Culture*, tr. from the 2d German ed. by Gilbert Highet, 2d ed. (New York, 1945), 1:286–331; E. Dupréel, *Les sophistes* (Neuchâtel, 1948); W. K. C. Guthrie, *A History of Greek Philosophy*, vol. 3 (Cambridge, 1969); and G. B. Kerferd, *The Sophistic Movement* (Cambridge, 1981).

it is the rhetorical world, or what we now think of as the logocentric world, that disturbs him, because of its refusal either explicitly or by implication to acknowledge the primacy of essence over appearance, of what is over what our languages produce.

Plato takes issue with the sophists and their worldview in a number of dialogues—indeed, they constitute the ever-present if frequently undenominated enemy—but devoted one work in its entirety to defining the character of the sophist and to exploring the ontological questions that a consideration of sophistry raises for a realist metaphysician. Ironically, the *Sophist* is one of the dialogues where Socrates, the arch antagonist of the sophists but also their peer in the exercise of purgative analysis if not of vainglorious eristic, occupies an entirely subordinate role.[2] His wonted place as interrogator and midwife is taken by a stranger from Elea, who is presented as a disciple of the great Eleatic monist Parmenides, and therefore as sharing in the sublime authority with which Parmenides was invested in Plato's eyes. This stranger Ficino identified with Melissus, a philosopher whom Socrates had referred to in the *Theaetetus* at 180E as a Parmenidean who espoused the language of monism— "Alone being remains unmoved, which is the name for the all"—and maintained indeed that "all being is one and self-contained." At 183E Socrates had again referred to him as a Parmenidean who believed that "all is one and at rest," though he accorded him less reverence than he accorded "the great leader himself, Parmenides, venerable and awful," whom he had once encountered as a youth and who seemed to him "to have a glorious depth of mind" (183E–184A). This is precisely the situation that Socrates recalls in the *Sophist* at 217C when he offers the Eleatic Stranger the choice between discoursing to them at length and using the method of asking

---

2. A. E. Taylor, *Plato: The Man and His Work* (London, 1926), pp. 380–381, even went so far as to identify Socrates with the "sophist of noble lineage," the sixth kind of sophist defined at 230E–231B and 231E as a "purger of souls." Sayre argues that "it seems likely that Plato intended to make the identification irresistible," and, furthermore, that Socrates practiced the cathartic method of the sixth sophist (an argument also propounded, with some qualifications, by Cornford, *Plato's Theory of Knowledge,* p. 182). He goes on, however, to observe that Plato intended to "chide" this method, "gently perhaps but also emphatically," by sharply contrasting it with the philosopher's dual method of collection and of division "according to kinds," i.e., separation of like from like (*Plato's Analytic Method,* pp. 151–152).

questions, "as Parmenides himself did on one occasion in developing some magnificent arguments in my presence, when I was young and he quite an elderly man."[3]

The foil to the Eleatic Stranger is not a sophist as we might expect, but rather the Theaetetus who had given his name to one of Plato's most dazzling dialogues, where, while still a youth, he is portrayed as Socrates' chief respondent. A disciple of Theodorus (the eminent geometrician who is the second respondent in the *Theaetetus* but a silent auditor in the *Sophist*). Theaetetus will soon fight heroically in a fatal battle at Corinth. Like Socrates, he is an ugly man with a divine soul: and in the *Theaetetus* at 143E-144B Theodorus describes him as exceptionally gifted, courageous, patient, modest, accounted far wider than his years, and as a brilliant mathematician. In the prologue, he is already reportedly at death's door, suffering from his wounds and from dysentery (142B). This admiring, almost heroic, portrait invests him with a seriousness of purpose that sets him quite apart from callow hotheads like Philebus addicted to sophistical games and aporias, to arguments for argument's sake. As one of Socrates' best and most distinguished pupils, Theaetetus is therefore untypical in all respects of the sophists' traditional prey. He is a significant choice for the chief respondent of the *Sophist*, a dialogue that Plato clearly intended as a successor to the *Theaetetus*, the main part of which records the conversation between Socrates and Theaetetus on the day prior to that depicted in the *Sophist*.

Even so, the *Sophist* is somewhat different in kind and superior in intellectual quality. It treats of the possibility of false belief, a subject it shares with the *Theaetetus*, in a much more sophisticated

---

3. Proclus refers to the Stranger merely as a member of the group about Parmenides and Zeno in his *In Parmenidem* 1.672.27–29 (ed. Victor Cousin in *Procli Philosophi Platonici Opera Inedita*, 2d ed. [Paris, 1864; reprint, Frankfurt am Main, 1962], cols. 617–1258; tr. Glenn R. Morrow and John M. Dillon, with introduction and notes by John M. Dillon, as *Proclus' Commentary on Plato's "Parmenides"* [Princeton, 1987], p. 57). What prompted Ficino to identify the Stranger with Melissus remains therefore a mystery, given that the *In Parmenidem* must have been his other principal source of insight, after Plotinus and the scholion, into the ancient Neoplatonic estimation of the *Sophist*'s concepts and themes (Proclus's own *In Sophistam* has not survived).

manner than the earlier dialogue, even as it further advances the notion of a dialectical method that can arrive at accurate definition and "catch" the elusive sophist in "a net." At the same time it treats of major ontological and meontological problems in a way that seems to be extending the critique Plato had already mounted in the *Parmenides* against the theory of Ideas. In this regard it goes beyond the cognate dilemmas posed by Parmenides, and the other Eleatic partisans of rest, on the one hand, and those posed by Heraclitus and the partisans of universal flux on the other, dilemmas also broached in the *Theaetetus*. By his own testimony in the *Sophist* at 216C–217B and 218B and in the *Statesman* at 257A ff. and 258B, Plato had intended to compose a trilogy of dialogues on the related themes of the sophist, the statesman, and the philosopher. The last was never written, and what we have is the obvious pair of the *Sophist* and the *Statesman,* along with the *Theaetetus* as a kind of prologue. The Eleatic Stranger is the protagonist in the two surviving members of the trilogy (and would probably have been so in the third), and in both Socrates appears briefly only to withdraw into the background as a silent auditor along with Theodorus. In the *Statesman* the chief respondent, incidentally, is the Young Socrates, who is introduced at 257C ff. as the namesake of the Socrates of history (Theaetetus had already identified him in the *Sophist* at 218B as his partner at the gymnasium). Scholars have dated the paired dialogues to relatively late in Plato's career, and they are thus loosely associated with the *Philebus,* the *Timaeus,* and the *Laws.* The *Sophist* in particular poses a number of interpretative problems, not least of which is Plato's reference to "the friends of the Ideas" at 248A, and thus its relationship in general to the *Parmenides*.

Marsilio Ficino undertook as his first labor in the instauration of Plato in the West to render the whole canon into Latin. With some dialogues—though not, incidentally, the *Sophist*—he could refer to previous translations, in the main by fellow humanists of the early Quattrocento and in particular by Leonardo Bruni, the great Florentine chancellor, whose translations he occasionally followed

rather closely.[4] He was also able to call upon the advice and guid-
ance of several of the most gifted scholars of his era—though not
all of them were Hellenists: the Byzantine expatriate Demetrios
of Athens (Chalcondylas), Giorgio Antonio Vespucci, Giovanni
Battista Boninsegni, Angelo Poliziano, Cristoforo Landino, and
Bartolomeo Scala, each of whom he thanks at the conclusion of the
preface he wrote for his *Platonis Opera Omnia* edition of 1484.[5]
Nevertheless, it was a monumental achievement and remains one
of the signal accomplishments of the Italian Renaissance, being
remarkable for its accuracy, its clarity, and its inclusiveness.[6]

---

4. For the humanist versions of various dialogues, see especially Eugenio Garin, "Ricerche sulle traduzioni di Platone nella prima metà del sec. XV," in *Medioevo e Rinascimento:
Studi in onore di Bruno Nardi* (Florence, 1955), 1:339–374; and James Hankins, "Latin
Translations of Plato in the Renaissance" (Ph.D. diss., Columbia University, 1984), app.
A and B. See also Paul Oskar Kristeller, *Supplementum Ficinianum*, 2 vols. (Florence,
1937), 1:clv–clvii; and, for Bruni's prefaces to his Plato translations, Hans Baron, *Leonardo Bruni Aretino: Humanistisch-philosophische Schriften* (Leipzig and Berlin, 1928), pp.
3–4 (*Phaedo*), 125–128 (*Phaedrus*), and 135–138 (*Letters*).

The extent of his indebtedness, if any, to the partial medieval Latin translation of the *Parmenides*, which is embedded in William of Moerbeke's rendering of Proclus's *In Parmenidem*, remains to be explored in the light of the research of Carlos Steel on that rendering in
his *Proclus: Commentaire sur le Parménide de Platon, traduction de Guillaume de Moerbeke*, 2 vols. (Louvain and Leiden, 1982–1985). In his introduction Steel notes that Ficino
had access to a MS of Moerbeke's work and "certainly knew" it; and that "it was only by
means of the Latin that Ficino was able to follow Proclus to the end of [his analysis of] the
first hypothesis." Steel also cites some passages in Ficino's own *Parmenides* Commentary
where, he claims, Ficino is paraphrasing from Moerbeke's rendering of Proclus's Commentary rather than working from the original Greek (1:38*–40*). This does not necessarily
imply, of course, that Ficino ever scrutinized Moerbeke's translation of the *Parmenides'*
lemmata embedded in that commentary. I am skeptical, moreover, of Steel's view that Ficino
was not familiar with the Moerbeke MS before 1489; for the argumentum which Ficino wrote
for his Latin version of the dialogue, and which demonstrates a familiarity with the entire
Proclian interpretation that could only have come from a knowledge of the *In Parmenidem*,
dates in all likelihood from July 1464.

The Latin *Timaeus* up to 53C was available to him, as to medieval cosmologists and
Platonists, in the translation by the late Middle Platonist Calcidius; see my "Ficino's Interpretation of Plato's *Timaeus*," pp. 404–408.

5. James Hankins, "Some Remarks on the History and Character of Ficino's Translation
of Plato," in Garfagnini, *Marsilio Ficino*, pp. 287–304 at 288–289.

6. This is not to deny that he made some mistakes, many of which he made a note of
and corrected later when working up his commentaries for publication. For the quality of
Ficino's scholarship, see Hankins, "Some Remarks," pp. 291–297; and idem, "Latin Translations," chap. 5. Sorting out errors in the manuscripts and editions of the Plato translations
that can be attributed to scribes or compositors obviously compounds the problem of determining Ficino's accuracy, as does determining scribal errors in his exemplars.

Ficino included in the volume as authentic all the *Letters* (though numbers 1 and 5 he
assigned to Dion), and the *Hipparchus*, the *Amatores*, the *Theages*, the *Alcibiades* 1 and 11,
the *Minos*, the *Hippias Major*, and the *Epinomis*.

Paul Oskar Kristeller, the distinguished doyen of Ficino studies, has argued that Marsilio translated the dialogues in the order in which they appear in the 1484 edition.[7] But this order is arbitrary and corresponds neither to the tetralogical arrangement which we associate with the manuscript tradition (and which Ficino, following Diogenes Laertius, associated with Thrasyllus) nor to the order in which the dialogues were studied in the Neoplatonic teaching cycle.[8] He has also argued that Ficino composed the introduction (*argumentum*) to each dialogue at the time he translated it, though returning subsequently to revise and to add cross-references to other dialogues and to his own works.[9] Ficino had begun his Platonic labors when he was given a codex by Cosimo de' Medici in 1462; but they were almost immediately interrupted when Cosimo asked him to lay aside the Plato until he had rendered into Latin the fourteen treatises of the *Corpus Hermeticum* appearing in a manuscript that had been

For its subsequent fortunes, see John Monfasani, "For the History of Marsilio Ficino's Translation of Plato: The Revision Mistakenly Attributed to Ambrogio Flandino, Simon Grynaeus' Revision of 1532, and the Anonymous Revision of 1556/1557," *Rinascimento,* 2d ser., 27 (1987), 293–299. There were five editions before 1532. Eighteen editions between 1532 and 1816 reflect the hands of various revisers, none with Ficino's level of scholarship. Finally, Immanuel Bekker's 1816–1818 edition of the Greek text of Plato included Ficino's original 1484/1491 Latin translation as did a London edition of 1826.

7. *Supplementum* 1:cxlvii ff.; Paul Oskar Kristeller, "Marsilio Ficino as a Beginning Student of Plato," *Scriptorium* 20 (1966), 41–54 at 44–46. The 1484 edition was financed by Valori.

8. This cycle has been explored by L. G. Westerink in the introduction to his *Anonymous Prolegomena to Platonic Philosophy* (Amsterdam, 1962); see chapter 3 below. The tetralogical arrangement is currently thought to derive from sometime between Aristophanes of Byzantium (c. 257–180 B.C.) and Marcus Terentius Varro (116–27 B.C.); but Diogenes Laertius attributed it to Thrasyllus (died A.D. 36) in his *Lives of the Philosophers* 3.56–61, and Ficino had no reason to doubt this. Ficino was familiar with Diogenes, incidentally, in Ambrogio Traversari's Latin translation, and it has been suggested that the Laurenziana's MS. 89.48 is the copy that he owned and annotated; see Sebastiano Gentile in *Marsilio Ficino e il ritorno di Platone: Mostra di manoscritti, stampe e documenti (17 maggio–16 giugno 1984),* ed. S. Gentile, S. Niccoli, and P. Viti (Florence, 1984), pp. 11–12 (no. 10)—hereafter *Mostra.* We might note, furthermore, that Diogenes' *Life of Plato* was also included in Ficino's principal Greek codex of Plato, the Laurenziana's 85.9, fols. 27r–32v (see chap. 3, n. 24 below). On the modern rejection of Thrasyllus, see J. A. Philip, "The Platonic Corpus," *Phoenix* 24 (1970), 296–308 at 298–300.

9. *Supplementum* 1:cxvi–cxvii, cxlvii ff. Raymond Marcel in his detailed biography, *Marsile Ficin (1433–1499)* (Paris, 1958), pp. 457–458, has challenged this hypothesis, resurrecting an old hypothesis of Arnaldo della Torre in the latter's great work, *Storia dell'Accademia Platonica di Firenze* (Florence, 1902), pp. 606–607, that Ficino wrote them in a block in 1475–1476 after all the dialogues had been translated. Kristeller replied to this challenge in his "Ficino as a Beginning Student," pp. 46 ff.

newly brought to Italy by Leonardo, a monk from Pistoia.[10] Ficino
accomplished this in a few months under the title of the first treatise,
the *Pimander*. Notwithstanding, by 1 August 1464, when Cosimo
died, he had succeeded in completing a rendering of ten dialogues,
culminating with the *Parmenides* and the *Philebus*. For he read
these two to Cosimo on his deathbed at Cosimo's special request
in the shared conviction that both were concerned with the One and
the Good, the supreme hypostasis in Platonic metaphysics.[11] Ficino
must have embarked on his rendering of the *Sophist* only a year or
two later and certainly by the first of April 1466 when he wrote to
Michele Mercati that he had already completed twenty-three dialogues.[12] For the *Sophist* appears as number 15 in the *tabula libro-
rum Platonis*, which immediately precedes his acknowledgments to
Chalcondylas and the others, the *Statesman* appearing, predictably,
as number 16 and the *Protagoras*, subtitled significantly "contra
sophistas," as number 17. The *Theaetetus* appears as number 13
and the *Ion* as number 14.

Ficino cannot have originally intended this anomalous position
for the *Ion*, however. In the versions of the *Sophist* introduction
printed in his own *Opera Omnia*, those published in Basel in 1561
and 1576 and in Paris in 1641[13]—though not, admittedly, in the
versions printed in his *Platonis Opera Omnia* editions—Ficino begins with the revealing bridging remark, "After the *Theaetetus*,

10. The exemplar has long been identified as the Laurenziana's MS. 71.33 (fols. 123–
145), which Poliziano later purchased from Ficino; see Gentile in *Mostra*, pp. 37–38 (no.
27), with further references. The "last" treatise, subdivided by modern editors into numbers
16, 17, and 18, was missing in this MS and was first rendered by Lazzarelli under the title
Definitiones; see Paul Oskar Kristeller, *Studies in Renaissance Thought and Letters* (Rome,
1956), pp. 227 ff. For treatise 15, a Renaissance composite, see A. D. Nock and A.-J.
Festugière, eds., *Corpus Hermeticum*, 4 vols. (Paris, 1945–1954), 2:228n.

11. See my *Philebus Commentary*, pp. 3–7. The other eight dialogues in order were: the
Hipparchus, the *Amatores*, the *Theages*, the *Meno*, the *Alcibiades* I, the *Alcibiades* II, the
Minos, and the *Euthyphro*. For a full analysis of the two earliest manuscripts of this first
decade, see Kristeller, "Ficino as a Beginning Student."

12. Kristeller, *Supplementum* 1:cil. Kristeller argues that under Piero, Cosimo's son and
successor, Ficino finished at least a first draft of all the dialogues.

13. The Paris edition was a reprint, confusingly, of the 1561 edition, and thus the 1576
edition, for all its errors, is the authoritative one. As is customary, all references to Ficino's
Opera will be to it. It was reproduced in Turin in 1959, 1962, and 1983 with a preface by
Mario Sancipriano and a brief bibliographical note (updated for the 1983 printing).

which concerns knowledge (*de scientia*), one should read the *Sophist,* which concerns being (*de ente*); for being is the object of knowledge" (*Opera,* p. 1284). He was, that is, following the avowed Platonic sequence. We must suppose, accordingly, that the *Ion* somehow or other got inserted in the fourteenth position by mistake or as a result of some printing exigency; though we might note that the rhapsode claims at 532B–533C to know all, an ironic comment on Socrates' critique of the kinds of knowledge possible in the *Theaetetus* (even so, the subtitle of the *Ion* is "de furore poetico"). Alternatively, Ficino may have turned to the *Ion,* since it was brief and easy, as an intellectual diversion before tackling the rigors of the *Sophist,* a dialogue which, like the *Philebus,* no medieval or Renaissance translator had tackled before him and which must therefore have been especially daunting, given the many intrinsic difficulties and given the relatively brief time he had been initiated into the Platonic mysteries and their exegesis.

One can arrive at an understanding of Ficino's preliminary interpretation of the dialogue by turning to the argumentum he wrote in the mid to late 1460s but first published, along with all his other argumenta and translations, in 1484. At first glance this introduction is unexceptional, but like others of Ficino's argumenta it betrays his Neoplatonic cast of mind and points to his own individual philosophical preoccupations and emphases. Although Ficino in general seems to have relied for his classification of the dialogues on the *Didaskalikos* of the second-century-A.D. Middle Platonist Albinus (whom he knew from the manuscript tradition as Alcinous) and for his subtitles on those that he found in his Greek manuscripts of Plato,[14] he nonetheless seems on occasion to have borne in mind

---

14. Kristeller, "Ficino as a Beginning Student," p. 53. For Ficino's Latin rendering of the treatise, see his *Opera,* pp. 1946–1962; on its date, manuscripts, and Greek sources (probably the Laurenziana's 71.33 and 85.9), see Kristeller, *Supplementum* 1:cxxxv–cxxxvi; idem, *Marsilio Ficino and His Work after Five Hundred Years,* Istituto Nazionale di Studi sul Rinascimento, Quaderni di Rinascimento, no. 7 (Florence, 1987), p. 130 (this is a revised version of the study that first appeared in Garfagnini, *Marsilio Ficino,* pp. 15–196). The customary assumption that the subscription "Alcinous" in the manuscripts of the *Didaskalikos* is a scribal error for "Albinus" and that Albinus is the author has now been challenged,

the Iamblichean precept that the *skopos,* or principal theme of the
dialogue must be defined positively.[15] This definitely seems to have
been the case later in his career after his intensive study of Proclus's
commentaries but may be true too for his work on the dialogues in
the 1460s; for we have evidence that he was already familiar with
Proclus's long and intricate commentary on the *Parmenides,* or at
least with the Latin version by Moerbeke, at the time he penned his
Parmenides introduction early in that decade.[16] The traditional subtitle for the *Sophist* was "de ente," and this Ficino accepts on the
grounds that "being is the proper object of inquiry for a philosopher," though, necessarily, this will also involve him in the study of
not-being, the theme that preoccupies the sophist. Since God alone
is "wise" according to Pythagoras and Plato, only the philosopher,
the lover of God's wisdom, is the true "imitator" of God, imitation
in this context being identified with loving. By contrast, the sophist
is not so much the "imitator" as the "emulator" of the philosopher.
Clearly, there is the possibility here that an individual sophist might
imitate a philosopher on a particular occasion rather than emulate
him, and that it might be difficult if not impossible to decide on the
borderline between the two modes of dependence. But the main
point is clear: the sophist is characterized by his ambition, presumably his desire for eristic victory, for money, and for power over
the young, and by his deceitfulness, his conscious manipulation of
appearances. He strives to emulate, to outdo, the philosopher, not
to imitate him diligently as a pupil imitates a master.

Ficino takes up Plato's six definitions of the sophist (summarized
at 231DE) and establishes a rationale for the process of definition.
We must distinguish initially between what is essential and what is
accidental and determine to which general class the object of inquiry
belongs along with the range of differences included in that class;

however, by M. Giusta, "*Albinou Epitomê o Alkinoou Didaskalikos?*" *Atti della Accademia
delle Scienze di Torino, Classe di scienze morali, storiche e filologiche* 95 (1960–1961),
167–194. See also J. Whittaker, "Lost and Found: Some Manuscripts of the *Didaskalikos*
of Alcinous (Albinus)," *Symbolae Osloenses* 49 (1973), 127–139.

15. Bent Dalsgaard Larsen, *Jamblique de Chalcis: Exégète et philosophe* (plus supplement, *Testimonia et Fragmenta Exegetica*) (Aarhus, 1972), pp. 435–446, esp. p. 441.

16. See n. 4 above.

for we cannot arrive at a definition without calling upon the process
of division. From our understanding of the class and its range of
differences, we can determine to which species the object belongs
and thus complete our definition of it. The whole process thus calls
upon the acts of dividing, compounding, and defining. Ficino sees
Plato, who is committed to the task of defining the sophist, having
to turn first to the problem of defining being and not-being; and he
cannot do this without reference to the ultimate metaphysical principle, the One, which Ficino sees behind the argumentation at
244B–245B. Hence the close link, as we shall see in Ficino's essentially Neoplatonic interpretation, between the *Sophist* and the
Parmenides. Plato is accordingly led to enumerate the five general
categories of being: namely, essence, identity, difference, rest, and
motion, categories which Ficino, following such passages in Plotinus's *Enneads* as 2.4.5.28–35, 3.7.3.8–11, 5.1.4.30–43, and
6.2.7–8, regarded as fundamental to Platonic metaphysics and as
prior to, and therefore underlying, the ten inferior categories explored, but not invented, by Aristotle.

Thus, according to Ficino, Plato is arguing, at 266B for instance,
that we can predicate "true essence"—that is, authentic being—of
incorporeals only, since corporeal objects possess an "imaginary essence" alone, meaning, I shall argue, something less than authentic
being but more than not-being, a being that engages our imagination
(in the pre-Romantic understanding of that faculty) rather than our
reason or intellect but which nevertheless has a kind of authenticity,
a kind of reality, however partial. Ficino always thinks of Plato as
waging war on the materialists and skeptics who affirmed the existence only of corporeal images and denied reality to the Ideas; and
at 246AB he interprets him as also contending against those who
were prepared to accept merely one or two of the five classes of
being. The followers of Heraclitus were obviously at fault here, but
so were those followers of Parmenides who had rashly insisted on
the universal sovereignty of rest over motion. We might note that
in his epitome of the *Cratylus* Ficino maintains that Plato's special
preeminence as a sage consisted in his having resolved the bitter
controversy between Hermogenes the Parmenidean and Cratylus the
Heraclitean by establishing that rest was the fundamental category

in the incorporeal or intelligible realm, while motion was the fundamental category in the physical.[17] Such skill in the art of resolving
and then perfecting contradictory views was typical of Plato's triumph as the greatest of the sages, the sixth in the Homeric chain
of golden philosophers deriving from Zoroaster and Hermes Trismegistus,[18] a succession, incidentally, that only indirectly embraced
the Eleatics by way of identifying them as Pythagoreans.[19]

Clearly, the *Sophist* treats of several lateral themes and motifs: the
distinctions between knowledge and opinion (the particular theme
of the *Theaetetus,* though it appears too in the *Gorgias* and the
Republic), between true and false oratory (a secondary theme in the
later part of the *Phaedrus*), and, more pertinently still, between
the substantive concept of being and the various functions of the
verb "to be." Nevertheless, the climactic moment of the dialogue
for Ficino is Plato's "divine concluding sentence" at 265C–E and
266B that all natural objects are not the illusory works of the devil
and his machinating demons but of God Himself: such objects cannot therefore be dismissed simply on the grounds that they are the
imitations of incorporeal realities, are the elemental images of sublime Ideas, since they too are the works that proceed from "the
divine wisdom" that "has been imparted to the world" (*mundo
infusa*). Ficino has in mind here Plato's complicated thesis concerning icastic creation which precedes the enunciation of this "divine
sentence," as we shall see in chapter 4, but the argument implies

---

17. *Opera,* p. 1310. Cf. the section, "Educatio, indoles, eruditio, sobrietas Platonis," in
the *Vita Platonis* (*Opera,* p. 764.1—misnumbered 774). This vita appeared originally as part
of the introduction to Ficino's first version of his *Philebus* Commentary completed in 1469
and extant only in MS Vat. lat. 5953; see Kristeller, *Supplementum* 1:xli, 30–31 (variants).
It was then transformed into a 1477 letter to Francesco Bandini now in the fourth book of
Ficino's *Epistulae* (*Opera,* pp. 763–770; there is an English translation by Members of the
Language Department of the School of Economic Science, London, in *The Letters of Marsilio
Ficino,* 4 vols. to date [London, 1975, 1978, 1981, 1988], 3:32–48). Finally Ficino used it
as the preface for his 1484 *Platonis Opera Omnia.*
18. In his epitome of the *Laws,* book 1 (*Opera,* p. 1488.2), Ficino argues that Plato reconciled the views of the contemplative Pythagoras and the active Socrates. See my "Marsilio Ficino on Plato's Pythagorean Eye," *Modern Language Notes* 97 (1982), 171–182 at
173–177.
19. Throughout his *Parmenides* Commentary, Ficino acknowledges Parmenides himself
as a Pythagorean—e.g., *Opera,* pp. 1137, 1138 "Parmenides Zenoque Pythagorici," 1153–
1154, 1166 "Pythagoreorum suorum more," etc. On the importance of Pythagoras generally
for Ficino, see my "Plato's Pythagorean Eye," with further refs.

the acceptance, at least in a limited or circumscribed sense, of the world of opinion, indeed of the world of material objects if not of matter itself. Ficino's Christian assumptions obviously oriented him towards such a highlighting of 265C–E and 266B; but he is also bringing to bear a number of assumptions he derived from his own complicated synthesis of Neoplatonic and Christian interpretations of Plato's *Timaeus,* and specifically of its architectonic myth of the Demiurge's creation of souls, of the Demiurge's sons' authorized creation of earthly bodies for certain of those souls, and of the subsequent forming of the corporeal world.[20] Such an interpretation aligns the *Sophist* with the immanent divinity of the Platonic book of Genesis rather than with the transcendental monism of the *Parmenides* as the Neoplatonists read it; and this surely helps to explain some of the fascination it held for Ficino (and thus for his contemporaries). For him it was a work of Platonic theology and one of the sublimest in the Platonic canon, fraught with arguments confirming Christian dogma on the Creator and His Creation.

Finally, the introduction argues that, just as natural objects possess an "imaginary essence" but are the work of God and his divine wisdom, and are therefore the legitimate concern of the philosopher who is the lover and imitator of God's wisdom, so by the same token things that are "shadowy" and "deceptive" must be the work of demons and their tricks. Ficino is here glossing the assertion at 266B7 that the images (*eidôla*) emitted by objects are the creation of a wonderful skill and "also owe their existence to divine contrivance" (*daimoniai kai tauta mêchanêi gegonota*), which he takes to be referring not to God but to the demons. This one instance alone of interpretative translation, incidentally, should alert us to some of the many problems facing an interpreter of Ficino's views on the dialogue and its themes, and to the necessity of referring constantly to Ficino's Latin version.[21] The theory of demonic illusions has pro-

---

20. See my "Ficino's Interpretation of Plato's *Timaeus.*"

21. This was originally dedicated to Michele Mercati before being rededicated to Lorenzo de' Medici (see Kristeller, *Supplementum* 1:cli with other examples). It can be found in the 1484 edition between sigs. N3v, col. 1 and O7v, col. 1; and in the 1491 edition between fols. 62r, col. 2, and 70r, col. 1.

For a chart indicating the locations of Ficino's own chapter divisions in the 1484 edition, see appendix 2 below.

found implications, as we shall see in chapter 5; but Ficino merely
notes here that they are the concern of the sophist, who is wrapped
in the "shadows of not-being in the sense of false being" and concealed from our gaze. By contrast, though he too is hidden from
us, the philosopher "is everywhere encompassed by the splendor
of authentic being, which is the splendor of divine truth." Thus
the divine truth conceals him in the sense that it is too dazzling for
the gaze of a vulgar soul, whereas the sophist is hidden from us by
the murk of shadows and demonic illusions. The two concealments
are, in other words, of a radically different order.

Even in the compass of this brief *argumentum*, we can see
Ficino's concern to establish the philosopher as the contemplator
of authentic being who must contend against the wiles of the sophist who is the champion of the realm of false being and of the illusions, shadows, and images that are the instruments of demonic
contrivance and deception.[22] But authentic being (*essentia vera*) and

22. Plato refers to the sophist "as a sort of wizard" (235A1: *tôn goêtôn . . . tis*; cf.
235A8, 241B6–7) and as belonging to the class of illusionists (235B5–6: *thaumatopoiôn*).
See Jacqueline de Romilly, *Magic and Rhetoric in Ancient Greece* (Cambridge, Mass.,
1975), chap. 2, "Plato and Conjurers," esp. pp. 28–32, for other Plato references to sophists
(and rhetors) as charmers, magicians, and conjurers. She briefly though aptly observes that
"the three notions of magic, sophistry, and imitation are used by Plato as being almost
synonymous" (p. 32). She does not treat, however, of the three sophist allusions that will
concern us below, the *Symposium*'s 203B ff., the *Cratylus*'s 403A ff., and the *Republic*'s
596C ff.

The oft-repeated charge that the sophists were confusing, ignorant, and ambitious (see,
e.g., Ficino's *Hippias, Protagoras,* and *Gorgias* epitomes, *Opera,* pp. 1271–1272, 1300,
1318) should be set first against the recurring notion that Socrates taught us how to exercise
our acuity in refuting them (see, e.g., Ficino's remarks in his epitome of the *Lysis,* "Nam
acuta ingenia redargutis falsis exiguo deinde vestigio vera venantur," *Opera,* p. 1272); and
second against Ficino's habitual association of clever if misguided Aristotelians in general
with sophists (see his letter to Giovanni Piero of Padua, *Opera,* p. 655, trans. in *Letters*
1:152) and of Averroist Scholastics in particular with them (see again his *Gorgias* epitome,
Opera, pp. 1315, 1318, etc.). This association necessarily follows, incidentally, if one
equates being Platonic with being wise and thus with possessing universal and hence ancient
truths. The sophist, whether callow or scholastically clever, is the introducer of novelty, as
Pletho had maintained Platonically in his *Laws* 1.2 (ed. Alexandre, pp. 32 ff.). But "novelty"
is an ambivalent if not a paradoxical concept in any educational context however conservative
(since the very process of maturation requires the adoption of facts and values that are "new"
to, or must be newly conceived by, a student); and it is no coincidence that the major impact
of the sophistic movement in antiquity (and hence its abiding interest for us) was in the field
of pedagogy. These shifting valences are all preliminary to the grand ambivalence that attends
the notion of a divine sophist; for which see chapter 3 below. The charge that the arguments
of Aristotle himself against Plato were disputatious and sophistical, that indeed he was a

false being (*non ens id est falsum*) are not the only two categories of being. In between them are the works of nature, the objects
created by the wisdom of God Himself as it was imparted to the
world; and these objects are possessed of an imaginary being (*essentia imaginaria*). In terms of the earlier distinction, they imitate
the incorporeal Ideas, while the illusions that obsess the sophists
merely emulate them. Since they occupy this strange middle ground
between true and false being but are nonetheless "the works of God"
(*opera Dei*), they and their contemplation raise a number of fascinating and complex epistemological, ontological, and theological
questions. However, Ficino was not to take up such questions with
regard to the *Sophist* itself until much later in his career when he
embarked on a formal commentary; and by that time the important
links with both the *Parmenides* and the *Timaeus* had become even
more apparent.

Before turning to this formal commentary, we should briefly consider three other dialogues, at least two of which demonstrably
supplied Ficino with an unexpectedly revealing perspective on the
Sophist, though a curious and irrelevant one to our eyes.

In the *Symposium* at 203B ff., in the course of recounting the
story of his instruction in the mysteries of love by Diotima of Man-
tinea, Socrates turns to the issue of Love's parentage. Just as his
father was Plenty, the son of Wisdom, and his mother Poverty, so
also, says Socrates, are Love's fortunes varied: like his mother, he
is always in distress, and like his father he is always plotting against
the fair and the good. Hence "he is bold, enterprising, strong, a
mighty hunter, always weaving some intrigue or other, keen in the
pursuit of wisdom, fertile in resources; a philosopher at all times,
terrible as an enchanter, sorcerer, sophist" (203D).[23] Furthermore,

---

discipulus ingratus, was an old one, though Argyropoulos, among Ficino's contemporaries,
had hastened to Aristotle's defense; see Arthur Field, "John Argyropoulos and the 'Secret
Teachings' of Plato," in Hankins-Monfasani-Purnell, *Supplementum Festivum,* pp. 299–326
at 317 and 320–321. Ficino was at pains to sort out the good from the bad—that is, the
sophistical—Aristotelians; see, for example, his famous letter of 1484 to Johannes Pannonius,
parts of which he later incorporated into the proem to his Plotinus translation (*Opera,* pp.
872, 1537).
    23. I am using the translation by Benjamin Jowett, *The Dialogues of Plato,* 4 vols., rev.

just a few pages later at 208C, Diotima herself is described as re-
assuring the astonished Socrates "with all the authority of an accomplished sophist." These two references struck a resonant chord in
Ficino as we can tell from his analyses in the *De Amore,* the long
and extraordinarily influential commentary on the *Symposium* which
he wrote with an eye glued to Plotinus's complex exposition in the
Enneads 3.5 and to other cognate passages in the *Enneads.* The
commentary he completed in 1469, translated himself into the ver-
nacular (taking the opportunity to make some revisions and additions), and included in his Plato edition of 1484 as an introduction
to the *Symposium* itself; signally, it and the *Timaeus* "compendium"
were the only commentaries so included.[24]

The *De Amore* 6.9 first presents the lemma, *incantator fascina-
torque, potens, veneficus atque sophista,* which a paragraph towards
the opening of 6.10 proceeds to explicate:

A *sophist* Plato defines, in the dialogue [the] *Sophist,* as an ambitious and
crafty debater who, by the subtleties of sophistries, shows us the false for
the true, and forces those who dispute with him to contradict themselves
in their speeches. This lovers as well as beloveds endure at some time or
other. For lovers, blinded by the clouds of love, often accept false things
for true, while they think that their beloveds are more beautiful, more

---

4th ed. (Oxford, 1953), 1:503–555. For another Platonic link between lovers and sophists
see the *Cratylus* 398C–E. Socrates, having argued that "hero" (*hêrôs,* "in the old writing"
herôs) denotes a demigod sprung from the love either of a god for a mortal woman or of a
mortal man for a goddess, declares that "the name heros is only a slight alteration of Eros,
from whom the heroes sprang" (398D3–5), and, furthermore, that "the noble breed of heroes
are a kind of sophists and rhetors" (398E2–3) (tr. Jowett, 3:58–59). Ficino, like the ancient
Neoplatonists, took the etymological play in this dialogue very seriously indeed; see below.

24. The standard critical edition of the Latin text, which follows the Vatican's autograph
manuscript, Vat. lat. 7705, without, however, recording Ficino's own variants in other
manuscripts, is by Raymond Marcel, *Marsile Ficin: Commentaire sur le Banquet de Platon*
(Paris, 1956); this includes an en face French translation. For the nature of Ficino's changes
and additions, see Kristeller, *Supplementum* 1:cxxiii–cxxv; James A. Devereux, "The Textual
History of Ficino's *De Amore,*" *Renaissance Quarterly* 28 (1975), 173–182; and Sebastiano
Gentile, "Per la storia del testo del 'Commentarium in Convivium' di Marsilio Ficino,"
Rinascimento, 2d ser., 21 (1981), 3–27.

Though it circulated in a number of manuscripts, Ficino's contemporaneous Italian version
was not published until 1544, when it appeared in Florence entitled *Sopra lo Amore o ver'
Convito di Platone.* The critical edition is by Sandra Niccoli, *Marsilio Ficino: El libro
dell'amore,* Istituto Nazionale di Studi sul Rinascimento: Studi e Testi, no. 16 (Florence,
1987). The editions by G. Ottaviano (Milan, 1973) and G. La Porta (Rome, 1982) merely
reproduce Giuseppe Rensi's edition of the 1544 text (Lanciano, 1914).

intelligent, or better than they are. They contradict themselves on account of the vehemence of love, for reason considers one thing, and concupiscence pursues another. They change their counsels at the command of the beloved; they oppose themselves in order to comply with others. Also the beautiful are often trapped by the craftiness of lovers, and those who have previously been obstinate become compliant.[25]

This gloss, for all its banalities, is important, since it assumes that the demonic nature of love, that the demon Love—and we recall Socrates' arresting correction of the views of the preceding speakers that Love was a god—partakes of the nature of a sophist, of the sophist's cleverness and of his deceitfulness, above all in forcing lovers and beloveds alike to accept the false for the true. Although Ficino seems here to be restricting himself to ordinary mortal lovers and their delusive fickle passions, there are larger implications that affect higher species of love, the desire for Aphrodite Urania as well as for Aphrodite Pandemos.

That Ficino was well aware of these larger implications is vividly demonstrated by his decision to link his gloss on love (or Love personified or deified) as a sophist to his gloss on love as a magician.[26] Indeed, the two roles are virtually interchangeable for him:

----

25. "Sophistam Plato in *Sophiste* dialogo ambitiosum et subdolum definit disputatorem, qui captiuncularum versutiis falsum pro vero nobis ostendit cogitque eos qui secum disputant sibimet in sermonibus contradicere. Hoc tam amantes quam amati quandoque perpetiuntur. Siquidem amantes amoris nebulis obcecati, falsa sepe pro veris accipiunt, dum dilectos suos formosiores, acutiores, meliores quam sint, arbitrantur. Sibimet ipsi propter amoris violentiam contradicunt. Aliud enim ratio consulit, aliud concupiscentia sequitur. Consilia sua ad amati imperium mutant, sibi ipsi ut morem gerant aliis, adversantur. Sepe etiam formosi amatorum astutia irretiuntur et faciles fiunt qui antea fuerunt pertinaces" (ed. Marcel, pp. 219–220). I am using the revised translation of Sears Jayne entitled *Marsilio Ficino: Commentary on Plato's Symposium on Love* (Dallas, Tex., 1985), p. 126.

26. "Preterea *sophistam* amorem vocat et *magum*" (ed. Marcel, p. 219). Cf. Plotinus, *Enneads* 4.4.40: "The true magic is the Love contained in the universe, and the Hate likewise." The resulting discord—and because of the presence of Love it is a concordant discord—is the universal sophistry of their union, the sophistical adultery of Mars with Venus that results in a daughter, Harmony, *discordia concors* herself. Indeed, all contrarieties—contrariety being the condition of the subintelligible, and therefore to varying degrees of the shadow, realm—are potentially reconcilable *sub specie sophistae,* as we shall see in chapters 3 and 5 below. See Edgar Wind's own magically suggestive study, *Pagan Mysteries in the Renaissance,* rev. ed. (New York, 1968), chap. 5, esp. pp. 85–89; and, more controversially, Ioan P. Couliano's *Eros and Magic in the Renaissance,* tr. Margaret Cook (Chicago, 1987), pp. 31, 87–88—this was first published as *Eros et magie à la Renaissance, 1484* (Paris, 1984).

sophistry is a kind of magic and magic a kind of sophistry, and necessarily so, since both fall under the domain of the demons and Nature herself is a demon mage and therefore a kind of sophist who works by way of "bewitchments, incantations and enchantments" that are the ways of love and of love's sophistries.[27] At 205BC Plato even argues that poetry or creation always signifies "the passage of not-being into being" and that the same is true for love. For Ficino, therefore, it too is suspended in the sophist's realm of illusory being, its desire being an imitation or an emulation of the beautiful and the good. Hence the felicity of Socrates' reference to Diotima's instruction of him in the art of love as partaking in a way of the art of the sophist.

The *Symposium* further contributed to Ficino's fascination with the links between the sophist and the demons and notably the demon Love and the demons employed by Nature to work her sympathetic magic by supposing that all the attributes of love adduced in the Poros-Penia episode can be predicated of Socrates himself, since he is the archetypal lover, the man possessed by the demon love. Thus in 7.2 of his *De Amore,* Ficino proceeds to apply the earlier lemmata to Socrates, including the cluster of *incantator, fascinator, veneficus atque sophista,* which he glosses as follows:

Certainly Alcibiades said that he was soothed more by the words of Socrates than by the melody of the excellent musicians Marsyas and Olympius. That a demon was familiar to him both his accusers and his friends testify. Aristophanes, the comic poet, called Socrates a Sophist also, and his accusers did also. Obviously because he had an equal gift of persuading or dissuading.[28]

---

27. "Quapropter nemini dubium est quin amor sit magus, cum et tota vis magice in amore consistat et amoris opus fascinationibus incantationibus veneficiis expleatur" (ed. Marcel, p. 221; tr. Sears Jayne, p. 128).

For a Neoplatonist the authoritative analysis of the traditional motif of Nature as mage is the *Enneads* 4.4.30–45 (cf. n. 26 above). Ficino refers to this section in his *De Vita* 3.26 (*Opera,* p. 570) and reiterates the motif elsewhere—e.g., in his *Apology* epitome (*Opera,* p. 1388, with a reference, incidentally, to Hermes Trismegistus). See Brian P. Copenhaver, "Renaissance Magic and Neoplatonic Philosophy: *Ennead* 4.3–5 in Ficino's *De Vita Coelitus Comparanda,*" in Garfagnini, *Marsilio Ficino,* pp. 351–369; and, for the motif in Pico's *Conclusiones Magicae,* Wind, *Pagan Mysteries,* pp. 110–112.

28. "Nempe Alcibiades ait se magis Socraticis verbis quam Marsye Olympiique excellentium musicorum melodia mulceri. Demonem vero illi fuisse familiarem et accusatores sui et

Plato refers to Marsyas and Olympus in the *Symposium* itself at 215BC, and the Aristophanes reference could be to one of several passages in the *Clouds*.[29]

The important allusion, however, is to what the Middle Platonists and the Neoplatonists thought of as Socrates' demon (what Socrates himself, according to Plato and Xenophon, called his *daimonion*), his warning voice, the prohibitory voice that "always forbids, but never bids" him to do anything. Plato adverts to this voice on a number of occasions, often in ironic contexts, most significantly perhaps in the *Apology* 31CD and 40A–C and the *Phaedrus* 242BC; but Xenophon confirms the seriousness with which it was regarded by both Socrates and others in his *Memorabilia* 1.1.2–4. Apuleius and Plutarch wrote at length on the nature of the monitory demon, and Ficino accepted their accounts and the complex demonology they implied. Here obviously he is linking together the twin notions of Socrates' demon and of Socrates as a sophist who "had an equal gift of persuading and dissuading." Indeed, one can see how on certain occasions an interpreter could identify Socrates' demonic powers with those of a higher kind of sophist, and correlatively identify particular demons as sophists or, vice versa, particular kinds of sophists as demons. Clearly, we are a far cry here from the pejorative uses of the term in much of Plato and indeed a far cry from the ordinary kind of venal professional sophist who is the recurring object of Socrates' censure and contempt. And Plato is not suggesting for Ficino what we now accept as the symbiotic relationship between Socrates and the First Sophistic, indeed the profound if combative indebtedness of Socrates and of Plato to the contemporary sophists, and even more so to those of the preceding generation, with regard both to debating methodology and to choice of content. Rather, Plato is presenting enigmas that require sub-

---

amici testantur. Sophistam quoque Socratem Aristophanes comicus apellavit atque etiam sui accusatores. Quippe cui equa esset hortandi et dehortandi facultas" (ed. Marcel, p. 244; tr. Sears Jayne, p. 157).

29. E.g., lines 102–115, 129–130, 144–153, etc. De Romilly, *Magic and Rhetoric,* pp. 32–37, deals, again briefly, with the notion of Socrates as a magician, citing in particular the *Meno* 80A–B, and the Marsyas and Siren references in the *Symposium* at 215B–C and 216A. Socrates, she writes, is pitting "the magic of implacable truth" against the illusionist magic of the sophists (pp. 36–37).

tle interpretation and partake of several senses. The sophist as the demon-inspired, enchanting Socrates, the sorcerer who casts a spell upon his youthful auditors, like a magus, like nature herself, and whose sophistries are not those of choplogic and dilemma designed to disturb, to impress, to win over, to deceive, but constitute rather the process, paradoxically, of authentic dialectic—this was the sophist that Ficino glimpsed behind certain lemmata in the *Symposium*. From the beginning it must have prompted him to approach the dialogue called the *Sophist* with heightened wariness and subtlety, and to search beneath certain phrases and images in the text for the presence of profound mysteries.

He would also have turned, I believe, to the discussion of Pluto-Hades in the *Cratylus* at 403A–404B. For there Socrates declares that it is his belief that "the office and the name of the god really correspond" (403B7–8). No one who has been down to Hades is willing to return because all are bewitched by the spell of his words, since "he is the perfect and accomplished sophist, and the great benefactor of the inhabitants of the other world" (403E–5), and even to us in this world he sends great blessings from below. He is also called Pluto because, having more than he wants, he gives away his wealth (*ploutos*) (403A3–5, E5–7). Hades will have nothing to do with men while they are still in the body but only when the soul has been liberated from the body's desires and evils; and this marks him as a philosopher. Hence, with the legislator (*nomothetês*) or skillful maker of names (389A1–3), we should think of Hades' name as derived, not from *aeidês*, "unseen," as is popularly supposed (403A5–6, 404B1–2), but from his knowledge (*eidenai*) of all noble things (*panta ta kala*) (404B2–4).

This eccentric etymological excursion thus provides Ficino with another even more mysterious sophist-philosopher to set beside the *Symposium*'s portrait of Love as a hunter-sorcerer-sophist-philosopher. Rich like the successful sophist, Hades is nevertheless mankind's "great benefactor" (403E4). Though people in general fear him, the wise know that he weaves the charm of his perfect sophistry around the philosophical soul, binding it with the desire for the true and the good. He is the god, that is, who sets his seal upon the famous definition of the philosopher in the *Phaedo* at 64A as a votary of dying and of death as the moment of the soul's liberation from the body's tomb. Such thanatological spells compel us to ask the insistent Platonic questions: Who is the shadow man, the living or the dead? What is the shadow world, the sensible cave or the intelligible Ideas? And who is the perfect sophist and what is the price that he demands? At all events, the *Symposium* and the *Cratylus* together must have convinced Ficino of the link for Plato between Love, Hades, and their respective sophistries and must have convinced him too that the *Sophist*'s ambivalent definitions of the sophist could be fully comprehended only by reference to them.

Ficino was confirmed in these convictions, moreover, by an anonymous scholion preserved at the head of all the manuscripts of the Greek text of the *Sophist* which he consulted, a scholion that, while citing the views of Iamblichus, was obviously indebted likewise to the references in the *Symposium* at 203D and in the *Cratylus* at 403E. Ficino attributed this remarkable scholion to Proclus and therefore invested it with the authority of the two greatest of Plotinus's Neoplatonic successors. I shall treat of it and of the whole matter of a higher sophistry in my third chapter, and of some of the demonological dimensions in my fifth.

In addition to the *Symposium* and the *Cratylus* we must also look to the *Republic,* the influence of which is evident throughout all of Ficino's commentaries. More particularly, the extended discussion of the nature of imitation towards the beginning of the tenth book clearly provided Ficino with a number of insights into the nature of "art" and probably served him as an introduction to, or as a gloss on, the *Sophist*'s complicated discussion of icastic and phantastic art. A more speculative debt, however, is suggested by a passing exclamation by Glaucon that may have caught Ficino's attention at the very beginning of the book and that a modern reader automatically dismisses, assuming that Glaucon intends it ironically or figuratively. At 596C Socrates raises the possibility of there being a supercraftsman who makes the "idea" or "form" of a couch or table on which the ordinary craftsman fixes his eyes in order to make the material objects. He describes this craftsman as someone who "makes all the things that all handicraftsmen severally produce" and goes on to surmise that he also produces "all plants and animals, including himself, and thereto earth and heaven and the gods and all things in heaven and in Hades under the earth." At this Glaucon admiringly exclaims at 596D1 (with a reference possibly to Euripides' *Hippolytus* 921 ff.), "A most marvellous Sophist." To a Neoplatonist this would immediately suggest that Plato is intimating that the Timaean Demiurge is a sophist and/or that beneath this supreme Demiurge exists a lesser, a sophistical, demiurge.

These complementary alternatives are buttressed by what follows. For Socrates then describes the "easy way," or rather the "many ways," by which the feat of actually reproducing the created world might be accomplished: "You could do it most quickly if you should choose to take a mirror and carry it about everywhere. You will speedily produce the sun and all things in the sky, and speedily the earth and yourself and the other animals and implements and plants and all the objects of which we just now spoke" (596DE). Glaucon pointedly replies, "Yes, the appearance of them, but not the reality and the truth." Some of the implications of the notion of creating worlds with a mirror will be taken up later, and we should merely note that, for a Neoplatonist, the interchange with Glaucon, occurring as it does in an important passage at the end of the *Republic,* seems to link the notion of a sophist, or at least of a higher sophist, with that of the maker of the world of appearance, the maker who produces a mirror image of the heavens and the earth in an "easy" and "manifold" way. Ficino would be led to identify such a maker with what the *Sophist*'s initial scholion, citing Iamblichus's authority, had referred to as "the sublunar demiurge," and thus with his imitators among men: the sophists, the painters, and the profane poets like Homer who set mirrors up to nature to catch the world of reflections and appearances.[30]

In sum, we must adduce passages from the *Symposium,* the

---

30. One should point out, however, that Ficino did not pick up Glaucon's exclamation at the time of writing his epitome for the *Republic* book 10 (where it would presumably appear in the *Opera* between pp. 1427 and 1428). But he does take up the issue of Plato's banishment of Homer "the prince of imitators" and of other profane poets, "the followers of the forms of things as they appear to the senses" (p. 1428). Elsewhere in the *Republic*—notably, for instance, in book 6 at 492A ff.—Socrates attacks the sophists with his customary contempt. Citations from the *Republic* are taken from the translation by Paul Shorey in the Hamilton-Cairns collection, pp. 820–821.

Cratylus, and the *Republic,* I believe, as well as from the *Parmenides* and the *Timaeus,* if we are to arrive at an adequate understanding of the Ficinian interpretation of the *Sophist* and, by extension, of the interpretation of the European Renaissance. This is an unexpected role for the *Symposium* especially, and therefore for the *De Amore,* Ficino's first sustained attempt as a mature scholar to enunciate the "theology" of the divine Plato.[31]

After he had translated it between 1464 and 1466 and written his introduction with its Proclian preface, Ficino did not return to the *Sophist* for several decades, except perhaps to polish his translation for the 1484 edition. Even so, it stayed in the forefront of his mind as an important dialogue since we find him making pertinent references to it in the *Platonic Theology* and in other works.[32] When he did take it up again in earnest towards the very end of his career, it was only after he had translated all of Plotinus, written extensive commentaries and notes upon the *Enneads,* and translated (or paraphrased) a number of other important Neoplatonic treatises and fragments, including Iamblichus's *De Mysteriis,* Porphyry's *De Abstinentia,* Synesius's *De Insomniis,* and Proclus's *In Alcibiadem.* To accompany this daunting work of translation and commentary, he turned once again to the task of commenting in full on the major Platonic dialogues in the manner of the commentaries he had already written in whole or in part for the *Symposium,* the *Timaeus,* and the *Philebus.*

The immediate stimulus was probably Lorenzo's promise to reissue the Plato edition, which had been reprinted in Venice in

31. It was superseded by the *Platonic Theology,* completely drafted by 1474. In his authoritative study, *The Philosophy of Marsilio Ficino* (New York, 1943; reprint, Gloucester, Mass., 1964; Italian version, Florence, 1953, 2d ed. 1988; German version, Frankfurt am Main, 1972), Professor Kristeller rightly bases his analysis of Ficino's thought in the main upon this huge apologetic masterpiece. Both earlier developments in Ficino's thought, as evidenced for instance in the commentaries on the *Symposium* and the *Philebus,* and later ones when he came increasingly to grips with the works of Plotinus and Proclus are, however, in need of further exploration.

32. Interestingly, these references always stress either the dialogue's ontology or its exemplification of the Platonic dialectic: e.g., *Platonic Theology* 8.15, 10.3, 17.2 (ed. Marcel, 1:325, 2:63, 3:151); *Philebus* Commentary 1.23, 27, 28, 29; 2.2 (ed. Allen, pp. 219, 257–259, 265, 273, 405–407).

1491—though without Ficino's supervision—together with Ficino's major work of apologetics and independent philosophy, the *Platonic Theology*.[33] This was to have been a deluxe edition with room for extensive additional commentary as well as for the original introductions and epitomes. But Lorenzo died in 1492 before the project could come to fruition; and Ficino had to content himself with what he probably envisaged as an interim solution. In 1496, two years after the Medici had been expelled from Florence, he published a volume composed of six commentaries alone: a long, complete, and extraordinarily difficult commentary on the *Parmenides,* which is deeply but by no means slavishly indebted to Proclus's even more difficult commentary on the same dialogue; a long and apparently completed commentary on the *Timaeus,* which was a revised and enlarged version of the *compendium* appearing in the 1484 and 1491 editions; a long but incomplete commentary on the *Philebus,* which he had first lectured on in the 1460s as part of his public inauguration of the Platonic revival in Florence; a commentary on Plato's discussion of the "fatal" and "nuptial" numbers in book 8 of the *Republic*; an important but incomplete commentary on the *Phaedrus*'s great charioteer myth, the first three chapters of which had already appeared in the form of an introduction to the dialogue in the two Plato editions; and *commentaria* on the *Sophist,* which began with the original introduction Ficino had written for the Plato edition (although omitting the scholion he had used as a preface for it) and which consisted otherwise entirely of chapter breakdowns and summaries. Ficino also included breakdowns and summaries for the other dialogues and further corrigenda for his translations of five of the respective six dialogues (the exception being the section on the *Republic*'s nuptial number). The volume did not contain the long and completed commentary on the *Symposium* as this was readily accessible in the 1484 and 1491 Plato editions.[34]

---

33. The 1491 edition incorporates all the corrigenda noted at the end of the 1484 edition.

34. Ficino may have intended to include a commentary on the *Theaetetus* too, for a note of Ficino Ficini, Ficino's nephew and amanuensis, in the Laurenziana's Incun. 5.10 indicates that he had written such a commentary by 1496, though it has not been preserved. The note is supported by an observation in Corsi's *Vita Marsilii Ficini* 14 (ed. Marcel, *Marsile Ficin (1433–1499),* p. 685; tr. in *Letters* 3:143) that Ficino "published commentaries not only on

Since Ficino was to die in 1499, and since the last three or four years of his life were devoted to commenting upon the Pseudo-Areopagite and upon the first few chapters of St. Paul's Epistle to the Romans, the 1496 volume constitutes the last monument to his labors as a Platonist and his last word on Platonic philosophy. Indeed, it marks the high point of his career as an exegete of the ancient poetic theology that had culminated in Plato. From the viewpoint of determining his mature interpretation of Platonic metaphysics, furthermore, the volume offers us more authoritative and complex analyses than those displayed in the *De Amore,* even though it had considerably less influence on the Renaissance, and made little of the imaginative impact that the earlier coruscating commentary had already made on Ficino's friends and contemporaries and was to continue to make on his followers throughout the sixteenth century.

In contrast with his prolonged if often discontinuous stints at commenting on the *Symposium,* the *Phaedrus,* the *Timaeus,* and the *Philebus,* Ficino does not appear to have attempted the task of commenting on the *Sophist* until the early 1490s, when the dialogue that dominated his attention was the *Parmenides.* As we know from a letter to a great friend, Germanus Ganaiensis (Germain de Ganay), he had finished his *Parmenides* Commentary by August 1494,[35] and it was then that he turned directly to comment on what he clearly regarded as its companion dialogue. No manuscript of his *Sophist* Commentary has come to light, and our principal evidence for the dating derives from this same letter.[36] What he ended up producing, however, was not really a commentary but rather (along with the original brief introduction without the "Proclian" preface) a breakdown and summary of the dialogue in forty-eight chapters. This

the *Parmenides,* the *Timaeus,* and the *Theaetetus* but on the *Philebus,* the *Phaedrus,* and the *Sophist* also." See Gentile in *Mostra,* p. 155 (no. 119); and Kristeller, *Ficino and His Work,* p. 144.

The hagiographical and tendentious aspects of Corsi's *Life of Ficino* have been exposed by Kristeller, *Studies,* pp. 191–211.

35. *Opera,* p. 957.2. The Vatican MS Regin. lat. 1619, fols. 73r–121v, contains excerpts from the Commentary apparently made by Joannes Brodaeus for Germain de Ganay. See Kristeller, *Supplementum* 1:xliii–xliv, cxx; and *Ficino and His Work,* p. 106.

36. Kristeller, *Supplementum* 1:cxx.

was on the model of the breakdowns and summaries he prepared
for the other commentaries in the 1496 volume (with the exception
again of the commentary on the section in the *Republic,* book 8);
and all were keyed by way of incipits to his 1484 translations. Still,
many of the summaries are revealing, and some constitute a body
of genuine commentary—the distinction between the two modes is
never a sharp one for Ficino—and a few are original excursuses on
particular themes suggested by the *Sophist.* Indeed, Corsi, Ficino's
first biographer, thought that Ficino had written a "commentary" on
the dialogue.[37] Though the briefest and least developed "commentary" in the 1496 volume, it is nonetheless a significant contribution to a significant publication. It bears witness to Ficino's sense
of the dialogue's high standing in the Platonic canon and to the
importance he had come to assign it in his program for the revival
of Platonic philosophy as a fitting—and arguably for the intelligent
and witty, the *ingeniosi,* a necessary—propaedeutic to the study of
Christian theology.

Though Ficino had arrived at this understanding of the *Sophist*'s
stature by way of his own prolonged immersion in Platonic studies
and had certainly intended to devote himself to a commentary on it
from the beginning of his career as a commentator, while continually
distracted from doing so by more immediately pressing intellectual
undertakings, he was eventually fired to the task by something more
particular than a general commitment to providing commentary on
Plato's major works, however long premeditated that commitment
had been. From the mid 1460s when he had drafted his public lec-
tures on the *Philebus,* the *Sophist* was first and foremost the dialogue
setting forth the theory of the five classes of being.[38] He was in-
trigued at that time by the problem of dovetailing this theory into
the *Philebus*'s theory of the primary dyad of the limit (*to peras*)
and the infinite (*to apeiron*); and the ontological dimension of the
dialogue continued to intrigue him as he deepened his understanding
of the hierarchy of principles elaborated by Neoplatonic metaphys-

37. See n. 34 above.
38. See the *Philebus* Commentary 2.2 (ed. Allen, pp. 405 and 407); also pp. 61 ff. below.

ics, a hierarchy derived by the ancient Neoplatonists in the main from the group of later dialogues that included the *Sophist*.

The same dimension also figured prominently in a controversy initiated in the months on either side of January 1490 by the brilliant Count of Mirandola, Ficino's friend, fellow enthusiast for the mysteries of ancient philosophy and gentile theology, and in many ways his philosophical rival rather than disciple. Indeed, Pico's introduction of the *Sophist* into the controversy was the immediate occasion for Ficino's decision to embark on an extended commentary even though he had been contemplating doing so for years. This is not mere speculation. For Pico's reference to the *Parmenides'* doctrine of being and the One in the same breath as his reference to the *Sophist*'s ontology had certainly been the immediate occasion for Ficino's decision to embark on a long and intricate commentary on the *Parmenides,* in the course of which Ficino mentions Pico by name and rebukes him for having the youthful temerity to attack the Neoplatonic, and by extension the Ficinian, interpretation of Plato's metaphysical masterpiece in favor of an erroneous Aristotelian position that Ficino had already rejected on philosophical and theological grounds. At the conclusion of chapter 49 he writes:

If only that wonderful youth [*mirandus ille*—punning on Pico's title] had diligently considered the disagreements and discussions I have treated above before he had the rashness to confront his own teacher and to espouse publicly an opinion so contrary to that of all the Platonists, an opinion which holds that the divine *Parmenides* is merely a work of logic and that Plato, followed by Aristotle, had identified the One and the Good with being.[39]

There is no comparable reference involving the *Sophist,* but Pico's account of it invites condemnation by association. Its correct interpretation is as much at issue as the correct interpretation of the

---

39. *Commentaria in Platonem,* f. 20v (i.e., *Opera,* p. 1164): "Utinam mirandus ille iuvenis disputationes discussionesque superiores diligenter consideravisset, antequam tam confidenter tangeret praeceptorem, ac tam secure contra Platonicorum omnium sententiam divulgaret et divinum Parmenidem simpliciter esse logicum, et Platonem una cum Aristotele ipsum cum ente unum et bonum adaequavisse." See my "The Second Ficino-Pico Controversy," pp. 430–431.

Parmenides, though necessarily subordinate to it and even, for a Neoplatonist, to a degree contingent on it.

In 1491 Pico wrote a brief treatise which he entitled "On Being and the One," though it was not actually published until 1496, the same year as Ficino's *Sophist* Commentary and other commentaries and two years after Pico's death.[40] Apparently it was intended as a preface for, or a section of, a much longer work of synthetic apology, where Pico would argue for the harmony of Aristotle's views and Plato's, at least on all fundamental issues. This irenic project by the Prince of Concordia, though commendable in itself and fully concordant with the ancient Neoplatonic tradition of attempting to reconcile the two great philosophers, was marred from Ficino's viewpoint by Pico's underlying assumption that Plato could be accommodated to Aristotle rather than the reverse. Ficino and the Neoplatonists had always insisted on the value of Aristotle as a propaedeutic to the study of Plato—indeed, on the necessity of an Aristotelian training in logic and philosophical method. In the preface to his Plotinus translation of 1492, Ficino had even gone so far as to praise Pico as an authentic Aristotelian following in the "pious" footsteps of Theophrastus, Themistius, Porphyry, Simplicius, Avicenna, and, surprisingly, Pletho along the path from which Alexander of Aphrodisias, Averroes, and their followers had impiously strayed (*Opera,* p. 1537). But this was a far cry from accepting all of Aristotle's ontology, at least as popularly and mistakenly understood. Reconciliation, that is, invariably signified the subordination of Aristotle to Plato. Those who rejected this subordination usually rejected Plato's metaphysics outright. Herein lay Pico's originality, at least in the Medicean context, and herein lay the most dangerous, because most intellectually appealing, threat to Ficino's entire re-

---

40. The standard critical edition (which includes an Italian translation en face) is by Eugenio Garin, *Giovanni Pico della Mirandola: De Hominis Dignitate, Heptaplus, De Ente et Uno, e scritti vari* (Florence, 1942), pp. 385–441. Some amendments and new variants are listed in his *La cultura filosofica del Rinascimento italiano* (Florence, 1961), pp. 278–279.

The *De Ente et Uno* has been translated into English by V. M. Hamm as *Pico della Mirandola: Of Being and Unity* (Milwaukee, 1943), and by P. J. W. Miller in *Pico della Mirandola: On the Dignity of Man, On Being and the One, Heptaplus,* tr. C. G. Wallis, P. J. W. Miller and D. Carmichael (Indianapolis and New York, 1965), pp. 35–62.

vivalist program, not just for Platonic studies but for commitment
to Platonic ideals and to Platonic metaphysics, insofar as they could
be modified to buttress Christian theology and particularly the orthodox dogmas on the Trinity and Creation.

Pico died in 1494, however, the year in which Ficino completed
his commentary on the *Parmenides* and commenced that on the
Sophist, and never lived to finish his irenic project. The treatise,
De Ente et Uno, is therefore a challenging position-paper rather
than a fully worked-through, or even thought-through, philosophical
treatise. It has been variously assessed. Eugenio Garin, Pico's most
influential and distinguished twentieth-century interpreter, has argued for its being the apogee of Pico's speculative achievement,
the treatise that constitutes a major breakthrough for Pico and a
signal departure from the vaguely Neoplatonic commitments of his
early maturity when he was deeply influenced if not dominated by
Ficino.[41] Giovanni Di Napoli has carefully unravelled for us Pico's
profound indebtedness to Thomist distinctions in his analysis of
being, essence, and existence and insisted generally on the degree
to which the preoccupations as well as the terms of Scholasticism
are molding Pico's entire approach.[42] W. G. Craven in a contentious
revisionist study has attacked Garin for what he sees as a misrep-
resentation of Pico's intentions and an overemphasis on the originality of his achievements. Instead of being a protomodern, or at least
a seminal, thinker, Pico is merely a typical Renaissance intellect,
stumbling perhaps at the threshold of novel conceptions but no
more.[43]

The treatise is dedicated to Poliziano, the great friend of both
Pico and Ficino and the most accomplished philologist in the Medi-

---

41. *Giovanni Pico della Mirandola: Vita e dottrina* (Florence, 1937), parts II and III, esp.
pp. 81–82 and 126 ff.

42. *Giovanni Pico della Mirandola e la problematica dottrinale del suo tempo* (Rome,
1965), especially pp. 217–223, 314–343; "L'essere e l'uno in Pico della Mirandola," *Rivista
di filosofia neo-scolastica* 46.4 (1954), 356–389, esp. 366-end; and "L'essere e l'uno in Pico
della Mirandola," in *Il pensiero italiano del Rinascimento e il tempo nostro,* ed. G. Tarugi
(Florence, 1970), pp. 117–129. Though identically titled, the two articles differ.

43. *Giovanni Pico della Mirandola, Symbol of His Age: Modern Interpretations of a
Renaissance Philosopher* (Geneva, 1981).

cean circle, and purports to grow out of a current debate in that circle. In the proem Pico observes revealingly:

Some days ago you told me what you and Lorenzo de' Medici had talked about on the subject of being and the One. Armed with the reasons of the Platonists, Lorenzo had argued against Aristotle, whose *Ethics* you are commenting on publicly this year. . . . But since those who argue that Aristotle is in disagreement with Plato are also in disagreement with me (who am committed to arriving at a philosophy that harmonizes both), you have asked me how Aristotle might be defended in this matter and at the same time how he might be held to agree with Plato, his master.[44]

The situation therefore involved four important people: Pico and Poliziano on the Aristotelian side of the debate, and Lorenzo and, by implication, Ficino on the Platonic.

Clearly, the issue at stake is signified by Pico's choice of title. The "Platonic" tradition, stemming in actuality from Plotinus rather than directly from Plato, was rooted in the assumption that Plato had elevated the source of all unity, hypostasized as the One, above the source of all being and existence, Being itself, hypostasized as Mind, the prime intelligible and the prime intellect. The later Aristotelian tradition, by contrast, and the authoritative formulations were derived from the *Metaphysics* (where Aristotle himself posits grades of primary substances, not a hierarchy of being), insisted that being was the apex of the metaphysical hierarchy, though it acknowledged that such being was one and could be thought of therefore as the One. Over this fundamental issue, an issue with profound implications for theology, the two traditions therefore seemed to be opposed or at least in disaccord. Ingenious attempts were made by the Platonists in particular to account for Aristotle's great error, and even to explain it away as not an error at all but a complicated presentation of the Platonic theory of the primacy of the One. Pico's treatise itself is ingenious and draws on ingenious distinctions in

---

44. "Narrabas mihi superioribus diebus quae tecum de ente et uno Laurentius Medices egerat, cum adversus Aristotelem, cuius tu *Ethicam* hoc anno publice enarras, Platonicorum innixus rationibus disputaret. . . . Et quoniam qui Aristotelem dissentire a Platone existimant, a me ipsi dissentiunt, qui concordem utriusque facio philosophiam, rogabas quomodo et defenderetur in ea re Aristoteles et Platoni magistro consentiret" (ed. Garin, p. 386). All translations from Pico are my own. Cf. di Napoli, *La problematica dottrinale*, pp. 221 ff.

order to promote a philosophy of harmony. But the issue remained controversial, and Pico must have realized that Ficino would not let his assault on the Platonic position go unanswered, even if its origins went back to a private discussion among friends—though they happened to constitute the intellectual principate of Quattrocento Florence—and not to a public polemic between rival schools.

One of the most notable aspects of the *De Ente et Uno* was its hostility to the *Platonici,* that is, to the Neoplatonists of antiquity who had espoused Plotinian metaphysics, and most notably Iamblichus, Syrianus, and Proclus. Pico attacked the *Platonici* in a particular context: in general because of their elevation of the One over being and their castigation of Aristotle for arguing that we can go no higher than the unity of being; but specifically because they had insisted on deriving the most persuasive arguments for their own doctrine of the primacy of the One from Plato's *Parmenides*. To the *Platonici* the *Parmenides* was a doctrinal work, not, as the Middle Platonist Albinus among others had claimed, an exercise in eristic.[45] As Plato's theological work par excellence, it was the culmination of his metaphysics, perfecting all the other dialogues and effectively subsuming them. As such, it had served as the climactic text in the ancient Neoplatonic teaching cycle; and Proclus for instance had argued that once it had been fully comprehended, then all the other dialogues could be set aside except insofar as they served to gloss or expand on propositions embedded in the fabric of the master dialogue, the dialogue, incidentally, governed by the great Eleatic himself as the mouthpiece of an essentially Pythagorean wisdom.[46]

Given Pico's commitment to reconciling Plato with Aristotle under an Aristotelian banner, and given his denial that there was any fundamental distinction hypostatically between the principle of being and the principle of unity, it was absolutely inevitable that he would take issue with the Neoplatonic interpretation of the *Parmenides*. The one thing that he could not do was ignore the work altogether. He had two options. He could argue that it did not pro-

---

45. See Albinus's *Isagoge* 3 and *Didaskalikos* 4.
46. Some of the reasons for this prestige accorded the *Parmenides* will be examined in chapter 2 below.

pound what the *Platonici* had always maintained that it propounded, namely the primacy of the One, though he could not deny that the work advanced a number of propositions that seemed to affirm that primacy. Or he could argue that it was merely an exercise in eristic and set forth a number of conflicting propositions about the relationship between the One and being without elevating any one of the propositions to the level of a dogma; and in this case he would be questioning its seriousness of purpose and adopting Albinus's view that it was not the medium of doctrine.

He opted for the latter. From being the profoundest, the most mysterious and perfect, the most theological of all the dialogues as it was in the Neoplatonic and Ficinian estimation, the *Parmenides* became for Pico what it had once been for the Neoplatonists' predecessors, a subtle dialectical game where, Pico affirms, "nothing is asserted positively at all." He concludes dismissively: "no more arbitrary or distorted commentaries exist than those adduced by people who wish to interpret Plato's *Parmenides* in any other sense than the eristical."[47] Pico probably had Ficino directly in mind and was baiting him at this point. Certainly Ficino was to lock horns with this "heretical" contention even while he was prepared to acknowledge a much greater element of jest and playfulness in the dialogue than the *Platonici* had seen there, and was prepared too to reject a number of their overelaborate interpretations of certain propositions and their overliteral readings of words or phrases that Plato had intended rhetorically or as "poetic flowers."[48] In his interpretation, the *Parmenides* reacquired its former majesty as the premier dialogue and the most complete presentation of Platonic metaphysics. By the time Ficino's defense had been finished and published, however, Pico had been in his grave for nearly two years.

The *Sophist* played a major supporting role in this controversy between Pico and Ficino, even though the center stage was occupied by the *Parmenides;* for it was the other principal dialogue adduced

---

47. "Certe liber inter dogmaticos non est censendus, quippe qui totus nihil aliud est quam dialectica quaedam exercitatio . . . ut nullae exstent magis et arbitrariae et violentae enarrationes, quam quae ab his allatae sunt qui alio sensu interpretari *Parmenidem* Platonis voluerunt" (ed. Garin, p. 390). See my "The Second Ficino-Pico Controversy," pp. 425–426.
48. Ibid., pp. 444–448.

by both parties. In the *De Ente et Uno,* chapter 2, Pico writes, "I find that Plato addresses the issue of being and the One on two occasions: in the *Parmenides* and in the *Sophist.* The Platonists argue that in both Plato elevates the One over being."[49] But the perspective that Pico had adopted with regard to the *Parmenides* was not feasible when it came to the *Sophist;* for the latter had never been adjudged a dialectical exercise, though it certainly served in part as a demonstration of the dialectical method. Pico had another line of attack. He felt confident in boldly asserting that the dialogue did not contain what the *Platonici* had said it contained, namely a declaration that the One was superior to being. "I do not find," he writes, "where Plato propounds such a theory"; to the contrary, "in the *Sophist* Plato speaks in support of the view that the One and being are equal rather than that the One is superior to being."[50] To bolster this contention Pico cites in Latin first the proposition at 237D6–7: "'For when you consider the matter thus, you must confess that the person who says something says some one thing'"; and then the proposition at 237E1–2: "'But the person who says not something necessarily says what is not one, that is, necessarily says nothing.'"[51] Plato's argument proceeds at 237E4–6, "Must we not even refuse to allow that in such a case a person is saying something, though he may be speaking of nothing? Must we not assert that he is not even saying anything when he sets about uttering the sounds 'a thing that is not'?"[52] (The Stranger had already got Theaetetus to

---

49. "De ente et uno duobus locis invenio Platonem disputantem, in *Parmenide* scilicet et *Sophiste.* Contendunt Academici utrobique a Platone unum supra ens poni" (ed. Garin, p. 390).

50. "Enim vero in *Sophiste* in hanc sententiam potius loquitur esse unum et ens aequalia, quam esse unum ente superius. Hoc enim ubi explicet non invenio, illud multifariam significat" (ed. Garin, p. 394).

51. "'Nam ita considerans confiteris necessarium esse eum qui aliquid dicit unum aliquid dicere' et mox 'eum vero qui non aliquid dicit necesse est neque unum quid, idest nihil dicere'" (ibid.). Significantly, Pico is citing accurately from Ficino's 1484 version (sig. N8r, col. 2, 14–12up and 10–9up). Here as elsewhere, we should bear in mind that Ficino was only familiar with the T variants (see chap. 3, n. 28 below) and that this is almost certainly true for Pico too. I am rendering Ficino's Latin. Cornford's translation of the original Greek reads: "Is your assent due to the reflection that to speak of 'something' is to speak of 'some one thing'? . . . necessarily to speak of what is not 'something' is to speak of nothing at all."

52. Ficino's 1484 edition reads, "Neque id concedendum hominem talem dicere quidem aliquid sed non unum quid, id est, nihil dicere. The. Atqui neque loqui dicendus est ille

agree at 237C7–8 that the term "what is not" cannot be applied to anything that exists; and at D1–2 that the term "something" must be applied to a thing that does exist.) The argumentation is clearly complicated and Pico is making a subtle but compelling point, though hardly one that he is prepared to follow up; for he proceeds immediately, "This is what Plato says. Therefore with Plato the not one and nothing are equals or rather the same, just as the one and something are equals."[53] We can see that Pico, in equating unity with being, is denying in effect the reality of the One as a sublime hypostasis and accepting oneness only as an attribute of being. We cannot therefore capitalize "one" here, since Pico is intending "one" as "one something" and not as "the One" beyond anything, anything and something being inseparable as concepts from that which exists or has being.

Nevertheless, Pico is not yet prepared to let the *Sophist* drop. For he sees a number of the related propositions in the following section at 238A–C as supportive of his rather than the Neoplatonic position. He continues, "After this Plato likewise proves that you cannot say that not-being is one, concluding, 'Being is not found with not-being. Therefore the One is not found with not-being' [condensing 237C7–11, 238A7–8 and B2–3, and 239A8–11]. But he is speaking about the one which he had said earlier is equal to what is something" (i.e., at 237D6–7).[54] Pico triumphantly concludes, "Therefore it seems to have been obvious to Plato that the One is being" (cf. 238A10–B1).[55]

Pico refers to the *Sophist* on four more occasions. In the process of asserting at the conclusion of chapter 3 that "the One cannot include more things than being unless it includes nothing itself," he

---

qui conatur non ens praeferre. Unde sermo extremum dubitationis haberet" (sig. N8r, col. 2, 8–3up). Notice that modern editors assign "Atqui . . . ens praeferre" (237E5–6) to the Stranger's preceding speech, not to Theaetetus's rejoinder.

53. "Haec ille. Aequalia ergo apud eum, immo eadem sunt non unum et nihil, aequalia item unum et aliquid" (ed. Garin, p. 394).

54. "Post haec item probat dici non posse non ens esse unum, atque ita colligit: 'Ens non enti non accidit; ergo unum non accidit non enti.' Loquitur autem de uno quod supra dixerat aequale esse ei quod est aliquid" (ed. Garin, pp. 394, 396, as emended in *La cultura filosofica*, p. 279).

55. "Videtur igitur pro confesso habere unum esse ens" (ed. Garin, p. 396).

remarks, "and this Plato denies in the *Sophist* when he says that not-being or nothing cannot be called one."[56] This is again a particular though slanted reference to 238B2–5 or in general to the whole line of argument from 237B–239A. He concludes by reiterating that being and being one are identical, and therefore that the One is being.

Much later, at the close of chapter 7, Pico makes the same controversial point: "Were the One more common than being, then it could happen that something might be either [a] not-being or nothing and yet be one; and in this event we would be predicating the One of not-being, a predication that Plato expressly denies in the *Sophist*."[57] And in chapter 8 he again refers to the *Sophist,* arguing that to the four universal categories of "being, the one, the true, and the good" the followers of Avicenna added two others, "something" (*aliquid*) and "thing" (*res*), and that this addition was accepted by the Averroists, who were otherwise often opposed to the Avicennists.[58] "These thinkers," he writes, "divide what is understood under [the category of] 'the one' into 'the one' and 'something.' And Plato would not find this offensive, for in the *Sophist* he includes 'something' when he speaks of the four universal categories; and what they divide into 'being' and 'thing' he includes under 'being' [see 237D1–7]."[59]

Finally, again in chapter 8, he reiterates his point:

If you grant something, then you are certainly granting that it is one [and therefore granting the One]. For the person who does not say the one [i.e.,

56. "Qua re plura eo ambire unum non potest, nisi ipsum ambiat nihil, quod Plato negat in *Sophiste,* cum dicit non ens sive nihil unum dici non posse" (ed. Garin, p. 398).

57. "si sit unum ente communius, fieri poterit ut aliquid sit non ens sive nihil, quod tamen sit unum, atque ita de non ente unum praedicabitur, quod expresse in *Sophiste* confutat Plato" (ed. Garin, pp. 424, 426). Garin refers us to 238D, presumably with 238D9–E3 in mind; but the reference is much more likely to be to the earlier proposition at 238B2–5 and/or to 239A8–11.

58. "Addita sunt his quattuor duo alia, aliquid scilicet et res, a posterioribus Avicennam secutis qui multis in locis philosophiam Aristotelis interpolavit, unde sunt illi cum Averroi magna bella pugnata; sed quantum ad hoc spectat, parva in re discordia" (ed. Garin, p. 426). Garin refers us to 251A–253B, but I think that it is once again to 237C ff.

59. "Dividunt enim hi quod sub uno intelligitur in unum et aliquid, quod a Platone non abhorret, qui in *Sophiste* inter has communissimas dictiones enumerat aliquid, et quod sub ente continetur partiuntur in ens et res" (ed. Garin, p. 426).

one something] says nothing, as Plato says in the *Sophist* [i.e., at 237E and 238A or 237B–239A as a block]. For whatever is, is something that is not divided from itself, but it is divided from others that are not itself. This is what we mean when we say the one; or, to use Plato's words, "it is the same as itself but different from others." And this he affirms in the same dialogue to be true of every thing.[60]

Here Pico is garbling the Stranger's contention at 254D14–15 that, since each one of the first three principal Ideas, namely being, motion, and rest, "is different from the other two, and the same as itself," we must admit two further principal Ideas, sameness and difference.

It is signal that Pico's only references to the *Sophist* and the *Parmenides* among the works published by Garin occur in the *De Ente et Uno* and that they occur essentially in tandem. Pico clearly thought of the two dialogues not only as linked—and the *Sophist* after all makes several critical references to Parmenides himself and to Parmenidean monism as the starting point for a consideration of being and not-being—but as the repository of Plato's most fundamental ideas on ontology. Even so, he has read the dialogue very selectively and makes no mention of what is demonstrably the crucial passage on the relationship of being to the One at 244C ff. where the Stranger asks, "Is [being] the same thing as that to which you give the name *one*? Are you applying two names to the same thing?" To this the Stranger himself responds that the person who asserts as his hypothesis the unity of being will not be wholly at his ease in answering this or any other question; for "to admit the existence of *two* names, when he has laid down that there is no more than one thing," is absurd.[61]

At 245A ff. the Stranger proceeds, even more convincingly from

---

60. "Da aliquid esse, certe et unum est. Nam qui unum non dicit nihil dicit, ut ait Plato in *Sophiste*. Est enim illud, quicquid est a se indivisum et ab aliis divisum quae non sunt ipsum; hoc autem intelligimus cum dicimus unum, sive, ut Platonis verbis loquamur, 'est idem sibi et ab aliis alterum,' quod unicuique rei congruere in eodem dialogo ipse confirmat" (ed. Garin, p. 428, slightly repunctuated).

61. Ficino's 1484 version reads, "Numquid idem quid unum nominibus ad idem duobus utentes? an aliud? [244C1–2] . . . Duo quidem nomina confiteri, cum unum dumtaxat ponatur, absurdum est [244C8–9]" (sig. 0 1v, col. 2, 8–6up and 3–1up).

a Neoplatonist's viewpoint, to distinguish carefully between the conditional unity that a whole may possess as the sum of its parts and the absolute unity of that which has no parts; and to argue that being possesses only the first kind of unity, the conditional, since it has parts according to the verses quoted from Parmenides comparing being to a sphere with a center and extremes. Admittedly, the Stranger then goes on to complicate the issue by forcing Theaetetus to hesitate over whether being (or what Cornford renders as "the real") is a whole with the attendant conditional unity or is not a whole:

For if the real has the property of being in a sense one, it will evidently not be the same thing as unity [or the One], and so all things will be more than one. . . . And again if the real is not a whole by virtue of having this property of unity, while at the same time wholeness itself is real, it follows that the real falls short of itself.

The further paradox is that "the real will be deprived of reality and will not be a thing that is"; or, in Ficino's Neoplatonic rendering, "being, since it is lacking in itself, will be not-being."[62]

The Stranger warily concludes at 245 DE, "And countless other difficulties . . . will arise, if you say that the real [i.e., being] is either two things or only one"; which can be interpreted to mean, "if you say that being is the One or is other than the One."[63] But the Neoplatonists, while admitting the difficulties, saw this as an irrefutable argument for the separation of the absolute One from the conditional oneness of being, however mysterious that conditionality, a conditionality that they glossed by reference to the famous apostrophe at 248E6 ff., "But tell me, in heaven's name, are we really to be so easily convinced that change, life, soul, understanding have no place in that which is perfectly real [i.e., which is perfect being]—that it has neither life nor thought, but stands im-

---

62. "Cumque ens unum esse admittat<ur>, cur non ens et unum idem apparet et plura omnia quam unum erunt [245B7–9]? . . . quod si ens sit non totum, ex eo quod illius susceperit passionem, sit autem ipsum totum, indigum ens sui ipsius efficitur [245C1–3]. . . . Enim vero secundum hunc sermonem, cum se ipso privetur, non ens erit ens ipsum [245C5–6]" (ibid., sig. 0 2r, col. 1, 14–7up).

63. "innumere quoque preter istas dubitationes adversus eum insurgunt, quisquis ens aut unum solum aut duo quedam ponit [245D12–E2]" (ibid., sig. 0 2r, col. 2, 8–10).

mutable in solemn aloofness, devoid of intelligence?"[64] For there
they were convinced that Plato was describing the supremely intelligible being as the fountainhead of mind, soul, life, and motion
itself, and thus as the Parmenidean "well-rounded sphere, evenly
balanced from the midst in every direction," of 244E with its constituent parts, parts that cannot be predicated of the indivisible One.[65]

In short, Pico's references to the *Sophist* were highly selective
and his interpretation flawed. Above all, he had not focussed on the
critical passages that supported the Neoplatonists' elevation of the
One over being.

This is the sum total of Pico's references to the *Sophist,* but they
are enough to demonstrate the critical role the dialogue played,
along with, and always in subordination to, the *Parmenides,* in the
great debate over the crowning concepts of Neoplatonic metaphysics. While modern interpreters have tended, at least until recently,
to agree with Pico's view that the whole of the *Parmenides* is "a
dialectical exercise" and to reject the contrary Neoplatonic view that
it presents us with the highest secrets of Plato's metaphysics,[66] by
the same token few would accept Pico's view of the *Sophist,* which,

---

64. "Quid vero, dic per Iovem revera motum, vitam, animam, sapientiam numquid ab
eo quod omnino ac vere est abesse prorsus existimandum? neque vivere ipsum, neque sapere,
neque venerandam [*em. of* venerandum] sanctamque mentem habere, sed immobile stabileque
esse?" (ibid., sig. 0 3r, col. 1, 8–13). Notice the difference between Ficino's and Cornford's
renderings of the phrase *alla semnon kai hagion* at 249A1–2. Cf. Plotinus, *Enneads* 2.5.3.22–
40, 3.6.6.10ff., 6.5.12, 6.7.12.

65. Cf. Plotinus, *Enneads* 5.1.8.14–23; see Wallis, *Neoplatonism,* pp. 56–57. We should
recall that in the *Metaphysics* 12 (Lambda).7.1072b26–29, Aristotle had declared that "life
also belongs to God; for the actuality of thought is life, and God is that actuality; and God's
essential actuality is life most good and eternal. We say therefore that God is a living being,
eternal, most good" (tr. T. Loveday and E. S. Forster in *The Complete Works of Aristotle:
The Revised Oxford Translation,* ed. Jonathan Barnes, 2 vols. [Princeton, 1984], 2:1695).
Plotinus also refers on occasions to his first principle, the One and the Good, as "God" (see
J. H. Sleeman and G. Pollet, *Lexicon Plotinianum* [Leiden and Louvain, 1980], s.v. *Theos*),
but his first principle of course is higher than Aristotle's. For Plotinus being, life, and
intelligence are the unfolding characteristics of the second hypostasis, *Nous.* For the threefold
implication of these characteristics in the later Neoplatonic tradition, an implication recognized by Ficino, see Stephen Gersh, *From Iamblichus to Eriugena: An Investigation of the
Prehistory and Evolution of the Pseudo-Dionysian Tradition* (Leiden, 1978), pp. 143–150.

66. But see Kenneth M. Sayre, *Plato's Late Ontology: A Riddle Resolved* (Princeton,
1983), for the persuasive argument that the second part of the dialogue exhibits the
mathematized metaphysics of the later Plato.

for all its opposition to the Neoplatonists, nevertheless seems to share in their basic assumptions about the kinds of ontological and epistemological solutions Plato is proposing. Indeed, it points to Pico's deep kinship with the Neoplatonic perspective on Plato and makes his view of the *Parmenides* seem curiously aberrant. One suspects he adopted it because it suited his tactics in the controversy of the moment, a controversy where his avowed aim was to reconcile the two great philosophers of antiquity and to present a unified account of their metaphysics and thus of ancient theology.

The *De Ente et Uno* was the immediate occasion for Ficino's decision to return to his commentaries on Plato, and specifically to interpret the *Parmenides* and the *Sophist*. It was not the only stimulus behind his decision, since he had been committed from the onset of his career to a comprehensive analysis of Plato and such masterworks as these two dialogues would obviously have to figure prominently in any such endeavor. Perhaps he had postponed treating them precisely because he assumed that the study of Plotinus would provide him with the keys for unlocking their every secret. Nonetheless, the impact of Pico's audacious treatise, which Ficino must have seen in manuscript or heard Pico describe, is incontrovertible, given Ficino's specific allusion to it in his *Parmenides* Commentary, and given his preoccupation throughout the opening years of the 1490s with exploring in comprehensive detail the complexities of Platonic—that is, Plotinian—ontology.

The wider impact of this domestic controversy between the two eminent Florentine intellectuals and their immediate friends was probably limited to the brief epistolary altercation between Pico and the Aristotelian Thomist Antonio Cittadini of Faenza, which was prolonged after Pico's death, again briefly, by Pico's distinguished nephew, Gianfrancesco.[67] It does, however, underscore the prominence accorded the *Sophist* by the philosophers of the Medici circle, and anyone embarking on an extensive study of Renaissance ontology will have to accord the Florentines' disagreements over the

---

67. See Garin, *Giovanni Pico* (1942), pp. 37–40; and di Napoli, "L'essere e l'uno" (1954), pp. 380–382, and *La problematica dottrinale,* pp. 223, 334–343.

dialogue center stage. Additionally, since the *Sophist* was one of the major texts in the forefront certainly of Ficino's mind in the last decade of his career, his interpretation of it necessarily provides us with valuable insights into his mature, his final judgments on a number of lifelong philosophical and paraphilosophical preoccupations.

Chapter 2: The Five Classes of Being

Preeminently Ficino saw the *Sophist* as containing one of Plato's major presentations of the theory of Ideas and therefore as a companion piece of the *Parmenides* and particularly of its first part. For us this is ironic, since we see Plato mounting in both dialogues a powerful critique of his own earlier theory and exploring alternative and certainly more subtle ways of analyzing intelligible reality. In Ficino's mind the two works were also linked to a third, the *Philebus,* the three constituting the core of Plato's metaphysics, of what Ficino and his disciples thought of as the triumph of ancient "theology." But the three were concerned with different aspects of this theology. The *Parmenides* was primarily concerned with the absolutely transcendent and ineffable principle of the Ideas in their collective totality, the One—although suppositions and indeed predications about subsequent ontological principles could be derived from its various hypotheses in the second part, where Plato's entire metaphysical system was set forth for those with the hermeneutical expertise to understand it. The *Philebus,* however, was concerned with the next step in the metaphysical descent: the emergence from the One of the two ultimate principles first explored by the Pythagoreans, the limit (*to peras*) and the infinite (*to apeiron*). Ficino had dealt at considerable length with the philosophy of the One in the *Parmenides* in his own long and intricate commentary on that dialogue. This he composed in one continuous stint between November 1492 and August 1494 after he had immersed himself in the study of Plotinus's *Enneads* and of two major works by Proclus, the *Platonic Theology* and the *Commentary on the Parmenides,* works that provided him with his fundamental insights into both the dialogue's structure and its theology.[1] Long before that, in his

---

1. For an introduction to the later Neoplatonists' complicated analysis of the *Parmenides,* see H. D. Saffrey and L. G. Westerink, *Proclus: Théologie platonicienne,* 5 vols. to date

Philebus Commentary, the first draft of which he wrote in 1469, he had treated of the limit and the infinite, and he had returned to the theme in the course of twice revising this commentary as well as touching on it in other works.

Nevertheless, it was to the *Sophist* that he principally turned for an understanding of the second step in the metaphysical descent from the One, the emergence or emanation of being. For at 254C ff. Plato had set forth the notion that five principal classes (*megista genê*)—and he seems to have thought of them as both "classes" and "Ideas" in his particular usage of the latter term (254A8–9)—were more universal than other Ideas and therefore fundamental in some way to them and thus to all being whether intelligible or sensible. These five classes, Plato had argued, were: being itself, rest, motion, identity or "the same," and difference or "the other." To comprehend Ficino's interpretation of this ontological scheme, we must first address Plotinus's views on the *Sophist*.

These views appear best in the *Enneads* 6.2 (forty-third in the chronological order). Ironically, Ficino himself does not comment on this treatise at any length in his own Plotinus Commentary, since long before he reached it he had been compelled, presumably under the pressure of time, to abandon extensive commentary at 4.3.14 and to restrict himself thereafter to providing guiding notes,[2] essen-

---

(Paris, 1968–), 1:lx–lxxxix; see also Dillon's account in his and Morrow's *Proclus' Commentary on Plato's Parmenides,* pp. xxiv–xxxviii.

For Ficino's debt to both Proclian works, see my "Ficino's Theory of the Five Substances," pp. 22–41; and "The Second Ficino-Pico Controversy," pp. 421–455. See also Paul Oskar Kristeller, "Proclus as a Reader of Plato and Plotinus, and His Influence in the Middle Ages and in the Renaissance," in *Proclus: Lecteur et interprète des anciens,* Colloques internationaux du C.N.R.S. (Paris 1987), pp. 206–209.

For modern views on the *Parmenides,* see Sayre, *Plato's Late Ontology.*

2. In July of 1489 Ficino wrote midway through his commentary: "Si enim longa similiter argumenta, immo et commentaria seorsumque ab ipsis Plotini capitibus disposita prosequamur, et confusa continget interpretatio et opus excrescet [in] immensum. Satis evagati sumus, satis multa iam diximus. Sat igitur erit deinceps breves quasdam annotationes, ut in Theophrasto fecimus, Plotini capitibus interserere" (*Plotini Enneades* [Florence, 1492], sig. aa 8v, i.e., *Opera,* p. 1738—the end of the commentary on 4.3.14). See Marcel, *Marsile Ficin,* pp. 503–504. For the reference to the "brief annotations" he had supplied for "Theophrastus," that is, for his translation of Priscianus's *Metaphrasis in Theophrastum,* see chap. 5, n. 19, below.

tially the same kind of summaries and annotations he was to provide for various Plato commentaries in his 1496 volume, the *Commentaria in Platonem*. Even so, we should observe that only two or three years elapsed between his having translated the *Enneads* 6.2 and his composition of the *Sophist* Commentary. Both the *Sophist* and the treatise must have continually come to mind, therefore, as he labored away at interpreting the *Parmenides* in that interim.

Of Ficino's indebtedness to Plotinus's account of Plato's "theology" there can be no doubt. In the proem to his 1492 translation of and commentary on the *Enneads* he speaks of the role of Plotinus in at last "laying bare" the theology of the ancients from under the veils that had concealed it thitherto; and of Plotinus as being the first and only man "who had been inspired by heaven to penetrate the secrets of the ancients." Even so, Plotinus had not exactly bared these secrets to the vulgar gaze: his "incredible brevity of style along with his equally incredible copiousness of ideas and the depth of his meaning"—and here Ficino was echoing Porphyry's comments in his *Life of Plotinus* 14.1–2—all required translation and elucidation in their own right, and hence Marsilio's decision to undertake both.[3] Again in the "exhortation" that prefaces his commentary proper, Ficino allows himself to speculate whether the divine Plotinus was not perchance Plato himself reborn, if not in the Pythagorean sense of being personally reincarnated, then in the sense of being inspired by "the same demon that had earlier inspired

---

3. "Plotinus tandem his theologiam velaminibus enudavit, primusque et solus, ut Porphyrius Proculusque testantur, arcana veterum divinitus penetravit. Sed ob incredibilem cum verborum brevitatem, tum sententiarum copiam sensusque profunditatem, non translatione tantum linguae sed commentariis indiget" (*Plotini Enneades,* sig. a 2v, i.e., *Opera,* p. 1537). This is a verbatim repetition of Ficino's comments in a letter to Joannes Pannonius of 1485 now in the eighth book of his letters, *Opera,* pp. 871–872.

For the history of the Plotinus translation and the various manuscripts and variants, see Kristeller, *Supplementum* 1:clvii–clix. For an identification of its first draft with an extant manuscript in the Biblioteca Nazionale of Florence (Conv. Soppr. E.1.2562), see Albert M. Wolters, "The First Draft of Ficino's Translation of Plotinus," in Garfagnini, *Marsilio Ficino,* pp. 305–329.

For the Plotinian Renaissance in the Quattrocento, see Eugenio Garin, *Rinascite e rivoluzioni: Movimenti culturali dal XIV al XVII secolo* (Bari, 1975), chap. 3, esp. pp. 100–112; and Françoise Joukovsky, "Plotin dans les éditions et les commentaires de Porphyre, Jamblique et Proclus à la Renaissance," *Bibliothèque d'humanisme et Renaissance* 42 (1980), 387–400; and eadem, *Le regard intérieur: Thèmes plotiniens chez quelques écrivains de la Renaissance française* (Paris, 1982), app. 1, "Ficin commentateur de Plotin."

Plato."[4] But there was a signal difference. Whereas Plato's inspiration flowed from "a particularly abundant spirit" (*spiritus uberior*), Plotinus's inspiration was "more circumscribed" (*angustior*). Nonetheless it was, if not "more august" (*augustior*) than Plato's—note the wordplay—then just as august and indeed "occasionally almost more profound."[5] This is tantamount to equating Plotinus with Plato, and Ficino invokes divine aid in order to interpret him.[6] He exhorts us to imagine Plato crying out in the words of God Himself at Christ's baptism: "Behold, this is my beloved Son, in whom I am well pleased. Hear him."[7] One could hardly find more startling testimony to Ficino's admiration for Plotinus, or to the religious

4. "Principio vos omnes admoneo qui divinum audituri Plotinum huc acceditis ut Platonem ipsum sub Plotini persona loquentem vos audituros existimetis. Sive enim Plato quondam in Plotino revixit, quod facile nobis Pythagorici dabunt, sive daemon idem Platonem quidem prius afflavit deinde vero Plotinum, quod Platonici nulli negabunt, omnino aspirator idem os Platonicum afflat atque Plotinicum" (*Plotini Enneades* [1492], sig. b 2, i.e., *Opera*, p. 1548.1). Cf. Augustine, *Contra Academicos* 3.18.41: Plotinus was "a man in whom Plato lived again." For the larger theme of a sage's palingenesis, see Wind, *Pagan Mysteries*, pp. 256–258 (Bessarion's letter to Pletho's sons).

5. "Sed in Platone quidem afflando spiritum effundit uberiorem, in Plotino autem flatum angustiorem; ac ne augustiorem dixerim, saltem non minus augustum, nonnunquam ferme profundiorem" (*Plotini Enneades*, sig. b 2, i.e., *Opera*, p. 1548.1). In his *Life of Plotinus* 14 and 18, Porphyry speaks of Plotinus's style as being "concise, dense with thought, terse, more lavish of ideas than of words," and as expressing itself most often "with a fervid inspiration"; and of his conversational air "entirely free from all the inflated pomp of the professor" (tr. MacKenna). Cf. Ficino, *Plotini Enneades*, sigs. a 7v . . . a 8v, "Scribit autem intentissimo quodam acumine et intellectu multiplici. Est quidem brevis sed sensibus ubique pluribus quam verbis abundans. Multa numine afflatus effundit, saepe ex ipsa re qua de agit mirifice patitur. Neque tam simplici disciplina loquitur quam animo ad rem ipsam ardenter affecto. . . . Ipseque Plotinus ab omni sophistica ostentatione fastuque erat alienus. In ipsisque disputantium coetibus non aliter quam in familiaribus colloquiis se gerere videbatur. Neque propere cuiquam necessarias argumentationum vires aperiebat in eius sermone latentes."

6. "Atque utinam in mysteriis huius interpretandis adminiculum Porphyrii aut Eustochii aut Proculi, qui Plotini libros disposuerunt atque exposuerunt, nobis adesset; spero tamen id quod admodum felicius est, divinum auxilium in traducendis explicandisque divinis Plotini libris Marsilio Ficino non defuturum" (*Plotini Enneades*, sig. b 2, i.e., *Opera*, p. 1548.1).

7. "Et vos Platonem ipsum exclamare sic erga Plotinum existimetis: Hic est filius meus dilectus in quo mihi undique placeo; ipsum audite" (ibid.). This corresponds only partially to the divine exhortation in Matthew 3:17, Mark 1:11, and Luke 3:22, see Wind, *Pagan Mysteries*, pp. 23–24. Even so, Plotinus never attained the mystery of the Trinity, Ficino asserts in his commentary on the *Enneads* 5.9.2, though he used all his powers to attempt to grasp and imitate it: "Plotinus apostoli Ioannis et Pauli mysteria saepe tangit, mysterium tamen Trinitatis non tam assecutus videtur quam perscrutatus et pro viribus imitatus" (*Plotini Enneades*, sig. kk 7r–v, i.e., *Opera*, p. 1770.1)!

gravity with which he embarked on the long and arduous task of presenting the Plotinian mysteries to his Florentine contemporaries.

Recently, Jean-Michel Charrue has taken a close look at Plotinus's interpretation of several major Platonic dialogues, among them the *Sophist*.[8] Normally Plotinus refers to the dialogues in an allusive and often elusive way, so much so that often there has been disagreement in the past as to what Platonic argument or phrase, if any in particular, Plotinus had immediately in mind. With the *Sophist,* however, or rather with the crucial section between 248A and 256D where the Stranger expounds the doctrine of the five ontological classes and their mutual relationships and focusses on the notion of what constitutes "complete and total being" (*pantelôs on*), Plotinus set about an almost systematic exposition in the treatise Porphyry later numbered 6.2. Other sections of the dialogue are ignored, and Plotinus omits all mention of the style, structure, interlocutors, or the theme of the sophist. He seems to have considered the *Sophist* essentially as a repository of ontological doctrine.[9] Plotinus's own treatise, moreover, has been described as "one of the most difficult and obscure of all the *Enneads,*"[10] and controversy attends much of its interpretation. Notwithstanding, Charrue has observed that it is "one of those rare instances where Plotinus has taken up a text and studied it in such a systematic way that it qualifies as a commentary."[11] Its importance for a full and accurate understanding of Plotinus's ontology and of his general estimate of the *Sophist* cannot be stressed too highly.

The reasons for this become immediately apparent. Following the lead of Alexandrian scholars, Plotinus thought of the dialogue as treating principally of being or essence at its most abstract—and the two terms *to on* and *hê ousia* are used interchangeably.[12] In the

---

8. *Plotin: Lecteur de Platon* (Paris, 1978). For the *Sophist,* see Charrue's chap. 4.

9. Ibid., p. 224, with further refs.

10. Ibid., p. 207, citing W. R. Inge, *The Philosophy of Plotinus,* 2 vols., 2d ed. (London, 1923), 1:194.

11. Ibid., p. 206. The treatise 6.2 is, of course, the central section of 6.1–3, Plotinus's larger treatise on the categories. For Plotinus's doctrine, see Pierre Hadot, *Porphyre et Victorinus,* 2 vols. (Paris, 1968), 1:215–222.

12. Charrue, *Plotin: Lecteur de Platon,* p. 213.

Plotinian metaphysical system the highest manifestation of being
is identified with mind in the sense of intuitive intelligence of the
highest order: the highest being is therefore identified with mind
hypostasized as Mind (*Nous*). Thus Plotinus assumed that the *Sophist* was treating of Mind and consequently of the various intricate
problems to which the concept gives rise when juxtaposed with
the first and third hypostases in his metaphysical system, the One
and Soul. Clearly, a number of the dialogues contained observations about being, and, from a Plotinian perspective, about being
hypostasized as Mind. But the *Sophist* seemed to constitute Plato's
major statement, with the exception, we must always assume, of
the *Parmenides,* where the whole of Plato's metaphysics—so
Plotinus perhaps and his successors certainly supposed—was defini-
tively and systematically presented. Given the preeminence of the
notion of Mind in Plotinus's metaphysics, and given the preeminence of ontology in Plotinus's philosophy, this means that the
Sophist, or at least the central portion of it to which Plotinus alone
refers, occupied an extraordinarily prominent role in his vision of
the Plato canon. After the *Parmenides,* it was proper to set it beside
the *Philebus* and the *Timaeus* as a masterwork containing the sublimest mysteries. At least, this is the impression that the later
Neoplatonists and Ficino both derived from their study of Plotinus's
comments.

The *Sophist*'s most important contributions to the edifice of a
Plotinian ontology are several. First, Plotinus sees its postulation of
the five fundamental classes of being as Plato's way of defining
the categories of the intelligible realm. Aristotle's ten categories,
by contrast, define the sensible realm and are thus subordinate to
Plato's five higher categories. Indeed, Plotinus devotes the preceding treatise 6.1 to discussing the role of the Aristotelian categories
and to demonstrating their insufficiency as concepts for defining the
realm of Mind and its modes of being and understanding. The five
classes are not Platonic Ideas in the same sense as Fortitude or
Justice, let alone lesser Ideas. Rather, they appear to be modes of
relationship that pertain among all Ideas that collectively constitute
the realm of Mind and thus to be modes of relationship within each
and every Idea. They enable us to grasp how the Ideas are mutually

associated and how each one exists with regard both to itself and to others. Charrue has hypothesized that for Plotinus the Ideas may participate in each other in ways that are analogous at least to those in which inferior entities participate in them; and they do so by virtue of their subjection to, if not exactly participation in, the five classes and the modes of being they define. Thus, he concludes, the five classes form "the infrastructure of the noetic realm."[13]

All this points to the role of the *Sophist* in the debate about the nature and reality of the Ideas and to Plotinus's sense that the dialogue provided the key to an understanding of Plato's ontology. Modern commentators tend to see Plato as engaged in controversy with "the friends of the Ideas" (248A4), that is, not with actual old teachers or friends so much as with his own earlier theory of the Ideas as propounded in the *Phaedo* and other middle dialogues—indeed, as having already abandoned the theory under the pressure of increasing doubts and scruples, notably those set forth in the first part of the *Parmenides,* where he mounts an exceptionally telling critique. Plotinus, however, and certainly his Neoplatonic successors were as committed to believing that the theory of Ideas was propounded in the *Sophist* as they were to seeing it also secretly but subtly vindicated in the *Parmenides*. One suspects, in fact, that they read the *Parmenides'* "critique" principally in the light of the *Sophist'*s ontology. Their justification for doing so was their understanding of the meaning of the second hypothesis in the *Parmenides'* second part, and—for the later Neoplatonists, certainly—of the first hypothesis as well. For Plotinus was the first philosopher to interpret the second hypothesis as concerned with Mind, that is, with the second hypostasis. Its topic was primary being and thus the same topic as the *Sophist'*s. In a manner of speaking it was the *Sophist'*s moment in the *Parmenides*; or, to reverse the perspective, the moment in the *Parmenides* that, among all the dialogues, the *Sophist* served to gloss most fully and explicitly.

For Proclus and the later Neoplatonists, the first hypothesis was also critical for an understanding of the *Sophist*. In denying any predication of the One, it was simultaneously presenting the predi-

---

13. Ibid., pp. 221–223.

cations of Mind, the hypostasis that Plotinus had defined as the one and the many. It could thus be used to gloss the second hypothesis, provided an interpreter had arrived at a comprehensive understanding of Plato's aims and methodology in the *Parmenides,* the inmost sanctuary of the Platonic vision and thus the climax of the ancient theology of which Plato was the most perfect theologian.

Ironically then, instead of being a dialogue in which Plato questions and arguably rejects his prior commitment to the theory of the Ideas, the Plotinian *Sophist* emerges as one of the cornerstones of the earlier theory. It is a text that students must master before they can arrive at the correct interpretation of the first two absolutely critical hypotheses in the second part of the *Parmenides,* where Plato had set forth the metaphysics of the One and Mind with especial profundity and thus the mode of all being's relationship to what Ficino necessarily interprets as God Himself.

Another signal contribution of the *Sophist* was the remarkable section from 248E to 249D, where the Eleatic Stranger contends that we cannot deny life and soul of that which is perfectly real or has real being: "Are we really to be so easily convinced that change, life, soul, understanding have no place in that which is perfectly real—that it has neither life nor thought, but stands immutable in solemn aloofness, devoid of intelligence?" Subsequently he concludes at 249B2–3 that "what changes and change itself are real things" and thus require that we postulate the five classes of being that allow for and explain both change and motion.[14] This enigmatic passage has prompted careful and extensive examination from a number of Plato's and Plotinus's most distinguished modern interpreters; and most, following the lead of F. M. Cornford, agree that Plato seems to be formulating a concept of mind and therefore of intelligible being that does not exclude life and motion.[15] Ancient

---

14. Ficino's 1484 version reads, "motum igitur et motionem tamquam existentia adesse fatendum" (sig. 0 3r, col. 1, 22–23). Cf. 249D3–4 "quotcumque vel stant vel moventur ambo simul ens et omne vocare" (ibid. 3–2up). For 248E ff., see chap. 1, n. 64 above.

15. *Plato's Theory of Knowledge,* pp. 244–246. For the impact of this passage on Plotinus, see the seminal article by Pierre Hadot, "Etre, vie, pensée chez Plotin et avant Plotin," in *Les sources de Plotin,* Entretiens Hardt, vol. 5 (Geneva, 1960), pp. 107–157; and idem, *Plotin ou la simplicité du regard* (Paris, 1963). See too Stephen Gersh, *Kinêsis*

Neoplatonists were likewise moved by this extraordinary passage and were driven by the radical nature of its propositions to predicate, again following the lead of Plotinus himself, being, life, and understanding in that order as a triad of powers within Mind. For Plotinus had repeatedly associated being with the concepts of life and understanding,[16] and spoken of Mind, in its compound integrity as one and many, as a hypostasis that embraces the powers of life and understanding and therefore, mysteriously, the powers of the principle of all motion and change, soul in its highest manifestation. Among a number of enigmatic references in Plato that sprang to mind in this context was the one in the *Philebus* 30D, where Zeus is endowed with a "royal intellect" and a "royal soul" and possesses the power of the cause. This follows on the question put just a few lines earlier at 30C, "And can wisdom and mind exist without soul?" to which Protarchus had instantly and correctly rejoined, "Certainly not."[17] In his remarkable commentary on the *Philebus* at 1.21, Ficino treats of the essence-life-understanding triad as it is paradigmatically present in Mind in terms of the familiar Neoplatonic formula that holds that each element in the triad is an aspect of the same hypostasis. Essence when at rest, it is life when it acts or is in motion; and it is understanding "insofar as it returns into itself." This triad is a variation on another basic triad, that of rest, procession, and reversion.[18]

---

akinêtos: A Study of Spiritual Motion in the Philosophy of Proclus (Leiden, 1973), on life and motion in Mind.

The Neoplatonists were accustomed to linking this passage to the *Timaeus'*s description of the world at 30B–D as an "all-complete" and "living" creature or animal endowed with soul and intelligence, since Plotinus had identified this "animal" with Mind. See R. T. Wallis, *Neoplatonism* (London, 1972), pp. 55, 65; also chap. 1, n. 65 above.

16. Charrue, *Plotin: Lecteur de Platon,* p. 212. Nevertheless, Plotinus did occasionally assign life the last position in the triad because of its association with Soul; see Wallis, *Neoplatonism,* p. 67.

17. Cf. *Laws* 10, 897C–D, where the Athenian Stranger argues that the universe must be governed by "the best soul" if it moves in a way that is akin to "the motion, rotation, and calculation of intelligence" (were it to move irregularly, on the other hand—which is clearly not the case, as he concludes at 898C—then of course it would be guided by an evil soul).

18. Ed. Allen, pp. 206–207. See Wallis, *Neoplatonism,* p. 66; also my *Platonism of Ficino,* pp. 73–75, 153 n. 18. In his *Pagan Mysteries,* p. 38 n. 9, Wind speculatively notes that Ficino and Pico changed the ancient triad of rest (*monê*), procession (*proodos*), and

The Plotinian concept of Mind therefore goes beyond the hypos-
tasization of the notion of a mind thinking ideas, or even of a
supreme Mind eternally intuiting the Ideas in Plato's special sense,
to embrace intelligibles such as life and soul that are not so much
Ideas (though Middle Platonists and Neoplatonists had wrestled
with the notion of an Idea of Soul, and Plato himself had postulated
an Idea of Life in the *Phaedo*) as they are powers in, or aspects of,
Mind. In this scheme the highest form of life is an aspect of the
purest form of contemplation and is thus a kind of mystical motionless motion or lifeless life, the issuing forth (*proodos*) of Mind from
and of and into itself.[19] Plotinus's emphasis on Mind and the extraordinary role it plays in his metaphysical system, by contrast with
Plato's emphasis on the Ideas that transcend any mind that might
contemplate them, obviously requires that we focus on this mysterious being and power of pure intellection, on this supreme rest-in-
motion of thought. It is here, with its evocative passage on the
need somehow to include aspects of life, motion, and indeed soul
as the celebrated principle of motion in the concept of Mind, that
the *Sophist* came into special prominence. For its concern from the
Neoplatonic viewpoint with the circling triadic powers of Mind,
rather than with the purity and absoluteness of the Platonic Ideas
that are the proper objects of Mind, constitutes one of the principal validations of the Plotinian concept of intelligible, of absolute being. To modern interpreters this passage in the *Sophist* at
248E ff. occupies a less pivotal role for one's understanding both
of the dialogue in particular and of Platonic metaphysics in general.
Nonetheless, scholars continue to find its arguments challenging
and even to share at times something of the Neoplatonists' fascination with Plato's adumbration of a paradigmatic life, a life that
consists in, or mediates between, the simultaneous rest and motion

---

reversion (*epistrophê*) into a new triad, procession (*emanatio*), conversion (*raptio*), and
return (*remeatio*), and in so doing radically altered the focus. In his *Cratylus* epitome (Opera,
p. 1312) Ficino associated the triad respectively with Uranus, Rhea, and Saturn, no doubt
with Plotinus's *Enneads* 5.1.7 and 5.8.13 in mind.

19. Charrue, *Plotin: Lecteur de Platon*, p. 212. On the problems in general of distinguishing Soul from Mind in Plotinus, see Wallis, *Neoplatonism*, pp. 72 ff., 81–82, 92, For Ficino,
see my *Platonism of Ficino*, pp. 160–161.

of intuitive vision and in which, as embodied souls, we can only occasionally participate.

For Plotinus and his successors this section in the *Sophist* from 248E to 249D, along with the first two hypotheses of the second part of the *Parmenides*, thus constituted Plato's authoritative pronouncement on the second hypostasis, and on the basic principles of ontology, the study contingent on that hypostasis. Indeed, Charrue goes so far as to assert that Plotinus's own ontology "found its principal resources in the ontology of the *Sophist*," a dialogue "consecrated basically to ontology."[20] In particular, the treatise 6.2 derived from the *Sophist* the notion that is fundamental to Neoplatonic metaphysics, namely that life and intelligence are what characterize true being and are therefore found in their paradigmatic forms in the supreme being, in the being that first emanated from the One. From Plotinus's point of view, the *Sophist* therefore contained one of the two or three most illuminating and profound passages in all of Plato's works, one that enabled him to formulate or at least to elaborate his pivotal metaphysical concept of *Nous*, and to suppose that it was not only Plato's authentic conception but in perfect accord with the hallowed theory of Ideas which it served to complement and frame.[21]

Marsilio Ficino's analysis of the *Sophist* embraces many more issues than those covered in Plotinus's treatise and deals, at least superficially, with the entire dialogue. Nonetheless, it is this Plotinian perspective, with its concentrated focus on ontology, that he espouses as genuinely Platonic. For him too the *Sophist* is the dialogue of the second hypostasis as surely as the *Parmenides* is the dialogue of the first. To illustrate, let us turn to his commentary chapters.

Much of Ficino's *Sophist* Commentary is concerned with analyzing the implications of Plato's theory of the five greatest classes or Ideas. He first introduces some key distinctions in chapter 17. The

---

20. *Plotin: Lecteur de Platon*, p. 223.

21. Charrue, *Plotin: Lecteur de Platon*, pp. 226–228, lists other passages from the *Enneads* indebted to the *Sophist*.

term "being" (*ens*) he thinks of as synonymous with "some one thing" (*unum aliquid*), but not with the absolute one, the One that is beyond all predication of being (229.16–19).[22] Being, he continues in chapter 19, is synonymous with what is true, and correspondingly not-being with what is false (233.4–6). The term "being," states chapter 34, "seems to signify something as it were concrete," whereas the term "essence" (*essentia*) "something abstract"; nevertheless, the two are often used interchangeably "for the sake of style" (*sermonis gratia*) (255.29–257.1). We should note that neither is to be identified with the term "existence" (*esse*). Ficino had already carefully set out these distinctions in his Commentary on the *Philebus* 2.2: "Plato means by the term 'being' (*ens*) something that is compounded from both 'essence' and 'existence,' although 'being' certainly refers more to that compound's existence than it does to its essence."[23] The distinctions had been finely honed by the Scholastics and are of crucial significance for an understanding, for instance, of Aquinas's thought. By contrast, Plato's deployment of various forms of the verb "to be" renders a number of his statements in the *Sophist* and elsewhere ambivalent if not ambiguous in terms of the Scholastic distinctions, and clearly in terms of the now standard differentiation between the significations of identity, attribution (or predication), and existence. Cornford believed Plato recognized only two of these, existence and identity, while others have claimed that he recognized all three, and still others that he did not distinguish the existential sense from either of the other two senses.[24]

22. Throughout this chapter and later chapters the references are by page and line to the text as edited below in Part II.

23. "Ens intelligit compositum ex essentia atque esse, quamquam nomen ens illius compositi magis exprimit esse quam essentiam" (ed. Allen, p. 405). For the Thomistic background of Ficino's careful distinctions, see Ardis B. Collins, *The Secular Is Sacred: Platonism and Thomism in Marsilio Ficino's "Platonic Theology"* (The Hague, 1974), chaps. 4 and 5. On the notions of being, essence, and existence in Plotinus, see G. Nebel, "Terminologische Untersuchungen zu *ousia* und *on* bei Plotin," *Hermes* 65 (1930), 422–445.

24. Cornford, *Plato's Theory of Knowledge*, p. 296. For other positions, see, e.g., Malcolm, "Plato's Analysis," pp. 130 ff.; Frede, *Prädikation*, pp. 9–11 and passim; Owen, "Plato on Not-Being," pp. 223 ff.; Sayre, *Plato's Analytic Method*, pp. 198 ff.; Bluck, *Plato's "Sophist,"* pp. 62–67, 119; Guthrie, *History of Greek Philosophy* 5:147–148; and Rosen, *Plato's "Sophist,"* pp. 229–244 (esp. p. 234, citing Frede). We might note the

In the *Philebus* Plato had postulated after the One the two apparently Pythagorean principles of the limit and the infinite. All things consist of these two principles, for, while the One is above all, these two are the source of all (*duo ex quibus omnia*).[25] Then Plato had turned, so Ficino argues, to postulate a third principle, one that is mixed from the limit and the infinite. But what causes this mixture? It is precisely such a consideration that had impelled Plato to postulate what appear in the *Sophist* as the five "elements" or "classes" of being. In the *Philebus* Commentary Ficino had taken care to explain why, given the obvious distinction between "essence" and "existence," the *Sophist* had not formally proposed six rather than five classes. The answer is that Plato had posited only five classes and omitted "existence" (*esse*) "because existence is what is primarily meant by the concept of being itself."[26] Hence "being" refers principally to the existence that is bestowed on infinity by the limit that transcends infinity. To such being Plato had attributed the five elements: essence (the infinity upon which the limit bestows existence), rest, motion, identity, and difference. In the case of every single thing that exists, these five elements—and this is one of Ficino's terms—are attributed to being, that is, to existence. Ficino then sees Plato assigning each of the resulting six elements either to the limit or to the infinite. Thus the limit, he argues, bestows existence, rest, and identity, while the infinite bestows essence, motion, and difference.[27]

---

obvious corollary that "not to be" may therefore signify nonidentity or nonattribution or nonexistence; see Owen, "Plato on Not-Being," *passim*.

25. Cf. Ficino's *Philebus* Commentary 2.2 (ed. Allen, p. 403).

26. "Posuit autem quinque et esse praetermisit, quia in expressione entis esse praevalet" (ed. Allen, p. 405). Cf. Ficino's *Timaeus* Commentary 37 (*Opera*, p. 1452).

27. Ed. Allen, pp. 405, 407. One may surmise that, as a Neoplatonist, Ficino would have aligned this analysis in the *Philebus* with Plato's description in the *Timaeus* at 35A ff. of the Demiurge's creation of soul from a blending of "indivisible" and "divisible" being and likewise of the indivisible and divisible kinds of the same and the different. Taking the three newly blended elements, the Demiurge "mingled them all into one form, compressing by force the reluctant and unsociable nature of the different into the same" (tr. Jowett in Hamilton-Cairns, *Plato*, p. 1165). Modern commentators, however, have been reluctant to use this enigmatic section of an enigmatic myth to gloss either the *Philebus*'s or the *Sophist*'s analyses of otherness. The Plotinian One is of course completely without otherness, as the *Enneads* 6.9.8.33–34 declares.

In chapter 34 of his *Sophist* Commentary, Ficino repeats this
formulation with the *Philebus* explicitly in mind: "In the *Philebus*
Plato appears to produce (*conflare*) essence from the following four
elements as it were: from the One and the many, and then from the
limit and the infinite" (257.2–3). Moreover, he conceives of the
Eleatic Stranger as having already accepted the formulation propounded in the *Philebus* that essence and existence together constitute the mixture that is being (even though existence predominates
in this mixture); and this would seem to imply what he elsewhere
rejects, namely the primacy, metaphysically speaking, of the *Philebus* over the *Sophist*. The four Phileban elements constitute the
ultimate causes of all being, while immediately subsequent to them,
as we have seen, are the *Sophist*'s five elements or Ideas of being.[28]
Ficino derives the following scheme of correspondences: "To this
essence Plato adds four elements that correspond in a way to the
first four: thus with the reason of the One and the limit are identity
and rest, with the reason of the many and the infinite are difference
and motion" (257.5–8). He notes in conclusion that we must always
take care to postulate three principal ontological classes, namely
essence, motion, and rest, and then to postulate two additional
classes, identity and difference. Following Plato, Ficino defines
them as "the five largest classes" (*amplissima quinque genera*)
(255.23), while continuing to refer to them as "elements" (as, for
instance, at (255.26, 27; 257.2, 5). The Platonic reasoning behind
the postulation of these classes, which Ficino replicates in chapters
34 through 37, need not concern us.

For Ficino, as it would seem for Plato, the five largest classes
are interdependent combinatory principles. In that he used the term
"idea" to refer both to the "Idea of Being" and to signify the nature
and status of what he then analyzes at 254C ff. as the five classes,
Plato, at least from the Ficinian perspective, apparently assumed
that the classes were Ideas and, furthermore, that they were the most
universal and all-embracing Ideas (and we could therefore elect to
capitalize them throughout). Thus we might suppose them to exist

---

28. Cf. Ficino's *Platonic Theology* 17.2 (ed. Marcel, 3:151–153).

entirely independently as the theory of Ideas would require, and to constitute the absolute principles of being. But Ficino assumes not only that Plato was presupposing the four causes of the One and the many, the limit and the infinite, as such absolute principles, but also that Plato had argued that the five classes define the relationship essentially of the Ideas to each other, and even more significantly to various aspects or modes of themselves. This at least was the Plotinian interpretation. In chapter 32 Ficino writes that, although identity is not difference and rest is not motion nor vice versa, and although no one of these Ideas can be its opposite Idea or even another of the Ideas, yet all these Ideas possess "some sort of communion or participation with each other" (251.7–10). Whatever single object appears to an observer to be under the dominion of one Idea in reality participates in several or even in many Ideas and does so simultaneously. In short, "Plato proves here that ideal beings (*entia idealia*) share in a certain mutual communion. For unless rest and motion themselves have some communication with essence itself, neither rest nor motion will possess being at all" (251.14–17). Neither will exist either as an independent reality or as what Ficino refers to, indifferently apparently, as *ens aliquod,* "some being" (251.16–17; 263.7; 265.2; 267.17), or as *ens aliquid,* "something being" (229.16, 19, 20; 263.31).

The precise nature of this "communion" and in general the relationship of the five principal classes, elements, or Ideas to other Ideas, to each other, and to the notion of being continue to arouse controversy. In this regard the theory of the five classes poses many of the same problems raised by Plato's postulation in the *Republic* and elsewhere of an Idea of the Good as an Idea that is superior to all other Ideas and is their principle and cause; or by his suggestion in the *Phaedrus* that there is both an Idea of Beauty which is the splendor of all the other Ideas, and an Idea of Truth which is simultaneously what all the Ideas constitute together. Certainly the five principal ontological Ideas do not have the same metaphysical status as the Ideas, say, of Justice or Fortitude, or the Ideas of classes of existing things like men or horses. Ficino prefers to think of them in chapter 34 as "the elements of universal being" (*elementa universi entis*) (255.26), and to link them with the two fundamental principles in the *Philebus* of the limit and the infinite, and with the analogous but even more fundamental principles in the *Parmenides* of the One and the many. The three dialogues together thus provide him with all the key concepts of the Platonic theory of being, and with an explanation of the emergence of being from the One. The theory of Ideas as such plays only a subordinate role in this grand architecture, since Ficino sees Plato intent upon erecting the principles that are fundamental to that theory and that the other Ideas participate in in ways that testify to the "communion" that the One bestows on the many.

Ficino also shared Plotinus's fascination with the *Sophist* as a dialogue concerned with Mind. Indeed, his interest in the five ontological classes, quite apart from their status as "more universal" Ideas than other Ideas—and this phrase occurs towards the end of chapter 33—has a direct bearing on their intricate relationship to the concept of "prime being" (*ens primum*). He notes in the same chapter that among the five classes the first and most embracing (*amplissimum*) is being. Included in the prime being are what he thinks of as "the oppositions among the classes" and "the differences among the Ideas" (235.26–27). I take this to mean that it must embrace the various oppositions that pertain among the five classes and govern their mutual relationships, and also the differences that distinguish not only the Ideas from one another but the "more universal" Ideas from the less—the highest genera, that is, from the lowest species. Given the argument in the *Sophist* that the oppositions among the five classes—and by extension the differences among the Ideas subsequent to these classes—are nevertheless offset somehow by the "communion" among them and virtually reconciled in the prime class of being itself, Ficino is led to suppose, in opposition to Pico, that Plato was arguing, not only that being and its antithesis not-being (defined in terms of oppositions and differences) are intertwined in human discourse, but that they are likewise intertwined in the prime being and ensure therefore the paradoxical presence of not-being in that being (235.28–29). Such a unified communion or mixture is inconceivable as a condition of the supreme hypostasis; and the One is thus beyond being and beyond the five classes that constitute being. But it is difficult to think of Ficino entertaining the notion of the Idea of Being as somehow distinguishable from the prime being. Conceptually separable and independent perhaps, as a universal Idea it not only participates in, and is participated in by, the other universal Ideas but also constitutes the hypostasizing of these Ideas "mixed" together. It is equally the hypostasis of the Idea of Being and of the communion of the five classes that in a way make up that Idea (though Ficino does not articulate the situation in these complementary terms).

The prime being is also the exemplar of being, given the metaphysical assumption that Ficino accepted from the Scholastics, namely that the first in any class is the fullest expression and perfection of that class and the model for all that is subsequent to it in that class.[29] But the highest conceivable kind of being from a Platonic perspective is intelligible being. Thus the prime being is necessarily defined by Ficino in chapter 25 as "intelligible" or as "the intelligible sphere" (237.26; 239.4), or in chapter 37 as "the intelligible world" (263.11), both "sphere" and "world" being understood in the figurative sense Ficino supposed Plato had intended in the *Timaeus*. In Neoplatonic metaphysics such intelligible being was theoretically identified with the prime intellect, and Ficino accepts this identification in chapter 30. Even so, he more often conceives of the prime intellect as thinking the prime intelligibles and thereby adopts the subtle Plotinian shift away from Plato's focus on the Ideas themselves to the Mind that thinks them and, by what seems to be an almost inevitable process of logic for a Christian philosopher, therefore exceeds them. For, although Plotinus and his successors identified the intelligibles with the prime intellect that thinks them, the effect of the Plotinian metaphysical system was to elevate Mind over the Platonic Ideas on the analogy of the human

---

29. See Kristeller, *Philosophy,* chap. 9, for the role in Ficino's thought of this important theory, which is rooted ultimately in the prevailing assumption in Greek philosophy that the cause must be more perfect than its effect (for which see proposition 7 of Proclus's *Elements of Theology*).

mind's sovereignty over its ideas. Platonic metaphysics was thereby accommodated to the Plotinian ontology and, for Ficino, to the personalism intrinsic to Christian conceptions of God and the soul.

In his *Sophist* Commentary chapters 27 and 30, Ficino also defines intelligible being as "true being, that is, eternal substance" (243.2–3) and as "the indivisible and eternal essence" (247.3–4). As such the prime being must contain all subsequent being. Thus in chapter 25 Ficino sees Melissus as contending that it is "one in essence, yet multiple in its essential powers and forms" (239.4–6); for it is "the model of this world" (239.1), and contains, he argues in chapter 23, "the oppositions among the classes and the differences among the Ideas" (235.26–27). Thus the prime being, he asserts in chapter 36, insofar as it cannot be the prime hypostasis, the One, must be both one and many; and insofar as it contains the many and their mutual differences, it contains not-being, even "infinite" not-being (261.28). The foundation for this hypothesis is the preceding analysis of the five classes as being "mixed" together or "in communion." Since the prime being must embrace, says chapter 23, the oppositions and differences that distinguish the five classes and indeed "less universal" Ideas, it must contain a mixture of being and not-being (*hic ens vel primum cum non ente commiscet*) (235.28–29).

It is interesting to see the notion of not-being thus linked with that of the onset of multiplicity: the prime being, Ficino asserts in chapter 26, is simultaneously many beings (*entia multa*) and necessarily has "parts" of which it is the whole (239.24–28). Moreover, as the "universal whole" (239.18), it is both the "origin of forms" and itself "omniform" (239.21) or "formally all things" (241.30). Again, as the "intelligible universe" (241.26), it is not only omniform but "fertile" (*fecunda*); for "the greatest possible multitude of essential reasons flourishes there; and from that multitude, as from a pregnant mother, the hosts of entities are everywhere born" (241.27–29). Indeed, the description of the prime entity as an intellectual and intelligible world burgeoning with "essential reasons" is in some respects reminiscent of the description in the *Timaeus* of the creation. It seems to run counter to Plato's initial conception of the Ideas as constituting a realm of supremely existent essences that transcend the many entities (possessing an inferior kind of existence) to which they give rise, essences that are neither affected nor perfected by such entities and to which the imagery of pregnancy and parenting is inappropriate (though Plato did use it of the Idea of the Good in the *Republic* 6.508B and 7.517C). We might also note that Plato's earlier theory of the Ideas seems not to have elaborated on the collateral if antithetical theory of the nonexistent, of not-being.

In this analysis Ficino is certainly calling upon Scholastic distinctions he had encountered during his early training in philosophy and logic and particularly during his study of Aquinas. First, he is well aware of the problem of using the term "being" equivocally. In chapter 27, in the course of tracing the history of the attempt to define the prime "eternal substance" and the role of the Pythagoreans in opposing the natural philosophers, Ficino contrasts the "corporeal mass" that the natural philosophers had postulated with "the proper incorporeal object of the intellect" postulated by their adversaries— that is, "true being" (*verum ens*) (243.12–13). He calls the corporeal notion of being "generation" and the incorporeal "essence." In chapters 28 and 29 he charts what he sees as Melissus's strategy in setting up a false argument for refutation, namely that "one and the same reason of being" exists both in bodies and in such incorporeal substances as souls (245.4–6). This reason or principle is the "prime essence," and it is the "prime power" both in the sense of acting and in that of being acted upon; as such it is present in each and every entity. Here he encounters a crucial distinction, for the Pythagoreans and Platonists agreed in their refusal to accept that "one reason of being is present equally both in eternal and in transitory things" (245.12–14). For the two schools, moreover, "being does not proceed as far as what is lowest [i.e., matter]"; but the One does so proceed, and therefore the One is superior to being (245.16–17). This is an argument Ficino had explored at length in his *Parmenides* Commentary. Hence, he contends, a Pythagorean or a Platonist predicates "being" absolutely of unchanging things but only equivocally of changing things, just as the term "man" refers absolutely to the person but only equivocally to his mirror image (245.18–19).

He returns to this line of reasoning in chapter 33. Having established the "most special species" and reduced them to the class "closest," that is, immediately superior to them (253.17–18), we arrive eventually at "the Idea itself of being" and finally, at the climax of the dialectical process, at the notion of the Idea of being as one and the same in all intelligible entities, and thus as common and univocal. For the fact that being can be present in some of these entities "first and in greater measure, but in others later and in less measure" does not prevent us from thinking of it univocally (253.21–25). The Platonic dogma is thus that in all intelligible entities there exists "one reason of essence"—that is, of univocal being. Sensibles, in contrast, are related to authentic entities as mirror images to the bodies they reflect. In other words, with regard to sensibles we can speak of being only if we mean the term "in an analogical or equivocal condition" (253.29–255.3). This is the outcome of our own mental limitations; for the "universal concept" we arrive at rationally is more limited than "the more universal idea" that exists in the prime intellect (255.9–12). Hence we cannot wholly understand "the reason of being" as it exists in its primary form.

The whole line of argument is predicated on the familiar Platonic assumption that we can make a fundamental division between the intelligible realm or universe of true being and the sensible realm of entities and their qualities, the realm of generation. But it supposes nevertheless that the latter possesses a kind of being, being in a conditional or relative sense. According to the wisdom of the *Sophist,* that is, anything inferior to the purely intelligible but superior to matter (as distinct from body or matter-in-extension) is at least partially real, partially in possession of being, however equivocally. Given the Plotinian principle elaborated most fully by Proclus that being's power does not proceed to matter while the One's does (simplicity being the unique predication common to the One and to matter), such logic implies, furthermore, that only when we arrive eventually at matter do we pass beyond the lowest limits of that equivocation and encounter privation, absolute not-being. The last element in the pentad of the five universal classes, the concept of difference, poses the question of the status of such not-being in its acutest form.

Ficino devotes chapters 35 through 38 to an analysis of difference. Unlike rest and motion that are "absolutes" and cannot easily
be mixed together, "either formally or denominatively," identity
and difference (or the same and the other) are "relative" and thus,
though opposites, can be easily mingled (261.7–9). But "the power
of otherness," having been mingled from the beginning in the
ideal forms, "makes negation" and "mixes not-being with being"
(261.12–13). This is to assert that we can in a way equate not-being
with otherness, and see the "communion" that pertains between
identity and difference in that each shares in the characteristic of
not being the other. This characteristic of not being something else
marks not only the mutual relationships pertaining between the five
classes but those pertaining among different aspects of the same
Idea. It means that even at the highest of ontological levels we must
predicate the communion of being with not-being, a communion
that is present from the very onset of intelligible reality and not
simply confined to the sensible realm. The first principles of ontology are necessarily those too of meontology.

But how can we reconcile the hallowed Plotinian definition of
matter as absolute not-being with what would seem to be both the
Sophist's argument and the logic of Plotinian ontology, namely that
if being and not-being are mutually dependent, or what we would
now think of as self-predicating, and if being extends through the
realms of Mind, Soul, Forms-in-Body, and even Body but not to
the One or to matter, then surely not-being, dependent as it is on
being, will also extend through those realms but not to the One or
to matter and cannot therefore be predicated of matter?

The obvious solution to this dilemma is to predicate univocal and
equivocal senses of not-being itself. Thus Ficino hastens to reject
the idea that the realms of Mind, Soul, Forms-in-Body (Ficino
sometimes refers to this realm as Quality), and Body constitute
a simple ontological pyramid where absolute being gradually de-
creases into equivocal being, thence into equivocal not-being, and
thence into absolute not-being. For this would have amounted, for
all its schematic tidiness, to a refusal again to confront the chief
interpretative challenge, or what Ficino would call the mystery, at

the heart of the *Sophist,* where Plato's argument clearly envisages
the copresence (if not coexistence exactly) of being and not-being,
not at the extremes of an ontological hierarchy but within each
existent in that hierarchy.

In chapter 37 Ficino argues that "otherness" in the *Sophist* seems
to signify "divisibility" and thus "deservedly it is also called not-
being" (263.2–4, 9–10). It can even be referred to as "the essence
or nature or power or origin of not-being," though the notion of
the "essence" of not-being has a paradoxical cast to it. This essence, furthermore, has been "sown in all beings": everything that
is also is not (263.9–11). But the issue of equivocation inevitably
arises. Surely difference, and therefore not-being, cannot be the
same (if we may accept this paradoxical formulation) with regard
to the realms of being on the one hand and to matter on the other?
Ficino observes: "Otherness in the intelligible world is as it were a
kind of matter; it is the cause there of any defect and difference,
just as the matter in the sensible world, along simultaneously with
dimension, is the cause of defect and disagreement everywhere and
of distance" (263.11–14). But, whereas the otherness in the intelligible realm is the cause only of relative not-being, the otherness by
contrast that is the foundation, the substrate of the sensible world
is the "beginning" (*initium*), not only, he writes, of relative not-
being, "the not-being of this or that" aspect or attribute or individual
entity in the sensible realm, but also of absolute not-being, that
is, of matter (263.14–16). Difference, therefore, is univocal with
regard to the realms of being in that they and their constituent individual beings differ relatively from each other, but equivocal with
regard to their relationship to matter in that they differ from it absolutely. Thus Ficino is led to think of difference in the intelligible
world analogously as a kind of matter since it is the cause of matter.
Presumably, this quasi-matter which is difference is the same as
Plotinus's intelligible matter as set forth in the *Enneads* 2.4.1–5,
where it is associated with the procession (*proodos*) from the One
(as elsewhere with the "indefinite dyad"), and where, interestingly,
two of the *megista genê,* motion and difference, are associated with
the descent into plurality that accompanies that procession.[30]

We might note that the Proclian interpretation of the *Parmenides,* which Ficino assumed was not only the interpretation of Plotinus but that intended by Plato himself, characterizes the last four of the nine hypotheses identified in the dialogue's second part as concerned with the consequences of supposing the not-being of the One.[31] None of the postulated consequences would follow, incidentally, from supposing the not-being of the prime being, because the prime being is not the One, and the concerns here are not those of the *Sophist*. Nevertheless, the four hypotheses as interpreted by the Neoplatonists do postulate degrees of not-being and also illuminate the related concept of "nothingness," a concept that haunts the *Sophist* in a way that is not true of the *Parmenides,* preoccupied as it is with the specter of the many. It would be interesting at some point to bring the theory of the five classes of being to bear on these negative hypotheses to see whether Ficino was directly influenced at all in his analysis of them by his reading of the *Sophist*.

That the seeds of not-being are present in the prime being itself, and infinitely and everlastingly so, is a tenet to which Ficino gladly subscribes for a particular reason. In chapter 36 he writes, "Therefore, not-being seems infinite in the first being"; and this is confirmation of the fact that the prime being is not what is absolutely first; for "no such discrepancy at all or as it were privation" can exist in what is absolutely first (261.28–30). However oblique, this "confirmation" of the One's total transcendence is surely one of the principal reasons why Ficino was eager to expatiate on not-being's presence in the second hypostasis. For proving the absolute primacy of the One was a lifelong Platonic commitment and something that preoccupied his later years when he was at work on the *Parmenides* and intent on refuting the Aristotelian challenge mounted by the opponent we have always supposed was his fellow Platonist, the

---

30. Wallis, *Neoplatonism,* pp. 48–50, 66–67, with refs. Note that intelligible matter in an Aristotelian context means something quite different, as Wallis observes (p. 66). Whereas Aristotle distinguishes in the *Physics* 1.9.192a4 ff., moreover, between the not-being *per accidens* which is matter and the not-being *per se* which is privation, Plotinus argues against him in the *Enneads* 2.4.14–16 that matter in the sense-world is identical with privation and thus with absolute negativity, having agreed with him against the Stoics in 2.4.8–12 that it is incorporeal and sizeless or dimensionless. When it accepts dimension, it becomes Body.

31. See my "Ficino's theory of the Five Substances," pp. 37–41; also "The Second Ficino-Pico Controversy," pp. 444–448.

count of Mirandola. At any event, Ficino acknowledged that not-being is not only intrinsic to all discourse and ubiquitously present in the sensible and animate realms, but is also ubiquitously present in the realm of the intelligibles and even within the very source of universal being, pure Mind itself. Indeed, not-being begins with, is even "infinite" in (as we have just seen), this being. The triumph of the *Sophist* for Ficino was to promulgate this challenging and unfamiliar doctrine as authentically Platonic, and its effect was to underscore the primacy and absolute simplicity of the One. Concomitantly, it severely undermined the Aristotelian position that equated the One with being, since such a position would also imply the One's equation with not-being, or at the very least the presence of not-being in the One; and this would negate the notion of the first hypostasis's absolute simplicity and thus prevent the One from being the One.

We can now appreciate more fully the reasons why Ficino immediately turned to this dialogue upon completing his huge *Parmenides* Commentary: it was obviously with the intention of focussing on its metaphysics, however briefly, for inclusion in the 1496 volume of commentaries. The issues at stake were fundamental to Platonism and its claim to be the perfection of ancient wisdom, but they also had profound implications for Christian theology and specifically Christology, and thus for Christian ontology and the doctrine of the creative Logos. Both Ficino and Pico realized this when they turned to invoke the authority of Dionysius the [Pseudo-] Areopagite, whom Ficino regarded as the "pinnacle of the Platonic discipline, the pillar of Christian theology,"[32] and equally as "the

---

32. "Platonicae disciplinae culmen et Christianae Theologiae columen" (*Opera*, p. 1013.3, i.e., the argumentum to Ficino's commentary on the [Pseudo-]Areopagite's *De Mystica Theologia*). John Monfasani deals with the interesting controversy surrounding the authenticity of Dionysius and the *Dionysiaca* in Bessarion's circle stemming from the criticisms of Lorenzo Valla in the 1440s and centered around Pietro Balbi and Theodore Gaza ("Pseudo-Dionysius the Areopagite in Mid-Quattrocento Rome," in Hankins-Monfasani-Purnell, *Supplementum Festivum*, pp. 189–219). At pp. 192–193 he notes, however, that Bessarion himself, like Ficino, nowhere hints at doubts and in his monumental *In Calumniatorem Platonem*, which Ficino received as a gift in 1469, asserts thrice that Dionysius was the disciple of St. Paul and the legendary Hierotheus, and twice, admiringly, that Dionysius had used Plato's own words (ed. Ludwig Mohler, *Kardinal Bessarion als Theologe, Humanist und Staatsmann*, 3 vols. [Paderborn, 1923–1942; reprint, 1967], 2:88.19 ff., 446.7 ff., 488.7 ff., 246.21, and 488.10).

sedulous observer of Parmenides,"[33] and "the supreme supporter" and interpreter of the dialogue Plato had named after Parmenides.[34] Both the Florentines were eager to appropriate the Areopagite's views on the *Parmenides* and to present them as their own, but we must also assume that Ficino thought of the Areopagite as the authoritative reader of the *Sophist*—as the thinker who had fully comprehended its central ontological doctrines and appreciated its close connection with the *Parmenides*. From his syncretistic perspective the Areopagite's celebrated "negative" theology would have been indebted therefore to both Platonic masterpieces.

We must now turn to Ficino's interpretation of the history of ontology as he deduced it from Plato's various comments in the dialogue. The secrets of the *Sophist* are expounded by the Eleatic Stranger whom Ficino, as we have seen, identified as Melissus at the head of his translation of the dialogue.[35] At 216A Plato had described the Stranger as belonging to the school of Parmenides and Zeno and as "devoted to philosophy," and at 216B Theodorus, in demurring to Socrates' youthfully overzealous suggestion that the Stranger might be a god "who intends to observe and expose our weakness in philosophical discourse, like a very spirit of refutation," had nonetheless accepted that he was certainly divine, since this was the title proper to every true philosopher. In his *Parmenides* Commentary, at the conclusion of chapter 37, Ficino had assumed that Plato had selected Melissus as his spokesman in the *Sophist* because he was godlike, and more importantly because he was a propounder of Parmenidean ontology and someone who scorned idle refutation and contention.[36]

Ficino habitually thought of Parmenides as a Pythagorean and

---

33. "Sedulus Parmenidis observator" (*Opera*, p. 1167, i.e., chap. 53 of the *Parmenides* Commentary).

34. "libri huius [sc. *Parmenidis*] summus adstipulator" (*Opera*, p. 1189, i.e., chap. 79 of the *Parmenides* Commentary). See my "The Second Ficino-Pico Controversy," pp. 448–453.

35. "Hospes Eleates qui forte Mellissus est" (1484 ed. sig. N 3v, col. 1, 2up; 1491 ed. p. 62, col. 2). See chap. 1, p. 11 above.

36. "In *Sophiste* Melissum Parmenidis sectatorem fuisse inquit a redargutionibus contentionibusque alienum, et ut deum veneratur* vel certe divinum" (*Opera*, p. 1154).

*The reading in the *Commentaria in Platonem* (1496), sig. c 2; the *Opera* has the corrupt "veneraretur."

his followers as also Pythagoreans. The opening summa for the *Sophist* describes Melissus himself as an Eleatic and as "a Pythagorean philosopher" (221.3). One of the most telling arguments turns on the question of genre. Ficino is at pains in the *Parmenides* Commentary to defend what he sees as Plato's playful mixture of metaphysical with dialectical concerns, a mixture that also characterizes the *Parmenides'* companion dialogues, the *Statesman* and the *Sophist*. With all three, and indeed with most of the other dialogues where Plato's custom was to mix together a variety of concerns (even if one of those concerns was overriding), we should take great care, he argues, not to be misled by the play of the dialectic into supposing an absence of seriousness; rather, the presence of the dialectic signals the presence of the highest matters. Ficino was convinced, that is, of Plato's debt to the Pythagoreans for providing him with a model for intertwining themes and for modulating in subtle and poetic ways from play to seriousness. On occasion, however, this symphonic methodology had given rise to confusion and error, most notably perhaps in its having suggested to Plotinus the unacceptable doctrine of metempsychosis. Also at fault was its misleading presentation of the doctrine of being—which is not to say that Parmenides or his followers were not in possession of the highest ontological truths.

The problem had been posed by the Eleatic Stranger himself at the onset of the ontological section in the heart of the dialogue. At 237A3 ff. he exclaims,

The audacity of the statement lies in its implication that "what is not" has being, for in no other way could a falsehood come to have being. But, my young friend, when we were of your age the great Parmenides from beginning to end testified against this, constantly telling us what he also says in his poem, "Never shall this be proved—that things that are not are."[37]

---

37. Ficino's 1484 version reads, "quia talis locutio id quod non est esse admictit; falsum namque haud aliter quod est fieret. Magnus autem Parmenides, o puer, dum pueri adhuc essemus, statim ab initio assidueque id predicabat. Sic enim carminibus passim iocatur. Numquam, inquit, et nullo modo sunt illa que non sunt, sed tu hoc tramite querens mentem cohibe [237A3–9]" (sig. N 8r, col. 2, 2–9). Again we should recall that Ficino was only familiar with the T variants.

The same dictum reappears at 258D. Having admitted at 258C that the course of their skeptical inquiry had carried them beyond the range of Parmenides' prohibition to the point even of questioning the grounds of that prohibition, the Stranger maintains at 258D that "we have not merely shown that things that are not, are, but we have brought to light the real character of 'not-being.' We have shown that the nature of the different has existence and is parcelled out over the whole field of existent things with reference to one another."[38] The point is a crucial one, given: first, the authority the prohibition is accorded in the dialogue and the Stranger's own express Parmenidean allegiances; second, Ficino's sense of Parmenides' august position in the prehistory of Platonism and his belief that Plato had deliberately chosen to honor him by naming his most profound work after him; and third, the Parmenidean stamp of Plato's own doctrine of intelligible being and his doctrine of the One. How was Ficino to interpret the Stranger's apparent rejection of the dogma concerning the absolute impossibility of not-being?

Plato himself had provided a clue at 242C. Having exacted a promise from Theaetetus not to regard him as a parricide for testing the philosophy of his father Parmenides (241D), and then for laying unfilial hands upon it (242A), the Stranger suggests that Parmenides and all who up to now had ever undertaken "to determine how many real things there are and what they are like"[39] had chosen to address their auditors "in rather an offhand fashion" as if they were children who needed to be instructed each with his own myth or story. At the onset of his chapter 22, Ficino takes up this ironic suggestion by insisting that the ancients had deliberately adopted "the light touch" when treating of being and had adumbrated their ideas "with poetic figments." In his Commentary on the *Parmenides* Ficino had reviewed the poetic devices used by Parmenides in the dialogue: his

---

38. "Numquam, nusquam, nullo modo sunt non entia. Sed tu querens ab hoc progressu cohibe mentem [258D2–3]. . . . Nos autem non solum non entia esse ostendimus, sed que sit non entis species demonstravimus. Cum enim ostenderemus alterius ipsius naturam esse perque omnia non entia divisam atque dispersam invicem [258D5–E1]" (ibid., sig. 0 5r, col. 2, 25–31).
39. "quot et qualia sint entia determinare est ausus [242C4–6]" (ibid., sig. 0 1v, col. 1, 8–9).

choice of nine hypotheses to explore in the second part as if they
were the nine Muses in the train of the One as Apollo (literally the
"not many" or the "not of many" in Neoplatonic etymologizing);
and what he interprets as the "poetic" meanings Parmenides had
assigned to various terms, and most notably to the "one" and the
"other." In the process Ficino discusses the relationship between
poetry and dialectic and the kinship between poets and dialecticians
as artists of metaphors and figures.[40] The figures themselves he
habitually thinks of, in the traditional manner, as "veils" that hide
the nakedness of truth from the vulgar gaze, or as a "rind" that
protects its sweet kernel. Occasionally, and more provocatively if
equally traditionally, he ponders their effectiveness as challenges to
the wit of clever men, as intellectual baits that will lure the subtle
into the paths of righteous inquiry. All this points to the suggestion
that when dealing with the ontology of Parmenides we are dealing
in effect with poetry and with certain ambiguities introduced by
poetic figures. There are veils that need to be drawn aside, but only
the adept, the Platonic philosopher-interpreter, is in a position to
do so with success: only he can reveal the naked purity of the truth
which Parmenides had seen but chosen to conceal.

But to conceal from whom? Among the ancients were numbered
the *physici,* the philosophers of nature. They had been among the
first to set out to determine the principles of being and to speculate
on what might constitute prime being. In glossing 242C ff., Ficino
writes in chapter 22 that the natural philosophers, among them
perhaps Thales if an emendation suggested to me by Professor
Kristeller is correct, had first postulated three prime entities: heat,
cold, and a mean defined as wetness. Then Anaxagoras had postulated four such entities by adding dryness, and by defining heat
and cold as active principles and wetness and dryness as passive.
Finally Heraclitus and Empedocles had postulated one prime entity,
matter, with diverse qualities sometimes in harmony, sometimes in
discord. While Heraclitus had argued that these were in a state of
perpetual flux, Empedocles had argued that harmony and discord

---

alternated from age to age: concord would first rule, and then discord would resolve all into chaos until concord was again restored. All these *physici* had been committed to the task of defining absolute being, but had been misled into doing so in entirely physical, or what Ficino thought of as sensible, terms.

The *metaphysici* by contrast, and this included preeminently the Pythagoreans and the Eleatics their followers, had dismissed the various entities postulated by the natural philosophers as not "true" entities (235.17–19) and had concentrated instead upon the principle that underlies them. But Ficino does not intend by this principle, interestingly, the One itself, though the One was Parmenides' preoccupation as a metaphysician, as Ficino was exultantly aware. Rather, he sees the metaphysicians as concerned with intelligible being as the prime and universal being that includes the natural philosophers' prime "beings" (even though they recognize that such beings are not true or real absolutely). While the natural philosophers, given their materialist premises, had arrived at various notions of a corporeal substrate, the metaphysicians, culminating in Plato and in his disciple Aristotle, had arrived at the much more profound and mysterious notion of an incorporeal prime matter which the later Platonic tradition, but not the Aristotelian, had identified with privation (and the authoritative text for Ficino as we have seen would have been Plotinus's *Enneads* 2.4.14–16). Paradoxically, this "metaphysical" history of prime matter and thus of notbeing takes us to the threshold of understanding prime being, the opposite of—but also, given the *Sophist*'s examination of the interrelatedness of the two concepts, the source of—"infinite" not-being.

Thus in chapter 21 Ficino interprets the Stranger as being in only apparent contradiction to his great "preceptor" (233.18–21). For he takes the Stranger to be arguing against what he calls in chapter 24 the "perverse interpretation" of those who interpret Parmenides' dictum that all being is one to mean that whatever is possessed of being must be entirely one and devoid of multiplicity, and therefore of difference and not-being (237.14–18). Hence, he writes in chapter 27, Parmenides, like all the Pythagoreans, had treated of "true being itself, that is, of eternal substance," though he had done so, again in the Pythagorean manner, poetically. Other philosophers, the *physici,* had treated of "what is not true, that is, of what has been generated." Accordingly, he asserts, Parmenides and the Pythagoreans had not spoken falsely about being, though some of them had pronounced "a few things rather obscurely" (243.2–7).

Ficino emphatically reiterates that in the *Sophist* we must realize that Plato's intention is to explain and resolve, not to confute, the views of the great Parmenides and indeed of any Pythagorean. For these metaphysicians had recognized that "only what is incorporeal and is the proper object of the intellect exists as true being" (243.7–13). In the process they had established the grounds for refuting those who erroneously supposed that the prime essence and being was "the corporeal mass [of the world] alone" (243.9), a theory that Ficino himself had first encountered in the great Roman *physicus,* the poet Lucretius, whose verses sprang instinctively to his lips whenever he spoke of the world's body and the atomic turmoil of its elements.

Again, for Ficino it was the Pythagoreans and their Eleatic followers, not Aristotle, who had discovered the difference between the univocal and equivocal senses of being and of not-being, and who had perceived the need to subordinate the philosophy of being to the philosophy of the One. They had thereby also arrived, says chapter 29, at a correct understanding of the foundations of epistemology and determined that intelligible being was the proper object of human knowledge (since knowledge of the One is not, strictly speaking, knowledge at all, but the outcome of an ascent to union that cannot be said "to be" or "not to be," given that it transcends the predication of being entirely).[41]

Finally, we must acknowledge their ultimate contribution to logic. Ficino argues in chapter 34 that just as it was an earlier Pythagorean, the poet Archytas, who had arrived at the ten categories for analyzing being later elaborated by Aristotle and his followers, so it was a later Pythagorean, Melissus, who had collected the ten categories into the five all-embracing classes, classes

---

41. On the problem of how we understand the One which is beyond understanding, see J. M. Rist, "Mysticism and Transcendence in Later Neoplatonism," *Hermes* 92 (1964), 213–225.

correctly understood only by the Platonists (as opposed to the Aristotelians) (255.21–25). This last observation is noteworthy, for it also suggests that the Eleatics refined upon the Pythagoreans and their followers, and thus that Ficino detected a subtle but fundamental distinction between the two schools.

The various accounts of Plato's career, most notably those familiar to Ficino in Diogenes Laertius's life, in the treatise *De Platone et Eius Dogmate* by Apuleius of Madaura, and in the notices in Aristotle, Cicero, and Augustine, tell the story of his youthful education in natural philosophy at the feet of such followers of Heraclitus as Cratylus, and in ethical and political philosophy at the feet of Socrates, though not necessarily in that order. Finally he had turned for instruction in speculative or contemplative philosophy to various Pythagoreans, particularly to mathematicians like Philolaus and Theodorus, and in Magna Graecia to Eurytus and Archytas of Tarentum. Subsequently, Plato had intended to visit the Indians and the Magi of Persia, Zoroaster being the first great magus and the originator of the Pythagorean wisdom, but was prevented from doing so by the outbreak of hostilities.[42] Instead, Apuleius says, he set about expounding the teachings of Parmenides and Zeno. Ficino certainly thought of these two masters as Pythagoreans, as he states in his *Platonic Theology* 17.4, and as we have already seen in the case of Parmenides.[43] Melissus, however, occupies a singular position as their pupil. In cutting Archytas's ten genera by half and thus arriving at five, the number signifying marriage and justice, he had not so much refuted his master as expounded his dictum correctly and explicated its enfolded poetry, Parmenides being the author, we recall, of what Ficino read as a poem full of Platonic secrets. Ficino observes in chapter 38 that Melissus "does not contradict Par-

---

42. Diogenes Laertius, *Lives of the Philosophers* 3.6–7; Apuleius, *De Platone et Eius Dogmate* 1.3; Aristotle, *Metaphysics* 1.6.987a29 ff.; Cicero, *Tusculan Disputations* 1.17.39; Augustine, *Contra Academicos* 3.17.37. Ficino incorporated these accounts of Plato's philosophical education and development into his own *Vita Platonis,* for which see chap. 1, n. 17 above; see also my "Plato's Pythagorean Eye," pp. 174–177.

43. Ed. Marcel, 3:168. Cf. Ficino's epitome of the *Laws* book 1 (*Opera,* p. 1488.2). We should bear in mind the tradition that Empedocles too was a Pythagorean and that for Ficino the source of all Pythagorean wisdom was ultimately Zoroaster.

menides but interprets him": he alerts us to the fact that when
Parmenides speaks of not-being we should take him to be referring,
not to "something that is not-being in any particular way," but to
"the absolutely nothing" (265.10–13). When Parmenides says that
"being is other than individual classes or all the classes," we must
understand him to mean being as a concept that the reason has
arrived at by abstraction, in other words to mean essence; "for being in the concrete is constituted as it were from all the classes"
(265.16–18). In short, the Eleatics would seem to be emerging in
this Ficinian account as Plato's most sublime masters. While Parmenides had initiated Plato into the highest reaches of monistic
metaphysics, Melissus had taught him the true doctrine of being
and not-being, a doctrine Melissus had learned from Parmenides
indeed but had made especially his own.

All this would be to attribute too much to Melissus, however,
and even to Parmenides at the expense of Plato. For Ficino nowhere
elevates Parmenides, let alone Melissus, to the company of the six
great sages which culminated in Plato and which included Philolaus
and even at a preliminary stage such a shadowy figure as Aglaophamus. This company never included Socrates either, and we must
suppose that Ficino did not consider him or Plato's Heraclitean
teachers or the Eleatics of the same stature as those in the chain of
pre-Platonic, "Pythagorean" Platonists originating in Zoroaster and
Hermes Trismegistus and passing through Orpheus, Pythagoras,
and Philolaus to Plato himself. We might note in addition that
Ficino does not think of Parmenides or Melissus per se as Plato's
teachers, though he does accept that Hermogenes, a follower of
Parmenides, had taught him.[44] The reason is, of course, chronology:
Parmenides was already an old man when Socrates was young and
Melissus also was his senior. It was Plato's custom, so Ficino had
argued in the *Platonic Theology* 17.4, following the biographical
tradition, to acknowledge his debt to the Pythagoreans whom he
had actually met, men such as Archytas of Tarentum, Eurytus, and

---

44. *Opera*, pp. 764.1 (misnumbered 774) (the *Vita Platonis*), 1310 (the *Cratylus*
epitome). For Hermogenes, Ficino's source was obviously Diogenes Laertius, *Lives of the
Philosophers* 3.6.

Philolaus, by introducing their teachers and other Pythagoreans into his dialogues as protagonists. Ficino specifically mentions Timaeus Locrus, Parmenides, and Zeno, but he might well have added Melissus too: "It is from their mouths that Socrates, in Plato's account, learns what he then transmits to others in the rest of Plato's works."[45] In effect Marsilio is blurring the nature of Plato's relationship to the great Eleatics and underplaying the debt. Whatever Plato had learned from them indirectly by way of his teachers he had made entirely his own. When they appeared in his dialogues propounding the secrets of being and the One, they were no longer voicing their own original ideas, or ideas they had inherited from the older Pythagorean tradition, but rather Plato's perfect transformation of those ideas: they were acting as spokesmen for his wisdom. That he had chosen them for such a role was a courteous acknowledgment of his general debt to Pythagoreanism and assuredly intimated the ancient origins of that wisdom; but it was also a facet of his playful, his poetic technique, and should in no way be held to diminish the sovereign authority we accord his works. In the *Sophist* Plato had indeed chosen a distinguished Eleatic Pythagorean as his protagonist, just as he had chosen another and even greater one for the *Parmenides*. But the complex ontology presented there is indubitably and luminously his own, and in particular the mysterious doctrine of not-being, which does not contradict the insights of Parmenides so much as go beyond them and refine and perfect them.

Ficino's arresting vision of the *Sophist* was, I suggested at the onset, the result of his encounter with Plotinus's *Enneads,* and specifically with the treatise 6.2. It shares in the Plotinian emphasis on ontology and deploys Plotinian arguments even as it reinforces them with concepts derived from Scholasticism. The Eleatic Stranger, the Melissus of the *Theaetetus,* is in many fundamental respects the voice of Ficino's Plotinus, the *Parmenides* and the *Sophist* being the two most Plotinian of Plato's works in the Floren-

---

45. Ed. Marcel, 3:168. See my "Plato's Pythagorean Eye," p. 174.

tine's interpretation. Was this perhaps one of the principal reasons why he chose to translate and comment on the whole of the *Enneads* before turning to comment on both major dialogues, the supposition being that he could not understand them correctly without Plotinus's insights? At any event, when Pico della Mirandola took up arms against the view that in the *Parmenides* and the *Sophist* Plato was subordinating being to the One, he was not only openly confronting his senior fellow Platonist but the majesty of Plotinus himself. This was fittingly ironic in that Pico had been the stimulus, by Marsilio's own testimony,[46] behind his having taken up the daunting challenge of rendering Plotinus into Latin in the first place, after the publication of his Plato translation in 1484. In short, we must align the *Sophist* Commentary with the *Parmenides* Commentary if we wish to appreciate, specifically, the range and depth of Ficino's response to Pico's *De Ente et Uno,* and generally, the unexpectedly pivotal role that the *Sophist* played both in the controversy that sharply divided the two great luminaries of Florentine Neoplatonism and in the remarkable revival of interest in Plotinus that preceded that controversy and was in many ways its cause.

---

46. *Opera,* p. 1537; see Kristeller, *Supplementum* 1:clvii. This may have been nothing more than a Platonic compliment.

Chapter 3: The Sublunar Demiurge

Though Ficino's principal guide to an understanding of the *Sophist* was undoubtedly Plotinus, there is interesting evidence that he was also cognizant of the later Neoplatonic concerns with the dialogue and perhaps influenced, in part at least, by them, more particularly since they addressed issues and motifs that Plotinus had apparently left aside. Furthermore, Ficino had in front of him the evidence of a brief but unusually suggestive text which he assumed to be from the hand of Proclus and therefore invested with his considerable authority. So convinced was Ficino of the importance of this text—in actuality an anonymous scholion—that he decided to translate it and to use it as the first half of an introduction he wrote for his *Sophist* translation in the great 1484 edition of Plato translations. The only piece of Neoplatonic commentary that he incorporated in this way, it testifies to the eminence Ficino accorded Proclus. Furthermore, since the Plato edition made an extraordinary impact on Ficino's contemporaries and had an abiding influence on the next two European centuries, it effectively promoted what all assumed to be the Proclian view of the dialogue, ironically more so perhaps than Ficino's commentary succeeded in promoting the Plotinian view, and despite Ficino's own qualifications, if not disclaimers, in the second half of his introduction.

For a sense of the role of the *Sophist* in Neoplatonism after Plotinus, let us turn to L. G. Westerink's prefatory comments to his edition and translation of some anonymous late antique prolegomena to the study of Plato. Originally lecture notes and not intended for publication, they were written apparently by someone after Proclus who must have belonged to the Alexandrian circle or school of Platonists, since there are links with the work of Ammonius and Olympiodorus but none with the sixth-century Athenian

Academy under Damascius.[1] The notes raise some significant issues. At 21.30 ff. the author observes that the theme of the *Sophist* cannot be the particular theme of the sophist but rather the more general theme of not-being: "For a sophist is something unreal, but nonexistence absolutely is more general than a particular unreal thing and, because more general, it is also more comprehensive, so that the more general theme comprises the more particular one."[2] With the same problem of having to define the principal theme in mind, the author also argues at 23.8–15 that

it is a mistake to say that the theme of the *Sophist* is the method of division [*diairesis*], though he does broach the subject there; he says for instance [at 235C] that nothing will glory in having escaped the method of division; he has also said of division [in the *Philebus* at 16C] that it is a gift of the gods to man through Prometheus. As this method is an instrument of the art of demonstration, it is one of the elements that contribute to the main plan [*skopos*]; we use it as a means to establish the central theme, but it should not be made the theme itself.[3]

Such comments alert us to the disagreement in antiquity over what constituted the dialogue's major theme (*skopos*). The Neoplatonists found both the suggestions that it was the human sophist and that it was the method of division equally unsatisfactory, because they were either too particular or merely instrumental to the main theme. Far more compelling was the notion that it was the comprehensive theme of not-being, but this too was rejected by some on the principle promulgated by Iamblichus, namely that no dialogue's theme could be a negative one. This led in turn to the proposition that the *Sophist* was primarily concerned, not with not-being, but with being, "de ente" having been indeed the customary subtitle for the dialogue in the Alexandrian school.[4]

Determining the *skopos*, however, was more than a matter of analyzing the dialogue internally: it depended too on how one

---

1. *Anonymous Prolegomena*, p. x.
2. Ibid., pp. 38–39.
3. Ibid., pp. 42–43.
4. Larsen, *Jamblique de Chalcis*, pp. 357–361. For Ficino, compare Diogenes Laertius, *Lives of the Philosophers* 3.58.

interpreted its relationship to other dialogues, and particularly to the two dialogues which Plato himself had linked with the *Sophist*, namely, the *Theaetetus* and the *Statesman*. The *Statesman* is its declared sequel in that both were intended to constitute the first two members of a trilogy treating respectively of the sophist, the statesman, and the philosopher. The *Theaetetus*, given that its theme was "knowledge," served as a kind of preface for this projected trilogy, and it came to Ficino certainly as the *Sophist*'s immediate predecessor in the second tetralogy. That he intended to retain this order in his own Latin translation of the dialogues is indicated by the opening sentence of his introduction to the *Sophist* as it appeared eventually in his *Opera Omnia*: "Post *Theaetetum* de scientia, legendus est *Sophista* de ipso ente, quod scientiae est obiectum."[5] Also linked to the *Sophist*, though less directly, wcrc the two greatest dialogues from the Neoplatonists' perspective, the *Parmenides* and the *Timaeus*, along with the *Philebus* as we have seen. Only after one had determined their primary themes could one settle upon the primary theme of the *Sophist*; for it had to complement theirs and play its part in the architectural whole of Plato's work.

In order to appreciate more fully the Neoplatonists' sense of the *Sophist*'s position in the canon, we must turn, not to chronological considerations to which they were largely indifferent, but to the structuring of their teaching cycle. Basing himself upon the "unimpeachable testimony" of Proclus's Commentary on the *Alcibiades* 11.15–17, Westerink argues that this was divided into two unequal parts.[6] The second part consisted of the *Timaeus* followed by the *Parmenides* as the climactic work of the whole cycle. Indeed, the Neoplatonists supposed that once a pupil had been educated to the level of being able fully to comprehend the structure, the method, and the substance of the *Parmenides*, then, from a strictly metaphysical or what Ficino thought of as a theological viewpoint, the pupil no longer really needed to study the other dialogues except insofar

---

5. See pp. 16–17 above.
6. *Anonymous Prolegomena*, p. xxxvii. See also Morrow and Dillon, *Proclus' Commentary on Plato's Parmenides*, p. xxxvii, where Dillon maintains that the scheme "is actually that of Iamblichus."

as they served to reinforce and gloss the lessons of the *Parmenides*. The elevation of the *Parmenides* to this unique status was the outcome of a long and complex series of attempts undertaken by generations of later Platonists, beginning with Plotinus and culminating in Plutarch of Athens, to analyze its structure correctly. At issue were the number and nature of the hypotheses in the dialogue's second part. By the time Proclus arrived in Athens at the end of the first quarter of the fifth century, Plutarch had triumphantly determined that Plato was presenting nine hypotheses, subdivided into five positive and four negative; and also that in each of the five positive hypotheses he was treating respectively of the five basic hypostases in what the Neoplatonists thought of as the Platonic metaphysical system: the One, Mind, Soul, Forms-in-Body, and Body (that is, matter-in-extension, matter actualized). An equally significant assumption was that Plato was secretly intending to take whatever was denied of the One in the first hypothesis in order to predicate it of Mind, the subject of the second hypothesis. Above all, the *Parmenides* owed its elevated status for the Neoplatonists to the fact that they were convinced that its *skopos* was the One itself, the first hypostasis of Platonic metaphysics and the key concept of all Platonic philosophy.[7] The *Timaeus* was the *Parmenides'* twin, not because of its concern with natural philosophy but because of its great myth of the Demiurge, whom the Neoplatonists, if not Plotinus himself, consistently interpreted as Mind. Of interest too was its treatment of the World-Soul and its creation by the Demiurge. The *Timaeus,* in other words, introduced the initiate to a proper understanding of the second and third hypotheses in the second part of the *Parmenides*.[8]

These two great dialogues were thought to be too difficult for the neophyte, however, and hence the rationale for the first part of the

---

7. Saffrey and Westerink, *Proclus: Théologie platonicienne* 1:lx–lxxxix; Morrow and Dillon, *Proclus' Commentary on Plato's Parmenides,* pp. xxiv–xxxviii. For Plotinus's interpretation, see Charrue, *Plotin: Lecteur de Platon,* pp. 43–115.

8. For the Neoplatonists' account of the *Timaeus,* see Matthias Baltes, *Die Weltentstehung des platonischen Timaios nach den antiken Interpreten,* 2 vols., Philosophia Antiqua, vols. 30 and 35 (Leiden, 1976–1978); vol. 2 is devoted to Proclus's views. For Plotinus's interpretation, see also Charrue, *Plotin: Lecteur de Platon,* pp. 117–155.

teaching cycle. According to Proclus's testimony, this part seems to have consisted of an introductory course of ten dialogues that culminated in a study of the *Philebus,* subtitled "On the Good."[9] In his Commentary on the *Gorgias* 4.23–5.5, Olympiodorus confirms that the first three dialogues were the *First Alcibiades,* the *Gorgias,* and the *Phaedo.*[10] The prolegomena assert that numbers four and five were the *Cratylus* and the *Theaetetus* and that numbers eight and nine were the *Phaedrus* and the *Symposium.* But, unfortunately, there is a lacuna in the prolegomena just where the author is about to declare what numbers six and seven were. At 26.31–32 he states merely that after the *Theaetetus* "we come to the . . . which deals with natural philosophy."[11] Westerink believes that the two missing dialogues were the *Sophist* and the *Statesman,* noting first, that Iamblichus, Proclus, and Olympiodorus (all three of whom adhered to the "regular program" of the teaching cycle) each wrote a *Sophist* commentary, though none has survived; second, that the *Statesman* figures prominently in the work of Proclus and is frequently cited as a source of Platonic "theology"; third, that the two dialogues were invariably linked according to Plato's plan; and fourth, that the decision to categorize both dialogues as "physical," meaning concerned with natural philosophy, is perfectly understandable if we see them as preparatory to the study of the *Timaeus,* the definitive Platonic treatment of all natural philosophy.[12] Moreover, Westerink continues, the initial group of ten dialogues can itself be broken down into the following scheme: an introductory dialogue, the *First Alcibiades,* and a culminating one, the *Philebus*; two ethical dialogues, the *Gorgias* and the *Phaedo*; followed by two logical dialogues, the *Cratylus* and the *Theaetetus*; followed in turn by two physical dialogues, the *Sophist* and the *Statesman*; followed in their turn by two theological dialogues,

---

9. For the significance for Ficino of the climactic position for the *Philebus,* see my *Philebus Commentary,* pp. 4–6 also my "Ficino's Lecture on the Good?" *Renaissance Quarterly* 30 (1977), 160–171.

10. Ed. Norvin (Leipzig, 1936), cited by Westerink, *Anonymous Prolegomena,* p. xxxvii.

11. Westerink, *Anonymous Prolegomena,* pp. 48–49.

12. Ibid., pp. xxxvii–xxxviii.

the *Phaedrus* and the *Symposium*. In the second half of the cycle the *Timaeus* perfects the logical and physical wisdom of the second and third pairs, and the *Parmenides* the wisdom of the ethical and theological wisdom of the first and fourth pairs.[13]

In this account the teaching cycle constitutes a neatly tailored and internally consistent pedagogical program that culminates first in the *Philebus* (on the Good), and then in the *Timaeus* (on Nature and the Demiurge) and the *Parmenides* (on the One). Remarkable for their absence are the *Republic*, the *Laws*, the *Meno*, the *Apology*, the *Protagoras*, and a number of the earlier Socratic dialogues. Nevertheless, the twelve selected dialogues do constitute a defensible core reading, at least for the later Plato. The exception perhaps might be the *First Alcibiades*, but this enjoyed considerable prestige among the Neoplatonists as the dialogue concerned with man's nature and his self-knowledge, a prestige reinforced for the Renaissance by the survival of a long and richly detailed commentary by Proclus and of an interesting commentary by Olympiodorus.[14]

The twelve dialogues also seem to have been of particular concern to Ficino, who was familiar with the Neoplatonic view of the Plato canon from his intensive study of Proclus. For six of the twelve he provided full-scale commentaries, and he took the considerable trouble required to provide an abbreviated translation of Proclus's *Alcibiades* Commentary into Latin.[15] For four others, the *Cratylus*, the *Phaedo*, the *Gorgias*, and the *Theaetetus*, he provided comprehensive introductions.[16] Finally, the *Statesman*, as we shall see,

---

13. Ibid., pp. xxxix–xl; see also Larsen, *Jamblique de Chalcis*, pp. 332–334.

14. For an introduction to the ancient Neoplatonists' interpretation of the *First Alcibiades*, see Larsen, *Jamblique de Chalcis*, pp. 340–347, and John M. Dillon, *Iamblichi Chalcidensis in Platonis Dialogos Commentariorum Fragmenta* (Leiden, 1973), pp. 72–83, 229–238. For Proclus's and Olympiodorus's commentaries see L. G. Westerink's two editions, *Proclus Diadochus: Commentary on the First Alcibiades of Plato* (Amsterdam, 1954), and *Olympiodorus: Commentary on the First Alcibiades of Plato* (Amsterdam, 1956). The Renaissance *fortuna* of Alcibiades and the two Platonic dialogues named after him (both of which are now usually considered spurious) has yet to be written but will have to begin with Ficino's epitome and comments in his *Opera* (for the *First Alcibiades*, subtitled "on the nature of man," on p. 1133, and for the *Second Alcibiades*, subtitled "on prayer," on p. 1134).

15. *Opera*, pp. 1908–1928. See Kristeller, *Supplementum* 1:cxxxiv–cxxxv; and *Ficino and His Work*, p. 130.

16. *Opera*, pp. 1309–1314 (*Cratylus*), 1390–1395 (*Phaedo*), 1315–1320 (*Gorgias*), 1274–1281 (*Theaetetus*).

interested him, as it had his predecessors, only because of the enigmatic myth propounded from 269A to 274E of the golden age of the "shepherd" Cronus, the succeeding miseries of the age of Zeus, and the cyclical alternation of divine care for and neglect of the rotations of the world.[17] Thus Ficino shared with the ancient Neoplatonists an interest in the same set of what we now think of as Plato's later dialogues where methodological and metaphysical themes dominate. We may surely predict that he would have acknowledged the appropriateness of the selection for the ancient teaching cycle could he have gained access to the kind of information appearing in the prolegomena.[18]

Nonetheless, the teaching cycle, however instructive for us, cannot have been the source of Ficino's understanding of the *Sophist*'s post-Plotinian reputation and interpretation; and the chances of his stumbling on such odd notices to the *Sophist* in Olympiodorus's commentaries as those adduced by Westerink are also fairly remote, though he was acquainted with the commentaries on the *Philebus* and the *Phaedo*. Rather, he was primarily, perhaps wholly, indebted to the anonymous scholion which he unhesitatingly attributed to Proclus, translated into Latin, and incorporated into the introduction he wrote for the dialogue as it appeared in his Plato editions of 1484 and 1491. In both these editions the scholion is entitled "Praefatio in Platonis *Sophistam* secundum Proculum a Marsilio Ficino translata" and the transition to Ficino's own remarks is effected without any kind of typographical break. A note simply states "Hactenus Proculi, deinceps Marsilii." This is immediately followed by the opening clause of the introduction, "Dum vero hic de ente disseritur." While the "praefatio" is notably missing from the 1496 edition of the *Sophist* Commentary, which therefore opens with the

---

17. See Ficino's epitome in his *Opera,* pp. 1294–1296.
18. According to Westerink, *Anonymous Prolegomena,* p. xxxvii, the prolegomena are the only extant description "of what was for more than two centuries the standard curriculum in the Platonic schools." They were known to the Renaissance in only one manuscript, which dates from the tenth century and is now in the Vienna National Library catalogued as Vindobonensis phil. gr. 314; they appear between fols. 29v and 50v. Though this manuscript was twice copied in the sixteenth century, Westerink notes that "it received little notice until the end of the 18th century" (pp. l–lii).

clause, "Dum in *Sophista* de ente disseritur," it reappears in the three *Opera Omnia* editions of Ficino's works. Again entitled "Praefatio in Platonis *Sophistam* secundum Proculum a Marsilio Ficino translata," it is now set off typographically from his own introduction and printed in italics. The introduction itself is preceded by a new heading, "Marsilii Ficini Commentaria et Argumenta in Platonis *Sophistam*. Argumentum," and opens with a new bridging sentence, "Post *Theaetetum* de scientia, legendus est *Sophista* de ipso ente quod scientiae est obiectum," before continuing as before with the clause, "Dum vero in *Sophista* de ente disseritur." The *Opera Omnia* editions contain, however, a number of corrupt readings. The text, with the variants, appears below in Part II.

Given the pitfalls involved in interpreting this preface, and in order to clarify its implications for Ficino (and he obviously encountered a number of difficulties), I offer an English translation of his Latin version as it was first published in the 1484 *editio princeps*.[19] We should bear in mind that it was this Latin version that was read throughout the Renaissance, since it invariably accompanied the various editions of Ficino's Latin translation of the *Sophist* itself.

Plato uses the term "sophist" to signify not only a particular man but also Love, Pluto, Jupiter; and he refers to the sophistic art as "most eminent." From this we may gather that the dialogue is concerned with a more noble subject than might first appear. For, according to the great Iamblichus, Plato's intention was to treat of the sublunar craftsman. For the sophist is a fashioner of idols, a purifier of souls, a shape-exchanger [*or* barterer] forever separating souls from contrary reasons [*or* arguments], and the mercenary hunter of rich young men. When he receives their souls, which come to him from the heavens laden with reasons, he accepts money from them, money which is the trade of animals [*or perhaps* money which is what we trade animals for; *or possibly, given the* "poiian" *in the* "zôopoiian" *of the Greek,* money which is the workshop of animals—in the sense that it makes animals out of men]. This money [*or* trade *or* workshop] is made according to the reason or method [not of the heavens

---

19. John Dillon provides a translation of the Greek in his *Iamblichi Fragmenta*, p. 91. For the text as it was known to Ficino, see appendix 1 below.

but] of mortals [*the Greek probably means* this money is the product of the way mortal men think; cf. 224CD]. The sophist devotes himself to [*or possibly in the literal sense* lies heavily on] that which does not exist because he begets [*the Greek probably means* fashions] what is in matter. He loves what is truly false, namely matter; but at the same time he regards what truly and really exists. The sophist is many-headed, since he lays claim to many essences and lives through which he arranges the variety of generation. This same sophist is also a mage in generation when he so enchants and entices souls with natural reasons [*the Greek probably means* with his speeches about nature] that they are only separated with great difficulty from generation. Love, moreover, is a mage, and nature is called a mage by some because of the reciprocal attractions and enchantments [*in Greek* repulsions] that proceed in the course of nature. Now, therefore, Plato means to proclaim the sophist in every way. For the philosopher too is a sophist in that he imitates both the celestial craftsman and the craftsman of generation. And the faculty that makes distinctions imitates the progress of things from the One, and the craftsman of generation imitates the celestial craftsman; wherefore he is a sophist. And yet man himself is a sophist: he is called a sophist because he imitates the great things. And therefore Plato called the sophist many-headed. Assume that the Eleatic stranger portrays [*Dillon's* should be conceived in the role of, *though the Greek might also mean* is thinking of] the father of both craftsmen—that is, the absolute, supercelestial father. But assume that the stranger's [two] auditors portray the twin understandings of that absolute craftsman: the one, the understanding of Jupiter; the other, being an interpreter and a geometer, the understanding of the angelic nature. And since craftsmanship, when it begins with the imperfect, ends in the perfect, so the stranger turns first to Theodorus and then to converse with his own Socrates [*in Greek* with the divine Socrates, *or, with Dillon,* with Socrates, who is analogous to Zeus; *Ficino probably read* "idiôi" *for* "diiôi"]. Thus far are the words of Proclus; those that follow are Marsilio's.

Where did Ficino first come upon this preface? He is rendering the scholion as it appears at the beginning of all three of the major Plato manuscripts containing the *Sophist*. For instance, in the oldest of these, the codex in the Bodleian, Clarkianus 39 (traditionally designated by the siglum B), which was transcribed for the Byzantine scholar Arethas, it appears at the foot of the first folium contain-

ing the dialogue.[20] This scholion, like other Platonic scholia, dates
back to the ninth century, but its ideas, in all probability, originally
derive from late antiquity. It was first edited by C. Fr. Hermann in
volume 6 of his *Platonis Opera*,[21] and then by William C. Greene
in his collection, *Scholia Platonica*.[22] This text has been reproduced,
with commentary, by John Dillon and by Bent Dalsgaard Larsen in
the course of their independent examinations of all the evidence
extant for determining the views of Iamblichus, and particularly his
views on individual Platonic dialogues.[23]

A glance at Greene's apparatus instantly determines that Ficino
was translating from the version of the scholion appearing in, or as
it was copied from, another of the three major manuscripts, the
codex in the Marciana, Venetus Append. Class. 4, cod. 1 (traditionally designated by the siglum T), which dates from the eleventh or
twelfth century. The third major manuscript, incidentally, is the
Vienna codex 54, suppl. phil. Gr. 7 (with the siglum W). Striking
evidence is his rendering of *kai ton Haidên* in T's first line (but
missing in the other two versions). Indeed, both B and W omit the
entire phrase *ton Erôta kai ton Haidên,* though B does leave a
lacuna for nineteen letters. T omits *Erôta* alone, leaving a superflu-
ous *ton* at the beginning followed by a lacuna, a lacuna Ficino could
easily fill by referring to the scholion's own contention at line 14
that "Love too is a mage" and by cross-referring to the *Symposium*'s
comment at 203D that Love is terrible as an enchanter, a sorcerer,
and a sophist as well as being at all times a philosopher and a mighty
hunter. Equally striking is Ficino's adoption of the T variant in line 7
logôn where B and W have *alogôn*: thus Ficino translates "he receives their souls, which come to him from the heavens laden with
reasons" (instead of "entirely deprived of reasons").

Ficino did not, however, have access to the Marciana manuscript.
Rather, in translating the *Sophist,* he worked principally, we now

---

20. See the facsimile of the codex by T. W. Allen, *Plato: Codex Oxoniensis Clarkianus 39 Phototypice Editus* (Leiden, 1898–1899), f. 113r.
21. Leipzig, 1853, pp. 249–250.
22. Haverford, Pa., 1938, p. 40.
23. Dillon, *Iamblichi Fragmenta*, pp. 90–91 (but omitting the scholion's first sentence, *hoti . . . dialogos*), 245–247; Larsen, *Jamblique de Chalcis,* pp. 357–361, and app., p. 86 (no. 175).

believe, from the Laurenziana's 85.9 given to him by Cosimo in 1462,[24] which was copied from the Laurenziana's 59.1 or its exemplar, either at the time of the great Ferrara-Florence council between the Roman and the Orthodox churches, or earlier in Greece.[25] Manuscript 59.1 itself did not show up among Lorenzo's books, incidentally, until it was brought to Florence by Janus Lascaris in 1492, long after Ficino's detailed work on the Plato text had been completed.[26] Both these Laurenziana manuscripts belong to the group that derives from the Marciana's T (as do two other Plato manuscripts Ficino may have occasionally used);[27] and we must assume that Ficino was therefore familiar only with the set of variants common to the T group.[28] It is therefore logical that, in translating the scholion, he would be rendering the T version as he found it on f. 78r of the Laurenziana's MS. 85.9. It too has *kai ton Haidên* in line 1 (with a lacuna for the preceding phrase *kai ton Erôta*); and it too has *logôn* in line 7. Additionally, MS. 85.9 has the other distinguishing features of the T version of our scholion and of other

24. On this manuscript, which contains abundant marginalia by Ficino, see Marcel, *Marsile Ficin (1433–1499)*, pp. 254 ff.; Martin Sicherl, "Neuentdeckte Handschriften von Marsilio Ficino und Johannes Reuchlin," *Scriptorium* 16 (1962), 50–61 at 51–52 and 59 (no. 7); Paul Oskar Kristeller, "Some Original Letters and Autograph Manuscripts of Marsilio Ficino," in *Studi di bibliografia e di storia in onore di Tammaro De Marinis*, vol. 3 (Verona, 1964), pp. 5–33 at 25; and Gentile in *Mostra*, pp. 28–31 (no. 22).

25. The views respectively of Aubrey Diller, "Notes on the History of Some Manuscripts of Plato," in his *Studies in Greek Manuscript Tradition* (Amsterdam, 1983), pp. 251–258 at 257; and of Sebastiano Gentile (who challenges Diller's arguments), "Note sui manoscritti greci di Platone utilizzati da Marsilio Ficino," in *Scritti in onore di Eugenio Garin* (Pisa, 1987), pp. 51–84 at 58.
On MS Laur. 59.1, see Marcel, *Marsile Ficin (1433–1499)*, pp. 254 ff.; Sicherl, "Neuentdeckte Handschriften," pp. 51–52 and 59 (no. 2); Kristeller, "Some Original Letters," p. 25; and Gentile in *Mostra*, pp. 29–30.

26. Diller, "Notes on the History," pp. 251–258; Gentile in *Mostra*, pp. 29–30; Kristeller, *Ficino and His Work*, pp. 72–73. Thus we must abandon the view first propounded by Marcel and Sicherl (see n. 25 above), that MS Laur. 59.1, which reveals no trace of Ficino's hand, was the principal exemplar for Ficino's translations. It cannot even have been a source for later corrections.

27. Laur. 85.6 and 85.7. See Sicherl, "Neuentdeckte Handschriften," pp. 53 and 59 (nos. 5 and 6); and Kristeller, "Some Original Letters," p. 25. These are now considered unlikely sources for Ficino; see Kristeller, *Ficino and His Work*, pp. 74, 138. Gentile, "Note," pp. 69 ff., has recently ingeniously demonstrated that Ficino collated the Laur. 85.9 with at least two other manuscripts containing either single dialogues or excerpts from Plato's works, the Laurenziana's Conventi soppr. 180 and the Vatican's Borgianus gr. 22; but neither involves the *Sophist*.

28. See Hankins, *Latin Translations*, chap. 5, n. 54.

scholia for the dialogue, including the obviously incorrect *katharsis* in line 5, for which Ficino correctly reads (with B and W) *kathartês*. Ficino did not translate the other scholia, incidentally, though they may have guided his interpretation and presumably possessed some authority for him. But then he chose not to translate any of the many scholia to Plato's other dialogues, and the signal exception is this prefatory one for the *Sophist* which is our immediate concern. In other ways unique, being one of the longest and summary in nature, it must have served indeed as a model, along with Bruni's *argumenta,* for the brief introductions that Ficino prefixed to most of his Plato translations. Quite apart from its prominent position at the head of the dialogue and its serviceability as an introduction, it bore the additional authority for Ficino of having been written by Proclus.

Why did Ficino so confidently attribute the scholion to Proclus when there is no specific attribution in the extant manuscripts? We do know from a reference in his Commentary on the *Parmenides* at 774.25–26 that Proclus wrote, or at least lectured, on the *Sophist*;[29] but, in reconstructing Proclus's views on the dialogue, scholars must perforce turn to the scholion and then work outwards towards odd clues in other texts. In 1880 T. Mettauer was of the cautious opinion that the scholion's source was "a certain Neoplatonist,"[30] and Greene was content to go along with this.[31] Recently Westerink and Dillon have drawn our attention to the Proclian parallels, and Westerink conjectures that the actual author of the scholion was probably someone in Proclus's circle, perhaps Olympiodorus, for his *Sophist* commentary was still available to the Arabic translators.[32] Dillon has gone so far as to note that "it is even possible that all of this passage after the initial sentence [*Esti gar . . . dêmiourgou*—meaning after the mention of "the sublunar demiurge"] is

---

29. Ed. Victor Cousin in *Procli Philosophi Platonici Opera Inedita* (Paris, 1864; repr. Frankfurt am Main, 1962), cols. 617–1244.

30. *De Platonis Scholiorum Fontibus* (Zurich, 1880), pp. 31 ff.

31. *Scholia Platonica*, p. xxvii.

32. Westerink, *Anonymous Prolegomena*, p. xxxviii (citing Proclus's *Platonic Theology* 1.5); idem, *The Greek Commentaries on Plato's Phaedo*, 2 vols. (Amsterdam and New York, 1976–77), 1:22; Dillon, *Iamblichi Fragmenta*, pp. 245–247. Cf. Larsen, *Jamblique de Chalcis*, p. 361n.

elaboration by Proclus."[33] But no one has been so unequivocally for Proclus as Ficino; and the decisive evidence for him must have been a statement by Proclus himself in the *Platonic Theology* 1.5 to the effect that the *Sophist* tells us about the sublunar world and the proper condition of the gods who have received it as their domain.[34] We must therefore recognize that this scholion was for him an authentic Proclian text. This surprising assumption, which has hitherto escaped the attention of scholars, must be duly taken into account when we seek to assess the impact of Proclus not only on Ficino but on the Renaissance at large.[35] For the *Sophist* scholion was part, if a minor part, of its Proclus canon and received special notice by virtue of its incorporation into Ficino's Plato translation, being the only piece of Neoplatonic commentary so honored.

We encounter a number of problems when we attempt to reconstruct the Iamblichean view of the *Sophist* from the scholion—the only evidence available for such a reconstruction—as Dillon and Larsen have rather differently demonstrated. And the situation is hardly easier when we attempt to arrive at the Proclian view, especially as Ficino interpreted it. Nevertheless, the attempt must be made, since the scholion had a vital role to play in Ficino's under-

---

33. *Iamblichi Fragmenta*, p. 247. We should bear in mind that Dillon omits the preface's first sentence, *hoti sophistên . . . ho dialogos*, from his text.

34. Ed. Saffrey and Westerink, 1:25.14–18. Proclus had obviously planned to write a systematic exegesis of both the *Sophist* and the *Statesman* in the later books of his *Platonic Theology*, but this, if it was ever composed, is lost to us; see Saffrey and Westerink's note *ad loc.* Interestingly, Proclus puts the *Statesman* prior to the *Sophist* here on the grounds that it provides us with the knowledge of the heavens' demiurgy and of the two universal periodic cycles and their "intellectual" (*noeros*), as contrasted with their "intelligible" (*noêtos*), causes (1:25.14–16), whereas the *Sophist* treats of the subheavenly realm. Both dialogues belong to the select group of eight dialogues he has just mentioned—the others being the *Phaedo*, the *Phaedrus*, the *Symposium*, the *Philebus*, the *Cratylus*, and the *Timaeus*—that "initiate us best into the divine mysteries, . . . being in their totality, so to speak, full of the knowledge that was divinely inspired in Plato" (1:24.12–19). These eight are still subordinate, of course, to the *Parmenides*. Less important are two other groups. The first consists of the myths of the *Gorgias* and the *Protagoras*, along with the material in the *Laws* on providence, and the material in book 10 of the *Republic* on the Fates and the world's revolutions; and the second consists of the *Letters* (1:24.19–25.2). This arrangement does not exactly correspond, obviously, to the Neoplatonists' teaching cycle.

35. For a comprehensive survey, which, however, does not mention the scholion, see Kristeller, "Proclus as a Reader," pp. 191–211.

standing both of the dialogue and of Proclus: it articulated a position
that he was equally careful to publicize and to distance himself from
in what constitutes a revealing instance of his ambivalence towards
the hermeneutics of later Neoplatonism.

The scholion begins with the general point that the dialogue has
"a more noble subject than might first appear" in that its theme is
not the human sophist merely but three higher sophists whose art
Plato is referring to when he describes it as "most eminent," presumably a reference to 223C1–2's "a great and many-sided art." In
ascending order these three higher sophists are Love (compare the
Symposium 203D), the god Hades (compare the *Cratylus* 403E),
and the father of all the gods and demons, Zeus, the brother of
Hades and Poseidon. Ficino, as we have seen, defined the theme
quite differently as treating, not of the sophist principally, but of
being. In so doing, he seems to have been more alert to and interested in the link between the *Sophist* and the *Parmenides* than between the *Sophist* and the "demiurgic" dialogue par excellence, the
Timaeus. But it is the Timaean dimension that had obviously struck
Iamblichus with all the force of a revelation; for his decision that
the *Sophist* is primarily concerned with "the sublunar demiurge" is
inexplicable without it and without the wealth of speculation that
had already swirled around its enigmatic myth of the great Demiurge, of his demiurgy, and of the "new" gods, his children.

For Ficino who is this mysterious "sublunar demiurge"? I believe
he is to be identified with the Hades of the scholion's first line.
We can explore this intriguing possibility by reference to the ancient text he would have turned to as the one most likely to cast
some light on the problem, namely Proclus's Commentary on the
Timaeus. We know he studied this complicated work from early on
in his career, for he refers to it a number of times in his *Platonic
Theology* published in 1482 but written in draft by 1474. Professor
Sicherl has identified Ficino's exemplar as the Riccardiana's Ricc.
24, a manuscript which he annotated and may have owned;[36] this

---

    36. "Neuentdeckte Handschriften," pp. 51, 60 (no. 11). See also Kristeller, "Some Orig-
inal Letters," p. 27; idem, *Ficino and His Work,* p. 82; Gentile in *Mostra,* pp. 109–110 (no.
85).

breaks off, however, at 191E at the word *sômasi* in the middle of the third book.[37]

The Platonic tradition long before Proclus had occasionally assigned the sublunar realm in its entirety to Hades—the realm, that is, of air that stretched from the terraqueous globe up to the limits of the first celestial sphere, the first sphere of pure fire (or, for the Aristotelians, of aether). We find such an assignment, for instance, in two treatises very familiar to Ficino, Plutarch's *De Facie in Orbe Lunae* 942C–F and *De Genio Socratis* 519A–C, and Dillon suggests that the idea may well go back to Xenocrates, the head of the Academy after Speusippus and the last one who could speak of Plato from personal acquaintance, or even possibly to Plato's *Laws* 10.904D.[38] Another important treatise by Plutarch, *De E apud Delphos* 393A ff., has Plutarch's teacher Ammonius declare that "some other god or rather demon" subordinate to the supreme god has been granted the office of dealing with nature "in her dissolution and generation," and this subordinate deity is then identified as Hades or Pluto.[39] Since change is traditionally confined to the sublunar world, Ficino would gather from Plutarch certainly, whom he regarded as one of the great Platonists, that Hades, in one of his manifestations at least, was the wise lord of the realm that begins

37. Ed. Diehl, 2:169.4; cf. 1:xi ff. We must assume that the second half of the commentary was therefore unknown to him, unless he had access to any of the twenty-one or so other extant manuscripts of the commentary, including three owned by Bessarion, the Marciana's gr. 190, 194, and 195. Past references by scholars, myself included, to Proclus's *In Timaeum* books 4 and 5 or to the later parts of book 3 should thus be rejected as probable sources for Ficino. Awaiting exploration is the question of Ficino's debt, if any, to William of Moerbeke's translation, which survives only in fragments and only in two manuscripts. See G. Verbeke, "Guillaume de Moerbeke traducteur de Proclus," *Revue philosophique de Louvain* 51 (1953), 349–373 (with an edition of the fragments on pp. 358–373); also Kristeller, "Proclus as a Reader," pp. 199, 209.

38. *Iamblichi Fragmenta*, p. 246n; idem, *The Middle Platonists, 80 B.C. to A.D. 220* (Ithaca, N.Y., 1977), pp. 172–174, 191, 216, 223, 288, 318. See also D. A. Russell, *Plutarch* (London, 1973), pp. 73 ff. (Plutarch even refers to the airy region as "the meadows of Hades").

39. Dillon, *Middle Platonists*, p. 191. In his *De Iside et Osiride* 28 and 78 (*Moralia* 361F–362B, 382E–383A), Plutarch identifies the three-headed Egyptian Serapis with Pluto. Julian's "Hymn to Helios" goes further and identifies Serapis-Pluto both with Helios and with Zeus. For the Renaissance interpretation of Serapis *triceps*, see Wind, *Pagan Mysteries*, pp. 259–262.

with the air beneath the Moon and is subject to coming to be (*gene-sis*) and passing away (*phthora*), the realm of change and motion.[40]

Whence, however, the more challenging notion that Hades was not just the lord of this realm but its sophistic creator who creates in imitation of a higher demiurge? The notion that the whole sublunar realm is the creation of a lesser demiurge, one who is subordinate to and perhaps even actively opposed to a higher demiurge and therefore less perfect and less powerful than he, is a notion fraught with snares. But Plato himself seems to have suggested it, even while rejecting it, when he observes in the *Timaeus* at 29A that it would be impious to suppose that there could exist a demiurge who gazes for his model "on that which has come to be" instead of on the eternal.[41] Anyone influenced by a dualistic philosophy such as that of the Persians would then be drawn to argue that such a lesser demiurge was evil like Ahriman.[42] But the Neoplatonists would not normally entertain such a negative view, given that the *Timaeus* itself had originated, or at least most fully articulated, the view that the Creator-Demiurge was also the guardian and preserver of a world that was intrinsically good and beautiful; and given that

---

40. The *Cratylus* surmises at 404CD that Persephone's name "means only that the goddess is wise (*sophê*); for seeing that all things in the world are in motion (*pheromenôn*), that principle which embraces and touches and is able to follow them, is wisdom. And therefore the goddess may truly be called Pherepapha . . . because she touches that which is in motion (*tou pheromenou ephaptomenê*), herein showing her wisdom. And Hades, who is wise, consorts with her, because she is wise" (tr. Jowett, in Hamilton-Cairns, *Plato*, p. 441).

41. See J. Mansfeld, "Bad World and Demiurge: A 'Gnostic' Motif from Parmenides and Empedocles to Lucretius and Philo," in *Studies in Gnosticism and Hellenistic Religions,* ed. R. van den Broek and M. J. Vermaseren (Leiden, 1981), pp. 261–314 at 293–303.

42. E.g., Plutarch, *De Iside* 369E, *De Animae Procreatione* 1014B ff., 1026B; and Atticus in Proclus's *In Timaeum* 1.381.26 ff. (ed. Diehl). Numenius may have entertained such a view on occasion; see frags. 11, 19, 20, 52 (ed. Des Places, Paris, 1973). The Platonic source for these "Gnostic" speculations is the postulation in the *Laws* 10.896E ff. of a maleficent World-Soul; but compare too the *Theaetetus* 176A, with its declaration that the sublunar world "is of necessity haunted by evil." See E. R. Dodds, *Pagan and Christian in an Age of Anxiety* (Cambridge, 1965), chap. 1, esp. pp. 12–17.

We might note, however, that Ficino, following Pletho, identified the Chaldaean trinity he found in Plutarch's *De Iside* 369E—Ohrmazd-Mithra-Ahriman (Oromasis-Mitris-Arimanis)—with the three Neoplatonic hypostases, and thus Ahriman with Soul. See his *De Amore* 2.4 (ed. Marcel, p. 150) and *Platonic Theology* 4.1 (ed. Marcel, 1:162); also Wind, *Pagan Mysteries,* pp. 242–243 and 250, with further refs.

Plotinus had promoted such an interpretation of the *Timaeus* in his *Enneads* 2.9 and had also launched an uncompromising attack on the Gnostics for their pessimistic dualism.

Nevertheless, the *Timaeus* at 42D had explicitly, if mysteriously, allocated the creation of the corporeal world to the "new or younger" gods, having first portrayed the Demiurge as the author not only of all souls but also at 32BC of the elements themselves. These "younger gods" are subsequently described at 42E as his "children," and he himself is several times referred to as a "father," a designation that Christian Platonists like Ficino himself found especially significant in the light of their Trinitarian preoccupations.[43] Plotinus's successors certainly (if not Plotinus himself, whose views now seem to us complicated and ambiguous)[44] had not been persuaded by Plutarch's theory that Plato had intended to identify the Demiurge with Zeus per se. After all, at 40E Plato has the Demiurge problematically address three generations of gods in the figures of Oceanus and Tethys, of Phorcys, Cronus, and Rhea, and of Zeus and Hera, the three generations themselves deriving from the prime generation of Earth and Heaven: at 41A the Demiurge begins, "Gods, children of gods, who are my works, and of whom I am the artificer and father." Rather, they identified the Demiurge with an aspect, albeit the jovian aspect, of Cronus—despite the identical problem posed by the Demiurge's address to a sequence of gods that includes Cronus!—and identified both with Mind, the second hypostasis in Plotinian metaphysics and the source of all being. Zeus in himself they identified with Soul, the third hypostasis, though Soul appears throughout the dialogue specifically as the World-Soul which is, strictly speaking, the first manifestation of Soul.[45] We should note that the Demiurge creates the World-Soul

43. Cf. Proclus, *Theologia Platonica* 5.16 (ed. Saffrey and Westerink, 5:52–59). See my "Marsilio Ficino on Plato, the Neoplatonists and the Christian Doctrine of the Trinity," *Renaissance Quarterly* 37 (1984), 555–584 at 568–571.

44. Charrue, *Plotin: Lecteur de Platon,* chap. 2, esp. pp. 123–127 and 133–139.

45. See Wallis, *Neoplatonism,* pp. 69–70; H. J. Blumenthal, "Soul, World-Soul, and Individual Soul in Plotinus," in *Le néoplatonisme: Colloque international du Centre national de la recherche scientifique, Royaumont, 9–13 juin 1969* (Paris, 1971), pp. 55–66; and

at 34B before there is any mention of "sons," but it was generally
assumed, nevertheless, that the World-Soul was the first and the
chief of the younger gods. Furthermore, in the *Enneads* 2.1.5.5–8
Plotinus adapts the *Timaeus* 42D ff. and 69C to argue that Plato
intends us to understand that after the World-Soul there is a minor
soul that is its emanating image and that "so to speak flows down
from above and makes the living things on earth" and hence man's
physical body.[46] Such a minor soul imaging the World-Soul could
obviously be equated with Hades, but then why not with Poseidon
as the second brother or with Hera the sister and spouse?

   Dillon draws our attention to two interesting passages in Proclus's
Timaeus Commentary for some light upon this question;[47] and we
may safely assume that Ficino had access to them, though not necessarily prior to 1484. At 1.156.5–7 Proclus refers to "the middle
demiurge" after "the first of the demiurges";[48] and at 1.74.15–18 he
refers to "the third demiurge" who must be Hades since, Proclus
argues, "the third demiurge associates himself with the creative activity of the second; for the whole of creation has absolute need
also of the contributions that come from the subterranean world."[49]
Dillon also draws our attention to three references much later in
Proclus's commentary to "the second demiurges," which he takes
to be Proclus's interpretation of the "new gods."[50] But Ficino would
not, I believe, have seen these, since they are all in the fifth book,
which was missing in the manuscript he consulted.

   In addition to these references, we might note that at 1.74.19 ff.

W. Helleman-Elgersma, *Soul-Sisters: A Commentary on Enneads IV.3 [27].1–8 of Plotinus*
(Amsterdam, 1980), pp. 57 ff. For Macrobius, who equated the third hypostasis with the
World-Soul, see Stephen Gersh's fine study, *Middle Platonism and Neoplatonism: The Latin
Tradition,* 2 vols. (Notre Dame, Ind., 1986), 2:551–552. Ficino also equated the two—see
my *Platonism of Ficino,* p. 115n—and may well have been influenced by Macrobius.

   46. I am quoting from A. H. Armstrong's translation in vol. 2 of the Loeb Plotinus, 7
vols. (Cambridge, Mass. and London, 1966–1988). We should note that Ficino's commentary
on this section at *Opera,* pp. 1598–1599, is too brief for us to determine what impression,
if any, it made upon him, though at p. 1596, when he is glossing 2.1.3, he writes that "the
heavens are the image (*imago*) of the World-Soul."

   47. *Iamblichi Fragmenta,* p. 246.

   48. Ed. Diehl; cf. the French translation by A.-J. Festugière, *Proclus: Commentaire sur
le Timée,* 5 vols. (Paris, 1966–1969), 1:208.

   49. Ed. Diehl; tr. Festugière, 1:109.

   50. 3:200.22–23, 313,6–7, 354.4 (ed. Diehl; tr. Festugière, 5:59, 193, 236).

Proclus speaks of the "middle demiurgy" and of the dyad and the triad among numbers being appropriate to it,[51] a "middle demiurgy" to which he has already adverted at 1.71.6.[52] This is presumably to be identified with "the demiurgy of the second rank" at 1.63.3 ff. which "resembles the first demiurgy and because of this is continuous with it," the two constituting a "demiurgic chain."[53]

In his note to 1.71.6 ff. in his French translation of the commentary, A.-J. Festugière adduces two further texts. The first is a scholion keyed to 1.71.21, which appears in the Paris codex Coislinianus 322 (Diehl's siglum C) at f. 39r, and which Diehl edits at 1.461.20 ff. This speaks of the third demiurgy as the work of Pluto just as the second demiurgy is that of Poseidon and the first of Zeus. Ficino was almost certainly ignorant of this scholion, but it does alert us to the import of the second text Festugière adduces and which he would have seen, namely 2.56.21 ff.[54] Here Proclus refers us to the three realms of the celestial, the sublunary, and the subterranean, assigning them respectively to Zeus, Poseidon, and Pluto. This should alert us in turn to a characteristically important distinction in Proclus's analysis of the demiurgy of the *Timaeus*: the distinction between the demiurgy in its primal unity and the triadic process to which it gives rise. And this is precisely the position Proclus advances in his *Cratylus* Commentary to which Dillon hesitatingly refers us.[55] There we have a Father of the demiurges—Mind, that is, in its primal and transcendent unity—who is, predictably, identified with Cronus; and under him a triad of demiurges, identified with the three Olympian brothers Zeus, Poseidon, and Pluto. Once again, however, it is Poseidon, not Hades, who is allotted the governance of the sublunar realm, being the earthshaker as well as the god of the sea, while Hades is allotted that of the

---

51. Ed. Diehl; tr. Festugière, 1:110.
52. Ed. Diehl; tr. Festugière, 1:106.
53. Ed. Diehl; tr. Festugière, 1:98.
54. Ed. Diehl; tr. Festugière, 3:88.
55. *Iamblichi Fragmenta*, p. 246, refers us to Pasquali's ed., pp. 84–87. We might speculate on the nature of the parallel, if any, between the three kinds of demiurgy and the postulation in the *Republic* 4.435B ff., the *Phaedrus* 246A ff., and the *Timaeus* 69C ff. of a tripartite soul governed by the *logistikon* as its highest part.

subterranean realm.[56] In other words, Proclus's subtle distinctions enable him to retain the identification of the Demiurge with the jovian aspect of Mind, with the Zeus in Cronus, while at the same time they enable him to identify Zeus in himself with Soul and thus the three Olympian brothers, the leaders surely of the "new gods," with the three realms of Soul: the celestial, the sublunar, and the subterranean.

How do we reconcile the Proclian assignment of the sublunar realm to Poseidon with the scholion's apparent association of "the sublunar demiurge" (in Iamblichus's designation of the *Sophist's* theme) with the sophist Hades? This is another way of asking whether we can reconcile Plutarch's assignment of Hades to the sublunar realm with Proclus's traditional assignment of him to the subterranean. With regard to Ficino's understanding of the scholion, there are two possibilities. First, he may not have associated the Hades of line 1 with Iamblichus's sublunar demiurge, but assumed rather that, just as we could apply the term "sophist" to a man, to the demon Love, to Hades, to Zeus himself, so we could apply it also to Poseidon, and that Poseidon was the deity Iamblichus had intended. But if so, Poseidon himself would have to be the primary theme of the dialogue, and this seems an unlikely assumption for Ficino (or for Iamblichus) to make, though not an impossible one, given that Poseidon rules over the oceanic "not-being" of the sublunar realm.

The second, much more likely possibility is that Ficino interpreted Iamblichus to be referring, for all intents and purposes, to a unitary figure, the lord of change, to a hybrid Poseidon-Hades. After all, Proclus himself in the *Timaeus* Commentary had em-

---

56. Like Festugière, Dillon also refers us to 2:56.21 ff. The most succinct Renaissance formulation of the Neoplatonic principle that every higher god exerts his power downwards in a triadic rhythm is Pico's eighth Orphic Conclusion: "He that understands profoundly and clearly how the unity of Venus is unfolded in the trinity of the Graces, and the unity of Necessity in the trinity of the Fates, and the unity of Saturn in the trinity of Jupiter, Neptune, and Pluto, knows the proper way of proceeding in Orphic theology" (*Conclusiones numero XXXI secundum propriam opinionem de modo intelligendi hymnos Orphei*, n. VIII; tr. Wind in his *Pagan Mysteries*, pp. 36 ff. and 248–249).

phasized not so much the distinction between the triple subordinate demiurgy of Zeus, Poseidon, and Hades and the unitary demiurgy of the sublime Demiurge, as that between what he calls "the new demiurgy" and "the older demiurgy." At 1.95.13 ff. Proclus compares the "more recent demiurgy that governs the renewal of all the kinds of being in the cosmos" with "the more ancient demiurgy that maintains steadfastly the cosmos's creative principles."[57] The "new demiurgy" is symbolized by Solon, the "more ancient" by the Egyptian priests.[58] Again, at 1.124.20 ff. Proclus writes that "the doctrine of the Egyptians signifies that all in the sensible realm that is steadfast, fixedly ordered, always likewise identical comes from the intelligible gods; by contrast, all that is in the process of becoming now this and now that, all that is born and dies, comes from the second demiurgy."[59] The doctrine is complicated, but as Festugière notes,[60] Proclus is obviously contrasting the "first" or "more ancient" demiurgy (with which the Demiurge fashioned the heavens) to the "second" or "more recent" demiurgy (with which the "new" gods fashioned the subcelestial—that is, the sublunar—world). Subsequently, one could subdivide the sublunar realm into the upper and lower domains ruled over by Poseidon and Pluto respectively; but this would be a scholastic elaboration of the major distinction between the demiurgy that created the translunar realm and that which created the sublunar one. That is, in contexts where the subdivision between sublunar and subterranean is of no importance and the focus is on the primary contrast between the intelligible and changeless and the sensible and transitory, we may think of the sublunar demiurge either as Poseidon or as Hades or as a hybrid Poseidon-Hades; and in this event the Plutarchan view of Hades can be le-

57. Ed. Diehl; tr. Festugière, 1:134.
58. Cf. 1.99.30–100.16 and 103.14–17; tr. Festugière, 1:142 and 146.
59. Ed. Diehl; tr. Festugière, 1:170. One wonders what Ficino would have made of the curious reference in the *Euthydemus* at 288B to Proteus, a deity we recall of the sea, as "the Egyptian sophist." The *Republic* 2.380D ff. rejects the notion that the Demiurge could be a lying wizard like Proteus. But Proteus, unlike Hephaestus, was too minor a deity to be even a possible candidate for the sublunar demiurge (since he signified merely one attribute of Poseidon); see n. 61 below.
60. Festugière, 2:25n; cf. 2:193n.

gitimately entertained. Such is the case here with the scholion to the opening of the *Sophist* at 216A.[61]

We are still left with the problem, inherited from Plotinus, of Proclus's identifying the Demiurge both with Cronus and with Zeus. But Ficino would not have regarded these apparently mutually exclusive alternatives as troublesome, since he was familiar with the Proclian strategy of interpreting deities of a subsequent generation, or in a subordinate familial position, as if they were powers in a

---

61. Another Proclian candidate for the sublunar demiurge may I think be safely dismissed as unlikely to have appealed to Ficino. In the process of commenting in his first book on the lemma in the *Timaeus* at 23D7–E2, Proclus discusses the lame god Hephaestus and assigns him the role of being the maker of the solid, sensible realm and of its particulars: he is the universal fabricator of "all the structure of Body," including the forging of the heavens themselves "of bronze" (ed. Diehl, 1:142.14–143.24; tr. Festugière, 1:191–192). Later, in his third book, in the course of analyzing the Demiurge's decision to make the world a sphere at 33B, Proclus asks, "How can the Demiurge also be the creator of all the shapes in the world?" To this he replies interrogatively, "Didn't the thrice-honored Hephaestus, after the Demiurge, form the shapes of all encosmic realities, the whole of heaven and the sublunar world, . . . fashioning (*schêmatizei*) with his hands the universe that the Demiurge had only willed?" (ed. Diehl, 2:70.6–31; tr. Festugière, 3:103–104). We might note that in both passages Hephaestus is assigned the making of heaven as well as of the sublunar realm. Accordingly, he cannot be the sublunar demiurge alone. In either event, Proclus is careful to restrict Hephaestus's making to the making of bodies, not of images, shadows, and dreams, and to characterize him as solely a making, not a vivifying or conserving, divinity; cf. *In Timaeum* 1:147.6–7 (ed. Diehl; tr. Festugière, 1:198 and note), where Porphyry is cited as defining Hephaestus as "the artisan intellect" (*nous technikos*).

In the *Statesman* 274CD Plato had affirmed that "in the old tradition" concerning the gods' gifts Prometheus had given men fire and other gods had given them seeds and plants, while Hephaestus had been the giver, with Athene, of the "secrets" of the crafts and arts (cf. the assertion in the *Laws* 11.920DE that the class of craftsmen who have furnished human life with the arts is under the patronage of both Hephaestus and Athene). On this theme see Ficino's comments in his epitome for the *Protagoras* (*Opera,* p. 1298, glossing 321D ff.). Vulcan, he says, signifies the effectiveness (*efficacia*) that serves Minerva's ingenuity (*ingenium*), while the fire in his workshop signifies the instrument. In his *Phaedrus* Commentary, chap. 10 (ed. Allen, pp. 118–119), Ficino obviously thinks of Hephaestus as merely "the provider for sensible things," but as subordinate now to Mars. Clearly a Poseidon-Hades-Hephaestus, or for that matter a Zeus-Athene-Hephaestus, or an Athene-Ares-Hephaestus triad, is always possible in what Wind has termed "the sacred *drôlerie*" of a Proclus-inspired system with its proliferating triadic subdivisions (*Pagan Mysteries,* p. 200); and the forging of an Achilles' shield can be viewed in certain lights as the product of a sophistical smithery (see chap. 4 below). We might note, moreover, that Proclus's first triad of hypercosmic-and-encosmic gods consists of Zeus, Poseidon, and Hephaestus, whereas the first triad of the purely hypercosmic gods consists of Zeus, Poseidon, and Hades (Pluto); see Saffrey and Westerink, *Théologie platonicienne* 1:lxvi–lxvii. This might have suggested to Ficino, had he referred to the requisite passages in Proclus's *Theologia Platonica* book 6, that Hephaestus was a power in Hades. The topic awaits investigation.

superior, older deity. In this, the most important case of all, Zeus is conceived of as a power, specifically the demiurgic power, in Cronus. While Cronus is the creator of Soul and souls and of the celestial realm, he is so by virtue of his demiurgic—that is, his jovian—power (as contrasted with his contemplative or uranian power, or his self-regarding or saturnian power). For the jovian power in any deity signifies the downward-regarding providential power in its fabricating, governing, and guarding modes (which Proclus of course distinguishes and assigns to yet lower gods or powers in Zeus). Thus, in a sense, Cronus signifies the uncreating Demiurge, the Demiurge contemplating all the principles and Ideas that will constitute life's paradigms and the paradigms even of Soul and of divine souls (since the Neoplatonists had taken up the notion debated by the Middle Platonists that there were Ideas of divine souls and an Idea of Soul in general).[62] The creation of Soul and the heavens does not take place therefore until Cronus turns to the jovian power, to the Jupiter, in himself. Thus Jupiter is twofold— and Plotinus had originated this important notion which he derived from the *Philebus* 30D.[63] He is a power in Cronus his father, specifically the demiurgic power, and therefore an aspect of Mind. As such he is the Demiurge. Yet Jupiter is also a deity in his own right at the lower ontological level of Soul, and as such he is the leader of the "new" gods. From Proclus's viewpoint, he is therefore the first of a demiurgic triad involving himself and his two sovereign brothers.

As Westerink has pointed out, the Iamblichean-Proclian theory of a sublunar demiurge imitating the sublime Demiurge, the jovian Cronus, would probably never have come about had it not been for Plato's declaration that the *Sophist* was intended to be the first of a trilogy and that the *Statesman* was the second member of that trilogy. The aspect of the *Statesman* that principally concerned the Neoplatonists was its provocative myth of the reigns of Cronus and

---

62. See Proclus, *In Parmenidem* 3.817.3–820.37 (ed. Cousin; tr. Morrow and Dillon, pp. 180–183, with Dillon's comments on pp. 151–152).

63. *Enneads* 3.5.8 and 4.4.9. Cf. 5.1.7, 5.8.4, and 6.9.7. Cf. Proclus, *Theologia Platonica* 5.23 (ed. Saffrey and Westerink, 5:84–87). See Wallis, *Neoplatonism*, p. 135.

Zeus which contrasts "a state of things in which law and order are immanent, the reign of Cronus, with the reign of Zeus, in which they are imposed precariously from above." Westerink goes on to assert that "Proclus identifies this Zeus with the Demiurge of the *Timaeus*, the universal creator, who thus became the supreme *Politikos*";[64] and refers us, interestingly, to Proclus's *Platonic Theology* 5.6–10[65] and to his Commentary on the *Republic* 1.68.24–26.[66] But in the latter Proclus declares that "the Statesman in the All is the one whom we celebrate as the 'great' Zeus and from whom derives, as Plato says himself, the political art." Ficino would have pounced, I believe, on this reference to "great." For in his Commentary on the *Phaedrus*, chapter 10, he carefully outlines what he sees as the Proclian distinctions between Zeus with no accompanying epithet and "great" Zeus, and between "great" Zeus and "greatest" Zeus.[67] "Greatest" Zeus is the jovian power in Cronus and thus the Demiurge of the *Timaeus*. "Great" Zeus is the third hypostasis Soul. Zeus with no epithet is either the planet Jupiter or a lesser manifestation of the jovian power in another god or demon. From Ficino's viewpoint, therefore, the *Stateman's* Zeus cannot be identified with the Zeus in Cronus but rather with the World-Soul. He declares this unequivocally in his introduction to the *Statesman*:

Plato calls to mind two reigns, those of Jove and Saturn, and puts the reign of Saturn before Jove's as the happier one. For he means by "the reign of Jove" human life and activity, but by "the reign of Saturn" the contemplation of matters divine. For Saturn is called in Greek *Cronos*, as Plato teaches in the *Cratylus* [396BC], and comprehends the inviolable

---

64. *Anonymous Prolegomena*, p. xxxviii. Cf. Proclus, *Theologia Platonica* 5.25 (ed. Saffrey and Westerink, 5:91–96, esp. 96.5–9).

65. As edited and translated into Latin by Aemilius Portus, *Procli Successoris Platonici in Platonis Theologiam Libri Sex* (Hamburg, 1618; reprint, Frankfurt am Main, 1960), pp. 258–265. For books 1 to 5 this Portus edition has been superseded, however, by Saffrey and Westerink's edition. Westerink's reference corresponds to pp. 24–35 of the fifth volume (Paris, 1987).

66. Ed. G. Kroll, *Procli in Platonis Rem Publicam Commentarii*, 2 vols. (Leipzig, 1899–1901); cf. the French translation by A.-J. Festugière, *Proclus: Commentaire sur la République*, 3 vols. (Paris, 1970), 1:84–85.

67. Ed. Allen, *Phaedran Charioteer*, pp. 114–115; see my *Platonism of Ficino*, pp. 126–128.

purity and integrity of the mind [or of Mind][B6–7]. But when he says that men lived happy lives when Saturn reigned, he is indicating that, when a man's divine mind reigns [over him]—man for whom actions have been ordered for the sake of contemplation—then the human race will be blessed. . . . But Jove, I believe, is what he calls the World-Soul by whose fatal law the manifest order of this manifest world is ordered. . . . But Saturn is the supreme intellect among the angels by whose rays the souls among the angels are illumined and inflamed and are raised continually with all their might to the intellectual life. As often as they are converted to this same life, to that extent are they said to live under the reign of Saturn, since they are living by understanding.[68]

The chapters in Proclus's *Platonic Theology* book 5, to which Westerink also refers us (especially chapters 6 and 7 and, I might add, 25) and which Ficino knew, would only serve to reinforce this general interpretation of the *Statesman*. For there Proclus explicitly refers to the *Statesman* and distinguishes between "great" and "greatest" Jove, having already used the *Cratylus*'s formula in chapter 5 to describe Saturn as "pure Mind, perfect and completely without matter," and yet possessed of a jovian power. He also considers the meaning of the two reigns in terms of the historical cycles of the cosmos and of the "periods" in the lives of particular souls.

Westerink's point is therefore well taken. For the Neoplatonists there was an inseparable connection between the *Sophist* and the *Statesman*'s great myth, and Iamblichus had probably felt impelled "to find a divine Sophist as a counterpart to the divine Statesman,"

---

68. *Opera,* p. 1296: "Commemorat et duo regna, Iovis scilicet et Saturni, regnumque Saturni regno Iovis tanquam felicius anteponit; siquidem sub Iove actio vitaque humana, sub Saturno autem contemplatio divinorum significatur. Saturnus enim Graeco nomine Cronos, ut Plato in *Cratylo* docet, puritatem integritatemque mentis inviolabilem comprehendit. Quod autem ait Saturno regnante beatos homines vivere, ostendit, divina quadam viri mente regnante, quo actiones gratia contemplationis instituas, humanum genus fore beatum. . . . Iovem, ut arbitror, animam mundi vocat, cuius lege fatali manifestus hic manifesti mundi ordo disponitur. . . . Saturnum vero supremum inter angelos intellectum, cuius radiis illustrentur inter angelos animae accendanturque, et ad intellectualem vitam continue pro viribus erigantur, quae quoties ad vitam eiusmodi convertuntur eatenus sub regno Saturni dicuntur vivere quatenus intelligentia vivunt." He would thus surely dispute Proclus's specific claim in the *Theologia Platonica* 5.25 (ed. Saffrey and Westerink, 5:95.22–96.24) that the *Statesman*'s Zeus is the demiurgic Zeus of the *Timaeus* 28A, the Zeus that Proclus also supposed the *Protagoras* 321D–322D and the *Philebus* 30D were referring to.

who was the Jove in that myth.[69] Indeed, such a divine Sophist would be a kind of second or lesser divine Statesman, as presumably the divine Statesman would have been a second or lesser divine Philosopher in the third member of the trilogy that Plato never completed. It is tempting to think of Ficino equating this triad of divine Sophist, divine Statesman, and divine Philosopher with another triad consisting of the sublunar demiurge (Hades), the celestial demiurge (Jove in himself), and the supercelestial Demiurge (Jove in Cronus or Saturn). Be that as it may, we still have the scholion's very different triad of Love, Hades, and Jove, a triad where, necessarily, each member partakes of the nature of its peers in some degree, or under some mode, and where we must therefore think not only of Love but of Hades and even of Jupiter as sophists in that they mysteriously imitate the intelligible world of the Ideas which constitutes the rule of Cronus. Sophistry, in short, is intrinsic to the notion of demiurgy, and certainly of the third demiurgy under the lordship of the demiurgic, the jovian Hades, the Jupiter in Hades, whom Iamblichus had invoked as the subject of the dialogue.

Following Plato, the scholion assigns the ordinary sophist seemingly contradictory roles.[70] He is a "fashioner of idols" (*eidôlopoios*; cf. 239D3), meaning a creator of images (of which more in chapter 5 below), and yet a "purifier of souls" (*kathartês*) in that he is "forever separating souls from contrary reasons," meaning reasons that impede or obstruct true knowledge (cf. 231E5–6), what Plato refers to at 230D2 as *doxai*, "opinions" or "prejudices." We recall that it was the Eleatic Stranger himself who had rather grudgingly conceded at 230BC that the sophist had a role as a "purifier" by virtue of his ability to undermine his interlocutor's intellectual pride and to bring about some recognition thereby of his ignorance. The sophist is also more familiarly the *transmutator* (in Greek *metablêtikos*; cf. 224C10 and E1), meaning, I take it, both a shape-changer in

---

69. *Anonymous Prolegomena,* p. xxxviii.
70. The subject of the section beginning "Nam est idolorum fictor" surely cannot be the sublunar demiurge of the preceding sentence, as Dillon's rendering suggests.

himself like Proteus and someone who exchanges or barters the shapes of others, metamorphosing them like a magician.[71] Finally, the sophist is the mercenary "hunter" after the youth of means. Ficino finds the T reading, *plêreis logôn,* "laden with reasons," entirely consonant with his Platonic assumption that souls are born with formulae for understanding the Ideas, an understanding that needs educating in the literal sense by the philosopher, who will, of course, refuse to accept money for what is already the supreme gift of the gods, the gift of young men endowed with the fundamental principles of philosophy. But all this is by way of response to Plato's declaration at 231C–E that we may define the sophist in at least six ways. Most noteworthy is the concession that the sophist can preside legitimately over constructive eristic, and particularly over the art of making distinctions, diacrcsis. In such a role he is not a verbal demiurge but rather a doctor who purges. When he does attempt to create, to put back together what he has divided, then he produces insubstantial images and dreams.

The scholion proceeds to treat first of the sophist who devotes himself to the nonexistent and "begets all that is in matter"; this is presumably the sublunar demiurge of the Iamblichean interpretation. The guiding image is that of paternity: such a sophist "lies on" what does not exist and then "begets" the material world and is "in love with" what is truly false, namely matter itself, even while he looks up towards what truly exists. Hence for the author of the scholion the significance of Plato's decision to call him the "many-headed" (240C4; cf. 226A6–7), given that he lays claim to "many essences and lives." I take Ficino to have understood by these enigmas that the sophist (like any demiurgic figure) must look up towards the intelligible species as he fashions material forms; this would be to locate him in effect at the level of the seminal reasons that are traditionally assigned the mediating role between the intelligible and the corporeal forms. For even in their lowest corporeal manifestation, forms exist in the sense that they come into being (*gignomai*), since the only thing that does not exist absolutely is matter itself

---

71. Dillon ignores these various mercantile and possibly magical connotations and translates "[he who is] able to produce change" (*Iamblichi Fragmenta,* p. 91).

prior to the imposition of any form—that is, matter in a chaotic state of potentiality for existence but not actually existent, not yet extended in space. If I am correct in thus associating the demiurgic sophist with the seminal reasons, it is tantamount to identifying him with Nature herself, to identifying a Hades-Natura who presides over the world of ever-changing forms subject to generation and death. Indeed, this conclusion seems inescapable when the scholion continues, "through the many essences and lives the sophist arranges the variety of generation"; that is, he operates like Nature in introducing form into matter and then marshalling the various corporeal forms into a various design, a multiform order. We recall that the scholion had begun by linking Love with Pluto as sophists; but barely fifteen lines later it is juxtaposing Love with Nature as great mages. The identification of Hades with Nature thus emerges as the central mystery in the Iamblichean interpretation.

It is difficult at first glance to see how one might reconcile the gubernatorial role for the sophist, the role associated with Nature in her sublimity as God's instrument, with the scholiast's collateral claim that the sophist is in love with the not-being of matter until we accept the Platonic view that such love implies that the sophist longs to bring the order of being into not-being's chaos, to bring form to matter.[72] Such a view is reinforced by the scholiast's description of the sophist as also a mage who rules by enchantment over the island of natural forms, a Circe who seduces souls into falling in love with "natural reasons" and devoting themselves to generation in matter rather than to contemplation of the pure Ideas.[73] Again this magic dimension brings the sophist into direct association with the arch mage, Nature herself, and also with Love, who rules over the affinities, the reciprocal attractions and enchantments of that Nature (and it is signal that Ficino substitutes *illecebrae*—an important notion in magic theory as his *De Vita* testifies—for the Greek *antipatheias* "repulsions" of line 15, despite the fact that the

---

72. See my "Cosmogony and Love," pp. 138–142, an analysis of Ficino's *De Amore* 1.3, where Cavalcanti expounds the complex Plotinian theory of "chaoses."

73. For Circe, see Porphyry's comments in Stobaeus, *Eclogae* 1.41–60; also Ficino's references to her *noxia pocula* in his *Protagoras* epitome (*Opera,* p. 1297) and in his letter to Cavalcanti of 12 December 1494 (*Opera,* p. 961.2).

Sophist itself introduces the Empedoclean pair of Love and Hate at 242E ff.). The sophist becomes a mage like Love and Nature; and conversely, Love and Nature become sophists. Thus at the lower end of the hierarchy the possibility is opened up that the sophist can be an enchanter who has some incantatory power, however limited, over the attractions and enchantments of the natural world and thereby can imprison us in that world with his deceptive verbal magic. Over such lesser enchanter-sophists rules the greater sophist, the demon Love, and over him the even greater sophist, the Hades of the *Cratylus* 403A–E, the wise lord of all of Nature's change and motion, whose enchantment, whose unseen rule over all her sympathies and antipathies, is a spell-binding sophistry. This sophistry ties the unphilosophical many in this transitory life to transitory things (as *ploutos* Hades gives man wealth from within the earth). However, it leads the philosophical few to love all that is true and good (*panta ta kala* 404B2) and to yearn for the liberating gift of dying to the magic of the sensible world in order to embrace that of the intelligible. Over and beyond Love and Hades, however, is the sovereign Jupiter, the divine and absolute Sophist, in whose paradigmatic image both Love and Hades are made, and after whom, however contradictory it might first appear, the human sophist is also made in pale imitation.

Taking his cue from Plato's willingness to entertain a number of definitions for the sophist, the scholiast proceeds to apply the term to all who imitate. Plato had begun at 216CD with the premise that the "true philosophers," as Homer had declared, "hover about cities . . . and sometimes they appear as statesmen and sometimes as sophists." The philosopher is therefore in a way a sophist (again compare the *Cratylus* 403A–E and the *Symposium* 203D, where Hades and Love respectively are assigned both roles). The scholiast adds that this is because he imitates the demiurge who made the heavens and also the demiurge of the sublunar realm. In the Proclian system neither of these demiurges, we should note, is the Demiurge of the *Timaeus,* who is supercelestial; they are rather imitations of that Demiurge, there being three demiurges in all as we have seen.

The scholiast turns next to the art of diaeresis, presumably as it is exercised by the philosopher in his sophistic role as distinction-maker. This art "imitates" the procession (*proodos*) of all beings from the One in the sense that it descends from prime genera to secondary genera to tertiary genera and so forth down to the species and thence to individuals, making finer and finer distinctions in an authentic sophistic. But this *proodos* itself at the sublunar level is the work of the third demiurge, who is imitating the *proodos* at the translunar level, which is the work of the second demiurge. This series in effect makes the philosopher exercising sophistic into the fourth demiurge; and insofar as the base sophist is the imitator of the philosopher, it implies that the sophist is the fifth demiurge, the demiurge concerned with the material world of not-being and illusion.[74] Thus man himself, even in his highest role as a philosopher, is also a sophist in that he imitates "the great things" (*ta megala*), meaning, I take it, the works of the higher sophists: of Nature, of Love, and above all of the two demiurges immediately subordinate to the arch Demiurge. For his imitation consists of making distinctions: the legitimate distinctions of the Platonic dialectician at one end of the scale down to the jejune distinctions of the venal sophist at the other. What commences in eternity as the procession of the sublime Ideas from the One terminates, so to speak, in the dancing mirages of a verbalist's persuasion and deceit.

All this is consonant with the curious but apparently originally Iamblichean assumption that the characters of a dialogue must be identified with the range of its themes.[75] The scholion argues that the Eleatic Stranger "portrays the father" of both the sublunar and the celestial craftsmen, a father whom it describes as "absolute" and "supercelestial." This cannot for Ficino be referring to the One, although the Platonists had frequently used the term "father" to refer to the One. Rather, it must refer to the second hypostasis, Mind, and more especially to the jovian power, the Zeus, in Mind, since such a power was identified by the later Neoplatonists and by Ficino with the Demiurge, meaning the first and absolute Demiurge of the *Timaeus,* the supercelestial craftsman.[76]

---

74. Ficino would doubtless have detected a Proclian propriety in my choosing to limit this study to five chapters!

75. Dillon, *Iamblichi Fragmenta,* p. 247.

76. Again cf. Proclus, *Theologia Platonica* 5.16 (ed. Saffrey and Westerink, 5:52–59).

The scholion next turns to the identification of the Stranger's auditors with the Demiurge's "twin understandings" (*tas dêmiourgikas noêseis*), understandings that we must suppose synonymous with the celestial and the sublunar demiurges. To equate the first with Jupiter in himself logically follows, since Jupiter is the celestial demiurge. But to equate the second understanding with Hades presents us initially with some difficulties, since the scholion equates it with that of "the angelic nature" (*eis tên angelikên*). Now the scholion has Socrates represent the jovian understanding and Theodorus represent the "angelic," since it is "an interpreter and a geometer." The notion of a geometer is highly appropriate to Theodorus, given the mention of his preeminence as a geometer in the *Theaetetus* at 143B (Socrates had impressed him, moreover, in the *Statesman* at 257B by drawing on the notion of a geometric ratio!). He is nevertheless subordinated to Socrates in the *Sophist,* and that is why Plato chose to start with him before turning to Socrates and thence to the Stranger. The understanding of the "angelic nature" Theodorus represents must therefore be subordinate in turn to Jupiter's understanding as represented by Socrates.

What of the term *tanquam interpretator,* however, which is Ficino's rendering of the Greek *hôs Hermaikos* meaning "as appropriate to Hermes"? Is there any way in which Hades or his understanding can be thought of as being "Hermaic"? Hermes played important roles as both psychopomp and divine messenger—and one thinks immediately of the opening of book 24 of the *Odyssey* or of the famous krater in the Metropolitan Museum in New York with its depiction of the dying hero Sarpedon being borne away by Hypnos and Thanatos under the presiding gaze of Hermes. The scholion, however, does not identify the second understanding with Hermes himself but says merely that it is Hermes-like in its role as angel in the literal Greek sense of messenger. Hence Ficino's decision to render *hôs Hermaikos* as *tanquam interpretator,* meaning like Hermes in his role as messenger and interpreter. But in Platonism the demons also are assigned the role of messengers and interpreters between the gods and men; and as such they can be thought of as Hermes-like. This is preeminently so, therefore, for Hades, their lord, more particularly since he is, in the Plutarchan interpretation, the lord of the air, the air being the principal seat of

all the demons and the mean between the celestial fire and the terraqueous orb. If the second understanding is to be identified with
Hades, moreover, it would be consonant with the scholion's claim
that it is also "geometric," that is, concerned with the three-dimensional corporeal world: for Hades would then govern it like a geometer and serve Hermes-like to interpret between his own sublunar
realm and the celestial realm governed by Zeus. Clearly, when Ficino chose to translate *eis tên angelikên* as *angelicae naturae,* he
did not, therefore, have the Christian angels in mind, and least of
all the angelic intellect viewed as a unitary hypostasis that he had
elsewhere identified with the Plotinian Mind. Rather, he selected
angelicus, which does not occur in classical Latin incidentally, simply to convey the original Greek meaning, "pertaining to a messenger." Thus Theodorus represents Hades, the sublunar demiurge,
just as Socrates represents Jupiter, the celestial demiurge, both these
demiurges being subordinate aspects of the great Demiurge, two
subordinate understandings of Understanding itself.

Finally, we should note that the scholion rather nicely intimates
that the *Sophist* too is the work of a demiurge. Given Plato's own
suggestion that the philosopher is a sophist, we can see Plato himself, the king of philosophers, as a sophist, and his work, above all
the work entitled *Sophistês,* as sophistry. This is to take "sophist"
and "sophistry" in the higher, more mysterious senses suggested by
Plato's decision to describe the sophist as "many-headed." Above
all, it is to emphasize sophistry's essence as imitation: the lower
demiurges create their realms by imitating the supreme Demiurge,
as the base sophist imitates the philosopher and the philosopher
imitates the gods. As a piece of demiurgic imitation, of creative
sophistic, the *Sophist,* the companion piece of the *Statesman* and
the *Timaeus,* begins, says the scholion, with the Stranger, who
represents the supreme Demiurge, interrogating the imperfect views
of Theodorus, who represents the sublunar demiurge, and then turning to the more perfect views of Socrates, who represents the celestial demiurge. Such an interpretation of the dialogue effectively
rejects the Iamblichean claim that it is only concerned with the sublunar demiurge; for it implies that it is primarily concerned with the
celestial demiurgy of Jupiter, though not with the supreme Demi-

urgy of the *Timaeus*'s myth. We recall the scholion's opening premise that Plato is dealing, *sub specie sophistae,* with Jove himself as
well as with Hades, Love, the philosopher, and the base sophist,
the many heads of the protean imitator of Mind and its Ideas, the
maker of all that can be called the shadow world in the grand Platonic sense of what is less than the Ideas.

In analyzing this elevated status accorded the Stranger, we should
again recall that for Ficino he was identified with Melissus, the
Parmenidean philosopher who was second only to Parmenides himself as the expounder of the most sublime and subtle mysteries of
Plato's metaphysics. Perhaps Ficino thought of him as a kind of
sophist and of the great dialogue which he dominates, given its
focus on not-being as well as being, as a sublime example of Platonic sophistry. But this is to extrapolate from the possible impact
of the scholion. We must always bear in mind that Ficino makes
no mention of the notion of a divine sophist in his own argumentum, nor, for that matter, of the sublunar demiurge. Indeed, the
Proclian scholion and the argumentum are the products of two very
different orientations towards the dialogue, being in many ways
incompatible; and it is difficult to suppose that he accepted all the
scholion's ideas without grave reservations.

Nevertheless, his signal choice to include the scholion in the
prominent role of a preface in his 1484 Plato translation—even if
it sprang in the first place from a wish to acknowledge its presence
in the manuscript tradition—must mean that he regarded it, at least
in part, as an authoritative interpretation. Certainly, his conviction
that it had been written by Proclus would invest it with the same
qualified esteem he accorded Proclus's interpretations of other dialogues; and his decision, moreover, to dovetail his own argumentum
onto it is surely manifest testimony to the value he himself attributed it. Most obviously, it set forth a scale of sophists that descended
from Jove, who imitates the intelligible Ideas in Mind when he
crafts the celestial realm, down through Hades, the lord of sublunar
nature who nonetheless charms us to abandon the corporeal tomb
and to become votaries of dying, to the demon Love who presides
over the magical attractions and enchantments of that nature, to the
philosopher who imitates the higher demiurgic sophists and is pos-

sessed by the great sophist Love, to the base and mercenary hunter of rich young men who may nevertheless serve as the "purger" of intellectual pride. This scale is, by Plato's own declaration, a scale of imitators of being who are involved in differing degrees also in the not-being that is mingled with it to form the half-being of all that is less than the pure Ideas; and even the Ideas, as we have seen, participate in difference, in the equivocal not-being of otherness.

Indeed, the scholion's focus on the "many-headed" sophist once again suggests the Platonic oxymoronic paradox of the "wise sophist" as one way of defining man made in God's image and likeness and the "wise sophistry" with which he turns to love and contemplate the divine. For the speculative Christian Platonist, mystical "reasoning" did not have to stop even here: for the Creation or the Cross or the whole scheme of Christ's Redemption of man could all be seen as the wonderful sophistry of God. Sophistry in other words, like St. Paul's Christian folly or Panurge's vision of universal debt or Sir John Davies's vision of the cosmic dance, possesses the potentiality for establishing a unique conceptual field, for becoming one of those ideas or images when bend or distort the intellectual and imaginative space around themselves, like the massive imploding stars of modern astrophysics. Certainly, the Renaissance had an eye for such authoritative "conceits." Whether Ficino derived from the scholion anything of this speculative order with regard to the sophist is doubtful. But the possibility nonetheless remains, given the mysterious linkages with which Plato had invested the role, as we have seen in other key dialogues besides the *Sophist* itself; and given too the antithetical pressure exerted by the imagery of shadows throughout Plato's philosophy, above all in those books so critical for a Neoplatonic understanding of the One and the Good, books 6 and 7 of the *Republic*.

In sum, the preface, bearing as it does the stamp of two of the very greatest of the Platonists, Iamblichus and Proclus, emerges as one of those texts from antiquity to which Ficino accorded esteem and a measure of credence. It is an eventful history for a mere scholion, and of considerable interest to the student of Renaissance Platonism, and especially, if unexpectedly, of Proclus's signal contribution to the formation and development of that Platonism.

Chapter 4: Icastic Art

One of the most intriguing issues raised by the *Sophist* is first broached at 234B ff. when the Stranger turns to the notion of imitation, and specifically to the painter's ability to make resemblances of real things, and proceeds to distinguish between the two kinds of image-making art (*eidôlopoiikê technê*): icastic, or the art of making a "likeness" (*eikôn*), and phantastic, or the art of making a mere "semblance" (*phantasma*) (236C3–7). He invokes the true painter or sculptor, the *eikastês,* who tries to reproduce absolutely faithfully the proportions of the original, and to render its colors. And he contrasts him with the falsifying artist, the *phantastês,* who strives to achieve a special optical effect or illusion in order to compensate for the height at which a statue or rendering is placed or for some other peculiarity of its position where, paradoxically, a perfectly proportional likeness and coloring would make an incongruous impression upon the viewer. To convey the illusion of perfect proportions such a falsifying artist has to devise subtly deceiving disproportions; and to convey the sense of authentic color he has unnaturally to heighten or modify his colors. Instead of remaining steadfastly committed to rendering the truth as he knows it to be, he strives to render appearances by using subterfuges that trick the eye.

This is not an obviously compelling argument, and it would seem to undermine the force of Plato's distinctions. For the artist of the appearances in question may be striving genuinely to render the truth to a disadvantaged spectator, and to exercise his skill in order to overcome a special set of difficulties. He may not be lying so much as making particular allowances in order to convey the same truth which an advantaged spectator would perceive and which a literal rendering would in fact distort or conceal from a disadvantaged one. At the heart of the problem lies Plato's sense of the absolute disjunction between what we see with the eye and what we know with the mind. For him the true painter strives to reproduce what he knows to be the correct shapes and colors even if we do not see them as such, while the falsifying painter strives to present the illusion of truth to the eye alone.

Plato returns to this crucial distinction between icastic and phantastic art much later in his dialogue at 264C4–5 ff.: "We distinguished two forms of image-making—the making of likenesses and the making of semblances." Now, however, he proceeds to define image-making or "imitation" further as "a kind of creation" or making of "images" (*eidôla*—which Ficino transliterates as *idola*); and to assert that there are two kinds of such secondary creation, human and divine. The world of nature is the creation of "a cause which, working with reason and art, is divine and proceeds from divinity" (265C8–9). This sentiment he repeats at 265E3: "the products of nature, as they are called, are works of divine art (*poieisthai theiai technêi*)." The things that man makes out of such natural objects become the works of human art.

Plato proceeds to align the basic distinctions. There are two kinds of divine art and two kinds of human: one is the making of true or verisimilar likenesses, the other of false images or semblances. Thus for Ficino God makes the objects of nature with his icastic art, such objects being the true, in the sense of verisimilar, likenesses of the Ideas of their species or kinds in the Divine Mind, the ultimate, the paradigmatic realities. The natural world, and this includes the celestial as well as the sublunar spheres, is an "imitation" of these realities, though imitation always implies, given the *Sophist*'s dictum at 240B, partial not-being and therefore some element of unlikeness or diminishment. If we hold to the earlier analogy with the true painter or sculptor, the natural world resembles the intelligible in terms, figuratively speaking at least, of both proportion and color. But the first and supreme creation was that of the intelligible world itself in its united but manifold nature as a series of Forms, an "all-complete animal," in God's Mind. The natural world is merely an imitation of that first creation which cannot strictly speaking, given Plato's definition, be analyzed in terms of "art." For God's first exercise of "art" was his creation, only in the restricted sense of making, of the natural world in imitation of His own Ideas, even perhaps of His one Idea of Nature.[1] Nature herself is the work, is the fabrication of His icastic art.

The *Sophist*'s distinctions accordingly require that, in a Christian Platonic context, we handle the traditional topos of the analogy between man the artist and God the Creator circumspectly. Man can imitate God only in the sense that he has the powers to imitate God the Imitator, the icastic Artist who made the natural world. Strictly speaking, he cannot imitate God the Creator in the ineffable sense of Him who conceived of the intelligible paradigm (or paradigms) of the natural world within Himself; for that paradigm was not the product, the fabrication, of imitation, and yet Plato deems the notion of imitation integral to the notion of the artist. We may refer to the natural world as "created" if we mean loosely that it was made, not out of preexistent matter, but rather out of the potentiality of "chaos" to receive form; but even then, strictly speaking, we should refer to it as being "formed" or "generated."[2] We might be hesitant to adopt this rigorous distinction between creating and the various modes of making, but we should be aware of it. All art is, according to the *Sophist*'s definitions, a making, not a creating: man imitates God the Maker when he too makes things from the sensible objects of the sublunar realm that God made in imitation of the Ideas of such objects in His own Mind, Ideas that are in turn sub-Ideas of the Idea of the world itself. If we introduce the famous analogy from the *Republic* book 10, 596A ff.,[3] man makes a couch but this couch is merely an image of the Idea of the Couch (or pos-

---

1. This was a debated issue in antiquity, but Proclus decided in favor of there being an Idea of Nature, given the testimony in the *Timaeus* at 41E that the Demiurge shows the souls "the nature of the universe." This Proclus took to be the paradigm of Nature in the Demiurge's mind: see his *In Timaeum* book 3, 270.16 ff. (ed. Diehl; tr. Festugière, 5:145) and *In Parmenidem* book 3, 820.38–821.33 (ed. Cousin; tr. Morrow and Dillon, pp. 183–184, with Dillon's comments on pp. 152–153).

2. For the all important distinctions between *creatio, formatio,* and *generatio,* see Ficino's *Platonic Theology* 18.3 (ed. Marcel, 3:188–189): "Mutatio quidem animae ex nihilo ad esse per Deum solum facta creatio est; mutatio vero corporis non viventis ad vitam ipsam ab anima capiendam formatio quidem corporis; animalis autem generatio nuncupatur." Cf. *Platonic Theology* 5.13 (ed. Marcel, 1:207–209).

3. The passage, we recall, that refers at 596D1 to a sophistical demiurge; see chap. 1, p. 30 above.

sibly of the unique God-made couch Socrates postulates at 597B–D
as participating in that Idea), which is itself a sub-Idea of a series
of more general Ideas. But what of the painter who then paints the
cabinetmaker's couch and is as it were at two (or, given the *Republic*'s unique God-made couch, at three) removes from reality? In
the *Republic* at 598A ff. he is dismissed as a deceiver and his
paintings as visual lies.

The issue is not quite so straightforward, however. Ficino takes
Plato's argumentation in the *Republic* to prove in fact that there is
no Idea of the Couch in the Divine Mind. For the Middle Platonists
and Neoplatonists had come to reject the notion that there could be
Ideas of artifacts (or of relative concepts, trivial objects, parts of
wholes, evils, and even individuals, though this last was a much
debated issue), despite the impression that the *Republic* seems to
postulate such Ideas.[4] Rather, for Ficino, God endows man's mind
with the formula of an ideal couch, a formula that is then activated
by the perception of a couch or couches, or by the memory of such
a perception, in ways that are developed fully in the psychology
and epistemology of Augustine and of his commentators among the
Scholastics. God also supplies via nature the materials, the natural
object(s), with which the cabinetmaker can make the couch using

---

4. Albinus's (Alcinous's) *Didaskalikos* chap. 9 (ed. Hermann, 163.20 ff.), which Ficino
knew and had translated, gives the traditional list of things without Ideas but caused instead
by *logoi*, reason-principles in Nature. See Morrow and Dillon, *Proclus' Commentary on
Plato's Parmenides,* pp. 145–156 (Dillon's introd. to book 3), for an analysis of the views
of Proclus, who also denied that artifacts could have Ideas. Another obstacle, besides the
Republic's mention of the Ideas of couches and tables, was the *Cratylus*'s introduction at
389B of the form (*eidos*) of a shuttle, and of the true or ideal shuttle.

While Plotinus recognizes Ideas of individuals, or at least of men and other living creatures, in his *Enneads* 5.7 (cf. 4.3.5, 5.9.12, 6.4.4.34–46, 6.7.12), it is unclear how consistently he holds to this doctrine. In a brief letter to Francesco da Diacceto dated 11 July
1493 (*Opera,* p. 952.1), Ficino observes circumspectly that "the Ideas of individuals are not
mutually distinguished in the prime Mind absolutely, but relatively" ("Non putas proprias
singulorum ideas in mente prima inter se absolute quidem sed quadam relatione distingui");
and that this accords with Plotinus's views as well as with Proclus's. In the *Timaeus,* he
concludes, sublunar individuals are constructed in the workshop of "the elder gods and
demons," following the mandate of "the architect" who contemplates the "ideal and eternal
model." For Ficino, a Christian Platonist, the "architect" is necessarily God the Father, and
the "model" is God the Son, who is the Idea of Man, and hence of all living things; see his
letter to Giovanni Cavalcanti (*Opera,* pp. 629–630; tr. *Letters,* 1:85–88).

the formula that has been activated in his mind. The craftsman who makes the couch is therefore the *icastes,* the maker of a verisimilar image. Is the painter who then paints the couch, though the imitator of an imitator, the imitator of an *icastes,* therefore exercising only a phantastic art? Surely he has the choice either of dutifully observing the couch's exact proportions and coloring and producing a picture that retains something of the truth of his original innate idea of a couch, or of consciously playing with the image of the couch in order to produce a three-dimensional illusion or some perspectival novelty or trompe-l'oeil. This is the step that the *Sophist* invites us to take. For the analogy it first introduces at 234B ff. introduces a critical modification of the whole notion of "image-making" which now validates the role of the scrupulously realistic painter, the artist who sternly eschews illusionist tricks even when they would serve to compensate for a spectator's skewed perspective. Henceforth the painter is not in himself a liar or false imitator. Indeed, he can be deemed on a par with the craftsman in that the theory of a "formula" of an Idea enables Ficino and others to argue that the painter also can respond not only to the visual presence of a wooden couch but to the image of a couch supplied to his mind's eye by the activation of his formula for such a couch, whether this formula is itself activated by the immediate visual perception of a couch or merely by the memory of such a perception in the past. Thus the painter can paint an "ideal" couch that corresponds to the one he sees in his mind's eye, the same ideal couch which the craftsman may perceive when he sets out to copy it in wood. In this view the two couches, the painted one and the wooden one, share the same ontological status as imitations of the idea of the couch as it exists in the human mind.[5]

Nevertheless, the activation theory would seem to require that at some originating point someone must actually see a wooden couch, preferably the unique God-made couch postulated by the *Republic* at 597B–D! Otherwise, one might argue that, after a while at least, a deterioration in perception must ensue. Craftsmen would be unable

---

5. See Plotinus, *Enneads* 5.8.1.

to make wooden couches eventually if all they could use to activate their formulas of such couches were pictures of them, not the
three-dimensional artifacts themselves. In other words, the wooden
couch, and therefore the cabinetmaker who makes it, would seem to
be in position of priority and therefore superiority over the painted
couch and the painter who paints it. But such an assumption proceeds from materialist premises. From an idealist perspective the
painted couch is no less real than the wooden couch: both share in
the illusory reality of the spatiotemporal world, and both imitate
the ideal image of a couch in one's mind with varying degrees of
fidelity and success. Indeed, a good painted couch can conceivably
be truer to that ideal image than a cabinetmaker's three-dimensional
couch if the latter is clumsily executed; though such a line of argument requires that we think of the three-dimensional world we inhabit as no more real than the two-dimensional plane of a painting
and contingent on the ideal dimensionless world in the same way.
Both the plane and the solid couch are products of a maker, be it
cabinetmaker or painter, knowing what it is that he is making and
thus what Idea or idea he is imitating (267B). For Ficino only a
materialist would demand that a couch must be solid for it to be
real. We can even see how a Platonist might well argue that the
painted couch, being one dimension less than the solid couch, is
that much closer to the ideal dimensionless couch that both the
painter and the cabinetmaker imitate as best they can. And this
is because it manifests such abstract qualities as virtue, beauty,
and goodness, those "primary" or perfective qualities of which
alone among qualities Ideas exist for the Neoplatonists.[6] As such
the painted couch may serve to activate the formula of the ideal
couch in our minds as well as or even better than the necessarily
defective product of the cabinetmaker.

   In brief, we can see how the *Sophist*'s sophisticated analysis of
the "being" of such phenomena as artifacts and their images and
the discourse concerning them, and the enigmatic mixture of such

---

6. "Secondary" qualities or accidents such as whiteness and sweetness are derived rather
from *logoi* in Nature; see Proclus's *In Parmenidem* book 3, 826.27 ff. (ed. Cousin; tr.
Morrow and Dillon, pp. 187–188, with Dillon's comments on p. 154).

being with not-being and with difference, considerably complicated the whole notion of imitation and radically undermined the positions earlier set forward in the *Republic,* positions that had too easily dismissed the painted couch's claim to a kind of being and thus the painter's claim to be the presenter of a kind of truth. Both the cabinetmaker and the painter now emerge as jointly the exercisers of two kinds of art: the icastic art of faithfully observing the known proportions and colors of an artifact that perfectly corresponds to its ideal form, to its idea in the mind, and then equally of failing to do so and lapsing into phantastic art. Ficino does not explore, incidentally, the further complications that would arise if one tried to analyze what a truthful painter would be doing were he faithfully to copy a cabinetmaker's defective couch, or indeed vice versa; or were a painter to use the ideal image in his mind to modify and thus correct his representation of a defective three-dimensional wooden couch; or a cabinetmaker were to do the same in working from a defective two-dimensional painting.

One of the *Sophist's* most fascinating suggestions concerns, however, the nature of phantastic art. At 266B such an art is attributed to God in addition to the icastic art by which He makes animate beings and the elements from which they are constituted. For the images or idols (in the technical sense) that such things emit are themselves the products of "divine contrivance" (266B7), and Plato gives as examples "appearances" or "phantasmata" (B9–10), those "dream images, and in daylight all those naturally produced semblances which we call 'shadow' when dark patches interrupt the light, or a 'reflection' when the light belonging to the eye meets and coalesces with light belonging to something else on a bright and smooth surface and produces a form yielding a perception that is the reverse of the ordinary direct view" (266BC). Thus the world of natural images or idols, the world of shadows and reflections, is conceived of as the making of God's phantastic art. This has extraordinary implications for Ficino as we shall see in the next chapter.

Again the issue becomes complicated when Plato turns to the human parallel. At 266C8–9 he identifies the art of building with the art of true image-making, but the art of drawing buildings once they are made with the phantastic art; for drawing is "as it were a man-made dream for waking eyes." We seem back at the stage in the argument presented in book 10 of the *Republic*. Plato suggests, moreover, that whereas the icastic art is the product of knowledge, the phantastic art is the product of opinion. Underlying this line of reasoning is the notion of the phantasy itself, which Ficino defines in chapter 43 of his *Sophist* Commentary as a passion (or passiveness), or as an "appearance (*apparitio*) which closely resembles opinion." Such "phantastic passion" "occurs with regard to things in the sense, first and always to those things in the inner sense," that is, I take it, in the common sense, "and also at times to those in the external senses" (269.4–7). It is contrasted with the reason, and occasionally with the imagination, while sometimes, confusingly, being identified with it.[7]

However, the phantastic art—which is not therefore to be identified with what Ficino refers to at the beginning of chapter 44 as "the imaginary art" (269.15), for this would seem to include both icastic and phantastic art insofar as both are concerned with image-making—is twofold. On the one hand it modifies our perception of what exists in the natural world, on the other "it feigns phantastic simulacra of what do not exist" (269.17–18). Ficino seems reluctant to force this distinction or even to suggest it in anything more than tentative terms. In chapter 15, for instance, he observes that there are two kinds of imitation: the first "looks at something that is true, and, determined to use the true as its exemplar, it fabricates likenesses, just as a painter and others do." The second "has not yet gazed upon the true and yet strives to fabricate images of it; in the process, however, it produces phantasms that appear perhaps to

---

7. For the distinction between the imagination and the phantasy, see Kristeller, *Philosophy,* pp. 234–236, 369. See also Marian Heitzman, "L'agostinismo avicennizzante e il punto di partenza della filosofia di Marsilio Ficino," *Giornale critico della filosofia italiana* 16 (1935), 295–322, 460–480; 17 (1936), 1–11, esp. 16:309–319; and Robert Klein, "L'imagination comme vêtement de l'âme chez Marsile Ficin et Giordano Bruno," *Revue de métaphysique et de morale* 61 (1956), 18–39. Aquinas considered the two faculties identical; but Klein argues for the inflluence of Avicenna and Albertus Magnus on Ficino and thus for Ficino's distinguishing, at least on some occasions (as in the *Platonic Theology* 8.1, ed. Marcel, 1:285–286), between the imagination as a faculty of the sensitive soul and the phantasy as a faculty of the rational soul that forms *intentiones,* that is, preliminary judgments of the images arrived at by the imagination from sense perceptions.

resemble realities but are not true likenesses" (229.2–7). Note that the painter is here separated from the maker of phantasms whom Plato identifies with the sophist. But is he now associating all painters with the icastic art? Obviously not. We must somehow fit in both the falsifying painter and the fabricator of what does not exist, the maker of nonrealities as contrasted with the perhaps well-intentioned distorter of realities.

These are dimensions that neither Plato nor Ficino wishes to pursue since their focus is upon trapping and defining the elusive sophist and the analogy with the perspective painter has been abandoned by the way. It is the sophist who is the preeminent practitioner of the phantastic art, what Plato calls at 268A6–7 the "ironical imitator" as distinguished from the naive mimic or mime, the "simple imitator." And Plato does eventually admit that he is concerned with only a subbranch of the phantastic art, with the sophist's art of "juggling words" (268CD). The sophist is the supreme instance of the maker who does not know what he is making and opining: he fabricates verbal simulacra and deluding "appearances"—the verbal equivalent of the trompe-l'oeils of the illusionist painter or of what does not exist. In terms of the *Sophist*'s ontological preoccupations, he understands neither being nor not-being, and Ficino so defines him in chapter 18. Hence he has no ability to differentiate true from false images, objects from their shadows and reflections, even though he is preoccupied with shadows and not-being. As Ficino writes in chapter 19, he deploys the phantastic art to "feign simulacra" of things that he does not really or truly see but merely invokes in the course of pursuing a persuasive line of argument (231.22–24).

Underlying this view of the sophist is a set of assumptions that associates him indirectly but logically with those who believe in blind chance, and thus in the absence of a divine providence. The sophist commits himself to eristic debate and the deployment of phantasms because he cannot see or will not see the truth. Unlike his antithesis, the philosopher, he is unperceptive of, or indifferent to, the providential beauty and design that governs the world and therefore should govern all authentic imitations of its presence in the world and the discourse that seeks to understand and convey it.

The shadowy nature of the sophist's false propositions are in stark contrast, therefore, both with all icastic art and with God's own phantastic art. They have no truth value because they are not based upon an understanding of the truth: the truth of God's shaping presence in the realm of Nature; the truth not only of natural genera and species but also, in however a qualified or partial a manner, of individual objects, parts, and accidents, even trivia;[8] and the truth of the language of the philosopher who has an understanding of such particulars and of the overarching providence that governs them and thus the nature of his discourse.

It is signal that Ficino paid especial attention to the proposition at 265E that affirmed the existence of a divine craftsman as opposed to the alternative corporealist view that nature was the result of "some spontaneous cause that generates without intelligence" (265C7–8). That Plato had affirmed the existence of a divine cause and thus of a providential order in nature was one of Ficino's most cherished convictions (the texts he habitually cites are the *Epinomis* 986C, the *Sixth Letter* 323D, and above all the *Second Letter* 312E and the *Timaeus* passim).[9] However much he might adopt the perspective of the *Phaedo* in his analysis of the intelligible realm, of what he thinks of Neoplatonically as the Ideas in the divine Mind, Ficino had also been persuaded by the *Timaeus*'s vision of a creating Demiurge, naturally enough given his Christian orientation, to insist in a way that is not characteristic of the *Phaedo*—despite Socrates' account at 97C ff. of how he had vainly hoped that reading Anaxagoras would explain to him in what way the world is "for the best"—on the beauty, variety, and plenitude of the generated world of nature. This world the God of Genesis had pronounced was good and thus, in some limited sense at least, possessed of authentic being. This is to say that we have an undeclared if predictable tension in Ficino between a number of idealist propositions he derived principally from the *Phaedo* and a Timaean-Christian affirmation of

---

8. In other words, of all those things, with the exception of evils and unnatural conditions presumably, of which the Platonic tradition had denied there were Ideas.

9. Indeed, the presence of these very motifs accounts in large part for the extraordinary prestige of the two letters and of the *Epinomis* in Ficino's eyes.

the natural world and with it of its individual objects, qualities, and parts—those things for which the ancient Platonists had declared there were only *logoi* or reason-principles in Nature, not sublime Ideas. Scholars have noted a similar tension in Plato himself and, to a lesser degree perhaps, in Plotinus; but it is necessarily more manifest in a Christian Platonist like Ficino, for whom the *Timaeus* is immeasurably strengthened by its association with, or more properly accommodation to, Genesis. Some obvious consequences ensue when we turn to apply the *Sophist*'s ontological categories. For the Timaean orientation authenticates God's and man's icastic arts, and not just those anagogic, elevatory, or intellectual arts like astronomy and geometry for which alone the Neoplatonists, following Plotinus in the *Enneads* at 5.9.11, had postulated Ideas.[10] Furthermore, it wholly authenticates God's phantastic art in the making of images that have a limited being, a being almost overwhelmed by the presence of not-being. Man emerges made in the image of God, the supreme Icastes, as preeminently himself an icastes. But he imitates God's demiurgy in a divided way, since he lacks the unitary nature of God or His angels. Hence the variety of man's arts and skills, and the limitations of their ability to form (in the Aristotelian sense) and to make: to weave being and not-being together in new and creative ways.

Ficino has a number of interesting things to say about man's icastic arts and skills, not so much in the *Sophist* Commentary as in the *Platonic Theology,* which he wrote in the lustrum 1469–1474 and first published in 1482. It was republished at the end of the second edition of his great Plato translation that appeared in Venice in 1491 and thus profited from the wide diffusion of that edition. This is his major work of philosophy and apologetics and was writ-

---

10. Again, the lesser recreational and material arts were derived from Nature's *logoi,* often, like the parts of the body, under the wardship of demons. See Proclus's *In Parmenidem* book 3, 827.26–829.21 (ed. Cousin; tr. Morrow and Dillon, pp. 188–189, with Dillon's comments on p. 154). For Ficino the argumentation in the *Sophist* ran counter to this traditional separation—or at least it made the dividing line between them more difficult to draw. Nevertheless, he was anxious, as we shall see, to retain a hierarchy for the arts.

ten in the years immediately following his profound immersion in Plato studies. His comments clearly involve a knowledge of the *Sophist*'s argumentation and constitute a testimony to its impact upon his thinking about the nature and dignity of man, his immortal soul, and his likeness to the Creator. Three important passages are worth special examination: the first from book 11, chapter 5; the next from book 13, chapter 3; and the last from book 10, chapter 4, where Ficino addresses the problem of establishing a hierarchy for the arts.

It is especially important, I believe, to juxtapose the first two passages if we are to appreciate fully: first, the care with which Ficino set about establishing important distinctions between the powers we predicate of God, of the angels, of Nature, and of man, whatever the appropriateness on occasion of analogizing between them; and second, the limitations with which he invested even his most optimistic and panegyrical portrayals of man the maker, the universal artist and icastes. The juxtaposition should serve to modify, in part at least, Professor Charles Trinkaus's influential view that 13.3 is "a culmination, as it were, of Renaissance encomiums of man as the builder and ruler of the earthly realm,"[11] and that for Ficino "the ultimate achievement of man" is "to become God Himself," though this "total fulfillment of human autonomy" remains beyond his powers.[12] Such a view does not sufficiently emphasize, I believe, the

11. *In Our Image and Likeness: Humanity and Divinity in Italian Humanist Thought,* 2 vols. (London, 1970), p. 484. See chap. 9 in general of this monumental study and notably pp. 482–486.

12. "Marsilio Ficino and the Ideal of Human Autonomy," in Garfagnini, *Marsilio Ficino,* pp. 197–210 at 209–210. This article, which deals with much of the same material as pp. 482–485 in Trinkaus's *Image and Likeness,* also appears in another recent collection of essays, *Ficino and Renaissance Neoplatonism,* ed. Konrad Eisenbichler and Olga Zorzi Pugliese, University of Toronto Italian Studies, vol. 1 (Ottawa, 1986), pp. 141–153.

For a contrary conservative, even minimalist, view of Ficino's contribution not so much to aesthetics (for "there is no real system of aesthetics in Ficino") but to a theory of the arts, a view that emphasizes the debt to Augustine and the ancients, see Kristeller, *Philosophy,* pp. 304–309. Here I shall be more skeptical than Trinkaus but less so than Kristeller about Ficino's originality.

A fascinating if perhaps overly speculative study of Ficino's impact on Renaissance painting is André Chastel's *Marsile Ficin et l'art* (Geneva and Lille, 1954); see also his *Art et humanisme à Florence au temps de Laurent le Magnifique* (Paris, 1961). For Ficino's theory of beauty, see Werner Beierwaltes, *Marsilio Ficinos Theorie des Schönen im Kontext des Platonismus,* Sitzungsberichte der Heidelberger Akademie der Wissenschaften: Philosophisch-historische Klasse, Jahrgang 30, no. 11 (Heidelberg, 1980).

range and nicety of the qualifications that Ficino consistently built into his propositions and that reflect the deeply rooted hierarchical assumptions underlying his Platonic ontology and anthropology. What I hope to do, therefore, is to point to the wider Platonic context for Trinkaus's penetrating observations on Ficino, focussed as they are on the humanistic theme or genre of the dignity of man.[13]

The eleventh book deals in general with the proposition that the soul is immortal in part because it is united with eternal objects, the Ideas, and receives from them the species that are entirely liberated from matter. In chapter 5 Ficino turns to what he calls the "signs" confirming the assertion concluding chapter 4 that "such seals are sown in the soul by the Ideas themselves and dwell there steadfastly and without changing."[14] In the course of considering the fourth of six confirmatory "signs," Ficino asserts that

since the species of humanity is common to all men in that they possess only one species of mind, then men must also share the same approbation of all pertaining to the mind. Thus every mind, directly it perceives a roundness in things, admires that roundness although it does not know why exactly. Similarly in the case of such buildings as churches, it admires in general the squareness, or the equality of the walls, or the ways the blocks of stone are arranged, or the opposition of the various angles, or the shape and placement of the windows.[15]

---

13. In general, besides his *Image and Likeness,* see Trinkaus's two wide-ranging articles, "The Renaissance Idea of the Dignity of Man" and "Themes for a Renaissance Anthropology," reprinted in his recent collection, *The Scope of Renaissance Humanism* (Ann Arbor, 1983), part 3, pp. 343–403. See also Kristeller's *Philosophy,* pp. 117–120, and an important article, "The Dignity of Man," first published in his *Renaissance Concepts of Man and other Essays* (New York, 1972), pp. 1–21 (esp. 9–11), and republished in his *Renaissance Thought and Its Sources,* ed. Michael Mooney (New York, 1979), pp. 169–181 (esp. 172–173).

14. Ed. Marcel, 2:125, "sigilla talia et ab ideis animo inserantur et ipsi haereant immobiliter."

15. Ed. Marcel, 2:128, "Quoniam vero una humana species est in omnibus, cum sit mentis species una, idcirco communis est eorum quae ad mentem pertinent approbatio. Omnis mens figuram laudat rotundam in rebus statim consideratam et cur laudet ignorat. In aedificiis quoque similiter talem vel quadraturam aedium vel parietum aequalitatem lapidumve dispositionem, angulorum oppositionem, fenestrarum figuram atque occursum." Cf. *Philebus* Commentary 1.19 (ed. Allen, pp. 196–197), "Visibilem quidem circulum animus corrigit cum in puncto planum non tangat, neque enim quiesceret umquam; et omnem artificiorum structuram musicaeque modulos vel probat vel damnat. . . . Veriores igitur habet formas animus, quibus de corporalibus iudicet. Perfectior enim iudex est quam quod iudicatur."

Notice that Ficino's perspective, which is indebted to Augustine's *De Vera Religione* to the point of stealing phrases and sentences from it, is based upon what he sees as our spontaneous response to the abstract properties of certain regular geometric shapes or arrangements, those properties for which traditionally there were Ideas. From this he proceeds to argue for our similar appreciation of the beauty and harmony present in the human form: "in the same way the human mind admires the proportions of the limbs in man and the concord of numbers and voices,"[16] meaning, I take it, the harmonies present in dance and vocal music. From the perception of these outward manifestations of what Ficino regards as intellectual form, "what the mind approves or admires," he turns to internal equivalents of roundness and squareness and geometric proportion: to the "decorum," the harmonious proportionality, of our characteristic moral attitudes and habits. Here the mind admires wisdom and truth and does so universally: "every mind everywhere and always approves of these even though it does not know the reason why: it cannot not approve; it approves instinctively and naturally."[17]

The tenor of the argument runs counter to the assumptions of modern psychology but is revealing of Ficino's Platonism in that it is based on the belief that the mind possesses species as if they were seals or stamps. It instinctively or naturally imposes these seals on sense perceptions and thus creates for itself the concord, the proportions, the satisfying shapes that constitute beauty; the more so because its imposition renders the perceptions into images, into imitations almost, of the Ideas in general and more particularly of mathematical or geometric Ideas like the Idea of a Circle or Roundness postulated by Plato himself in the *Seventh Letter* at 342C (such Ideas to be kept distinct from the "mathematicals" themselves). The sensible realm, and by extension the realm of human affairs and human behavior, is thus made to conform by the mind to the forms,

---

16. Ed. Marcel, 2:128, "Laudat insuper eodem pacto certam quamdam sive membrorum humanorum proportionem sive numerorum vocumque concordiam."

17. Ibid., "Commendat morales gestus et habitus tamquam decoros. Commendat sapientiae lucem et veritatis intuitum. Si quaelibet mens haec omnia semper et ubique asciscit illico et quam ob causam asciscat ignorat, neque potest non asciscere, instinctu asciscit necessario prorsus et naturali."

the species or seals in itself, and hence to the intelligible realm that bestowed such forms on man in the first place. But this is not to postulate an exclusively subjective idealism even with regard to the sensible world. For while we do indeed impose our forms on our perceptions, or more simply form our perceptions, two factors prevent such forming from being peculiarly ours.

First, since our forms are derived from the Forms of the intelligible world, they are the same forms for all men. Therefore all men, so Ficino's argument goes, should share the same aesthetic criteria and by implication perceive the same forms in things, perceive the same intelligible structure to sensible reality. Therefore they should share essentially the same perceptual and epistemological criteria. Therefore they should always agree on the nature of truth and beauty, their minds working in the same way and according to the same canons, being equipped, to use Ficino's image, with the same seals. Furthermore, Platonic physics is of a piece with Platonic metaphysics in Ficino's view and requires that the ideal Forms have replicated versions of themselves in men's minds and have thus provided men with species or what he elsewhere calls "formulae" or "reasons" of themselves; and have also replicated themselves, not necessarily in inferior modes or degrees, in the sensible world. We perceive shape and proportion in things because our perceptions are formed by our internal "seals" and also because shape and proportion, form in the general Platonic sense, actually abide in things. Platonism had articulated a hierarchy of such replications that corresponded to its hierarchizing of being.

Finally, Ficino accepts the central theory of a correspondence (what he sometimes refers to scholastically as an *adaequatio*)[18]

---

18. For instance in the *Philebus* Commentary 1.15 (ed. Allen, pp. 166–169): "veritas est adaequatio rei ac mentis; et veritas mentis est eius ad res adaequatio; veritas rerum est rerum adaequatio menti. Duae sunt mentes: divina, humana. Duae res: opera divinae mentis, opera mentis humanae. . . . Veritas humani operis est adaequatio eius ad hominis mentem, id est, ut tale sit ut ideae artificis correspondeat. Veritas operis naturalis quod est divinae mentis opus adaequatio ad divinam mentem. . . . Veritas mentis humanae adaequatio rebus, non operibus suis, sed divinae mentis operibus. . . . Mentis autem divinae veritas adaequatio rebus non his quae infra se sunt, sed his quae intra, id est, seminibus rerum in sua essentia existentium." Note that this revealing passage does not appear in the manuscript of the first version of the commentary.

between the psychic forms and the forms as they dwell in matter. Our formulae or reasons are imitations or images of the supernal Forms, but so are the forms in matter, the material species. Our formulae and the material species are thus adapted to each other, or rather our formulae can be activated by the perception of the material forms precisely because, though closer to the pure intelligible Forms, they have been bestowed upon us in order that we might perceive the truth of the sensible world, and move from that limited and contingent truth up the ladder of perception to an understanding of the immaterial source of all the material forms in that world. Underlying the entire set of assumptions is the belief in a universal harmony that radiates outwards or downwards from the intelligible to the sensible, and that privileges man as the bond or knot whose mind receives both the perceptions of material forms and the prints or images of the purely intelligible Forms and then fits or justifies the one to the other.

What, however, of man the icastes as distinct from man the perceiver and thinker? What special kind of correspondences does he make between the highest Forms and their lowest manifestations in matter? And how do such correspondences differ, if they differ at all, from those we arrive at in the course of knowledge? Why, in short, should we accord the artist any kind of privileged role, even if we accept the premise that man is an artist by his very nature and an image of God the Artist?

Particularly relevant here is Ficino's recourse to our experience of geometric shapes and patterns. In theory we are held to respond with intellectual approbation to such shapes whenever and wherever we perceive them in the sensible world, in the works of nature or the works of man. But Ficino obviously has the achievements of architects specifically in mind, and more especially and predictably of the great Florentine architects who were his contemporaries and immediate predecessors and who had discovered and appropriated the Vitruvian canons in their quest for satisfying balance and harmonious proportions, for complementarity of mass, shape, angle, and line. Of course, Ficino's argument could equally well apply to man's perception of the architecture of wood and hill, of the deep romantic chasms of the natural world, but in actuality the context is almost exclusively anthropocentric. It is man's architecture—literally with regard to his highest achievements in building in the external world, the designing of churches; then to his personal outer architecture, the articulation of limb and voice; and finally to his inner architecture, the edifice of "moral attitudes and habits of the soul"—that Ficino looks to with such enraptured gaze. It is there that he comes upon the universal concords, the forms that are universally acknowledged and provoke an intellectual delight and assent.

All such architectural, musical, and moral "shapes" in the world of man are the products, however, of human art and skill, of the application of *technê* in the undifferentiated sense it had in ancient Greek, though applied here in what we would regard as a figurative sense to the molding of a man's character and virtue, to the forming of his moral nature. At this point the argument comes full circle. Just as human art makes the forms and harmonies of the city, of the life of the citizens within that city, and of the individual souls of the citizens, so too do the minds of the citizens instinctively respond with admiration to the perception and recognition of those forms, forms which man has himself imposed upon the world and which are the product of his art. This is not a narcissistic delight, for the forms without our minds are not uniquely or peculiarly our own, but the stamps and seals derived from the divine Forms. Moreover, as Ficino makes clear at the beginning of the discussion, in mankind there is only "one species of mind"; and thus the forms that one man has created in designing a temple, another in cultivating the dance, another in rendering himself just or courageous, can all be recognized by other men as if they were their own. In this sense man is the measure of all things: it is his forms, made and contemplated and remade, that perfect the circle. This is not to say that the forms of Nature herself are essentially ancillary or inferior to man's forms, or that human art, even when fully exercising its potential, can improve on her forms by making them its own; but rather that man adds his forms to Nature's, fills to overflowing her cornucopia, thereby reassuming his original Adamic powers and setting his seals beside the seals of the natural world to recreate, if only in part, the lost harmonies of Eden.

In that he begins with the model of Renaissance civic and eccle-
siastical architecture as somehow the most explicit demonstration
of the presence of the *sigilla idearum* in man, Ficino presents us
with the archetype of man as architect and thus with the connotations
such an image conveys. Perhaps he was influenced here by Plato's
recurring references to geometry, to its importance in education,
and to the geometric properties of the elements (as Ficino read
about them in the *Timaeus* and in the *Timaeus* commentary tradition
stemming from Calcidius). But this was assuredly reinforced by his
daily exposure to the masterpieces of Alberti, of Brunelleschi and
Michelozzo, to the geometry of Florence's greatest age. It is interesting to note, too, that among the wonders that most struck him,
as he records in a letter to Paul of Middelburg dated 13 September
1492, was "the Florentine machine showing the daily motions of
the heavens."[19] The machine's mobile geometry reproduced the intricate orbits of the Ptolemaic spheres and thus enabled the onlooker
to contemplate the circles, squares, and angles, the placements and
proportions that make up the most sublime of all God's buildings,
what Marlowe's Tamburlaine would call the wondrous architecture
of the world. The effect of Ficino's praise is not to direct our
attention to the heavens above so much as to the Archimedean
machine below: to the human art that had made as it were a talisman,
a model of the celestial world, and had then impelled it into motion,
thereby recreating the heavenly geometry in a way that testified to
the glory of human art as well as to the excellence of God's original
design. It is one of the most revealing witnesses to Ficino's anthropocentrism, to his approbation of man the maker. Man is the maker
or remaker not only of himself but of the elemental world below
and of the shapes and spaces of the circling spheres above; and in

---

19. *Opera*, p. 944.3. This is the famous letter announcing the new golden age and prais-
ing the return of the Platonic discipline, the discovery of printing, and the production of
astronomical tables enabling one to see in an hour a century's heavenly permutations. Ficino
had also been struck much earlier, he tells us in the *Platonic Theology* 2.13 (ed. Marcel,
1:122), by a German artisan's mechanical display of figures of various animals and birds, a
display he could set in motion by one mysterious godlike movement. A similar account
occurs in the *Disputatio contra Iudicium Astrologorum* of 1475; see Kristeller, *Supplementum*
2:11–76 at 13 ff.

setting them all in motion he becomes a kind of primum mobile. The argument, however, is based strictly upon analogy.

When Ficino turns in this same chapter 5 to what he calls the fifth *signum* confirming that "the seals are sown in the soul by the Ideas themselves,"[20] he addresses the subject of *ars*. "Every art," he writes, "because it orders its artifact (*opus*) by way of a particular reason or rationale with a particular end or goal in mind, must itself be a rational faculty. And if this rational faculty is innate in every irrational nature, then there is even more reason to suppose that it is innate in every rational nature."[21] Ficino proceeds to express his admiration for the "artful" way that even the elements seek out their own appropriate places: "with what a fine geometric art they preserve the straightest of lines in their ascent and descent; with what great architectural care the rain contracts itself into spherical drops; with what subtle cunning the air rushes to nature's help lest a vacuum should occur in her!"[22] Ficino is now attributing the circles, lines, and proportions, which the preceding, the fourth, *signum* had confined to man's world and art, to the art of Nature; he is remaking Nature in the image of man the icastes.

He proceeds to draw up a traditional list of Nature's arts: those associated with the silkworm, with the spider and its web, with the swallows and their feats as natural potters, with the swans and their music, with the bees and their architecture in wax, with the cranes and their living in a community, with the lions and their feats of war, with the foxes and their skill in hunting. But it is with this qualification: "the souls of animals in their sundry individual species only practice individually separate arts";[23] that is, in the main at

---

20. Ed. Marcel, 2:125, "sigilla talia et ab ideis animo inserantur et ipsi haereant immobiliter."

21. Ed. Marcel, 2:129, "Omnis ars quia certa ratione ad certum finem ordinat opus, rationalis facultas est. Facultas rationalis, si omni naturae irrationali est ingenita, multo magis ingenita est omni rationali."

22. "Elementa quam artificiose situm repetunt suum. Quanta geometriae arte rectam lineam in ascensu servant atque descensu? Quanta architecturae industria pluvia se in orbiculares guttulas cohibet? Quanta aer sagacitate rerum naturae succurrit, ne quid in ea vacuum relinquatur?" (ibid.).

23. "Ipsae quoque brutorum animae singulis in speciebus singulas artes exercent" (ibid.).

least, the foxes only practice the art of hunting, the lions that of war. Neither species practices the art of another, there being enough arts to go around, presumably, for all the various natural species. The goal of the argument is not Plinian description, however, but rather to assert that "nearly all" the arts known to man and to his world can be found in the world of Nature, though individually distributed to the species. Man is still the measure of art and its varieties.

Ficino then asks rhetorically, "Could you therefore maintain that only the rational nature is artless [*inertem,* meaning without any art and consequently helpless] and because of this skill-lessness from the onset rendered irrational?" Obviously not. Rather we must assert that "all the arts must be in the possession of man considered as a rational species, since each individual art is innate in the separate species of irrational animals."[24] The arts are admittedly divided up among individual men, but they are all possessed collectively by the one species, man.[25] The angel is necessary to cap the argument: for, since all the animals viewed collectively possess all, or nearly all, the arts, and since man as a species possesses all of them, accordingly we must acknowledge the necessary existence of an individual being who possesses all of them and this must be the angel. But in the angel the arts are still divided up "according to the forms,"[26] meaning, I take it, that they are still individually separate in the mind of the angel—who is all mind but nevertheless multiform in his thinking. Thus for its completion the scheme requires that God in His uniqueness possess all the arts but "under His one divine form alone," God as Creator being omniform and

---

24. "Quis autem dixerit, modo ista consideret, solam naturam rationalem inertem fuisse atque ex inertia irrationalem ab initio constitutam? Immo vero si debet rationalis sedes [species?] multo prius et magis artem capere rationalem quam sedes [species?] irrationalis, oportet omnes rationali hominum speciei artes innasci, postquam singulae innatae sunt singulis irrationalium speciebus. Omnes enim ferme in genere brutorum universo congregantur, sed aliae species artium per alias animalium species disperguntur" (ibid.). I am indebted to Professor Kristeller for the suggestion that "sedes" be emended to "species."

25. "Omnes ergo in unica rationali hominum specie colliguntur, licet per singulos dividantur" (ibid.).

26. "Omnes iterum in uno speciei angelicae singulari, in quo tamen dividuntur secundum formas, quoniam multiformis est angelus" (ibid.).

uniform. Hence in God all the arts and skills are one, are the divine Art.[27] In this scheme the concept of art or skill spans the arch of being from God (if He can be said to be) to the elements seeking out their natural places in the straightest of lines. By implication such art is virtually the same as any activity or operation that bestows order, harmony, beauty in imitation of God's original bestowal of such attributes or essences at the time of the world's creation. We recall that the word *kosmos* in Greek signifies the imposition of order and beauty on chaos. Thus the very notion of the world implies the notion of art, the creation of the kosmos being the supreme work of art, the art of arts, the original and paradigmatic manifestation of art. I wish to stress the element of activity and operation, because Ficino concludes his discussion of his fifth "sign" by bringing to bear the contrasting Aristotelian categories of having the disposition or capacity for (*habitus*—the Greek *hexis*) and of actually practicing (*actus*—the Greek *energeia*) the arts.

He marshals his argument thus: the arts are divided up equally with regard to potentiality and act among all the species in the general class of animals, since no one animal species exercises all the arts or has the potentiality for exercising them all; each species has the disposition for and practices only one art. Accordingly, in mankind as a species the arts must be in actuality distributed among its various individuals, since individuals devote themselves to different arts.[28] We might note that the argument at this point makes no allowance for the cognate notions of one man being a master of a number of arts and skills, and of a group of men being devoted to the study and practice of the same art; or for the separate but more important notion that some arts are much more proper and profitable than others to all men. While each individual usually devotes himself to the practice of a single art, mankind as a class practices all the arts. Each individual, however, has the potentiality (initially at

---

27. "Cunctae [artes] denique in uno singulari Deo atque una dumtaxat Dei forma" (ibid.).

28. "Quapropter artes dividuntur invicem in brutorum genere secundum habitum atque actum, quoniam nulla brutorum species aut artes omnes exercet actu aut omnes infusas habet, sed quaelibet eorum species unica utitur arte et possidet unicam. Artes igitur dividantur oportet in hominum specie secundum actum, quia alii alias meditentur, non tamen secundum habitum, quia singuli cunctas possideant" (ibid.).

least) for devoting himself to any one of the arts. In sum, both the individual and the species are capable potentially of cultivating all the arts, but the species is capable of cultivating them all simultaneously, the individual only one of them (or certainly only a few) at a time (since it is difficult for us to conceive of even a Methusaleh having the time, capacities, or inclination to practice all the arts).

Again, the angel is required to mediate between man the icastes and God the Icastes. In any one angel the arts are all potentially present and all may be exercised in actuality. The angel as an individual being corresponds in this regard to man as a species and, we might add, to the irrational animals as a class. Each angel "studies all the arts," that is, contemplates their potential use, and may exercise them all in practice, though habitually exercising only one of them, or possibly one group of them, "since each angel governs the world in a different manner."[29]

Finally, Ficino asserts, with a reference to 1 Corinthians 12:6, that the arts are united in all conceivable ways in God Himself: "He possesses and sees and practices all the arts; for, as Paul the theologian writes, He works all things in the workings themselves of all things."[30] Unlike the angel, that is, God always exercises all the arts and is not customarily devoted to one of them or to one group of them.

Notice that Ficino's logic requires that the arts in practice be di-

---

29. Ed. Marcel, 2:129–130, "Siquidem in angelo quolibet uniuntur cunctae habitu atque actu. Quilibet enim illorum quaslibet meditatur,* sed dividuntur executione, quoniam alii aliter gubernant mundum."

*The reading in the *Opera*, p. 256; Marcel has "mediatur."

The problem for the Scholastics of whether each angel is an individual or a separate species—St. Thomas holding the latter, St. Bonaventura and other Franciscans the former—had revolved around the intricate hylomorphism controversy. Ficino's ideas are deeply indebted in many ways to Aquinas even as his Platonic assumptions drew him toward the Augustinian-Franciscan tradition. See my "The Absent Angel in Ficino's Philosophy," *Journal of the History of Ideas* 36.2 (1975), 219–240 at 221 ff., 223 ff., 227–229; and, more generally, Kristeller, "The Scholastic Background of Marsilio Ficino," *Traditio* 2 (1944), 257–318 (reprinted in *Studies*, pp. 35–97); idem, *Le thomisme et la pensée italienne de la Renaissance* (Montreal, 1967), esp. pp. 93–104, 109–124; and Collins, *The Secular Is Sacred*, pp. 15–16, 20–23, 30–34, 38–39 and passim.

30. Ed. Marcel, 2:130, "Cunctae in Deo modis omnibus uniuntur, quia et habet, et videt, et exequitur universas. Nam in omnibus operantibus, ut inquit theologus Paulus, omnia operatur."

vided among the brutes and men, while remaining unified among the angels and in God. Among the brutes the arts are divided in potentiality and actuality; among men in actuality. In the angel they are united in potentiality though not in actuality; but in God they are united in actuality. As we have seen, the scheme effectively equates the status of the angel here with that of mankind viewed as a species, though certainly not as an individual.

All the arts are simultaneously natural, human, and divine. The realm of Nature is therefore a gallery for us to contemplate their various perfections. Man exercises no art, or almost no art (and Ficino leaves himself a loophole), that is not also somewhere evident in Nature. Conversely, Nature has no art that does not have its equivalent among men (and Ficino feels no need to provide for a possible exception). Ficino considers all the arts as *fabricationes* or *operationes,* and his paradigms, as in the Scriptures, are the potter and the architect.[31] He is not concerned in this immediate context with the completely different motif of "inspiration" in art stemming as it does primarily from the Platonic theory of poetry as interpreted by the ancient Neoplatonists, above all by Proclus, and revived by such Italian predecessors and contemporaries as Bruni and Landino. For the plastic arts this notion has never been as appropriate or significant as it has been for poetry and music; and Ficino seems to have confined the central notion of the "divine fury," following Plato in the *Phaedrus* at 245A ff., to a consideration of prophecy, priesthood, poetry, and love.[32] This is not to deny the inspiration necessary to excel in the plastic arts, but it is to insist on its being a different kind of rapture from the Orphic or Davidic rapture that Ficino associates with lyric poetry, with the divine hymn, and with the experience of preternatural ecstasy. Concomitantly, Ficino seems reluctant to think of poetry and music as merely "arts," and the introduction of poetry in particular serves to undermine the supposition, which has hitherto seemed pivotal, that any single man may, or at least does, only exercise one art, since only

31. See Ernst Robert Curtius, *European Literature and the Latin Middle Ages,* tr. Willard R. Trask (New York, 1953; reprint, New York and Evanston, Ill., 1963), pp. 544–546.
32. See my *Platonism of Ficino,* chap. 2.

in mankind as a species, in the angel, and in God can we anticipate the exercise of many or all the arts.

An illuminating text in this regard is Plato's *Ion*. In this curious and witty exchange between Socrates and a naively overenthusiastic rhapsode, the rhapsode claims that he personally knows all the arts because Homer, his hero and unceasing preoccupation, knew them. Socrates demolishes this claim to omniscience on the part of Ion but leaves the supposition that Homer was omniscient essentially intact. This may well be because Plato's goal was either quite simply to provide us with a delightful vignette of wisdom and folly in animated conversation or to poke fun in general at rhapsodes and their pretensions. It seems unlikely that he intended in this dialogue to attack Homer himself, even though common sense might suggest that no poet is omniscient or possesses all the arts, or even perhaps more than the one art of poetry. Certainly Ficino's working scheme would substantiate the extension of Socrates's objections to Ion to Homer himself, were it not for his Neoplatonic doctrine of the divine fury, which quite clearly allows for the poet to utter more than he knows and to achieve in poetry a profundity and universality of understanding that is quite beyond him in normal waking life. Indeed, the doctrine seems to have been generated in the first place to take account of the palpable discrepancy between the habitual ignorance of the natural man and the momentary wisdom of that same man when visited by Apollo and the Muses.

One way out of this dilemma is to regard poetry not as a human or a natural art (and the idea that birdsong is the natural manifestation of poetry can be fondly dismissed) but as a divine art that man does not share with the angels and God (if we think of the universe as the product of God's Word) so much as receive from on high as a gift. In the receipt, moreover, he may be momentarily apotheosized. But the notion that art in general may render us angelic or almost divine is an independent theme, and one to which Ficino would only have subscribed with reservations. While he accepted the Platonic doctrine of the soul's fall from a state of angelic bliss into the prison house of matter, there to labor until its reascent, equally he accepted the Platonic theory of the soul's difference from the pure angelic intelligences and its perpetual and essential involvement in motion, however intellectually conceived. In the experience of divine fury or ecstasy, and thus of poetic ecstasy that is one of its four manifestations, the soul may reacquire something of its original angel-like status, if only transiently, but it does not actually become an angel. This qualification enables him to keep intact the basic conviction that, while the angels may exercise all the arts individually and as individuals, souls can only separately exercise separate arts. Still, the thrust of the argument implies that the ecstatic soul may acquire in sublime moments, and certainly the eventually purified and glorified soul will indeed acquire, the power to exercise each and every art, albeit seriatim. At the time of redemption, or possibly in the rapturous ascents that immediately precede or even anticipate the redemptive state, the individual soul may therefore come to possess, however proximately, the powers of mankind viewed collectively as a species, and thus to wield, in some sort, the powers of individual angels.

Obviously, the questions of what the arts will be like in the wholly redeemed world, and what man as icastes will be and do in such a world, are highly speculative, and turn upon the manner in which we think of the angel and of God as artists. Nevertheless, the issue of poetic ecstasy, and therefore, by implication at least, of poetic art, does invite speculation; and we must acknowledge that the boundaries that Ficino invokes here in order to plot his distinctions gradually become indeterminate, even if we confine ourselves to traditional Platonic criteria. That the soul as an individual fallen being, not man as a species, may ever be in possession actually of all the arts is an assumption Ficino takes care to avoid making, for it goes too far in identifying man the artist with the angel, let alone with God. But it is an assumption which nevertheless haunts his arguments and provides him with, if you will, an emotional context for his consideration of man's elevated powers and for his passionate belief that man is, in the words of the Eighth Psalm constantly on his lips, only a little lower than the angels.[33]

---

33. Psalm 8:4–7, "Quid est homo, quod memor es eius? aut filius hominis, quoniam visitas eum? Minuisti eum paulominus ab angelis, gloria et honore coronasti eum. Et constituisti eum super opera manuum tuarum. Omnia subiecisti sub pedibus eius, oves et boves universas, etc."

After all, the ease with which he habitually slips from a discussion of man as an individual to consideration of man as a species, from man's soul to Soul in general, makes him vulnerable to blurring the line between what an individual artist or artisan might achieve and the skills exercised by mankind. Even so, we must acknowledge the presence of his caveats and qualifications and give them due credit. Whatever the implications his theses might bear if carried forward too rigorously, Ficino himself is aware of the limitations we must apply to our image of man the artist. In the universal hierarchy, man occupies the median position and his art is less than the art of the angel, whatever that might be, and therefore, in the original Platonic system, less than the art of the demons later identified by Christian Platonists with the angels or at least the lesser angels. Though Ficino's vision is anthropocentric and partially coincides with what we now regard conveniently as the Burckhardtian vision of Renaissance man, it is not that essentially Romantic vision. Man is a maker, not a creator, and above him are the demonic intelligences of much greater makers, intellectual artisans whose works render the works of man but those of a child.

In arguing that "the rules of the arts" are "naturally innate in us," Ficino observes later in chapter 5 that, whereas in the beasts they are "imprinted by the celestial and the corporeal nature" (a distinction we shall shortly address), and whereas in God "they emanate from His pure essence," in man they are implanted or infused in our minds along with the "species of things." I take this last phrase to mean along with the formulae of such species as the species exist in the Divine Mind, formulae that we are endowed with as soon as we issue from God, like the angelic intellects themselves, and that we bring with us into this world from our antenatal existence. Whereas the beasts receive "the rules of the arts" from "the celestial Nature," man receives them directly from God without the mediation of Nature.[34] Moreover, each man receives all the rules, while

---

34. Ed. Marcel, 2:133, "ut quando audimus artes nobis inesse natura, non intelligamus vel a natura caelesti corporalique impressas vel a mera animae essentia fluere (siquidem a tali natura impressas habent bestiae, ab essentia autem mera manantes solus possidet Deus),

each species of animal receives just one rule alone.[35] Finally, the beasts "are compelled to exercise the various arts at a certain time and according to a necessary impulse of their nature. While we may choose to exercise any one art or several according to the free judgement of our reason," and, by implication, at any time.[36] Again these observations might suggest that Ficino deems human art superior to the art of Nature; but this would be to misinterpret him grievously. The argumentation allows that man's arts can be superior to those exercised by the individual animal species, though arguably no spinning is more perfect than the spider's, no architecture more intricate than the bee's. But this does not mean that man as artist is superior to Nature herself. To the contrary, in a number of passages in earlier books of the *Platonic Theology,* Ficino subordinates human art to Nature's art, arguing in 1.3 and 2.13 that hers excels ours,[37] and in 2.7 that as human art is to Nature, so Nature is to God.[38] This is a traditional proportional comparison that de-

---

sed intelligamus nostris mentibus statim ex Deo natis infusas fuisse species rerum et regulas artium, ut in Timaeo tradit Plato, non aliter quam angelicis mentibus infundantur . . . a Deo sine medio nos eas accipimus, illae [bestiae] natura caelesti intercedente."

35. "quisque nostrum accipit cunctas, bestiarum species singulae singulas" (ibid.).

36. "bestiae necessario quodam impulsu naturae ad suae artis usum certo tempore compelluntur, nos autem libero rationis iudicio tum artis unius, tum plurimarum usum eligimus" (ibid.).

37. Ed. Marcel, 1:49, 120, "Nempe ex eo quod natura efficacius meliusque materiam suam movet quam ars suam, coniicimus principalem formam in natura* materiae suae magis dominari quam principalem formam in arte materiae suae. Si dominatur magis duo concluduntur, tum quod propius quam ars adest materiae secundum situm, tum quod magis quam ars secundum substantiam excellit materiae suae, magisque potest per se sine illa existere" (p. 49); "Proinde partes mundi et corpuscula quaelibet ad certum finem per viam ordinatissimam et commodissimos modos, aut semper, aut plurimum ita proficiscuntur, ut peragant saepissime opera sua quanto melius effici possunt, perinde ac si artem intus haberent, et artem quidem absolutissimam; immo tam mirabili ratione progrediuntur, ut humanam artem, rationemque ex<s>uperant" (p. 120).

*The reading in the *Opera,* p. 84. Marcel's "arte" is clearly wrong as his translation indicates.

38. Ed. Marcel, 1:94, "Sicuti se habet ars ad naturam, sic et natura ad Deum. Artium opera eatenus permanent incorrupta, quatenus vi naturae servantur. . . . Et sicut natura operibus suis infert motum, sic Deus naturae praestat esse. . . . Tamdiu igitur existit natura, quamdiu Deus servat eam in existendo." Cf. *Philebus* Commentary 1.2 (ed. Allen, pp. 84–85) with a garbled reference to Plato's *Statesman* 269C–270A ff.: "Natura enim ut dicit Plato in *Politico* vel Dei ars est vel artificiosum Dei organum." For Cicero's equations of God with Nature and with the cause of Nature, equations with which Ficino must have been familiar, see Gersh, *Middle Platonism and Neoplatonism* 1:93–99, with further refs.

pends on our substituting for the limited notion of the animal species even in their totality the grander notion entirely of Nature.

We can think of her, he writes in 5.4, as a sublime artist-artisan having at her disposal "a matter as yet deprived of all forms but nonetheless equally prepared to receive all forms."[39] Moreover, Ficino asserts in 2.13 that, since she is responsible for the wonderful beauty of the world, she "must have a rational sense."[40] For she organizes matter from within, he writes in an important passage in 4.1, while man merely organizes it from without in imitation of her art; and she does so by way of "intellectual reasons" which instill in her seeds a "force for life" (*vis vivifica*).[41] That she "generates" or "draws out" the "substantial forms" (*educere formas substanti-*

---

39. Ed. Marcel, 1:177, "Ergo et ipsa natura, rerum artifex, subiectam quamdam sibi materiam habet omnium expertem formarum, ad omnes suscipiendas pariter praeparatam."

40. Ed. Marcel, 1:124, "oportere . . . artificem omnium naturam sensum habere, sensum, inquam rationalem."

41. Ed. Marcel, 1:146–147, "Proinde, si ars humana nihil est aliud quam naturae imitatio quaedam, atque haec ars per certas operum rationes fabricat opera, similiter efficit ipsa natura, et tanto vivaciore sapientioreque arte quanto efficit efficacius et efficit pulchriora. Ac si ars vivas rationes habet, quae opera facit non viventia, neque principales formas inducit, neque integras, quanto magis putandum est vivas naturae rationes inesse, quae viventia generat formasque principales producit et integras. Quid est ars humana? Natura quaedam materiam tractans extrinsecus. Quid natura? Ars intrinsecus materiam temperans, ac si faber lignarius esset in ligno. Quod si ars humana, quamvis sit extra materiam, tamen usque adeo congruit et propinquat operi faciundo ut certa opera certis consummet ideis, quanto magis ars id naturalis implebit, quae non ita materiae superficiem per manus aliave instrumenta exteriora tangit, ut geometrae anima pulverem quando figuras describit in terra, sed perinde ut geometrica mens materiam intrinsecus phantasticam fabricat? Sicut enim geometrae mens, dum figurarum rationes secum ipsa volutat, format imaginibus figurarum intrinsecus phantasiam, perque hanc spiritum quoque phantasticum absque labore aliquo vel consilio, ita in naturali arte divina quaedam sapientia per rationes intellectuales vim ipsam vivificam et motricem ipsi coniunctam naturalibus seminibus imbuit, perque hanc materiam quoque facillime format intrinsecus.

"Quid artificium? Mens artificis in materia separata. Quid naturae opus? Naturae mens in coniuncta materia. Tanto igitur huius operis ordo similior est ordini qui in arte est naturali, quam ordo artificii hominis arti, quanto et materia propinquior est naturae quam homini, et natura magis quam homo materiae dominatur. Ergo dubitabis certorum operum certas in natura ponere rationes? Immo vero sicut ars humana, quia superficiem tangit materiae et per contingentes fabricat rationes, formas similiter solum efficit contingentes, sic naturalem artem, quia formas gignit sive eruit substantiales ex materiae fundo, constat funditus operari per rationes essentiales atque perpetuas. . . . Haec omnia significant adesse ubique per terram et aquam in natura quadam artificiosa vitalique spiritalia et vivifica semina omnium." Cf. *Philebus* Commentary 1.18 (ed. Allen, pp. 186–187), "Et quia natura agit vi superioris essentiae, omnium seminum quae in natura sunt sunt et in ea essentia rationes, quas Ideas vocamus."

ales is a traditional scholastic formulation) from the seeds within matter, in contrast with man who imposes "contingent" forms on matter externally, is evidence of her superiority over man; for she has "essential" reasons while he only has "contingent" reasons. We should be aware of two sets of distinctions here. First there is the threefold distinction between the totally inert, unformed matter of the primordial chaos; the matter on earth which has received certain primary forms and qualities but has not yet been "seeded" to become anything in particular; and the already seeded matter which brings forth a myriad of forms of its own accord. Second there is the crucial quadruple set of distinctions between substantial and contingent forms, and essential and contingent reasons. Essential and contingent reasons are what Nature and man respectively bring to bear on matter: essential reasons correspond to forms already potentially there and actualize them as substantial forms; contingent reasons are imposed by man artificially on matter and merely actualize contingent forms.

The argument in 11.5 recognizes, however, two basic but contrasting kinds of human art, one consisting of the imposition of contingent forms, the other aligning man with Nature as the artisan who assists her in bringing forth substantial forms. Thus, some men apply themselves to a matter "which has no inherent principle that will make it into anything in particular," and Ficino gives as examples clay or marble awaiting the potter and sculptor.[42] But other men facilitate the inherently natural processes of healing and growing and so forth. Hence Ficino argues that the informed matter of man's own earthly body always heals itself but is helped by the physician's art; and a similarly subordinate ancillary role is accorded the art of the farmer who assists Nature in bringing forth crops.[43] Ironically, this approach elevates the doctor and farmer and their "artistic" skills over the artisan who makes something; for they are, as it were,

---

42. Ed. Marcel, 2:130,, "Duo sunt artium genera. Aliae sunt quarum materia circa quam versantur nullum habet in se principium operis effectivum, sicut lutum aut saxum ita subesse videntur figulo et sculptori ut manum dumtaxat expectent artificis, ipsa vero suapte natura nihil momenti habeant ad opus efficiendum."
43. Ibid., 2:130–131.

little Natures, and must in part at least be bringing to bear like her, and along with her, "essential" and not "contingent" reasons. Even so, such artisans seems eminently dispensable, and one is led to ask why Nature has need of man's arts at all, since she can do so eminently well without them (and Ficino ignores the doctrine that Nature fell with Adam's fall).

The dispensability of man's arts seems even more obvious when one turns to the larger role of Nature in establishing the world's beauty and harmony (*convenientia*). At such moments Ficino calls upon the traditional topos that Nature is God's instrument, the instrument, that is, of the divine art. He argues in chapter 13 of his *Argumentum in Platonicam Theologiam,* a short treatise he included, along with others, in his second book of letters, that it was "the rational art or rather the artificial reason [in the literal sense of artificial]" that gave shape and beauty to a world that is both uniform and omniform and must depend therefore upon a uniform and omniform art.[44] This art is not to be equated with Nature or with Nature's art, for it is God's alone as the supreme Creator; but Nature is its instrument, and her art imitates this supreme divine art and is likewise the bestower of uniformity and omniformity and thus of order and harmony as well as of fullness and variety. We should recall that Ficino was always in essential agreement with the Greek and then the Augustinian notion that the most admirable aspect of any artifact is its harmony.[45] Thus Nature's harmonious art puts her above man, just as his skills ensure his place above the beasts even viewed in their totality.

One is led to wonder at this point about what, if anything, differentiates the art of Nature conceived of in this sublime way that associates her, I believe, with the World-Spirit if not with the

---

44. Ed. Marcel in an appendix to his *Théologie platonicienne* 3:277, "ratio probat artificium hoc mundi . . . esse regique ab arte quadam rationali artificiosaque ratione, . . . artem illam mundi effectricem esse rationem quamdam et unam et universam, uniformem, ut ita loquar, et omniformem. Rationem, inquam, mundi totius rationes omnes in seipsa omnium mundi partium complectentem."

45. Cf. *Platonic Theology* 12.5 and 6 (ed. Marcel, 2:174–187), where Ficino quotes extensively, as Marcel's notes demonstrate, from Augustine's *De Vera Religione* and his *De Musica.* Kristeller discusses these quotations briefly in his *Philosophy,* pp. 306–307.

World-Soul, from the art of the angel. Ficino does not, to my knowledge, address this question directly, but we may observe that his argumentation does appear to equate the two: the angelic art is effectively the same as the art of great creating Nature; or at least we must suppose the angels to preside over Nature and in doing so to exercise their artistic powers, Nature being the proper, and some would surmise perhaps the only, arena for that exercise. Human art, by contrast, is good insofar as it imitates the art of Nature, and specifically the way in which Nature works through the "intellectual reasons" and then by "rational seeds," the image of the reason as seed and the seed as reason being the controlling image in the whole line of argument which stresses the rational in the formal and the formal in the rational.[46] At the same time, imitation of Nature's art brings with it imitation of the "power of life" which she implants in the seminal reasons. In the plastic arts this puts the stress on the dynamic interplay of shape, mass, angle, line, color, and tone, and on the skills that convey a sense of movement and life. We are back at the *Sophist*'s affirmation of the presence of life and soul in Mind—of vital, spiritual motion in the realm of angelic tranquillity. Presumably, the angels, like Nature, are able to exercise a supremely living and moving art and to render, if we can suppose them to be concerned at all with the plastic arts, supremely vital plastic forms. Such is the realm of Nature herself. Counter to it is the realm of discordant formlessness, the abode of death, where, if motion exists, it is chaotic motion: no art regulates, no seed germinates, no rational form or formal reason bestows beauty or life. For Ficino's argumentation implies, however paradoxical it may first appear, that, after the divine art itself, Nature's art is the supreme exercise of art fabricating the supreme artifice; and that "naturally" and "artificially" mysteriously qualify the same action when applied to her bestowal of authentic form and motion on the world.

The second of Ficino's three most revealing passages on the arts in the *Platonic Theology* occurs in book 13, chapter 3, and is the

---

46. Cf. *Platonic Theology* 4.1 (ed. Marcel, 1:147 ff.).

passage most susceptible to a Promethean interpretation. Book 13 as a whole explores four aspects of human endeavor that bear witness to the soul's immortality: the "affections" of the phantasy and then of the reason (including the four divine furies and their recipients and what Ficino calls the seven "vacations" that come to the soul), the manner in which man practices the arts and government, and the manner in which he accomplishes miracles. Chapter 3 itself appears to present us with a less qualified vision of man the artisan than 11.5, and to comprise one of the most anthropocentric moments in Ficino's oeuvre, "a paean of praise to the status of civilised man," to borrow Trinkaus's apt formulation.[47] It would be colorful to speculate that the Romantics' elevated vision of man the artist, in the specific sense of someone who excels in the practice of the fine arts as defined by their predecessors in the Enlightenment, only became possible after Ficino and his contemporaries had arrived at an elevated vision of man the artisan, of man the artist in the older classical and medieval sense of the term "art": to speculate that the Ficinian vision of man as the supreme craftsman made in God's image was a precondition for the nineteenth century's vision of him as the supreme artist, Romanticism's elevation of the latter deriving from the Renaissance's elevation of the former. But the title is clouded and the truth, I believe, more gray.

Ficino begins his chapter by once again contrasting the beasts, which "either live without art" or are restricted to the exercise of one particular art "by the law of destiny" (an exercise where, incidentally, they never improve—or lose?—their skills), with men, who are "the inventors of innumerable arts" and everywhere exercise

---

47. *Image and Likeness,* p. 484; cf. p. 482: "[this passage is] reminiscent of Manetti's eulogy of the works of man. . . . Ficino's praise of *homo faber* is fulsome." Another arresting phrase in Trinkaus's "Ideal of Autonomy," p. 206, namely that this same passage is "a threnody for *homo faber,*" seems less appropriate in that it suggests that Ficino is mourning the death of an ideal.

Note that Trinkaus provides translations of a number of key passages from 13.3 often *in extenso.* There is also a translation of the first part of 13.3 (ed. Marcel, 2:223–226)—along with translations, incidentally, of the *Platonic Theology* 3.2 and 14.3, 4—by Josephine L. Burroughs in an article by Paul Oskar Kristeller, "Ficino and Pomponazzi on Man," *Journal of the History of Ideas* 5 (1944), 227–239 at 232–235. I have kept an eye on these renderings while attempting my own.

them at will (*suo arbitrio*). Individual men, moreover, may practice many arts, not just one, and by doing so may continually improve (or alternatively lose?) their skills.[48] At this juncture Ficino launches into apostrophe: What a marvel it is that the human arts of their own accord fabricate all that Nature herself fabricates! It is as if we were not Nature's servants but her rivals![49] And he parades the traditional Plinian instances of Zeuxis painting grapes so surpassingly that they deceived the very birds; of Apelles depicting a mare that provoked passing stallions to whinny with desire and a dog that caused other dogs to bark; of Praxiteles sculpting a Venus for a temple who was so lifelike that she aroused the lust of those who gazed upon her; of Archytas, who devised a wooden dove that actually flew; of the Egyptians, who, according to Hermes Trismegistus, created statues that moved and spoke; of Archimedes, who constructed a bronze celestial sphere that reproduced the motions of the seven planetary spheres and moved like the heaven itself; of the Egyptians' pyramids and of the monuments in stone, metal, and glass erected by the Greeks and Romans. "In a word," he sums up, "man imitates all the works of the divine nature, and perfects, corrects, and amends all the works of the lower nature."[50]

A sentence later he reiterates this distinction between the "higher nature" (*natura altior*) and the lower "corporeal nature" (*natura corporalis*). Presumably, Ficino has in mind the distinction we have

---

48. Ed. Marcel, 2:223, "Caetera animalia vel absque arte vivunt, vel singula una quadam arte, ad cuius usum non ipsa se conferunt, sed fatali lege trahuntur. Cuius signum est quod ad operis fabricandi industriam nihil proficiunt tempore. Contra homines artium innumerabilium inventores sunt, quas suo exsequuntur arbitrio. Quod significatur ex eo quod singuli multas exercent artes, mutant, et diuturno usu fiunt solertiores." See Trinkaus, *Image and Likeness*, p. 482; idem, "Ideal of Autonomy," p. 206.

49. Ed. Marcel, 2:223, "et quod mirabile est, humanae artes fabricant per seipsas quaecumque fabricat ipsa natura, quasi non servi simus naturae, sed aemuli."

50. "Denique homo omnia divinae naturae opera imitatur et naturae inferioris opera perficit, corrigit et emendat" (ibid.). In referring to the Orphic "Hymn to Nature" (no. 10 in Quandt's edition) in a letter to Germain de Ganay dating from sometime between 1494 and 1498, Ficino alerts his disciple to the "ancient mystery" concerning Nature—namely, that we must understand "nature" in four different senses depending on whether we are thinking of the realms of Body, Soul (World-Soul), Mind, or the Good. Universal Nature herself is "the creative power of good things, the mother of all that pertains to essence, motion, and life" ("Natura universalis est fecunda potestas bonorum genitrix ad essentiam et motum vitamque pertinentium"). See Kristeller, *Studies*, pp. 54 (commentary), 96–97 (text).

already been alerted to between the "celestial" and the "corporeal" nature. The first is the Nature that works through "intellectual reasons" in a way that is angelic and even perhaps presided over by the angels—the Nature that is God's instrument and therefore paradoxically the supreme artisan-artist below God and the artist upon which man himself as artist is effectively modelled. The second is the nature that works through "seminal reasons" and is formed and quickened by the higher Nature. But these are in actuality just two aspects of the same nature, since the term has traditionally been used both of the World-Body and of the World-Spirit and even sometimes, though incorrectly, of the World-Soul. Ficino is hypostasizing not so much two separate beings as two operations or levels of making that should probably be predicated of just one Nature. Even so, he inherited the traditional medieval distinction, deriving from Averroes, between *natura naturans* and *natura naturata*; and, if he preferred on some occasions to view them as two aspects of one Nature, he prefers to think of them here as two natures, principally, I would maintain, because it enables him to insert man between them. While man is obviously inferior to the higher Nature, he can entertain the notion, therefore, that he is superior, at least in origin and in potentiality, to the lower, corporeal nature that governs the world of animals, plants, minerals, and the elements.

The insertion of man between the two natures persuades Ficino to set aside the notion of man as the "imitator" of nature to explore the more adventurous but biblically sanctioned theme of man the artisan as the imitator of God the Artisan who works through nature. Thus he reasons: "Man's powers [as an artist-artisan] are almost like those of the divine nature."[51] He is impressed here with man's abilities, not only to improve his physical lot by way of growing food, of making clothes, bedding, homes, furnishings, and arms, and of devising various pastimes and pleasures, but to turn his "discursive and ingenious reason" (*cogitatrix ratio*) to the creation, often at the cost of great hardship and trouble, of masterpieces of

---

51. Ed. Marcel, 2:224, "Similis ergo ferme vis hominis est naturae divinae, quandoquidem homo per seipsum, id est per suum consilium atque artem regit seipsum a corporalis naturae limitibus minime circumscriptum, et singula naturae altioris opera aemulatur."

weaving in wool and silk, and of paintings, sculptures, and mighty monuments.[52] In the process man utilizes all the materials present in the world and from every provenance: he transforms them into "many forms and shapes," and unlike the beasts, he is not content with a single material but uses them all "as if he were the lord and master of all."[53] He plows the earth and furrows the sea with his keels and ascends the air in his high towers—the haunting image of San Gimignano must have floated before a Florentine's eyes—and this is to leave aside, writes Ficino, the story of the winged flight of Daedalus and his son. He has even harnessed the fourth element, fire itself, bringing delight to his hearth. However, it is right and proper that "the celestial animal alone should be delighted with the celestial element"; thus man "with his celestial power [his discursive *ratio*] ascends and measures the heavens themselves." Finally, with his supercelestial mind or angelic intellect [his intuitive *mens*], he passes beyond the heavens altogether, meaning the eight celestial spheres.[54]

Here Ficino again breaks into admiring eloquence, moved by the idea that man not only uses but adorns the elements:

How marvellous is man's cultivation of the earth throughout the globe. How stupendous is his erection of buildings and cities. How cunning is his ability to channel rivers and streams. Man plays the part of God in all the elements and cultivates them all. While present on the earth, he is still not absent from the aether. Indeed, he uses not only the elements but all the animals that inhabit them: those on the earth, in the waters, and in the air for food, comfort, and pleasure; and those in the supernal and celestial regions [the demons] for doctrine and the miracles of magic.

---

52. Trinkaus, *Image and Likeness*, pp. 482–484, gives a translation of the entire passage that appears in Marcel's ed. at 2:224–225 "Similis ergo ferme . . . et proculdubio immortalis"; cf. his "Ideal of Autonomy," pp. 206–209 (with much of the same translation).

53. Ed. Marcel, 2:224, "homo et omnes et undique tractat mundi materias, quasi homini omnes subiiciantur. Tractat, inquam, elementa, lapides, metalla, plantas, et animalia, et in multas traducit formas atque figuras; quod numquam bestiae faciunt. Neque uno est elemento contentus aut quibusdam ut bruta, sed utitur omnibus, quasi sit omnium dominus."

54. Ed. Marcel, 2:224–225, "Terram calcat, sulcat aquam, altissimis turribus conscendit in aerem, ut pennas Daedali vel Icari praetermittam. Accendit ignem et foco familiariter utitur et delectatur praecipue ipse solus. Merito caelesti elemento solum caeleste animal delectatur. Caelesti virtute ascendit caelum atque metitur. Supercaelesti mente transcendit caelum."

Man, moreover, "rules over the beasts not only as a cruel tyrant, he also governs, cherishes, and teaches them"; and in thus imitating the universal providence of God, "who is the universal cause," he is a god (*est quidam deus*) providing "universally for all things, animate and inanimate." Certainly he is a god for the animals in that "he makes use of them all and rules over them and instructs (in the sense of tames) many of them"; and "he is a god with regard to the elements also since he inhabits and dwells in them all"; and "he is the god of all materials since he works with them all and changes and forms them." Ficino concludes, "He who thus rules over the corporeal [world] with regard to so many and such great things and plays the part of immortal God undoubtedly must himself be immortal."[55] Despite the grammatical possibility that Ficino could be intending by "god" the unique deity of Christianity and not the Greek, and specifically the Platonic, notion of a divine being (and Marcel has capitalized the "Deus" which I have printed in the lower case in the phrase "est quidam deus"), I nonetheless believe that he means to imply that man can become a divine being, a god in the Platonic sense, but not that he can become a God Himself. This latter conceit Ficino would have found entirely unacceptable, except perhaps in mystical utterance. The potential ambiguity of the term "god" in any Platonizing discourse has occasionally misled modern commentators, but the Renaissance Platonists were well aware of the need to introduce and maintain rigid distinctions. After all, they could turn to the extensive patristic commentaries on such familiar texts as the declaration in Genesis 1:26 that man is made

---

55. Ed. Marcel, 2:225, "Nec utitur tantum elementis homo, sed ornat; quod nullum facit brutorum. Quam mirabilis per omnem orbem terrae cultura! Quam stupenda aedificiorum structura et urbium! Irrigatio aquarum quam artificiosa! Vicem gerit Dei qui omnia elementa habitat colitque omnia, et terrae praesens non abest ab aethere. Atqui non modo elementis, verumetiam elementorum animalibus utitur omnibus, terrenis, aquatilibus, volatilibus ad escam, commoditatem et voluptatem, supernis caelestibusque ad doctrinam magicaeque miracula. Nec utitur brutis solum, sed et imperat. . . . Non imperat bestiis homo crudeliter tantum, sed gubernat etiam illas, fovet et docet. Universalis providentia Dei, qui est universalis causa, propria est. Homo igitur qui universaliter cunctis et viventibus et non viventibus providet est quidam deus. Deus est proculdubio animalium qui utitur omnibus, imperat cunctis, instruit plurima. Deum quoque esse constitit elementorum qui habitat colitque omnia. Deum denique omnium materiarum qui tractat omnes, vertit et format. Qui tot tantisque in rebus corpori dominatur et immortalis Dei gerit vicem est proculdubio immortalis."

in God's image and likeness and not merely in the likeness of an angel or a higher demon; or the divine assertion to men in Psalm 82:6, recalled by Christ himself, that we are gods, and all of us children of the most High.[56] Christology, furthermore, had necessarily honed to a cutting edge their perception of the difference between the orthodox Pauline exhortation that we, being many members, nevertheless "are one body in Christ" (Romans 12:5) and the blasphemous madness of claiming that man is the Christ, is the Son in the triune God.

Ficino next turns to the superior arts of "government"—governing oneself, and one's family, administering the state, ruling over nations and exercising sway over the whole globe—which imitate God's sovereignty in other less material, less fabricatory ways; and then to the witness of the liberal arts and sciences (*scientiae liberales*), including, predictably, the old quadrivium of arithmetic, geometry, astronomy, and musical theory, as well as natural philosophy (*naturalium inquisitio causarum*) and metaphysics (*diuturnorum [divinorum?] investigatio*), oratorical eloquence, and, surprisingly, "the frenzies of the poets." While one can appreciate the appropriateness of including the accomplishments of oratory, the "frenzies" of the poets seem out of place here, given Ficino's understanding of these frenzies as God-bestowed and transcending human art entirely. One must suppose he included them because he was not thinking so much of the incandescent furies themselves as of the cooler art with which the poet subsequently shapes their vision, Horace's labor of the file; the same labor, or almost the same, that the orator continually deploys in his art of persuasion. "In all these arts," Ficino observes, "man's soul despises the mere ministry of the body, because one day the soul will be able to live without the body and even now it has begun to live without the body."[57] The inclusion of astronomy prompts the conclusion that

---

56. "Ego dixi: Dii estis et filii excelsi omnes"; cf. John 10:34: "Jesus answered them, Is it not written in your law, I said, Ye are gods."

57. Ed. Marcel, 2:226, "In iis omnibus animus hominis corporis despicit ministerium, utpote qui quandoque possit et iam nunc incipiat sine corporis auxilio vivere." There are recurring pessimistic notes in Ficino interestingly and curiously at odds sometimes with his fundamental optimism, for which see my *Platonism of Ficino,* pp. 93–94, 181–184, 192–194, with further refs.

Since man has seen the order of the heavens, whence they are moved, whither they proceed and in what measures, and what they give rise to, who would deny that he possesses, so to speak, the genius, or almost so, of the author of those heavens; and that he would be able, almost as God has done, to fabricate those heavens, could he acquire the instruments and, to accompany them, celestial matter? For he fabricates the heavens now: though he uses another kind of material, yet he endows them with almost the same order.[58]

Here Ficino seems to be ignoring the role of the higher Nature and of the angels ministering to that Nature with their respective arts, while bringing man the artist-artisan as close as he dare to the Creator Himself, asserting that man has the power to make the heavens, though he lacks the means—that is, lacks an instrument of the caliber of Nature, God's instrument—to do more than fabricate a conceptually accurate model of them like Archimedes.[59] Nevertheless, even here in this most panegyrical of moments, we should take note of the recurring and familiar qualifications—*ut ita loquar, pene eodem, quodammodo*—and the careful use of conditional expressions.

Finally, he enumerates the four qualities deemed essential for excelling in the liberal arts: "divine penetration" and "quickness of understanding" (he cites the examples of blind Homer and blind

---

58. "Cum igitur homo caelorum ordinem unde moveantur, quo progrediantur et quibus mensuris, quidve pariant, viderit, quis neget eum esse ingenio, ut ita loquar, pene eodem quo et auctor ille caelorum, ac posse quodammodo caelos facere, si instrumenta nactus fuerit materiamque caelestem, postquam facit eos nunc, licet ex alia materia, tamen persimiles ordine?" (ibid.). See Kristeller, *Philosophy,* p. 119, with further refs.; and Trinkaus, *Image and Likeness,* p. 485.

59. Trinkaus, "Ideal of Autonomy," pp. 209–210, seems to me to have gone considerably beyond Ficino's line of argument when he concludes, "The ultimate achievement of man, to become God Himself, remains beyond the powers of the human species, so that man's autonomy is not complete. Yet Ficino so yearns for this total fulfillment of human autonomy that he speculates that, given the proper instruments and material, mankind could recreate the universe itself." Admittedly, Trinkaus is speaking to Ficino's sense of man's aspirations and of the ideal and not to his sense of the reality or even of the possibility of human autonomy, but even so I believe this overstates the case.

Kristeller writes more guardedly, "Ficino insists on the universality of the human mind and sees in this its basic affinity with God. . . . the soul tries to become God, and this is its divinity. It is, however, inferior to God, since God actually is all things, whereas the soul merely tends to become all things" (*Renaissance Thought and Its Sources,* p. 173).

Didymus of Alexandria); breadth and retentiveness of memory; "the most wise skill in the prediction of the future" (meaning, Ficino later makes clear, the mathematical learning associated with Chaldaean and Egyptian astrology); and skill with language. For "language has been given us that we might achieve the most excellent work: it serves as the mind's interpreter and as the herald and infinite messenger of infinite discoveries," given that the mind is "the author of endlessly varied discoveries" and "conceives within itself by understanding all that God has made in the world by understanding."[60] Ficino concludes the chapter by claiming that the soul is assuredly divine since it is thus God's emulator in the liberal arts and in the arts of government.[61] We recall that the topic of the arts was introduced in the first place because it provided a further opportunity for Ficino to argue for the soul's immortality, his primary concern throughout the *Platonic Theology.*

Ficino's sustained admiration for the range, variety, and marvellous excellence of man's handiwork inevitably raises the issue of form, external and internal, and the complex metaphysical problems that attend the notion.[62] Just as inevitably, it recalls the myth of the world's forming in Genesis and in the *Timaeus,* and the attendant

---

60. Ed. Marcel, 2:227–229, "Ideo ad excellentius aliquod opus est nobis sermo tributus, videlicet tamquam mentis interpres, infinitorum inventorum praeco et nuntius infinitus. . . . Verum mens hominis infinitarum distinctarumque inventrix rerum. . . . Ergo tot concipit mens in seipsa intelligendo, quot Deus intelligendo facit in mundo" (pp. 228–229). Cf. Trinkaus, *Image and Likeness,* pp. 485–486.

61. Ed. Marcel, 2:229, "Quapropter dementem esse illum constat, qui negaverit animam, quae in artibus et gubernationibus est aemula Dei, esse divinam."

62. Collins, *The Secular Is Sacred,* pp. 9–11, 47–54, 58–61, 68–70, and 73–74, explores Ficino's debt in the *Platonic Theology* to Thomistic concepts of form. For the complex role of this and other concepts of form (as specific, as substantial, as seminal reason, as celestial figure, etc.) in the *De Vita* and generally in Ficino's theory of magic, see Brian P. Copenhaver's two important articles, "Scholastic Philosophy and Renaissance Magic in the *De Vita* of Marsilio Ficino," *Renaissance Quarterly* 37 (1984), 523–554, esp. pp. 536–546; and "Renaissance Magic and Neoplatonic Philosophy: *Ennead* 4.3–5 in Ficino's *De Vita Coelitus Comparanda,*" in Garfagnini, *Marsilio Ficino,* pp. 351–369, esp. pp. 363–end. See also his two cognate studies: "Hermes Trismegistus, Proclus, and the Philosophy of Magic in the Renaissance," in *Hermeticism and the Renaissance: Intellectual History and the Occult in Early Modern Europe,* ed. Ingrid Merkel and Allen G. Debus (London and Toronto, 1988), pp. 79–110; and "Iamblichus, Synesius and the *Chaldaean Oracles* in Marsilio Ficino's *De Vita Libri Tres*: Hermetic Magic or Neoplatonic Magic," in Hankins-Monfasani-Purnell, *Supplementum Festivum,* pp. 441–455.

motif of man's forming in the image of the Creator and his duty in
turn to form himself, others, the world. The instrument of such a
duty is not so much the potter's supple hands as the suppler reason
that guides them, the "rational art" that man exercises in imitation
of the supremely rational art with which the Logos, the supreme
reason, molded all things. But even as Ficino raises these issues,
so just as surely does he determine the limits of the analogy between
the art of man's reason and the supreme art of the Logos. Man imitates the higher Nature and even in a way God Himself, but he does
not become them. He becomes perhaps like them for a fleeting
moment, becomes indeed their emulator and "rival," but only in the
artisan's sense of being their apprentice or pupil. We should note
that the focus is on the reason and its role, not on the mind (*mens*);
consequently the paradigm is man as artist-artisan, the active fashioner of things, not as tranquil philosopher, the passive contemplator
of the author of all such things. It is possible to align the two paradigms and to suggest a third synthetic possibility, the philosopher-
artist. Ficino could certainly turn to ancient magus figures like
Zoroaster and Hermes Trismegistus for such a possibility, since the
magic "art" as they had reputedly practiced it was the ultimate
achievement of man's skills as an artisan even as it was only achiev-
able by a sublime philosopher. But this is not the occasion to explore Ficino's complicated and shifting conceptions of such ancient
high magic and miracle-making, and its sister "art" of theurgy, since
it would take us far beyond the range and relevance of the *Sophist*'s
icastic/phantastic distinction and what Ficino habitually understood
by the notion of *homo faber*. For all his declared allegiance to the
life of contemplation, sanctioned as it was by the twin authorities
of Plato and Aristotle, and exemplified in the lives of certain *Platonici* as well as numerous Christian saints and contemplatives,
Ficino was still too much a child of his own marvellous age not to
be struck by the achievements and virtues of the life of making.
Florence, with its ordered columns, its domes and arches, its public
statues and private paintings, its civic ceremonies and triumphs, all
the eloquence of its many forms, clearly moved him to more than
admiration—indeed, when he contemplated them in their totality,
to an almost religious awe. Once, paradoxically, keyed to the ideal

of inner contemplation, such awe was now being occasioned by the external contemplation of the daily transformation of the Tuscan metropolis and its surrounding countryside into the forum of an active, making life[63]—a forum that had come to replace both the monk's cell and the blessed grove of the Platonist as the paradigmatic setting for the exercise of man's rational powers and for the philosopher's meditation on those powers.

The last passage I wish to focus on here is concerned with an interesting lateral issue: the grounds for establishing a hierarchy among the arts. It will cast some light on a major topic already explored by Professor Kristeller in a long and important article on the emergence in the eighteenth century of the notion of the "fine arts" as sharply distinguished from the classical and medieval notion of the *artes,* the arts and crafts of men everywhere.[64] It will also serve to underscore the implications of the *Sophist*'s attempt to distinguish between two kinds of "likeness-making" and yet to insist that both kinds are exercised by the divine.

The passage occurs at the beginning of chapter 4 of book 10 of the *Platonic Theology,* where Ficino is reacting to the erroneous Epicurean contention that there can be no forms separate from matter and that no form can act outside of or beyond matter. Against this materialistic assumption Ficino adopts what he believes to be the Platonic position, but one confirmed also by Aristotle, namely that "all the works of nature . . . are perfected by a divine intelligence, which rotates the spheres of the heavens as its instruments and impels, in Plato's words, the celestial chariot and thus forms as it does so the inferior matter of the elements."[65] On the one hand

---

63. Trinkaus, "Ideal of Autonomy," 207, points to the impact that "the rich artisanal and artistic environment of Florence" must have made on Ficino; cf. his *Image and Likeness,* p. 482.

64. "The Modern System of the Arts." This was originally published in two issues of the *Journal of the History of Ideas* 12 (1951), 496–527, and 13 (1952), 17–46, but has been republished twice. I am using the version in Kristeller's *Renaissance Thought and the Arts* (Princeton, 1980), pp. 163–227 (this book first appeared in 1965 as a Harper Torchbook under the title *Renaissance Thought II*).

65. Ed. Marcel, 2:68, "Nos autem omnia naturae opera, sicut Plato in *Philebo* scribit Aristotelesque confirmat, a divina quadam perfici arbitramur intelligentia, quae quidem

is the totally immaterial divine Intellect that, though motionless itself, moves the celestial spheres, presumably by means of the first such sphere, the primum mobile (and we can see why Ficino was drawn to equating the Logos, Reason, with such an Intellect because it enabled him, as it enabled others, to account for the otherwise inexplicable generation of discursive motion, the characteristic of Soul, from what is traditionally considered the motionless intuition of pure understanding). On the other hand is base matter that serves as the material to be formed or informed by the motions deriving from the Logos-Intellect but mediated by way of the heavens. These heavens themselves consist of forms having informed a celestial matter normally identified with the Aristotelian aether or with the Platonic pure fire. This higher matter is first informed when the Intellect imparts a perfect circular motion to it and thus creates a moving, rotating sphere, the primum mobile, and thence moves the subordinate celestial spheres, the imposition of form entailing from the beginning the idea of motion.

To elucidate, Ficino turns to what he sees as the three aspects of such informing:

Just as the form first exists in the artificer's mind, and is then imparted to the tools he is using, and thence to the matter those tools have fashioned, so the forms of things, which God generates or creates here below by means of the motions of the heavens (which transfer the forms hither or prepare them), have their source first in God Himself, and then flow down through the heavens as through streams or channels, until, finally, they enter this lower matter. But such matter, since it is thus set in motion by the divine understanding, must receive and exhibit any one of the most exact forms of the divine understanding.[66]

---

caelos velut instrumenta sua revolvens et citans, ut Plato inquit, caelestem currum, inde inferiorem hanc elementorum format materiam." Marcel identifies the references as being to the *Philebus* 28E, 30C–D, and to the *De Caelo* 2.6.288ab.

66. "Atque ut in arte operis forma triplicem habet gradum: est enim primum in artificis animo, secundo in instrumentis ab eo agitatis, tertio in materia inde formata*. Ita formae rerum quas Deus per caeli motus vel traducentes vel praeparantes hic generat aut creat, primum in ipso sunt Deo, deinde in caelis tamquam rivulis aut sedibus, postremo in hac inferiori materia. Oportet autem materiam hanc, quandoquidem a divina intelligentia sic agitatur, suscipere ac prae se ferre exactissimam aliquam divinae intelligentiae formam" (ibid.).

*The 1576 reading; Marcel has, incorrectly, "formae."

The material creation exhibits, accordingly, the divine forming in a more perfect and precise way than any material can sustain and then exhibit the form imposed upon it by a human artist or artisan. As such it must be recognized as the greatest, most perfect, and most exact work of art.

Since the form of the work must always reflect, however inadequately, the form already present in the mind of the producer of that work, and since that internal form is always superior to its external reflection, so the logic requires that the instrument that serves to transfer the one to the other be the medium of an intermediate form. But does this mean that Michelangelo's chisel was somehow superior in itself to the New Sacristy's figures of Dusk or Dawn? Or should we extend the notion of "instrument" to include the painter's own hand and indeed body? Neither seems satisfactory. However, when we extend the notion of an instrument to embrace the highest aspects of Nature, according to the ancient maxim God's instrument, then we are dealing with a different set of factors, and we can readily acknowledge that the forms in the heavens are superior in kind to those that inform lower things; that the heavens, and preeminently the prime spheres of the Sun or the fixed stars, are the supreme instrument of God's divine art.[67]

But where do these forms exist? How are they conveyed to the sublunar realm? And how do we perceive them in the heavens or know of their presence? At times Ficino entertained the notion that the shapes of the familiar constellations constituted a selection of such forms and that many other forms in less obvious constellations had been detected among the fixed stars or their presence hypothesized by the ancients, and notably by the Indians, Egyptians, and Chaldaeans in their descriptions of the decans and the decan demons.[68] But this would only account for a limited number of forms. Now the heavens are ruled by the highest souls (and Ficino was

---

67. See Copenhaver, "Scholastic Philosophy," pp. 535–538, 544 ff., 550; and idem, "Renaissance Magic," pp. 355, 363–365.

68. *De Vita* 3.18 (*Opera,* p. 556) notes that, in addition to the zodiacal signs and the constellations that everyone can see, "there are multitudes of forms which we do not so much see as imagine that we see, and that the Indians, Egyptians, and Chaldaeans looked at in the faces of the signs, or imagined extended across them." The example Ficino gives is that of the beautiful girl in the sign of Virgo. See my *Platonism of Ficino,* p. 136n.

never happy with the originally Aristotelian notion that the spheres were governed by pure intelligences, because such intelligences were, from a Platonic viewpoint, completely divorced from motion and could not therefore be supposed to move their spheres directly).[69] The forms must therefore exist in the minds of such souls and be thence translated somehow through the spheres, as though through the spirit linking soul to body, down to the body of the sublunar world. This in turn implies that such souls think the forms as they are imaged or replicated in their minds, on the analogy of the formulae of the ideas which the Platonists and Augustine had postulated in the human mind. We thus have, within the larger notion of the heavens as instrument between God and the corporeal forms, a model for that instrument which reproduces the three fundamental stages in the whole artistic process. In this smaller model the "reasoning powers" within the celestial souls serve as the means for transferring the forms in the formulae of the celestial souls to the influences which the planetary spheres rain down upon us as they rotate, and which serve in the larger model as the basic instruments for informing the sublunar world.

Thus astrological assumptions are intricately tied in with the way in which Ficino thinks of the artistic process and particularly of the notion of instrumentality. In a very real if surprising sense the heavens, ruled by the Sun, constitute the paradigm for the artist-artisan's instrument. In raining down influences on inferior matter and continuing, like the subtle motions of the first influences, to inform that matter with images of the higher forms, they are the paradigmatic instrument and exercise the highest form of art. Moreover, by virtue of the familiar retroactive effects of analogy, man's artistic instruments—his chisel, his hand, his whole body—emerge as the heavens, or specifically the Sun, responding to the art of reason and influencing matter and perhaps by extension other men who witness the resulting artifacts. Thus art is derived from the stars and the stars exercise the highest art: both are aspects of a sublime aesthetico-astrology or astro-aesthetics. These are unexpected but

---

69. See my "The Absent Angel in Ficino's Philosophy," pp. 230–232. For the pertinent situation in Macrobius, see Gersh, *Middle Platonism and Neoplatonism* 2:554n.

fruitful consequences of Ficino's mode of reasoning and the analogies he draws upon.

The notion of a gradation that leads from the pure form in God's mind, and by analogy, in an artist's mind, down via an instrument to its embodiment in, or better its reflection in, matter predictably leads Ficino to suggest a gradation for the arts themselves. Some works, he argues,

are as close as possible to the soul while others are completely distant and others still are midway. Almost all the works pertaining to the sight or to the hearing most fully declare the genius or wit of the artificer; while those that pertain to the three lower senses declare it least. For in the fabrication of perfumes or tastes and flavors or in the construction of beds and baths [that is, those things that most obviously pertain to the touch] the artificer's intention least or hardly appears. Certainly, in pictures and in buildings his deliberation and prudence are exhibited; indeed, the disposition and the shape as it were of the soul itself is made manifest. For in such works the soul expresses itself and figures itself forth, just as a man's countenance, when he gazes into a mirror, figures itself forth in that mirror. But the artificer's soul is most fully manifest in the works that pertain to the hearing: in speeches and poems and vocal music. For in these the disposition and the will of the entire intelligence is present for all to see. For whatever the artificer feels, such are the feelings that his works usually arouse in us: if his voice is tearful, we are moved to cry; if angry, to rage; if lascivious, to lust. So the works that pertain to the sight and to the hearing come closest to conveying what the artificer has in mind; those that pertain to the three other senses are furthest away, as we declared; but in between are those that pertain to exercising the body, whether for war or for sport.[70]

---

70. Ed. Marcel, 2:69–70, "Verum per haec artificis animus tria quaedam exsequitur: nonnulla sibi quam proxima, remotissima alia, alia media. Omnia sane artificis opera quae ad aspectum pertinent aut auditum totum pene artificis declarant ingenium. Quae ad sensus tres reliquos, minime. Nam in odoribus saporibusque conficiendis aut stratis lavacrisque temperandis paulum aut vix artificis apparet intentio. In picturis autem aedificiisque consilium et prudentia lucet artificis. Dispositio praeterea et quasi figura quaedam animi ipsius inspicitur. Ita enim seipsum animus in operibus istis exprimit et figurat, ut vultus hominis intuentis in speculum seipsum figurat in speculo. Maxime vero in sermonibus, cantibus atque sonis artificiosus animus se depromit in lucem. In his enim tota mentis dispositio et voluntas planissime designatur, et qualis est affectus artificis, talem nobis affectum opera eius solent

We thus have a hierarchy for the arts: at the bottom are those that pander to the nose, the palate, and the touch; in the middle are those that promote bodily health and strength; and at the top are those that concern the hearing and the sight. The curious aspect of this hierarchy is, at first glance, the intermediate status of the exercising arts, martial, athletic, and presumably callisthenic; and it is possible that this signal position in Ficino's hierarchy of the arts was one of the factors contributing to the new humanist emphasis upon the educational role and importance of physical exercise and training. One has only to think of Gargantua's multifariously exhaustive workouts in the afternoons under the coaching of Ponocrates. It would certainly serve as a validation of the martial and athletic arts in the curriculum of the training of a prince or governor, and reflects the hierarchy of values and accomplishments espoused by Federico da Montefeltro and his many emulators among the princes and condottieri of the age.

The hierarchy itself reflects the three tiers of the traditional division of society into the learned, the knights, and the artisans: the arts that pertain to the sight and hearing being the concern of the first, the martial and athletic arts of the second, and the remaining arts of the third. But Ficino does introduce at this point a significant further subordination by subjecting sight to hearing even though this reverses the traditional elevation of sight (particularly when we think of it figuratively), and even though he returns to the traditional elevation just a few pages later.[71] For he subordinates the plastic arts of painting, sculpture, and architecture to the arts of eloquence and oratory, of poetry and music for the voice. The rationale is that these arts of the hearing more fully express the mind that governs them, are more exactly correspondent to the mind's forms or formulae than the arts of the sight can be, and are thus closer to the world of the purely intelligible Forms.

excitare, flebilis vox flere, furiosa furere, lasciva lascivire saepe compellit. Haec igitur opera cum ad visum tum ad auditum spectantia artificis menti sunt proxima; illa vero quae ad tres reliquos pertinent sensus, ut diximus, remotissima. Mediae autem illae operationes sunt, quae ad corporis exercitationes, ludicras aut bellicas pertinent."

71. Ed. Marcel, 2:74.

They are closer, furthermore, because they are not required to shape base matter but rather the air; and the air is infinitely more malleable than paint or stone and thus capable of expressing intelligible form with infinitely more precision and fidelity. Hence the subtlety of the astral influences that rain down on us through it. The air enters our bodies not only through our lungs but through our ears; and sounds can pass thence to our "airy spirit." This is the almost incorporeal, refined, and subtle mixture of air and pure fire that constitutes for Ficino and his contemporaries, as for the ancients, our rarefied body, the body in which we enter purgatory to have even the airy parts purged away, so that we may eventually enter paradise itself in a purely fiery body, the glorified body of the resurrection and eternal life.[72] The arts that pertain to the hearing are therefore for Ficino the "spiritual" arts in the literal sense of spirit as understood in the Galenic and Platonic traditions. They transmit forms through the air, that subtle carrier of shapes, and thence the air transmits them to the airy spirit in our inner ear and thence to our intelligences.[73] On occasion Ficino even toys with the dangerous notion that the demons play a role in this process of transmission by actually contorting their airy—their spiritual— bodies into sounds before entering into our ears and thence our phantasies in order directly to form or inform our spirits. At one point in his *De Vita* 3.21 he suggests that musical sound is a demon; that music is a consort of demons riding the air and pouring into our ears.[74] But, by the same token, this notion is restricted to the purely airy and fiery, the higher, demons, since only they are truly rarefied and refined, subtle and flexible enough to serve in this

---

72. See my *Platonism of Ficino*, pp. 102–103, n. 29.

73. See D. P. Walker, *Spiritual and Demonic Magic: From Ficino to Campanella* (London, 1958; reprint, Notre Dame, Ind., 1975), chaps. 1 and 2; idem, "The Astral Body in Renaissance Medicine," *Journal of the Warburg and Courtauld Institutes* 21 (1958), 119–133; and idem, *Music, Spirit and Language in the Renaissance,* ed. Penelope Gouk (London, 1984). Of general interest are M. Putscher, *Pneuma, Spiritus, Geist* (Wiesbaden, 1973), and the collected conference papers in *Spiritus,* ed. M. Fattori and M. Bianchi (Rome, 1984).

74. *Opera,* p. 563. See Walker, *Spiritual and Demonic Magic,* p. 10; and my *Platonism of Ficino,* pp. 25–27.

capacity, the watery and earthy demons being too gross. Thus the idea of a demonic agency brings with it no necessary implications of temptation, seduction, and fall. To the contrary, given the habitual equation of such higher demons and spirits with the angels of Christianity, it stresses rather the divine nature of the arts of the hearing, or at least of their highest manifestations, presumably those that attract the notice and concern of the highest and best of the angels ministering to men.

Underlying this entire line of argument is the assumption that the hearing arts are the arts of the word and thus those that best speak to the soul and its powers of understanding and intuition. Hence Ficino's care to emphasize that he has vocal music, not instrumental music, in the forefront of his mind, the music that is essentially allied with poetry and constitutes the *carmen* that he himself presented in his own musical recitals as he sang invocatory odes to the Sun, to Light, to Justice, to the Good, and to other high Platonic entities, while accompanying himself, rapturously by all contemporary accounts, on an Orphic lyre.[75] It is the spirit-borne, spirit-shaping word that justifies the elevated status of hearing and the arts it subtends and promotes, arts that we hear with the inner ear.

At the same time Ficino also assumes, without giving any indication of perceiving the positions as incompatible, that the seeing arts are almost as capable of conveying the artificer's mental forms and conceits. This assumption is given an extra fillip by the dominance of the metaphor of God's choosing to reflect his image in the material world as in a mirror. The visual beauty of the cosmos is thus a mirror image of the intelligible beauty of the Forms in the Divine Mind. In particular, the beauty of the heavens by day and by night constitutes a visual language as it were for the devout to meditate upon (and for Zoroaster and Hermes to imitate when they wished

75. Walker, *Spiritual and Demonic Magic,* pp. 12–24, with further refs.; idem, *The Ancient Theology: Studies in Christian Platonism from the Fifteenth to the Eighteenth Century* (London, 1972), pp. 24–25; and John Warden, "Orpheus and Ficino," in *Orpheus: The Metamorphoses of a Myth,* ed. John Warden (Toronto, Buffalo, London, 1982), pp. 85–110. See also my "Summoning Plotinus: Ficino, Smoke, and the Strangled Chickens," forthcoming.

to give a sacred, hieroglyphic language to their priests).[76] Even
so, two factors work against the unqualified elevation of sight over
hearing (and the question of their primacy endured as an academic
diversion for centuries).[77] The first factor derives from Ficino's understanding of the Platonic argument that it is the rational soul that
most fully reflects God's "countenance" in the mirror of creation;
and we recall the opening hypothesis that inserts the celestial spheres
of the heavens between God and the sublunar creation and attributes
to each of the spheres a supremely rational soul. Such a soul cannot
be seen although it is the mover of a celestial sphere and of a planet
that can be seen and heard as it sounds its concordant note in the
greater harmony generated by all the spheres. Once again we are
back with the nexus that binds reason to words, thoughts to their
articulation. The second factor is a related one: behind the visual
drama of the heavens and sublunar creation lies the all-creating
Word of Genesis: God had said "Let there be Light," the Word
preceding all things, sound and thought preceding the very light that
makes sight possible. Of course, at this level of mystery all references to hearing and seeing must perforce be supremely figurative,
and we cannot put much trust in analogizing to the quotidian world
of the senses. Nevertheless, the Logos is Ficino's ultimate paradigm
for all musical as well as verbal utterance: God's divinely harmonious Word in its eloquence, poetry, and music was what created the
cosmos, and its sublime beauty was first heard in chaos not seen.
The first ordering of the cosmos was the response of chaos to the
divine *carmen*; and the primacy of that ordering was reflected in
Ficino's and his contemporaries' abiding sense that the plastic arts
were subject to the aural ones. Thus the creation of the world by
the all-creating Word serves as the ultimate paradigm for all the
arts, as the supreme Art, but also vindicates the claim of the aural
arts to be the most proximate to that primal Art. In terms of the
Sophist's distinctions the Word was the first likeness-maker, the
first Icastes, and the orator, poet, and singer are first in the ranks

---

76. Ficino, *Philebus* Commentary 1.29 (ed. Allen, pp. 270–273).
77. See my *Platonism of Ficino,* pp. 51–57.

of its human imitators. For human reason and language together are a more faithful, a more verisimilar image and likeness of God than the human form itself, however divinely proportioned, however compelling its plastic beauty.

We are now in a position to appreciate why the *Sophist*'s discussion of icastic art raised a number of critical issues for Ficino: from the nature of God's creation and the ways in which that creation reflected the sublime Ideas, to the nature of hearing and the status of physical exercise. It led him to postulate a hierarchy for the arts that assigned the primacy to those centered upon the word and music, but at the same time duly to acknowledge the claims of the arts of design, above all of sacred architecture. In all these arts man the maker exercises almost godlike powers and thereby approximates most closely to his Adamic nature as a being made from the onset of the world, like the angels, in the image and likeness of God the Maker. That the most revealing texts on these themes occur in the *Platonic Theology,* which was completely drafted as early as 1474, is indicative of the *Sophist*'s subtle impact on Ficino long before he actually sat down to pen a formal commentary upon it. For the dialogue, as we have seen, advances positions that go well beyond those adumbrated in the *Republic,* which to this day is commonly taken to present Plato's best-considered thoughts on the whole subject of artistic imitation, even though its decision to subordinate the artist to the artisan is merely a preliminary stab at a series of problems that continued to fascinate Plato throughout his career. At first glance, this may seem to be assigning a primacy to the *Sophist* that runs counter to its less than central position in the popular view of Plato and the canon, however questioned and modified in recent years;[78] and I do not wish to exaggerate the role of a text that Ficino was certainly acquainted with from the 1460s but did not refer to with the same frequency and enthusiasm as he did to the *Symposium,* the *Phaedrus,* the *Parmenides,* and even the *Philebus.* Still, we should accept the probability (and it is more than

78. See Introduction, n. 3 above.

a possibility) that the *Sophist* had a far-reaching influence on the age by way of Ficino's own thought, principally because of its presentation of man made in the image of the icastic Creator. We have only to think of Philip Sidney's notable treatise, *The Defense of Poesy,* and its immediate offspring, George Puttenham's *The Art of English Poesie,* where both critics juggle carefully with the notions of icastic and phantastic art and with the complex ramifications of the analogy between man the maker and the Maker of all likenesses. In this regard it is instructive to note that they ran into some of the same confusions and contradictions that Plato himself had encountered in the *Sophist* and Ficino after him, and that are clearly inseparable from the way Plato had chosen to approach the whole question of what kind of truth is present not only in human art but in the fabricated world, which is the product of divine art and which serves as the seedbed of, and a model for, all human art.

Plato's decision to link his discussion of image-making to a probing examination of the nature of being, not-being, and difference had been a momentous one. In the Renaissance certainly it generated a series of searching questions about being that went far beyond a concern with the nature of tangible reality, and with the ways in which we perceive, mold, and attempt to reproduce or add to it, in order to wrestle with the more intricate intangible reality of what might be or might have been, the reality of the feigning that the age required of its artistic makers. Ficino and his Platonism had no small part to play in the dissemination of these ideas and in the debate that swirled around them. He was thus one of those primarily responsible for laying the philosophical foundations both of the Renaissance's apology for poetry as a representative of all the arts and of its rapturous, though in his case carefully qualified, defense of man's poetic achievements in the rich, original sense of the term *poiêtikos.* In short, I believe we should add the *Sophist,* and more particularly the Ficinian *Sophist,* to that select group of Platonic texts which went to the composition of Renaissance aesthetics and poetics and, more significantly still, to the development of its central notions of the dignity of man the maker and of the hauntingly divine—in the Greek sense of the demonic—nature of the masterworks of his reason, ear, and eye.

Chapter 5: Phantastic Art, Magic, and the Idola

Whatever his reservations concerning the Iamblichean notion of the sublunar demiurge, Ficino did not entirely set it aside; for it raised a number of fascinating questions about the nature of sublunar reality with its myriad illusions and about its status as an imitation of the intelligible reality that alone possesses full and authentic being. When the *Sophist'*s Eleatic Stranger, who we recall Ficino supposed was Melissus, had dared at 237A and again at 258D to question the dictum of his great mentor Parmenides that "never shall this be proved, that things that are not are," and had ventured into an examination of the "forbidden" word "not-being," he was addressing the necessity of having to assign to sublunar reality the status of possessing something more than not-being if less than full being. As we saw, furthermore, when we examined Ficino's argumentum, Plato had affirmed at 265C ff. that the works of nature were still the works of divine art and were subject to God's providential design, not to some "spontaneous cause that generates without intelligence" (265C7–8) as postulated by the atheist and materialist. Indeed, the whole dialogue confronts the Parmenidean, or at least the extreme Parmenidean, position—the Stranger even prepares ironically to defend himself against the charge of parricide at 241D—and proceeds to affirm the necessary involvement of being with not-being and the existence, in some mode, however limited, of illusion and falsehood. This affirmation entails as an inevitable corollary the acceptance of the workings of the imagination and the phantasy and their power to deceive but also to instruct us.

In his *Parmenides* Commentary, in the course of examining the last four of what the later Neoplatonists had seen as the nine hypotheses of the *Parmenides'* second part, Ficino reiterates the Proclian view that Plato had used these four hypotheses to examine the consequences that would follow from supposing that the One does not exist absolutely.[1] The eighth hypothesis argues that, were the One to exist only in part—that is, were it to exist perhaps as the transcendent One but not immanently in being—then material species—that is, forms in matter, the corporeal forms—would not exist, and the distinction between form and substance necessarily would be done away with altogether. We would be left with the possibility of the existence of "shadows and dreams" and of matter (participating in the One but not being and thus partaking of a unitary but insubstantial nature).[2] But the ninth and last hypothesis argues that, were the One absolutely not to exist, then "there would not even be the shadow of anything anywhere" and matter would not exist in its unitary but illusory way.[3] We should note the Plotinian assumption most fully elaborated by Proclus that, since it is higher than being, the One embraces more than being and is more universal than being. Thus it not only transcends and is immanent in but also subtends being, since that which is less than being, that is, matter, is nevertheless one.[4] Consequently, matter participates in the One but not being. For the last realm to participate in being however partial is the realm of Body, of matter in extension, along with its material species, while the first realm to be is the intelligible realm of Mind, of Being itself. Both the One and matter can be said to exist, but only in the figurative senses that the One exists beyond the actuality of being and matter exists merely as the potentiality for being. Thus both can be said to be prior to being and therefore to possess notbeing, the One existing as it were above being, matter below being. It follows from the whole set of negative hypotheses in the Neo-

---

1. *Opera*, pp. 1165–1166, 1199v. See my "Ficino's Theory of the Five Substances," pp. 36–41; and "The Second Ficino-Pico Controversy," pp. 444–448.

2. *Opera*, p. 1166. Ficino treats in detail of the eighth hypothesis in two chapters at the very end of his commentary, *Opera*, pp. 1201–1202. Having toyed with the notion in the *Enneads* 3.5.9.49 ff. that we should identify matter with the Penia of the *Symposium* 203B, Plotinus defines it in the memorable passage at 3.6.7.12 ff. as "truly not-being . . . a ghostly image of bulk, a tendency towards substantial existence . . . a phantom which does not remain and cannot get away either . . . but is lacking in all being . . . a sort of fleeting frivolity . . . it seems to be filled and holds nothing" (tr. Armstrong). Aristotle, in his *Physics* 1.9.192a, declares that, like a female, it has a perpetual appetite for form.

3. *Opera*, p. 1166; cf. pp. 1202–1203 (an analysis of the ninth hypothesis).

4. Cf. Ficino's *Philebus* Commentary 1.30 and 31 (ed. Allen, pp. 284–287, 300–303).

platonists' *Parmenides,* however, that, since the One exists both absolutely and immanently, then not only do the realms of Mind, of Soul, of the corporeal forms, and of body itself exist but also, in a unitary if insubstantial way, does the realm of shadows and of dreams; and it exists immediately subordinate to the realm of corporeal forms or material species upon which it directly depends and of which it is an imitation.

The scheme articulated in the *Parmenides* in Proclus's interpretation requires, in other words, that we accept in some limited sense the unitary existence of phenomena that do not exist in the fuller sense in which the material forms can be said to exist and certainly not in the fullest sense in which the intelligible Forms exist. Such phenomena are imitations of the material forms that are in turn imitations of the intelligible Forms, the truly and authentically existent beings. The issue of what, therefore, has being or is an imitation— and in what way and at what remove—is a necessary accompaniment of the scheme. It necessarily involves in its series of qualifications the concomitant notion of "illusion," concomitant because an inverted pyramid of the kinds of illusion shadows the pyramid of the kinds of being and existence. The situation becomes more complicated still when we attempt to introduce, as Plato does in the great myth of the *Timaeus,* a Demiurge who copies the intelligible Forms in order to make the world, and who deputes some of his creative duties to his sons, the younger gods. For they become in effect lesser demiurges who imitate their father and involve themselves not only in the realm of corporeal forms but in the realm that imitates it, the realm of illusions, shadows, and deceitfulness traditionally assigned not to the gods but to the demons in their train.

Ficino takes up some of these spiralling complications in chapter 46, the longest chapter in his *Sophist* Commentary, and, interestingly, one that can be independently assigned to 1492 or later on the basis of internal evidence. It addresses issues raised by Plato at 265E ff. There, as we have seen, the Eleatic Stranger returns to the notion of two kinds of "art," the divine and the human, and proceeds to subdivide them into the icastic art, which creates true likenesses, and the phantastic art, which creates deceiving similitudes. In the case of the divine icastic art it results in the making (Ficino uses the term *effectio*) of corporeal things that are the true likenesses of their intelligible Forms. Their likenesses in turn, it follows, will be "images and shadows" (271.11), two phenomena that are not to be equated but that seem to share the same ontological (or meontological?) status. These also will be the product of divine art, but of divine phantastic, not divine icastic, art. Nevertheless, Ficino seems understandably reluctant to assume that they are the works of God directly, though he refers to them as *opera divina* (271.12). Rather, with the *Timaeus*'s myth in mind, he assumes that they are the works of the "creative art" (*ars effectrix*) (271.5) of lesser, "younger" divinities, whom, given his Platonic categories, he identifies with the demons in the neutral, technical meaning of the term. Divine works broadly speaking, Ficino defines them more specifically as "demonic works" (*opera daemonica*) (271.13), with Plato's phrasing at 266B7 obviously in mind. Indeed, he argues, just as the demons follow the gods, so do the "likenesses of things" (*similitudines rerum*) follow things themselves, "which are the followers of the prime divine works" (271.15).[5] Thus they are as it were "demonic contrivances or tricks" (*daemonica machinamenta*) (271.16). Note that Ficino is not referring to the deceptions and illusions of dreams or dream-related states in waking consciousness, though Plato speaks in the same breath, confusingly, of shadows, of reflections in water, and of dream images as if they were phenomenally kin. Rather, he is arguing that the demons are the makers, the creators in the restricted sense, of the whole realm of images, reflections, and shadows in the natural world; and he is probably not referring directly or perhaps at all to the demons, or to a particular class of demons, who deceive men with dream images. His concern, in other words, is with our perception of demonic agency in the waking world, however obvious and paramount its presence in the world of nocturnal or diurnal sleep.

The waking world, the entire world of nature including the night

---

5. The "which" here can refer either to things or to likenesses; but I take it to refer to likenesses, and thus that Ficino is arguing that likenesses follow things, God having made things first. I do not believe he would have ever thought of the sublime Ideas as "divine works," a necessary consequence if "which" refers to things.

world under the moon and stars, is governed, however, by light; and our understanding of the role of the demons in manipulating the "likenesses" in that world is inextricably bound up with our understanding of the role and nature of light. Ficino argues, "Just as the nature of the demons is midway between higher beings [the gods] and lower beings [men], so is light the medium between incorporeals [the intelligible Forms] and corporeals" (271.16–18). This is not, furthermore, simply a conventional analogy. Ficino goes on to assert that there is in light itself "a certain demonic power" (*in lumine potestas quaedam est daemonica*), which is "the maker of images and shadows." For the demons "are accustomed to reveal certain wondrous sights to men not only when they are asleep or bemused but also when they are fully awake" (271.18–21); and their only way of presenting such "sights" is by means of working "tricks" with light.

We might assume that in speaking of the "demonic power" of light Ficino was speaking entirely figuratively, were it not for the evidence first adduced by D. P. Walker that demonstrates, as we have seen, that Ficino regarded sound, and in particular musical sound, as likewise possessed of demonic power, being the subtle and harmonious movement of the air, whose three zones—fiery, purely airy, and misty—are dominated by the demons, its proper inhabitants. Indeed, at times Ficino may even have regarded music as an actual demon or a chorus of demons working in concert.[6] Sound he certainly imagines as entering, like a demon, into the ear and reshaping the airy spirit within the inner ear and thereby affecting the whole spiritual body of a listener. The eye also functions by means of spirit, and can accordingly serve, if not in the same way exactly as we shall see, as an aperture for demonic entry and reshaping of the soul's spiritual envelope. For light, like sound, is a demonic medium, and both are associated preeminently with the air, the sphere dominated by the demons and their natural abode. Hence, Ficino can argue, for instance in the fourth chapter of his

---

6. Cf. *Phaedrus* Commentary, summa 11 (ed. Allen, pp. 138–141).

Commentary on St. Paul, that the Platonists had postulated five kinds of cult:

the lower spirits inhabiting the misty air are customarily solicited by way of animal sacrifices and the offering of fruits and corn. The spirits dwelling in the pure air are invoked by way of perfumes, instrumental music, songs and chants, and lights. And the spirits dwelling in the fiery air of the aether are cultivated by way of prayers accompanied by lights. The pure intelligences, however, who are completely separated from the body, are worshipped only by the powers and motions of our understanding. The father of these, finally, is worshipped by that understanding only in an ecstasy and by an ineffable impulse (*affectus*) of our will.[7]

Hence, Ficino observes, Iamblichus had been led to condemn the Egyptians for their cultivation of the airy lower spirits and to subordinate them to the Chaldaeans, who worshipped the disembodied intelligences and the father of those intelligences.[8] We have here an implicit hierarchy pertaining to the faculties: the lowest demons accept what we smell and taste; the middle demons what we smell and hear and see; the higher demons what we see and think; the disembodied intellects what we think; and God Himself what we think and will in ecstasy. While the two orders of demons dwelling

---

7. *Opera*, pp. 432–433, "species quinque cultus esse disputant pro quinque speciebus spirituum qui coluntur. Spiritus enim infimos crassum aerem habitantes sacrificiis ex frugibus animalibusque coli solitos. Spiritus autem purum aerem incolentes vaporibus sonisque et cantibus atque luminibus. Aetherea vero numina orationibus luminibusque simul. Sed intellectus a corporibus separatos intelligentiae viribus atque motibus. Horum denique patrem excessu quodam mentis et ineffabili voluntatis affectu."

8. "Iamblichus inter haec damnat Aegyptios, quod materiali cultu prae caeteris uterentur, aeriorumque daemonum cultores essent. Anteponit autem iis Chaldaeos, qui spiritalem cultum potius sequerentur, utpote qui separatas a materia mentes patremque earum praecipue colerent. Haec quidem illi viderint" (ibid.).

This argument lay behind Ficino's mature decision, as I have argued elsewhere, to assign the primacy to Zoroaster, the master of the Chaldaeans, in his enumeration of the six-linked chain of "ancient theologians" culminating in Plato, and to subordinate Hermes Trismegistus, the founder of Egyptian cult, to Zoroaster, even though he acknowledged that Hermes was probably not responsible for the various corruptions introduced by his priests ("Marsile Ficin, Hermès et le *Corpus Hermeticum*," in *Présence d'Hermès Trismégiste*, ed. Antoine Faivre [Paris, 1988], pp. 110–119). Though both Ficino and Pico would have encountered anti-Egyptianism in Pliny and other well-known ancient sources, they were probably also familiar with Pletho's contention in his *Laws* 3.43 (ed. Alexandre, pp. 252 ff.) that the Egyptians' demonolatrous mysteries were degraded; see Wind, *Pagan Mysteries*, pp. 279–280.

in the two upper reaches of the air are both cultivated by way of "lights," we accompany the one with prayers, presumably silent prayers, alone, but the other with incense and music. That is, the offering of light reaches higher than the offering of musical sound and mediates between the corporeal and the incorporeal realms, between what we perceive with our senses and what we think with our understanding. To abandon light for prayer alone is to go beyond the realm of the demons entirely. By the same token, the highest demons are susceptible to propitiation by way of light.

But what does such propitiation imply? The airy demons are moved by a variety of sounds, by instrumental and vocal music, by the shaping and twisting of the air into many demonic forms, as the lower mist- and murk-dwelling demons are moved by a variety of sacrifices and, presumably, by the dense, rich smokes that rise from them. Similarly, we must suppose the airy and particularly the aethereal demons are attracted by various kinds of light and lightplay: not only by the presence of lighted tapers and other fire offerings but by the refractions, reflections, and shadows to which their rays give rise as they pass through prisms of various kinds, or are caught by the tilt of faceted stones and gems, or are angled or focussed or dispersed by mirror surfaces, convex, concave, perfect, distorted, brilliant, or dim. In short, the entire realm of optical effects becomes a way of attracting the higher demons because they have a natural affinity with light and the power to shape it just as they have an affinity with and power over musical sound.

Both Genesis and the *Timaeus* assign the actual creation of light to the Maker himself; and since we usually think of the sun as the source of light, the study of light necessarily involves a philosophy of the sun, or what for the ancients and even for Ficino was a solar theology.[9] But the demons who do the Demiurge's bidding hasten

9. See Eugenio Garin's chapter on the connections between the Platonists' solar theology, deriving in the main from the *Republic* book 6, and the Copernican revolution in his *Rinascite e rivoluzioni*, pp. 255–282. See also, among recent studies, Fernand Hallyn, "Copernic et platonisme ficinien," in *L'invention au XVIᵉ siècle* (Bordeaux, 1987), pp. 135–151; idem, *La structure poétique du monde: Copernic, Kepler* (Paris, 1987). Of particular importance are Ficino's two treatises, *De Sole* and *De Lumine* (*Opera*, pp. 965–986). For Ficino's notes on Julian's "Prayer to the Sun" in the Riccardiana's manuscript 76, see Garin's edition and

to the frontier where the pure light of the sun crosses over into the darkness of the corporeal realm and, along the boundary line, plays with the darkness and half-forms it into fleeting images and transient shadows. The demons should not be condemned for patrolling this boundary and taking charge, in effect, of the light-play that characterizes it—for playing with light itself, their fellow demon as it were. Rather, they are doing the Demiurge's bidding, or, in Christian terms, they are fulfilling their appointed role in God's providential plan, which includes the "creation" or "making" of optical effects and their accompanying shadows. For the shadow and reflection world is also God's: like the world of material objects around which it dances, it too is an *opus divinum*.

It follows from this that we have to adapt the ontological scheme that Ficino inherited from Plato and that runs from the Ideas through the formulae in our minds to the corporeal species and to the seminal reasons of such species in seeds. For there is no obvious place in this scheme for the shadow and reflection world and what Parmenides had designated its not-being, the world which the Eleatic Stranger had come to argue has a kind of minimal, equivocal existence, a phantastic, imaginary being. The faculty that enables us to perceive such a severely qualified being is the imagination since it is the faculty that organizes and processes images from the data given it by the five senses. Ficino writes, "our imaginations (*imaginamenta*—an Italianism) also are possessed, in a way, of a demonic power. This is both because the demons excite the imaginations in ourselves by way of their own creative imaginations (*efficaces imaginationes*) and tricks, and also because what imagines in us is in some respects a demon (*quod in nobis imaginatur est quodammodo daemon*)" (271.21–25).

Two possibilities are being presented. First, the demons can excite (*suscitare*) our imaginations by way of their own imaginations, tricking and deceiving us with their devices (*artificia*).[10] But how

---

commentary, "Per la storia della cultura filosofica del Rinascimento," *Rivista critica di storia della filosofia* 12.1 (1957), 3–21. For an exploratory note on Ficino's Augustinian light metaphysics, see Chastel, *Ficin et l'art*, pp. 103–104.

10. Cf. Ficino's *Phaedrus* Commentary, summae 9 and 11 (ed. Allen, pp. 136–141); also his opening summa for Plotinus's *Enneads* 3.4 (*Opera*, p. 1708). In the latter, however,

precisely? The demons must somehow attune our imaginations to their own by making them vibrate as it were in sympathy, on the analogy of musical strings vibrating together. But to achieve this, do they have to enter into us? Entering might be particularly easy when we are asleep or distracted and our imagination is unguarded by the higher faculties of the reason and the intellect. Then perhaps our imagination is as easily invaded as our limbs by warmth or cold and excited or pacified by the images the demons present to us. Certainly, sleep or sleeplike states are particularly vulnerable times for us, unless we have purified ourselves by fasts and vigils in the hope of obtaining a dreamless and imageless sleep. Man is vulnerable to actual penetration through the ear as we have seen, but the infection of the imagination turns out to be a more complex matter; and Ficino may have in mind as a model the passage of light through transparent or translucent materials. Our material bodies would be open to such subtle demonic penetration everywhere since we live inside a flesh of glass. Like light, like sound, with light, with sound, the demons would then affect, in the sense of actually enter like light into, our image-making power. Alternatively, for shadows, if not for images, the model might be simply that of the demons casting shadows on the wall of our imagination, blocking out the light of the reason and afflicting it with the likenesses that they project. In either case, the demons affect our imagination, our image-making power, by way, says Ficino, of their own image-making power: they use their powerful imaginations, not their higher powers, as tools to deceive us. Tricked by their imaginations' images, we replicate or mirror them; and thus we become enslaved to the demons' image-making powers, become indeed extensions of them.

The second possibility is equally intriguing and follows as a corollary. Ficino suggests that in us what does the imagining is, so to speak, a demon. This is a gloss on the claim that "our imaginations

---

he takes up the specific question of personal demons, and postulates a cloudy demon to work upon our imagination through its imagination, a purely airy one to work upon our reason through its reason, and an aethereal one to work upon our understanding through its understanding. The higher demon works "more secretly" and "more tranquilly" than the others. Note that for Porphyry, apparently, the body of a demon was the object of its own imagination; see Dodds, *Proclus: The Elements of Theology*, p. 319.

too are possessed in a way (*quodammodo*) of a demonic power."
Notice the qualifier. Ficino is apparently speculating with the notion
that we become demons in the limited sense that our imaginations
create their own realm of images and shadows and do so usually
independently, though on occasion they may merely replicate that
of the demons who temporally possess them. In terms of the *Sophist*'s all-important distinction, they imitate the world of "likenesses"
produced by the demons' divine phantastic art by creating their own
phantastic likenesses. In the process our imaginations become creating demons, agents "in a way" of the divine phantastic art (at
least the distinction between divine and human becomes increasingly blurred at this juncture). We cannot restrict this claim to the
notion that we become only like the lower demons, moreover; for
"lights" as we have seen are alluring to the highest of the demons,
who, presumably, possess the most powerful of all imaginations.
Certainly, we could postulate a scale of imaginations in human
beings, ranging from the lowest kind in Chaucer's miller to the
highest kind in Porphyry's Plotinus, that would correspond to the
scale that stretches from the subterranean demon to the aethereal
demon closest to a god. But Ficino did not indulge in such a notion
and surely opted for the traditional Platonic theory that as one ascends the scale, one becomes more perfectly governed by the highest
faculty, the intuitive intelligence, until, for all intents and purposes,
the imagination, one of the lowest faculties, is set aside if not
completely abandoned.

   That Ficino means to accord the human imagination an authentically demonic power to create and manipulate images and shadows
is further evidenced by his decision to enhance the preceding arguments by adducing the "Platonic School's" threefold division of the
demons into those veiled in purely fiery or celestial bodies, those
wrapped in such bodies tempered to the utmost with air, and those
enveloped in bodies compounded "from the quadruple vapor of the
elements" (271.25–29). When you gaze inwardly, claims Ficino, at
your soul "clothed as it were in spirit," then you will suppose perhaps that you are gazing on "a triple demon." For you will gaze on
the soul itself and on the celestial vehicle, that is, on the body composed of pure fire (or of the fiery air Platonists refer to as the aether).

You will also gaze "on the same vehicle covered entirely with a fiery and an airy veil," but principally airy; and on the same veil enveloped in spirit, that is, in spirit "compounded from the vapors of the four elements," in other words from the four humors, though, one assumes, in varying proportions (271.29–273.3). Notice the movement outwards from soul to inner fiery vehicle to the airy veil that wraps it, and thence to the enveloping spirit made from the airy essences of the bodily humors of bile, blood, phlegm, and black bile, associated respectively with the four possible combinations of the qualities linked with the four elements (hot and dry: fire; hot and wet: air; cold and wet: water; cold and dry: earth). The theory that the two lowest elements have airy essences enabled Ficino (and other Platonists, incidentally) to accommodate the lowest kind of demons, the watery, the earthy, and even the subterranean, by alloting them differing proportions of such essences. The fact that they were still thought of as "airy" essences guaranteed the integrity of the more general theory that all demons were in essence creatures of the air. The fire demons presented another, cognate problem, but this was solved by defining their kind of fire as "aethereal" and then defining aether Platonically as the fieriest form of air. The ultrademonic gods alone had purely fiery bodies, though the borderline between them and the demons closest to them was perhaps indiscernible to mortals. Even Ficino, who was careful to preserve demonological distinctions, often speaks of the highest demons as if they were possessed of bodies of absolutely pure fire like the gods ruling over them. Part of the problem stemmed from the widely accepted Aristotelian definition of the aether as the purest form of fire, the celestial fire, an assumption that Ficino had always to remember to correct against the Platonic definition, most clearly educed in the *Epinomis* and the *Timaeus* and then taken up by Calcidius.[11] The *Epinomis* we now reject as spurious, but Ficino

---

11. The *Epinomis* at 981C and 984B–E refers to the aether as a fifth element but inserts it between the air and the fire; see Ficino's epitome, *Opera*, p. 1527. The *Timaeus* at 58D describes the aether as "the brightest part of the air" but obviously does not regard it as a separate fifth element since it supposes at 31B, 32BC, 40A, and 81E ff. that the Demiurge needed only four elements to build the universe. For Calcidius's views see his *In Timaeum* c. 178. See my *Platonism of Ficino*, pp. 11–13.

accepted it without question as the thirteenth book of, or the appendix to, the *Laws,* and therefore possessed of the authority of the one work written, like the *Letters,* in Plato's own voice.[12] Clearly Ficino is not thinking here of the soul as being in possession of three separate vehicles but rather of its having the fiery body, the glorified body of the resurrection, concealed behind two veils, the airy and the compound. Elsewhere, however, he speaks of our airy body and our elemental body; and while we can certainly see the distinction between the corporeal body and the spirit compounded of vaporized humors, it is more difficult to see any point in distinguishing between an airy body and an airy veil. Indeed, they must be one and the same.

We thus have in descending sequence: the soul, its fiery vehicle, the airy veil or airy body, the vaporous spirit, the vapors themselves of the four bodily humors, and finally the corporeal body compounded of the four elements. Moreover, the postulation of water demons would seem to require that we insert between the airy veil and the spirit compounded of four vapors another veil compounded of air and water vapor alone; and in his most Proclian moments Ficino would probably have acceded to this. In practice, however, he works with the scheme that consists of the fiery vehicle, the airy veil, the vaporous spirit, and the elemental body. The first three at least are not so much separate entities (though Ficino occasionally speaks of them as such) as manifestations of the same "body" or "spirit" in various states of purity and rarity or rarefaction. When we ascend the mount of purgatory, the vapors of the baser elements are burned away and we inhabit, not a different and a higher body, but the body we have always possessed, now stripped of ugly ac-

---

12. Ficino refers to it as the thirteenth book of the *Laws* at the end of the preface to his *Platonis Opera Omnia* of 1484 (*Opera,* p. 766.2 "Libri Platonis"), and as the *Laws'* appendix in the title to his epitome for the dialogue, *Opera,* p. 1525.2 (*epinomis* means, of course, an addition or appendix to a law). On several occasions he affirms that it was only in the *Laws,* the *Epinomis,* and the *Letters* (excepting the first and fifth) that Plato elected to speak in his own person—e.g., *Opera,* pp. 766.2 (again the Plato preface), 1488.2 (epitome for book 1 of the *Laws*), and *Platonic Theology* 4.1 and 17.4 (ed. Marcel, 1:165, 3:168–169).

Leonardo Tarán, *Academica: Plato, Philip of Opus, and the Pseudo-Platonic Epinomis,* Memoirs of the American Philosophical Society, vol. 107 (Philadelphia, 1976), pp. 133–139, attributes the authorship of the *Epinomis* to Philip of Opus or another member of the early Academy.

cretions and the weight of matter, and also of its veils of mist and
air. For it was never Ficino's intention to deny the ancient definition
of man as a soul united with a body, a definition accepted by the
Church, though variously defined, and one that required therefore,
rather than merely vindicated, the doctrine of the resurrection of the
body—the resurrection, that is, of the aethereal or fiery bodies that
alone are truly ours.

Given the vehicle, the airy veil, and the vaporous spirit, we must
accordingly suppose three levels of operation for the imagination.
For we should know, Ficino writes, "that the soul primarily and effectively exercises the imagination in the celestial vehicle, and prepares (*expedire*) all the sense through the whole vehicle" (273.3–5).
This means, I take it, that in the celestial vehicle sensation is no
longer differentiated among the five senses and confined to them
but that there is a ubiquitous "common" or "universal" sense, which
Ficino elsewhere identifies with the imagination.[13] We should bear
in mind that Ficino thinks of the celestial vehicle as entirely circular
and thus of sensations, or rather a unitary sensation, as being conveyed from the circumference to the center; and of images generated
by the imagination as being conveyed from the center to the circumference. Moreover, given the rarity and purity of the celestial vehicle, it can respond perfectly to the imagination and represent the
images it projects with the utmost subtlety and fidelity. Thence we
descend the ladder of distortion; for the soul frequently uses the
vehicle itself as if it were a seal "to impress"(*imprimere*) its images
on the second veil; and uses the second veil similarly "to fashion"
(*conformare*) the third veil (273.5–7). In other words, the vehicle
projects the images onto the airy veil and the airy veil in turn projects them onto the vaporous spirit. Like a series of mirrors, the
three envelopes thus serve to reflect the soul's images; and in the
triple process, the images become more and more distorted and
indistinct.

It will be clear from all this that the imagination per se is not a
faculty confined to the fallen world and to the fallen elemental body,
but rather that it is best exercised in the "body" furthest removed

---

13. *Phaedrus* Commentary, summa 11 (ed. Allen, pp. 138–139).

from terrestrial limitations. It is indeed a faculty that, with others, we share with the highest of the demons and that they use in the best, the paradigmatic, way. Consequently, we must acknowledge that the demons are meant by providence to possess and use the imagination: first as a way of communicating perfectly among themselves but also as a way of communicating with men. But how can this be when the model is that of a Chinese box of "veils" or envelopes where each veil serves as wax for the images imprinted in it by a superior veil until we reach the celestial vehicle itself that responds directly to the imagination? For there seems to be no room here for an external agent. The demons must be able to impress their images on us, however, as well as on one another (though demonological hierarchy would seem to require that higher demons can impress their images more powerfully on men and lower demons than lower demons can on men and on one another). The impression cannot be upon our faculties directly but must occur at a time when the images are being impressed by one vehicle on another. Presumably, that ordinary men have vapor-laden vehicles renders them the easiest prey, while airy "demonic men" like philosophers and other demons would be vulnerable only to the impress of alien images through the airy vehicle. And still higher fiery demons would impress each other's fiery vehicles in the most perfect play of imaginations conceivable. All that Ficino says at this juncture, however, is that we can assume that "the images that are innermost in you, since they are made by this spiritual and demonic animal, proceed from a certain demonic contrivance [or mechanism]" (*machinatio quaedam daemonica*) (273.7–9). In this cryptic sentence I take it he is referring to the notion that as long as it is the spirit as a higher animate "body" (and thus as an "animal") that is the first receptacle of the images we perceive (and thus that we are not dealing simply with sensation and ordinary sense images), then we must assume that the source of such images is either the demons themselves or the demonic power possessed by our own imagination. For this power consists in generating images quite independently of sensations and projecting them, though mediated through the other vehicles, onto the vaporous spirit. We might note, incidentally, that one of the sources of enduring confusion lies in Ficino's failure to differentiate consistently between images that come from within, or from the demons working within, and images derived directly from the senses.

We should not assume that all images impressed by higher demons either in us ór in demons above us are necessarily or even predominantly bad or deceptive. To the contrary, Ficino would maintain on familiar Platonic grounds that the higher demonic imagination was supremely good and that we could on occasion be flooded by good images. Even our own imaginations, when we play demons, as it were, to ourselves, are not intrinsically flawed and do not invariably function as agencies of deception. At times they may furnish us with sublime and liberating images for our contemplation. Nevertheless, Ficino is not anticipating the vision-making power of Coleridge and the Romantics but describing a faculty that in us, at least, is vulnerable, often fatally so, to infiltration by demons intent on misleading us. Arguably, it is even vulnerable, as we shall see, to the demonic machinations of other men.

Melissus now turns, in Ficino's analysis, to examine the nature and status of external images. The cognate problem of shadows is subordinate to this larger question, for shadows are merely the effects of an obstacle blocking the light, which "proceeds ultimately from the celestial fire," though some shadows can have expressive or suggestive shapes and can provide evidence on occasion of the kind of obstacle blocking the light. This is notably the case with shadows in the midst of fires that can be caused by salamanders or other unfamiliar beings or objects, where the rays of light, prevented from proceeding directly, "burst out" around the obstacle and bear "some shadowy shape that has been immediately but invisibly (*e conspectu*) stamped upon them" (273.10–14). Such a shape is close to being an image. But Ficino defines the "more distinct images" as the products of a "double light," not solely of a light radiating around an obstacle. This double light consists first of "the common light" that is everywhere suffused externally around corporeal objects, and second of "the proper or peculiar light," which Ficino glosses to mean the light "from the nature (*indole*), color, and shape

of a face already surrounded with the common light" (p. 273.14–
17). He continues,

Each of these lights when it strikes a mirror surface creates an image there.
Furthermore, you can achieve a manner of looking surpassing the one you
commonly and habitually achieve. For, in addition to the fact that, at a
straight glance, you customarily observe the mirror and the [your?] image
simultaneously, you also descry simultaneously the things behind your
back, when the [your?] visual ray, that is, has been reflected back directly
from the mirror (273.17–22).

This is a difficult set of propositions, and can best be understood
by reference to Plato's equally difficult account of the origin and
nature of vision in the *Timaeus* 45B–46C, as Ficino himself alerts
us when he refers to his own exposition of the problems elsewhere.
The particular analysis he has in mind is not in his *Timaeus* Commentary proper but rather in the section of chapter breakdowns,
summaries, and comments (*distinctiones capitum in Timaeum et
summae capitum atque commentariola*) that he had obviously already compiled for the projected deluxe edition of all his Plato
translations and commentaries which was never realized. Since he
had begun this section by 7 November 1492 and had probably finished it by year's end,[14] we therefore have the first of two pieces of
internal evidence for dating this forty-sixth chapter at least to a
period subsequent to 1492.

Chapter 30 of the section is a long one and treats of the crucial
passage in the *Timaeus* 45B ff. where, inter alia, Plato discusses
the theory of the two lights, or what he calls the inner and the outer
fire: the one is the fire of everyday life, the other is the fire that
streams out of our eyes. When the two lights or fires coalesce, then
we are able to see objects in our line of vision, until, at nightfall,
we lose the outer fire and our eyelids close in sleep in order that
we might retain the inner fire. Moreover, Plato continues, "from

---

14. Kristeller, *Supplementum* 1:cxxi, marshals the evidence for the dates of the addition
of this section to a commentary that Ficino had been engaged on intermittently throughout
his career.

the communion of the internal and external fires, and again from the union of them and their numerous transformations when they meet in the mirror, all these appearances necessarily arise, when the fire from the face coalesces with the fire from the eye on the bright and smooth surface" (46A–B). Ficino comments in the opening of chapter 30 that

the animal spirit, which is the senses' instrument, is solar by nature and is principally raylike or radial, especially in the eye. A ray of it which is very pure escapes through the pupil and mingles with the external light that is like itself and does so in that part of the air especially in which it is concentrated through the sight. Having thus coalesced there with the external light on one form, the ray, if it touches anything that resists it at all, rebounds as it were directly back into the spirit and thence from the spirit into the soul.[15]

Ficino is consciously adopting not only the traditional ray-based optics of what he lists as "Democritus, Heraclitus, the Stoics, the majority of the Aristotelians and geometers along with the Platonists" but also the Calcidian identification of the inner fire with the "animal spirit" with its solar and hence radial nature. This is an aspect or extension of the same spirit as that which constitutes the

---

15. *Commentaria*, f. 84v (i.e., *Opera*, p. 1472), "Spiritus animalis sensuum instrumentum natura solaris est, et praecipue radiosus praesertim in oculo. Ubi per pupillam radius eius purior evolans cum externo lumine simili commiscetur in ea praesertim aeris parte in quam intenditur per aspectum. Ibi igitur in unam speciem cum hoc lumine coalescens siquid attigerit quod quoquomodo resistat quasi resilit prorsus in spiritum, atque ex hoc ad animam." For Ficino's optical-ray theory, which derives from book 6 of the *Republic* as well as from the *Timaeus* 45B ff., see also his *Philebus* Commentary 1.30 (ed. Allen, pp. 302–303). For the medieval context, see David C. Lindberg, *Theories of Vision from al-Kindi to Kepler* (Chicago, 1976), and the various articles reprinted in his *Studies in the History of Medieval Optics* (London, 1983), especially no. 1.

The role generally of *spiritus* in Ficino's thought is at the center of Couliano's provocative new study, *Eros and Magic*. He claims that "the spiritual magic of the Renaissance—Marsilio Ficino being its first and most influential representative—is built on the principle of universal pneumatic sympathy" (p. 127) and argues that "the focal concept in Ficino's astrology and psychology is spirit" (p. 28). In the process he is led to deny Walker's distinction between a spiritual and a demonic magic (p. 156) and to stress the central role of "phantasms" and the "phantasmic" (pp. 28–32, and passim). Even so, little in his argument impinges on the specific concerns of this chapter, or indeed of this book; and a number of his claims, at least with regard to Ficino, though fascinating and often arresting, are open to refutation or qualification.

vehicles, envelopes, or veils used by the soul's imagination to project its images. Here it serves as the senses' instrument, illuminating the corporeal world and conveying images of it back to the imagination and thence to the soul. External sight is the result of a ray from our own spirit or inner fire transmitting back to us "spirit images," or what Ficino thinks of understandably as ray-borne or "radial images."

Later in chapter 30 he takes up another, more speculative theory: namely, that even "certain Platonists," and not just the materialists and atomists, had postulated "material images" of natural objects in addition to "radial and spiritual images." These would be the images or films that Democritus and Empedocles had supposed "flowing out through the pores of bodies and preserving for a certain interval not only a body's quality but also its shape." They imperceptibly act upon the spirit of any man who is close by, and thence they act upon his imagination "especially if it is frail (*debilis*) and easily fashioned." It is precisely these actions of material images streaming out of the "pores" of objects that "are detected and observed for the most part by magicians," though such are not his immediate concern.[16] The radial images, by contrast—and he refers us specifically to the *Sophist* (266B–D?) and to the *Republic* book 7 (532B–C?) as well as to the *Timaeus*—are borne in the rays of the common light. They possess such "an extremely thin essence" that they cannot become clearly visible to our eyes unless it be in mirrors. For in mirrors such images are rendered "uniformly steady," and are "restored and illumined" and "receive a measure of their pristine power and mode of shape" with which to proceed. Indeed, so great is the "friendship" of light for the mirror that lights and visual rays and radial images are not dissipated or weakened in it, but immediately enhanced and strengthened. Thus intensified, he argues, the light instantly illuminates a wall opposite. Our visual

---

16. *Commentaria,* f. 85r (i.e., *Opera,* p. 1473), "Imagines vero naturalium Platonici quidam non solum radiales spiritualesque invenerunt, sed materiales etiam, quales Democritus et Empedocles per poros corporum effluentes servantesque ad certum spatium non solum qualitatem corporis sed figuram, et clam agentes in spiritum propinqui hominis et imaginationem praecipue debilem et conformem. Actiones eiusmodi a magis praecipue depraehenduntur et observantur."

ray not only sees the mirror but also, "having been reflected powerfully from the mirror as if it were flashing out once again from the
eye itself," surveys what exists outside the mirror's immediate field
of view. The radial image of an object is now unfolded and wit-
nessed in its pristine form, after thus being transported "enfolded
in rays" to the mirror. Our own images, Ficino observes, "become
radial in mirrors because of the common light and at the same time
because of the likeness (*effigia*) of the body carried there by the
light."[17] He then proceeds to discuss the problems of inverted images and of left- and right-handedness as raised by Plato in the
Timaeus at 46BC.[18]

Let us return, however, to chapter 46 of the *Sophist* Commentary. Marsilio next considers the objections of those who deny the
existence altogether of specular images. He argues that Plato and
his followers had postulated the specular image as an independent
"something" on the grounds that "otherwise no objects could appear
in mirrors unimpaired" (273.23–26). Besides the *Sophist,* one of
the principal texts for the claim that "the idola are not the same as

17. Ibid., f. 85r–v (i.e., *Opera*, p. 1473), "Radiales imagines in *Timaeo, Sophista,* septimo de *Republica* Plato tetigit, quae quidem nimis exilem habent essentiam, ut non aliter
palam ostentare se oculis possint quam in corporibus specularibus, aequabiliter stabilitae,
redintegratae, illustratae pristinam vim quandam modumque formae unde processere recipi-
ant. . . . Tanta profecto amicitia luminis est ad speculum, ut in hoc ipso lumina, radii visu-
ales, radiales imagines non frangantur quidem sed ita protinus invalescant, ut hinc statim
multiplicatum lumen oppositum illuminet parietem, ac radius visualis non solum videat speculum, sed etiam illinc valide replicatus, quasi rursus ex oculo micans, quae e conspectu speculi
sunt attingat atque circumspiciat. Et radialis imago rei obiectae speculo hucusque provecta
radiis implicata, hic iam in formam pristinam explicetur atque cernatur. Fiunt autem imagines
nostrae radiales in speculis ex communi lumine simul et effigie corporis lumine vecta."
18. This section of the dialogue had been extensively commented upon by Calcidius, undoubtedly Ficino's most accessible and important source. Calcidius devotes sections 239 and
240 to the general topic of mirrors; but he devotes the whole of part 10, that is, sections 236
to 248, to the topic of sight; and the whole of part 11, that is, sections 249 to 263, to the
topic of images, sections 257 to 259 specifically to specular images.
Ficino was familiar with Calcidius's *Timaeus* Commentary from his earliest years as a
student of philosophy, and was deeply indebted to it long before he had learned Greek. A
manuscript of the work which he himself copied out, annotated and owned is now in the
Ambrosiana shelved as S. 14 sup.; see Kristeller, *Supplementum* 1:liv. However, he later
consciously distanced himself, I believe, from some of Calcidius's "faulty" metaphysics,
after he had returned to the *Timaeus* himself on several occasions and had become acquainted
with the first half of the huge and important commentary on the dialogue by Proclus.

bodies"—meaning "that they possess their own nature but that they do not have matter" (273.26–29)—is the *Timaeus*. However, even more important, says Ficino, is the argument in book 6 of the *Republic*—he is referring to 509D ff., the section on the divided line— where Plato maintains that as mirror images are to their objects, so are mathematical figures to the divine Ideas. Like little ideas, the idola with their matterless nature have "as it were their own act and mode," just as mathematical figures have theirs (273.30–32). Here in his *Sophist* Commentary, as at a similar point in the argument in the middle and at the end of chapter 30 of his *Timaeus* commentary (*Opera*, pp. 1473 and 1474), Ficino refers us to "Theophrastus's treatise *De Anima*" and to the comments of Iamblichus and of Priscianus upon it. The reference is in fact to Priscianus Lydus's *Metaphrasis*, which he had himself translated around 1488.[19]

19. Priscianus Lydus was probably a student of Damascius who taught at Athens until Justinian's edict in A.D. 529 expelling the pagan philosophers. Thereupon he departed, along with Damascius, Simplicius, and four other Neoplatonic teachers, to seek refuge at the court of Chosroes I of Persia, until the king negotiated their return to Athens in 533. Two extant works are attributed to him: the *Solutiones Eorum de Quibus Dubitavit Chosroes Persarum Rex*, which survives only in a Latin translation dating from the sixth or seventh century and which was known in the Middle Ages and the Renaissance (though often wrongly attributed to Priscianus Caesariensis, the grammarian); and the *Metaphrasis in Theophrastum*, a work that contains some genuine Theophrastian doctrine but also much from other, particularly Neoplatonic, sources. The *Metaphrasis* first became known to the West only after Ficino himself had gained access to a Greek manuscript of the work and translated it into Latin. Along with his commentary, it appeared: first, in the 1497 and 1516 Aldine editions and in subsequent editions of his *Iamblichi De Mysteriis et Alia*, where it accompanied both his treatise, *De Voluptate*, and his translations of other Neoplatonic pieces; and then eventually in his own *Opera* on pp. 1801–1835. Divided into two parts, the *De Sensu* and the *De Phantasia et Intellectu*, it is apparently based upon the fourth and fifth books of Theophrastus's eight-book *Physica* (which has not survived, except perhaps in extracts, but which is listed by Diogenes Laertius in his *Lives* 5.42–50 as among Theophrastus's writings). However, Ficino's important prefatory letter of 25 March 1489 to Valori (*Opera*, pp. 1801, cf. 896.3; for the date, see Kristeller, *Supplementum* 1:35) describes the work as "a brief but diligent exposition of Theophrastus's book on the soul." As a remark in the commentary itself makes clear (*Opera*, p. 1807.1), Ficino thinks of Priscianus as a true Platonist and as a follower of Plotinus, Iamblichus, and Proclus; but he valued him especially, as he says to Valori, because he had convincingly demonstrated that Plato, Aristotle, and Theophrastus held the same opinion about the nature of the soul although they used different formulations. Priscianus had thus provided him with the "concordist" solution to a problem that had long troubled him; see Frederick Purnell, Jr., "The Theme of Philosophic Concord and the Sources of Ficino's Platonism," in Garfagnini, *Marsilio Ficino*, pp. 397–415 at 413–414. Here he may be referring specifically: either to the *De Sensu* cap. xxxiii, where his commentary defines an idolum as "quasi specimen sive exilis quaedam species a specie perfectiore proveniens" (*Opera*, pp. 1816–1817); or, more probably, to the *De Phantasia* in its entirety,

Even more revealingly, he refers us to Proclus's Commentary on the *Republic,* specifically on books 6 and 7. He had gained access to this only in 1492, after Lascaris had brought a manuscript to Piero de' Medici directly from Greece. The evidence here is a letter Ficino wrote on 4 August to his great friend Martinus Uranius (alias Prenninger) and also an autograph entry in the loan register of the Medici's private library noting that he had borrowed the manuscript on 7 July.[20] This manuscript, now the Laurenziana's 80.9, is incomplete and contains the first twelve only of Proclus's seventeen extant treatises.[21] We should accordingly dismiss the possibility that the last five, in many ways the most important five, treatises were ever known to Ficino (as scholars have too confidently assumed in the past). Ficino's letter contains extracts from and epitomes of the twelve treatises, which cover the first six books and the beginning of the seventh book of the *Republic* as Ficino himself acknowledged when he set about gathering "flowers from their most delightful meadows."[22] The late date of Ficino's encounter with this particular Proclus commentary should not lead us to suppose, incidentally, that he was not familiar with other commentaries from relatively

---

especially to chapters 1 and 2, which actually adduce the views of Iamblichus on the phantasy and its *phantasmata* (*Opera,* pp. 1824–1825).

Priscianus's two extant works were first joined by I. Bywater in his still standard critical edition, *Prisciani Lydi Quae Extant: Metaphrasis in Theophrastum et Solutionum ad Chosroem Liber,* in *Supplementum Aristotelicum,* vol. 1, part 2 (Berlin, 1886), the *Metaphrasis* appearing on pp. 1–37. In general, see Charles B. Schmitt's article—to which this note is greatly indebted—entitled "Priscianus Lydus," in *Catalogus Translationum et Commentariorum: Mediaeval and Renaissance Latin Translations and Commentaries: Annotated Lists and Guides,* vol. 3, ed. F. Edward Cranz and Paul Oskar Kristeller (Washington, D.C., 1976), pp. 75–82; see also Gersh, *Middle Platonism and Neoplatonism* 2:767–775.

For the dating and manuscripts of Ficino's translation and commentary in particular, see Kristeller, *Supplementum* 1:cxxviii–cxxix; idem, *Ficino and His Work,* pp. 69, 73, 74, 84, 101, 111; and Gentile in *Mostra,* pp. 125–126 (no. 97), 128–129 (no. 99). For the two Greek manuscripts Ficino may have used, the Laurenziana's 87.20 and Munich's Bayerische Staatsbibliothek's cod. Monac. gr. 461, see Kristeller, *Ficino and His Work,* pp. 75, 95, 128, 147; also Gentile in *Mostra,* pp. 123–124 (no. 96).

20. *Opera,* pp. 937.2–943.1. See Kristeller's edition of Ficino's third catalogue in his *Supplementum* 1:3; idem, *Ficino and His Work,* pp. 126–127; Sicherl, "Neuentdeckte Handschriften," pp. 50 and 59 (no. 4); Gentile in *Mostra,* pp. 151–152 (no. 117–the manuscript); Viti in *Mostra,* p. 189 (no. 160—the library entry).

21. See Festugière's note to his translation at 2:105.

22. *Opera,* p. 937.2, "ex amoenissimis horum pratis flosculos passim discurrendo collegi religionem sanctam prae caeteris redolentes."

early in his career. Indeed, the argumentum he wrote for the *Parmenides* in 1463 contains informed references to Proclus as does the *Timaeus* Commentary's initial draft in the 1484 Plato edition. The mention of Proclus's comments on the *Republic* undoubtedly provides us, however, with another piece of internal evidence for dating the *Sophist* Commentary, or at least this forty-sixth chapter, to sometime after 1492.

In his epitome of the opening of the twelfth treatise, where Proclus is commenting on the section on the divided line, Ficino had been struck by evidence that seemed to confirm the "opinion" in the *Sophist* that "visible images consist of certain substances of certain simulacra and are fabricated by demonic machination."[23] As testimony there were Proclus's descriptions in the same treatise: first, of the hyena held to have trampled on the shadow of a dog crouching above it, thereby causing the dog to tumble down immediately and become its prey;[24] and second, taken from Aristotle, of the menstruating woman who had looked at herself in a mirror until

---

23. *Opera,* p. 941.2, "Dicendum ergo secundum sententiam Platonicam in *Sophista* apparentes imagines esse substantias quasdam quorundam simulachrorum machinatione quadam daemonica fabricatas."

Note that Ficino occasionally errs, as in this passage which begins "Plato in septimo de *Republica* rerum ordinem lineae comparat," in thinking of the section on the divided line (509D ff.) as occurring in book 7. The reason may well be that Proclus does not treat of the section until the opening of his twelfth treatise, which then goes on to treat of the myth of the Cave in book 7. The section and the myth are of course intimately connected anyway, and Plato returns at 533E ff. to the divisions of knowledge established by the section. In "Some Remarks," pp. 294–296, James Hankins analyzes Ficino's translation of 509D–511E, and provides on pp. 298–304 the Latin text from the 1491 Venice edition along with Ficino's Greek text from MS Laur. 85.9. He notes that "the translation comes down firmly on the side of the Neoplatonic interpretation of the passage. Ficino chooses to translate the two main divisions of the Line (*tmêmata, genê*) as *genera* and their subdivisions (confused throughout with the Forms or *eidê*) as *species*—a translation sanctioned by classical and medieval precedent, but always apt to be confused with the logical *species* of Porphyry and the *species intelligibilis* of Aristotelian psychology" (p. 295).

24. *Opera,* p. 941.2, "Nam hyenam ferunt calcantem canis in alto sedentis umbram, illum ex alto praecipitare statim atque devorare." The reference is to Proclus's *In Rempublicam* 290.18–19 (ed. Kroll). Festugière, in a note to his translation at 2:98–99, refers us to Pseudo-Aristotle's *De Mirab. Auscult.* 145.845a24–27—the obvious source—and to Aelian's *De Nat. Anim.* 6.14 (ed. Hercher, p. 98.26 ff.), though the hyena in Aelian's account projects its own moon shadow onto the dog. An authentic work by Aristotle, the *De Hist. Anim.* 8.5.594b3–4, claims to the contrary that a hyena "will inveigle a dog within its reach by producing a retching sound like that of a man vomiting." The hyena is, of course, an important magical animal.

the mirror and the image it reflected assumed the color of blood.[25] Ficino had concluded his epitome by noting that Plato had confirmed (with Proclus agreeing) that such specular or imagined images are substances of a kind on the analogical grounds that as mathematicals are to intelligibles, so are images to the visibles we actually see. Both are "species" in themselves, images being "particular and natural effluences from things in nature, and thus possessed of their own nature."[26] Ficino must have been alerted by Proclus himself to the relevance of these observations in the twelfth treatise for an understanding of the passage in the *Sophist* at 266B ff. For Proclus had referred to the *Sophist* just a few lines earlier at 290.8–10 in speaking of *hypostaseis eidôlôn*, that is, of the substantive nature of images. At all events, this allusion to the hyena and the dog's shadow (though not to the menstrual woman and the mirror) clearly stuck in Ficino's mind, for he repeats it here in his *Sophist* Commentary and refers us directly to Proclus's *Republic* Commentary in the context of arguing for the fact that shadows and images "have a power (*vis*) and nature as it were of their own" (275.2–4).

---

25. *Opera*, pp. 941.2–942.1, "Atque Aristoteles inquit mulierem in purgatione menstrui sanguinis constitutam foedare sanguine quodam obiectum, speculum et imaginem." A commonplace in the Middle Ages, the motif derived ultimately from Aristotle's treatise *On Dreams* 2.459b27 ff., which argues that it is easier to wipe off the "bloodshot cloud" if the mirror is an old one and therefore less reflective, and that a woman's eyes are affected during her period and hence affect the air at the mirror's surface. Ficino's reference is again to the *In Rempublicam* 290.19–22 (ed. Kroll; tr. Festugière, 2:99).

Interestingly, he had referred to the Aristotle passage in his *De Amore* 7.4 (ed. Marcel, p. 247) in the course of discussing the spirit, mirrors, and rays. There he had defined the spirit as "a vapor of the blood," and thus as "blood that is so thin that we cannot see it" until it is "thickened" on the surface of a mirror ("spiritus, qui vapor sanguinis est, sanguis quidam tenuissimus videtur esse, adeo ut aspectum effugiat oculorum, sed in speculi superficie factus crassior clare perspicitur"). Couliano refers to this in terms of an "ocular hemorrhage" (*Eros and Magic*, pp. 29–30). For the phantasy's ability to "form" in the sense of infect or contaminate its own and foreign bodies, see also Ficino's *Platonic Theology* 13.4 (ed. Marcel, 2:233–235).

26. *Opera*, p. 942.1, "Imagines denique substantias quasdam esse Plato confirmat ubi ait: Sicut cogitabilia ad intelligibilia sese habent, sic imaginalia ad visibilia corpora. Cogitabilia vero, id est mathematica, res in se quaedam speciesque sunt, similiter imagines, cum sint naturales quidam ex rebus naturalibus effluxus, naturam quoque suam habent." Note that in the *Platonic Theology* 6.2 (ed. Marcel, 1:228) Ficino says that "numbers are spiritual" and in 14.3 (ed. Marcel, 2:256) that "we live the life of the demons when we engage in mathematical speculation," that is, contemplate "cogitabilia." The implications of the connection between the demons' rule over images and their obsession with mathematics are far-reaching.

Marsilio also refers us to Solinus, that is, to the third-century-A.D. geographer-phantasist C. Iulius Solinus, who had noted in a work which is basically a digest of Pliny and Mela, the *Polyhistor* or *Collectanea rerum memorabilium* 27.24, that a dog cannot bark in the shadow of a hyena.[27] Pliny observes in his *Natural History* 8.106, a work that Ficino does not refer to but certainly knew, that "when a hyena's shadow falls on dogs, they are struck dumb." He adds that the hyena possesses certain magical powers by which it causes any animal it gazes upon to stand rooted to the spot, and then repeats the Aristotelian story that the hyena imitates the noise of a man vomiting.[28]

Ficino goes on to note Proclus's claim in the twelfth treatise of the *Republic* Commentary that magicians are accustomed to "affecting" things' images and shadows "in marvellous ways."[29] Having affected the images, they are able similarly to affect the things themselves. It is as if images and shadows possessed a nature of their own which, in some unspecified manner, reaches or corresponds to things, and that "through this nature a certain mutual sympathy (*compassio*) can be achieved" (275.6–10). At first sight this affecting by way of mutual sympathy might appear to involve neither a spiritual nor a demonic magic, but solely a natural image or shadow magic. However, given the sovereignty that the demons exercise over the whole realm of shadows and images, we must assume that the magician who wishes to affect this realm necessarily

---

27. Ed. Th. Mommsen (Berlin, 1864; rev. ed., 1895), p. 135.14–16. The work is contained in a manuscript in the Laurenziana, Pluteo 22.2, and someone should explore the possibility of Ficino's having had access to it. However, there are other possibilities, since some one hundred or so manuscripts survive from the fifteenth century alone (about half of which are of Italian provenance) and at least two hundred survive from earlier centuries; and the *editio princeps* appeared in Venice in 1473. See Mary Ella Milham, "C. Julius Solinus," in *Catalogus Translationum et Commentariorum,* vol. 6, ed. F. Edward Cranz, Virginia Brown, and Paul Oskar Kristeller (Washington, D.C., 1986), pp. 73–85 at 75. The *Polyhistor* was translated, incidentally, into English in 1587 by Arthur Golding and had a considerable impact on Elizabethan compilers of natural history and lore.

28. Festugière at 2:99n again refers us to Aelian's *De Nat. Anim.,* this time to 3.7 (ed. Hercher, p. 40.37), where Aelian is merely noting, however, that nature has enabled hyenas to stop hounds from barking. It is very unlikely that Ficino knew this passage, and Pliny and Solinus are his obvious sources.

29. Ed. Kroll, p. 290.8–16 (tr. Festugière, 2:98).

must have dealings with the demons. Of particular curiosity are
"the marvellous ways" by which he does so. The analogy with the
mathematicals might suggest that one such way involves mathematical formulas. But in all probability other "marvellous" ways for
Ficino involved mirrors and the power of mirrors to rejuvenate and
strengthen even matterless, radial images. The magician has the
knowledge and ability either to employ a mirror to concentrate and
direct rays, or even in a mysterious way to use himself as a mirror.
Again, the analogies with the workings of a hyena's shadow or the
gaze of a menstrual woman might suggest comparable techniques.

Ficino himself moves hesitantly, declaring, "although I do not
venture to lay claim myself to these effects, yet I will hazard the
opinion that such things could happen for magicians"—if, that is,
we accept the existence of the simulacra posited by Lucretius in
addition to the radial and spiritual images that are the result merely
of light. Even when light has been removed, Lucretius claims, these
simulacra stream forth from objects and "drag along with them the
matter and the nature of bodies" (275.10–15). For these Lucretian
simulacra Ficino could have turned to a number of passages in the
De Rerum Natura.[30] This great philosophical poem he had enthusias-
tically quoted from in his youth, when he had entertained a number
of Epicurean propositions and had felt able to ignore the implications
of the atomism and agnosticism at the heart of the work. He had
also written a formal commentary on the poem, though he had later
set fire to it, in imitation perhaps of Plato, who had incinerated his
own youthful tragedies and elegies as a token of his conversion from
poetry to philosophy.[31] In later life Ficino consistently rejected Lu-

30. Lucretius introduces the simulacra:
> quae, quasi membranae summo de corpore rerum
> dereptae, volitant ultroque citroque per auras,
> atque eadem nobis vigilantibus obvia mentes
> terrificant atque in somnis, cum saepe figuras
> contuimur miras simulacraque luce carentum,
> quae nos horrifice languentis saepe sopore
> excierunt; ne forte animas Acherunte reamur
> effugere aut umbras inter vivos volitare.
(4.31–38)
31. See Ficino's letter to Uranius, which accompanies his rendering of two of the less
dangerous Orphic hymns, *Opera,* pp. 933.2–935.1; also Kristeller, *Supplementum* 1:clxiii.

cretius, along with Epicurus, Democritus, and the atomists, as an unbeliever in the soul's immortality, and personally as a poet driven to madness and suicide by the excesses of love melancholy.[32] Concomitant with the onset of reservations concerning Lucretius's philosophy and the increasing awareness that he was one of the enemies of Platonism is Ficino's growing reluctance to mention Lucretius at all or to quote from the poem, a reluctance all the more remarkable given the frequency of references in the first decade or so of Marsilio's scholarly career.[33] This late reference, accordingly, is notable, though obviously relevant, given the prominence of the simulacra at the beginning of the poem's fourth book where Lucretius also considers mirrors and the problems of right- and left-handedness reversal.

Ficino seems to be stressing the distinction between radial or spiritual images, the images he usually thinks of as idola, and the Lucretian simulacra. But we must move circumspectly here, since in the lexicon of Lucretius, a materialist, the two terms predictably signify the same thing; and in the Latin tradition generally, including the Latin Platonists with whom Ficino was familiar from the onset of his intellectual career, the two terms were often indifferently deployed, in Platonic contexts confusingly so.[34] What impresses Ficino most is that Lucretius's simulacra can be perceived in the absence of light. He has in mind not only the stimuli that enable us to smell, taste, or hear something at a distance, but the shapes that we seem to see in darkness and to which the poet is referring at 4.168 ff., when he describes the gloomy storm clouds becoming a canvas at night for "faces of black horror."[35]

Lucretius was a tainted if familiar authority, however, and Ficino refers in addition to two celebrated Platonists: to Proclus, "who seems to have secretly signified the existence of the simulacra," and

---

32. *De Amore* 7.6 (ed. Marcel, p. 251), "Lucretius amantium omnium infelicissimus." Ficino proceeds to quote a dozen lines from book 4 of the *De Rerum Natura* (1052–56, 1108–14) on the shameful frenzies of physical passion.

33. See, e.g., the important quotations in the *De Amore*, the *Philebus* Commentary, and the *Platonic Theology*, all works of the 1460s and early 1470s.

34. In the Lucretius lexicon "simulacrum" (Epicurus's *eidôlon*) means the same as "imago," "effigia/es," and "figura."

35. *De Rerum Natura* 4.168–175, "inpendent atrae formidinis ora superne" (173).

to Synesius (A.D. c. 370–c. 414), a native of Cyrene, who had studied at Alexandria under Hypatia, then married a Christian wife, and became three years or so before he died the bishop of Ptolemais in Libya (despite the likelihood that he had not yet been baptized!). The work of Synesius that Ficino has in mind is the treatise *De Insomniis* (referred to sometimes as the *De Somniis*) on the causes and meanings of dreams, a work that probably predates Synesius's conversion but is certainly redolent of piety if not of Christian spirituality. Ficino took the considerable trouble to translate this difficult treatise from the Greek into Latin for Piero, the son of Lorenzo de' Medici, and it was eventually published along with a number of other Neoplatonic treatises and extracts in the 1497 and 1516 Aldine and subsequent editions of Ficino's *Iamblichi De Mysteriis et Alia,* and then again at the end of his *Opera Omnia.*[36] Ficino worked from a very defective text, as he himself complained in a letter to Aldo Manuzio, and his translation accordingly is fraught with difficulties.[37] Synesius himself he regarded as both a Christian and a Platonist, and he refers to him on various other occasions.[38] In particular he thought of him as the author of Platonic hymns and as an authority on the controversial topics of the soul's "vehicles,"[39] the faculty

---

36. *Opera,* pp. 1968–1978. In the splendid second edition of 1516, it occurs between fols. 43v and 50r. Kristeller dates its composition to 1484; see his *Supplementum* 1:cxxxvii–cxxxviii (on p. lxix he describes the 1497 and 1516 eds.).

37. Della Torre, *Storia dell'Accademia Platonica,* p. 621; Kristeller, *Supplementum* 1:cxxxviii; and Gentile in *Mostra,* pp. 55–57 (no. 43) and 130 (no. 100.1). For the letter to Manuzio, dated 1 July 1497, which is preserved in the Vatican manuscript Reginensis lat. 2023 at f. 173, see Kristeller, *Supplementum* 2:95–96, and Gentile in *Mostra,* p. 131 (no. 101). We might note, incidentally, that the Englishman John Free had already produced a Latin translation in 1461–1464; see Roberto Weiss, "New Light on Humanism in England during the Fifteenth Century," *Journal of the Warburg and Courtauld Institutes* 14 (1951), 21–33 at 27–31. For a critical edition of the original Greek text, see Nicolaus Terzaghi, *Synesii Cyrenensis Opuscula* (Rome, 1944), pp. 143–189; and for an English translation, A. Fitzgerald, *The Essays and Hymns of Synesius of Cyrene,* 2 vols. (Oxford, 1930).

38. In the index to both the Italian and the German versions of his study of Ficino's philosophy, Kristeller cites the following Synesius references: in the *Opera,* pp. 531, 549, 562, 570 ff., 896, 898 ff., 901, 904 ff., 961, 1293 (the ref. in the *Sophist* Commentary), 1684, 1690, 1968 ff. (i.e., the translation of the *De Insomniis*); and in the *Supplementum* 1:3, 66, 104 ff.; 2:95. Couliano asserts—with some considerable justification, it seems to me, though the issue awaits further exploration—that "Ficino is a Synesius" (*Eros and Magic,* p. 128).

39. See Robert Christian Kissling, "The *ochêma-pneuma* of the Neo-Platonists and the *De Insomniis* of Synesius of Cyrene," *American Journal of Philology* 43.4 (1922), 318–330;

of the phantasy, and the related subject of idola, all three topics being of course fundamental to Neoplatonic oneirology.

Ficino presents us with Synesius's comments on images in a chapter of his translation entitled, "The simulacra flow out of all things, and the mirror and the receptacle of these simulacra is the phantastic spirit itself."⁴⁰ There are many difficulties in this chapter, but Ficino seems to be understanding Synesius as saying that "the marvellous nature of images" is such that those who possess them "are effected [*or* formed] by things that are not yet effected [*or* formed] themselves."⁴¹ There can be no ampler a receptacle for indefinite images than our divine spirit; and hence in sleep, as in waking life, we must "strive to set some term to indeterminate things," that is, we must establish "an art with regard to the idola or images."⁴² Notice that here Ficino seems to be equating idola with simulacra.

Luckily, the best gloss for these enigmatic propositions is itself chapter 46 of the *Sophist* Commentary. Ficino writes, "For Synesius supposes that the sensible species [i.e., form] in the body is extended along with the matter [of the body]" (275.17–18). Thus, when "a certain vaporous matter is exhaled through motions," then the "species mingled with it" proceeds with it also. The result is a vaporous "efflux" from "the special body," that is, from the body informed by the sensible species; and the efflux is still so formed or so in-

---

and Jay Bregman, *Synesius of Cyrene, Philosopher-Bishop* (Berkeley, Los Angeles, London, 1983), chaps. 4 and 5. For a more general consideration of the whole complicated topic of the soul's vehicle, see the second appendix to E. R. Dodds's *Proclus: The Elements of Theology,* 2d rev. ed. (Oxford, 1963); Paul Moraux, "Quinta Essentia," in Pauly-Wissowa-Kroll, *Realencyclopädie der classischen Altertumswissenschaft* 24.1 (1963), at cols. 1251–1256; and now John F. Finamore, *Iamblichus and the Theory of the Vehicle of the Soul,* American Classical Studies, no. 14 (Chico, Calif., 1985).

For Ficino and Synesian magic theory, see Copenhaver, "Iamblichus, Synesius and Ficino," pp. 446–448.

40. The 1516 ed., f. 48v (i.e., *Opera,* p. 1976.2), "Ab omnibus profluunt simulachra, quorum speculum receptaculumque est spiritus ipse phantasticus." The *Opera* incorrectly reads "species" for "spiritus." For the spirit as mirror, see Couliano, *Eros and Magic,* p. 29.

41. "Mirabilis quidem natura imaginum ita se prorsus habentium ut a rebus nondum effectis efficiantur" (ibid.), translating "θαυμαστά γέ τοι τὴν φύσιν ἐστὶ καὶ οὕτως ἔχοντα, ὅτι ἀπὸ μήπω γενομένων ἐγένετο" (ed. Terzaghi, p. 178.8–9).

42. "age iam vel in rebus indeterminatis terminum aliquem perquiramus, hoc est, artem circa idola, id est, imagines statuamus" (ibid.), translating "φέρε τινὰ κἂν τοῖς ἀορίστοις ὅρον ζητήσωμεν, τοῦτ' ἔστι τέχνην περὶ τὰ εἴδωλα συστησώμεθα" (ed. Terzaghi, p. 179.5–7).

formed by the presence of that sensible species that we must call it
an "idolon." The Greeks refer to the species itself as an "idos"
(*eidos*), and therefore by "idolon" they mean a little "idos." It is so
to speak either "the specimen" that proceeds from the species, or
an "attenuated" (*tenuis*) species (275.18–22). Since, Ficino continues, this attenuated species "is fashioned from [*or possibly* wrested
from] the entire body that has already been shaped," the Platonists
suppose that "it is revealed with that shape" and, moreover, that it
preserves that particular shape "over a certain distance and for some
time" (275.22–24). He speculatively and obscurely observes that
"the matter probably proceeds still farther than the shape [the spe-
cies] mingled with it" and that "a certain immaterial species so to
speak and spiritual mode of the shape probably proceeds still further
than the matter." The Aristotelians, for instance, hold that "an intention of scent and of sound is propagated much further than the
material efflux" (275.24–29).

This analysis seems to be postulating above matter itself three, or
possibly four, kinds of subintelligible being: the species "mingled"
with matter and called the "sensible" species; the "attenuated" species that flows out of the body informed by the sensible species and
is as it were the "specimen" of that species; and the "immaterial
species" further defined as the "spiritual mode" of the sensible species and paralleled by (though not perhaps equated with) the "intentions" of Aristotelian and Scholastic physics. Above these lowest
manifestations of species or form exist of course the pure Ideas (the
intelligible Species) and their "formulae" or reasons in men's minds
and in the minds of higher souls.

But where on this scale do we locate the idola and simulacra?
And what are their mutual relationships and those of the "attenuated"
specimens, the "spiritual modes," and the Aristotelian intentions?
Ficino's reading of Synesius's model for action at a distance provides us with a clue. The sensible species is entirely restricted in
time as well as space and is more confined in this regard than the
matter it informs, since the matter will become subject eventually
to other forms. But the images that flow out of such a confined
species are far less restricted and extend a greater distance than
either their parent species or their matter; they can even extend "for

a certain interval of time." Such images are of two kinds. The Lucretian simulacra or Epicurean idola are more material or still retain a degree of matter in them and are therefore to be thought of as "material effluxes." The Platonic idola, however, are wholly immaterial or spiritual and can exist independently of their source both for a while in time and out to a certain distance. They resemble, though they apparently are not to be equated with, what the Aristotelians call the "intentions" of smell and sound—that is, the refined images of the "material effluxes" that the phantasy transmits to the reason for it to refine still further into thoughts. Ficino seems to imply that although such spiritual idola are normally so attenuated as to be invisible, nevertheless, by the cunning use of reflective surfaces that trap, rejuvenate, and strengthen them, they can on occasion be rendered visible.

On such occasions, however, the reflective surfaces in effect turn the idola back into "material effluxes," that is, into Lucretian simulacra; or at least they "thicken" or "make more weighty" as it were their attenuation, render them closer to their source in the sensible species, and thus blur the distinctions between spiritual, radial, and materially effluent images. At all events, given the restrictions in time and space for even the most attenuated idola, the process, the ultimately magical or demonic process, of capturing and manipulating both the simulacra and the wholly spiritual idola is an exceptionally delicate one and requires that the magician choose his time and place with care and expedition. Even then, the successful operation will depend not so much on the magician's own lore and skill as on the physical conditions governing the origin of the images; and it will always be subject to the pressure of passing time, to the fading power and ultimate decay of both kinds of images when far from their origin.

Ficino now returns to the question of capturing the simulacra: "Just as radial images, which are so to speak empty (*vanae*) when elsewhere, are restored in mirrors, so such simulacra, which are so to speak torn apart from each other (*divulsa*) when elsewhere, are thought to be collected together and reformed in the animate and phantastic spirit as though in a mirror of their own." And he suggests the analogy with the characters on the front of a closed book which disappear when the book is opened but reappear directly it is closed (275.30 ff.). Here Ficino supplies us with the missing key to the whole scheme, namely what in either a man or a demon is somehow equivalent to a mirror. The radial images, being purely visual, can be reflected by the naturally magical power of a plane mirror or focussed by one that is convex or concave. The simulacra, however, can only be reflected or focussed in "the animate and phantastic spirit" (275.32), that is, in the *spiritus phantasticus* of Neoplatonic pneumatology and more particularly for Ficino of Synesian oneirology. This vaporous spirit may vary in shape and assume convex or concave (or indeed conical) forms, and, like the surface of water, serve as a living mirror to trap and focus the simulacra (though, like a mirror presumably and depending on its shape, it too must reverse the relationship of right- to lefthandedness). Since this spiritual envelope even in its densest, most vapor-laden form is thought to extend beyond the limits of our elemental body, the bodily senses can on occasion perceive phenomena that seem to us to be outside the body but are in actuality being mirrored by our spirit. Hence the apparently "objective" reality of many occult and demonic experiences that are being assembled and focussed, and not merely perceived, by our spiritual vehicle.

At this point we should recall the complex relationship between the faculty of the phantasy or imagination and that of the *spiritus phantasticus,* a relationship essentially of power to instrument. On the one hand, we have the vehicle focussing the scattered simulacra as they stream through the air, even in darkness; on the other, we have the driver of that vehicle. Ultimately this is a soul (our own or that of a more powerful being), but proximately it is the phantasy itself, potentially any phantasy, but preeminently that of a magician. Such a phantasy can strengthen the simulacra and redirect their flow by using its spirit as the most subtle and effective of mirrors. Hence it can produce various real and imagined effects at a distance. Furthermore, since the demons also possess these mirroring *spiritus phantastici,* indeed possess them in a more eminent and potent degree, they too can perform similar magical and illusory effects. Once again we should recall that a logical consequence of the whole scheme is the controversial notion embraced, for example, by Avicenna that one phantasy can affect another: that a more powerful imagination, be it of a demon or a mage, can mold the images that strike our spirit and hence our phantasy or can reflect others onto it. Even so, this kind of enslavement is limited to the sublunar realm, and it is limited too by the transitory life of all images, of all half-species. The magician's power to function using his vaporous spirit as a powerful reflecting mirror is therefore as passing as it is real, and the same is fortunately true of the still more potent imaginations of the demons, the lords of the mirror world.

However, Ficino obviously does not wish to elaborate upon these lines of argument since he is apprehensive of appearing to be an advocate of what Prospero was to designate a "rough magic." He therefore concludes this remarkably suggestive chapter by tossing out, in a manner that had become habitual with him over the years, a number of speculations and suggestions for further inquiry as if they were matters that he could not spare the time to go into at that moment:

I set aside the problem of how some things are affected by others by way of the efflux and the conflux of the idola, and how imaginations may be moved through these idola by absent things almost as though they were approaching us, and how dreams occur. If the idola have any power at all, and to the extent that they endure as material effluxes, then it is likely that they affect the spirit naturally. But to the extent that they issue (*evadere*) as spiritual effluxes, then it is likely that they affect the soul by way of knowledge, and are thus in harmony with (*congruere*) the imagination in the same way as radial images are in harmony with the eye (277.3–10).

Ficino is asserting that our imaginations can be moved by distant or even absent objects because of the power that their images exercise over us. Nevertheless, he seems happier to assume that this happens in dreams, even though the theory allows for such "moving" of our imaginations at all times and not just in dreamlike states of suspended consciousness such as occur in trance or syncope. It is interesting to see him distinguishing between "efflux" and "conflux," the first signifying the initial issuing forth of the idola, radial and material alike, from the sensible species, the second their being refocussed and strengthened in the mirrorlike spirit under the power of the imagination. Once again, he is also distinguishing between the simulacra or "material effluxes" which, as vaporous but still material half-species, would have a natural, that is, a material, effect upon the vaporous nature of our own spirit, and the "spiritual" idola that do not impinge so much on our spirit, even in its purest or most rarefied form, as on the lowest faculty of the rational soul, that which governs the spirit, the phantasy or imagination. Even more significantly, they affect this faculty as if they were thoughts, not *naturaliter* but *cognobiliter*. This is surprising, given the fact that in the medieval faculty-psychology Ficino inherited and usually accepted, at least for the inferior faculties where Aristotelian rather than Platonic notions prevailed, the imagination is the processor of images, not of thoughts, and passes on images in a refined form as intentions to the higher faculty of the reason. The spiritual idola specifically, however, are the proper objects of the imagination, and there exists a perfect harmony or agreement between them. They provide it with a kind of knowledge, the opinions that we form about the material world and check against the intuited knowledge that we possess innately of the intelligible world.

At this point it is appropriate to ask about the relationship, if any, between the idola of our inquiry and the soul's *idolum,* a faculty that Ficino derived in the first place from his reading of Plotinus and particularly of the *Enneads* 1.1.5–12, and that would seem at first glance to be the perfect receptacle of the idola. Ficino's ideas concerning the idolum are not consistent, as is often the case with some of the technical terms he encountered in Neoplatonic discourse. In the concluding chapter of his authoritative study of Ficino's philosophy, Professor Kristeller deals with the idolum in a section devoted to the parts of the soul.[43] The three higher faculties of the soul in men in descending order are: the *unitas* (though it is not strictly speaking a faculty but "a privileged element within the *mens*"),[44] the *mens,* and the *ratio.* Inferior to the *ratio* is a group

---

43. *Philosophy of Ficino,* pp. 371–375.
44. Ibid., p. 369.

of faculties which Ficino collectively calls the idolum.[45] In descending order again the faculties in this group consist of: the *phantasia* or *imaginatio*, the *sensus*, and the *vis vitalis* or *nutritiva*. For men the rational soul consists of the three higher faculties and of these faculties constituting the idolum. Beneath the idolum we find the spirit or vehicle in its three states of purity as aethereal, purely airy, and mist-laden. At the bottom of the scale we reach the elemental body and infused through it the *natura* or *complexio vitalis*. Ficino usually thinks of this "natura" in man as the irrational soul,[46] though in beasts, which do not possess of course a rational soul, the irrational soul must consist apparently of the nature plus the idolum,[47] presumably without the attendant spirit vehicle, at least in its threefold form. This might seem straightforward enough, and for men at least the idolum is preeminently the faculty of the phantasy or imagination,[48] the purveyor of refined images to the faculty immediately superior to it, the reason. Such is the scheme outlined in Ficino's *Platonic Theology* books 6, 7, 8 and above all 13.2,[49] which serves as the foundation of Kristeller's analysis—properly so, given the authority and centrality of the work in the articulation of Ficino's philosophy.

However, Kristeller also notes a recurring and confusing Ficinian definition of the idolum as the image (*simulacrum* again) of the rational soul cast or reflected onto the aethereal body of the spirit in a manner that parallels the reflection of the *natura* onto the earthly body. Moreover, this *simulacrum* gives life, is indeed a kind of life containing within itself "the seeds of all qualities and motions that are unfolded in the body by the soul," as Ficino argues in the *Platonic Theology* 13.2.[50] Kristeller cites two passages from the *Platonic Theology,* which define "the life impressed by the Soul upon the aethereal vehicle as upon an eternal mirror" as something that

---

45. In his *Platonic Theology* 13.2 (ed. Marcel, 2:209–210), Ficino calls it "the foot of the soul." See Trinkaus, *Image and Likeness,* pp. 476–477.

46. Kristeller, *Philosophy of Ficino,* pp. 370–371.

47. Ibid., p. 385. See also my *Platonism of Ficino,* pp. 219–220.

48. See chap. 4, n. 7 above.

49. Ed. Marcel, 2:207–210.

50. Ed. Marcel, 2:207.

"always accompanies the impressing Soul" in contrast with the life
that the *natura* impresses upon the earthly body, which is subject
to mortality. The ancient theologians, furthermore, had not claimed
that "the rational part of the Soul is directly inherent in the vehicle, but that the rational Soul . . . sends into the vehicle an animat-
ing act, which we have often called the *idolum* of the Soul. . . . For
as the light of the moon in a cloud produces paleness out of itself,
so the Soul produces in the celestial body the *idolum* as a comet
produces its tail."[51] The idolum in this usage is thus not so much a
faculty as the activity of the rational soul that gives life by impressing the aethereal spiritous body with life. At the same time,
still more confusingly, it serves a vital epistemological function as
the mediator of images derived from sense perception which it transmits to the reason. Finally, it has, as we have seen, a critical role
to play in the realm of the demon, the magician, and the sophist, a realm which they inhabit neither in the aethereal vehicle nor
in the elemental body but in the airy spirit in either its pure or
moisture-laden forms. In such spiritual states the phantasy itself,
like other faculties, is no longer localized but common to the entire
spiritual vehicle as the *sensus universus*.[52] Hence the vehicle may
serve as a perfect instrument for the phantasy, a perfect mirror upon
which the idolum, itself the image of the rational soul, can project
images in dream or waking vision; and a mirror through which as
through a window it can receive the sensations it will turn into
images and thence into intentions. The vehicle thus serves the
teasing double function of the Renaissance glass as both mirror and
window: one can look through it and at it and sometimes both at
the same time, with the uncanny but nevertheless familiar effect of
double imaging.

As the umbrella term for the lower faculties, the idolum has therefore little immediate connection with the quite distinct theory of the
idola. Nevertheless, as "a vivifying act" imparted to the aethereal

51. *Philosophy of Ficino*, pp. 371–372, citing *Opera*, pp. 149 ff., and 404 ff., i.e., the
end of chapter 13 of book 5, and chapter 4 of book 18. In Marcel's edition they are to be
found in 1:208–209, and in 3:193–196. For 18.4, see also my *Phaedran Charioteer*, pp.
230–235 (text and translation), and *Platonism of Ficino*, pp. 218–220 (analysis).
52. It is so defined in the *Phaedrus* Commentary, summa 11 (ed. Allen, p. 139).

vehicle, the act itself implying preeminently the gift of life and moreover of an "irrational but immortal" life, it raises a number of speculative possibilities. Not least is the possibility that such an act consists of flooding the vehicle with idola, the idola now being images of the formulae of the species in the reason and the idolum itself an "image" of the rational soul. Underlying this second quite distinct if not contradictory conception of the idolum is again the notion of light: the paleness, in Ficino's own image, that the moon's splendor casts onto a passing cloud, or the head of a comet onto its tail. For the act of life is conceived of in terms of being illumined. The whole theory of the idola indeed implies light and its manipulation, concentration, and reflection. Ficino probably thought of the idolum as the faculty that operates precisely at that mysterious ontological point of transition where intelligible becomes sensible light, where the light of Truth, having already entered our intellectual eyes, enters our physical eyes as the light of the Sun. Certainly, the knot that the *Republic* had tied in books 6 and 7 between the twin notions of knowing and seeing and of truth and light makes a transitional zone necessary and inevitable. The idolum as the phantasy operates precisely at that zone; and the idola are precisely those mysterious entities which mediate between ideas and images like the Aristotelians' intentions. Attenuated forms, not fully embodied ones, they flow out of bodily forms and pass through the eye and on into the spirit and thence to the phantasy. As such they possess as it were an equivocal life.

These are speculative possibilities that Ficino failed to elaborate here, but they collectively add up to a theory of influences, in the older astrological sense, that has radical implications for magic theory. It suggests a kind of magic that should be distinguished from, if subordinated to, the higher magic he had discussed in the *De Vita* and that involves the stars and the star demons.[53] In the

---

53. I realize that this is a novel claim, but I believe we have hitherto dismissed wonder-working through illusions and images too easily, as if for Ficino it were a simple minor magic. Illusions and shadows may indeed be the work of thaumaturges rather than theurges (for which see Copenhaver, "Iamblichus, Synesius and Ficino," p. 449), but they are nevertheless, as Ficino's analysis of the *Sophist* demonstrates, exceedingly complex ontologically (and astrologically!) and require a correspondingly complex thaumaturgy. We have hardly arrived at the threshold of understanding this unfamiliar dimension of his thought.

Platonic Theology 13.2 Ficino had asserted that the idolum connects us with Fate as the *mens* with Providence and the *natura* with universal Nature, the *ratio* as the peculiar faculty of the soul being free to ally itself "now with this faculty, now with that."[54] When it allies itself with the idolum and the nature, it falls prey to sensations and the distractions they occasion. In doing so it becomes enmeshed not only in the world of sensible things but in the more mysterious Fate that governs our illusions, those of our waking as well as our sleeping lives. It becomes the victim of the sophistry that trammels the phantasy rather than the reason and that rules over the haunting quasi-dialectic of dreams and images. Only later, when this dialectic was transformed into the Romantic and then the Freudian theories of the workings of the imagination, could the persistent sense of the presence of something external about images be wholly exorcised. For Ficino, however, the idola, like so much else in the *Sophist,* were equivocally real, equivocally in possession of being and its attendant not-being. As such they constituted an absolutely vital component in his worldview and in the complex pneumatology, demonology, and various magics that it embraced with such guarded but enduring fascination.

---

54. Ed. Marcel, 2:209–211. See Kristeller, *Philosophy of Ficino,* p. 375.

Epilogue

From our viewpoint the *Sophist* is clearly concerned, apart from the important but qualified admission of the sophist's role sometimes as a purger of intellectual error, with an essentially negative figure, the venal deceiver. Ficino concludes his *Sophist* Commentary by defining him in Plato's original terms as "the ironic imitator" (268A7), who possesses "great duplicity in himself." While some sophists are "cowards" (*ignavi*)[1] and can therefore be suddenly detected and seized, others are "extraordinarily crafty and adroit" and can elude capture for a long time. But the ordinary sophist, for all the appearance of being wise, is essentially "ignorant" (as Plato suggests at 268A3–4); he is a "craftsman and juggler of phantasms" (*phantasmatum fictor et praestigiator*) and a greedy and ambitious refuter (*redargutor*).[2] Long ago, in the *Philebus* Commentary 1.28, Ficino had accused him of exercising the worst vices of the "rival discipline" that passed either too rapidly or too slowly from the One to the many and captivated the adolescent mind with its destructive ingenuity. For the sophist fails to enumerate the species and their subdivisions and thus to understand the Platonic Ideas and their crucial role as a finite many in mediating between unity and multiplicity.[3] Without the Ideas he cannot exercise dialectic, the "coping stone of the sciences" (*Republic* book 7, 534E), and is therefore a deceiver not a teacher, a profane poet perhaps but not a philosopher.

Yet Neoplatonic assumptions about all the dialogues and their themes compelled Ficino to entertain, at least in part, a positive interpretation that had to be the more subtle as the superficial in-

---

1. One should resist the temptation to emend to *ignari*.
2. Ficino is echoing the Stranger's summary definition at 268C8 ff. Cf. Ficino's *Phaedrus* Commentary, summa 24 (ed. Allen, p. 167), "sophista philosophum simulans."
3. Ed. Allen, pp. 260–263.

tention of the dialogue so obviously militated against it. The principal subject of one of Plato's masterworks, his tour de force of ontology, could not have been the wretched human sophist, therefore, though he was assuredly one of the lesser concerns. It was far more intriguing and appropriate that it be a figure as mysterious as the sublunar demiurge, the sophist deified and paradigmatized, and to whom one could attribute sophistries possessed of some measure of truth, some measure of authentic imitation of the intelligible sublime.[4] To accept such an elevated interpretation was effectively to justify Melissus's parricidal attack on Parmenides' precipitate distinction between being and not-being, and to accept his contribution to the edifice of Platonic metaphysics—indeed, to indicate the degree to which that metaphysics had gone beyond the great Eleatic and achieved a more perfect account of reality and of man's amphibious existence between opinion and knowledge. That the philosopher, that Love, that Hades or Poseidon or a hybrid Hades-Poseidon, that Jove himself were all sophists was too striking and profound a mystery for Ficino to reject out of hand, even if he was willing to accept the Alexandrian designation of the *skopos* as concerned with being. Nevertheless, to take up these Proclian mysteries, even in part, required a mastery of Platonic sophistry, just as an understanding of the ontological subtleties required a mastery of Platonic diaeresis. The ideal interpreter must be able to accommodate the two in the greater discipline of Platonic dialectic.

We should bear in mind that many of Ficino's references to the *Sophist* prior to the *Sophist* Commentary itself draw attention to its dialectical method. In another commentary, the Commentary on the *Parmenides,* Ficino propounds an interesting variation on the theme of dialectic by arguing that Plato and his predecessors in the "Platonic" tradition of *prisci theologi* had made use of dialectic sophistically in order to protect the mysteries from the insolence of the professional sophists. In the proem he writes, "It was the custom of Pythagoras, of Socrates, and of Plato to everywhere conceal the divine mysteries in figures and veils, and modestly to hide their

---

4. Ficino, moreover, was not alone in entertaining the notion of a sophist-demiurge. In his *Commento* (ed. Garin, p. 548), Pico observes that the ancient Platonists were accustomed to referring to "the maker of sensibles" as a sophist.

wisdom from the insolence of the sophists: to jest in seriousness and to play in great earnest."[5] The philosophers, in other words, succeeded in out-sophisting the sophists by dissimulation.[6] All this suggests again a much more complex relationship between dialectic and sophistry, and between the philosophers and the greater sophists, than might first appear: not opposition so much as the just appropriation by philosophy of all that is best and meaningful in their sophistry. In a way, the higher sophistry emerges as a propaedeutic to philosophy and thus as the first legitimate step in a triadic process that goes, as Plato had first suggested, from the sophist to the statesman to the philosopher. The key to its proper mastery is, ironically, the dialectical method, which is both discussed and amply demonstrated in the *Sophist,* where Plato sets out to trap the base sophist dialectically, to cast a modest net about his temerity and arrogance.

In this elevated interpretation of the dialectical *Sophist,* Ficino was careful to insist upon just one reservation. While it is true that the *Sophist,* along with the *Statesman* and the *Philebus,* treats of "divine matters" in conjunction with consideration of the "art" of dividing and defining, the two "inferior skills" in the exercise of dialectic, Ficino nevertheless declares in the proem to his *Parmenides* Commentary that the *Parmenides* is superior because it treats of divine matters in conjunction with a higher dialectical skill, the "art" of demonstrating.[7] For this art, chapter 34 of that Commentary declares, enables the highest dialectical skill, the power to resolve

---

5. *Opera,* p. 1137.2, "Pythagorae, Socratisque et Platonis mos erat ubique divina mysteria figuris involucrisque obtegere, sapientiam suam contra Sophistarum iactantiam modeste dissimulare, iocari serio et studiosissime ludere." See my "The Second Ficino-Pico Controversy," pp. 437–440. For the larger context of Neoplatonic "veiling," see Wind, *Pagan Mysteries,* introduction, chap. 1, and conclusion.

6. An interesting pointer to this ambivalency is the view of Aristotle propounded by Ficino's elder contemporary, the influential Renaissance scholar and teacher John Argyropoulos (c. 1410–1487). Argyropoulos, who was an accomplished translator and sympathetic expounder of Aristotle's works, regarded Aristotle's critique of Plato's theory of Ideas as merely an exercise in sophistic even as he recognized that Aristotle hated the sophists intensely! See Field, "John Argyropoulos and the 'Secret Teachings' of Plato," pp. 317 and 320–321. Perhaps it is not entirely incidental that Botticelli, the painter most imbued with Ficinian concepts, was described by Vasari as a *persona sofistica* (as noted by Wind, *Pagan Mysteries,* p. 126)!

7. *Opera,* p. 1137.2, "Divisivam [artem] quidem et diffinitivam in *Philebo* et *Politico* atque *Sophiste,* demonstrativam in *Parmenide* similiter copulat cum divinis."

(*resolutoria facultas*), to lead us directly to an understanding of the Ideas in Mind itself.[8] While the *Sophist* certainly revels in distinction-making and the requisite divisions and subdivisions and terminates with a successful definition of the base sophist, it only looks towards the philosopher's higher arts of demonstration and resolution, the focus of the *Parmenides*. It thus remains, like the other dialogues, an ancillary work. In the light of its important ontological doctrines, however, it is ancillary only to the *Parmenides*.

This position in the implicit hierarchy of the Plato canon is underscored by an important letter that Ficino wrote as a preface to his *Commentaria* edition of 1496 and addressed to Niccolò Valori, his ardent young disciple, the *Commentaria*'s dedicatee, and a future Florentine statesman.[9] This concludes with a rationale for the arrangement (*dispositio*) of the commentaries in that edition, an arrangement which, he says, follows that of the universe itself. The *Parmenides* is treated first because it deals with the universal principle, the One; the *Sophist* next because it deals with being and not-being and thus with the second hypostasis, Mind; the *Timaeus* third because it deals with the natural world; the *Phaedrus* fourth because it blends consideration of matters divine with matters natural and human; and the *Philebus* fifth and last because it too blends matters divine, natural, and human, but has a briefer discussion of matters divine than the *Phaedrus* and is less divinely inspired.[10] I

---

8. *Opera,* p. 1152, "concludemus per divisionem, definitionem, demonstrationem nos proprie ad cognoscendas ideales formulas pervenire in intellectibus post primum expressas. . . . Ideas autem intelligibiles, primas scilicet species in mente prima, quoniam a compositione motuque distinctissimae sunt, non per illos dialecticos gradus, qui in compositione motuque versantur, statim posse cognosci, sed post eiusmodi disiunctiones, quae propinquius ad ideales formulas ducunt, purissimam in nobis mentem ideas iam primas per simplicem intelligentiam intueri, ad quam sane resolutoria facultas potius quam definitiva, vel divisiva, vel demonstratio confert." In the *Philebus* Commentary 1.23–25 Ficino gives a detailed analysis of Platonic dialectic and at one point seems to elevate demonstration (ed. Allen, pp. 226–229; cf. pp. 33–34)! For Proclus's complicated analysis of Platonic dialectic, see his *In Parmenidem* 5.980–1017 (ed. Cousin; tr. Morrow and Dillon, pp. 332–367, with Dillon's comments on pp. 324–329). For the Renaissance, see N. W. Gilbert, *Renaissance Concepts of Method* (New York, 1960), pp. 24, 104–105.

9. In the *Opera* it appears on p. 1136.2 immediately after Ficino's epitome for the *Euthyphro* and prior to his *Parmenides* Commentary. Note that Ficino also dedicated the tenth and eleventh books of his *Letters* to Niccolò; see Kristeller, *Supplementum* 2:353.

10. *Opera,* p. 1136.2, "Nunc vero quinque nobis perpetuo commentaria in primis disponenda videntur, in quorum dispositione, si sequimur ordinem universi, primum erit in

have suggested elsewhere that this is, to a certain extent, an *ad hoc* arrangement designed to justify the fact that Ficino had only found time to work up materials for the five dialogues in question: and it leaves aside the separate appearance in the same book of the treatise on the fatal number of the *Republic* book 8 and the publication elsewhere of the *De Amore,* the acclaimed commentary on the *Symposium.*[11] Even so, it is interestingly justified, and it pairs the two "metaphysical books," placing the *Sophist* second only to the great capstone of the whole Platonic canon, the *Parmenides,* "that heavenly work in which Plato seems to have excelled even himself and which he appears to have brought forth in a divine manner from the sanctuaries of the divine mind and from philosophy's innermost shrine."[12]

That the *Sophist,* one of the less familiar dialogues for the majority of readers now who are not analytic philosophers, was accorded such eminence has important ramifications, most obviously for an understanding of Proclus's profound impact on the Renaissance by way of Ficino's mediation. More immediately, however, it should alert us to the fundamental reorientation that is required of anyone who wishes to arrive at a full understanding of Renaissance Neoplatonism but who comes to its study armed only with the Burckhardtian, but still prevalent, assumption that the *De Amore* conveys the essence of Ficino's philosophy. Certainly, Ficino made an

---

Parmenidem, tanquam revera primum, de ipso videlicet uno rerum omnium principio tractans; secundum in *Sophistam* de ente disputans et non ente. Hos autem libros metaphysicos atque divinos *Timaeus* physicus sequi debet. Quartum vero locum teneat expositio *Phaedri; Phaedrus* enim divina cum physicis humanisque permiscet. Quintum autem enarratio habeat in *Philebum*; nam, etsi *Philebus* etiam quodammodo haec miscet omnia, *Phaedrus* tamen in hoc ordine prior erit, ob longiorem videlicet divinorum disputationem, praecipuumque divini furoris munus *Philebo* divinior. Horum autem commentariorum quinque digestionem sequetur index atque catalogus dialogorum omnium Platonicorum humano quodam ordine deinceps disponendorum."

11. *Phaedran Charioteer,* p. 48n.

12. *Opera,* p. 1136.3 (the argumentum to the *Parmenides* Commentary): "cumque in aliis longo intervallo caeteros philosophos antecesserit, in hoc tandem se ipsum superasse videtur, et ex divinae mentis adytis intimoque philosophiae sacrario coeleste hoc opus divinitus deprompsisse." Cf. Raymond Klibansky, "Plato's Parmenides in the Middle Ages and the Renaissance," *Mediaeval and Renaissance Studies* 1 (1943), 281–330 at 313–314 (reprinted in his *The Continuity of the Platonic Tradition during the Middle Ages* [Munich, 1981]; this preserves the original pagination); also my "The Second Ficino-Pico Controversy," pp. 433–434.

enormous impression on the 1460s with his interpretation of the *Symposium*, but his philosophical stature in later years sprang from the universal recognition that he held the keys to even more arcane and difficult but sublime works from the Athenian master: namely, the *Parmenides,* the *Sophist,* the *Timaeus,* the *Phaedrus,* and the *Philebus,* the five dialogues which, along with the writings of St. Paul and the Areopagite, he devoted the last decade of his life to expounding. Ficino's *Sophist* thus emerges, unexpectedly but unquestionably, as one of the masterpieces of the ancient theology that had culminated in Plato. Most notably, it adumbrates some of the magical themes and preoccupations that were to obsess Platonizing mages, artists, and philosophers for two centuries after Ficino's death as they strove to acquire demiurgic as well as philosophical powers, to become true image-makers under a Moon that Copernicus eventually was to displace in their imaginations as momentously as her brother the Sun, thereby nullifying the whole extraordinary notion of a sublunar demiurge and with it the cognate notion of the demonic sophistry of optical and shadow magic. Perhaps, with his essentially Plotinian preoccupations, Ficino would not have been dismayed. Nevertheless, one must recognize that, for him and for the Florentines he tutored in its mysteries, the *Sophist* was a visionary and, after the *Parmenides,* a definitive work of metaphysics, a work that is distinctly different, moreover, from the one that is admired in the skeptical academy of modern analytic scholarship.

Part II

Marsilii Ficini Commentaria in Platonis *Sophistam* (A Critical Edition with Translation)

Headnote and Sigla

The following is a critical edition and translation of Ficino's *Sophist* Commentary as it appears on folios 53r to 59r in his *Commentaria in Platonem* (Florence, 1496)—the *editio princeps*. It has been collated throughout with the text, albeit frequently corrupt, as it appears on pages 1284 to 1294 of the widely available second edition of Ficino's *Opera Omnia* published in Basel in 1576 (and reproduced by photo-offset in Turin in 1959, 1962, and 1983).

Also edited is the preface Ficino attributed to Proclus. This appears in an authoritative manuscript, the Laurenziana's 82.6, fol. 119v, which contains the first half of Ficino's Plato translations and their accompanying argumenta, and was probably transcribed before 1484 (Kristeller, *Supplementum* 1:xi, clv; and Gentile in *Mostra,* pp. 113–116 [no. 89.1]—see chap. 1, nn. 4 and 8 above). It also appears in the two great editions of Ficino's *Platonis Opera Omnia* published in Florence in 1484 and Venice in 1491; and it was included in the 1576 Basel edition of Ficino's own *Opera Omnia,* while being omitted from the 1496 *Commentaria* edition. Included too is the introduction or argumentum as it appears following directly on the preface in the Laurenziana's MS. 82.6, fol. 120r, and in the 1484 and 1491 Plato editions, and then separately in the 1496 *Commentaria* and 1576 *Opera Omnia* editions. As the authoritative texts I have taken the Laurenziana's for the preface and the 1496 *Commentaria* edition's for the argumentum. Note that the only other fifteenth-century manuscript containing these two introductory pieces is the British Library's Harleianus 3481, fols. 127r–128r, which presents them as separate paragraphs. Kristeller believes, however, that this manuscript was probably copied from the 1491 Plato edition (*Supplementum* 1:xxxii [Lo 1]; *Studies,* p. 159 [no. 5]—see chap. 1, n. 10 above; *Ficino and His Work,* p. 92—see chap. 1, n. 14 above; and "The First Printed Edition of Plato's

Works and the Date of Its Publication [1484]," in *Science and History: Studies in Honor of Edward Rosen,* ed. Erna Hilfstein, Pawel Czartoryski, and Frank D. Grande, Studia Copernicana, vol. 16 [Wroclaw, Poland, 1978], p. 33n). He has shown moreover that a later, a sixteenth-century manuscript containing them, Düsseldorf's Universitätsbibliothek, cod. F. 10, fol. 3r, was certainly copied from the printed edition (*Iter Italicum,* 3 vols. to date [London and Leiden, 1963–], 3:522; *Ficino and His Work,* p. 69). We might note that another important manuscript containing Ficino's *Sophist* translation, the Vatican's Urb. lat. 1317, does not contain the preface or the argumentum. For a translation of the preface, see chapter 3 above; and for the Greek original, see appendix 1. I have consulted the copies at UCLA for the 1484 and 1491 Plato editions (the preface and introduction appearing on sig. n iii r–v and on p. 62 respectively); and the copy at Yale for the 1496 *Commentaria* edition. No manuscript of the Commentary itself is extant.

As is customary, I have omitted all notice of the texts of the Commentary and the argumentum as they appear in the first (Basel, 1561) and third (Paris, 1641) editions of Ficino's *Opera Omnia,* since the third edition is a reissue of the first and both yield authority to the second edition of 1576. The punctuation throughout has been modernized, though the paragraphing is that of the 1496 *Commentaria* text. Contractions and diacritics have been silently expanded and the spelling has been regularized (with the *u/v* and *ae/e* distinctions). Ficino commences each chapter (*summa*) with an *incipit* from his own Latin translation of the *Sophist* in order to indicate his position in the text; very occasionally, however, his wording in the 1496 *Commentaria* edition differs slightly from that in the 1484 and/or 1491 Plato editions. In brackets before each *incipit* I have provided the standard Stephanus designation (the line numbering being that of the Oxford edition of the Greek text by John Burnet, vol. 1, pp. 357–442). For a guide to Ficino's breakdown of the dialogue into chapters, see appendix 2 below.

The following sigla have been adopted: L = MS Laur. 82.6, F = ed. 1484, V = ed. 1491, H = MS Harl. 3481, Y = ed. 1496, and

Z = ed. 1576. A few *o*'s in Y are broken and resemble *e*'s; in the instances where this suggests possible variants in Y, the apparatus will indicate such with a bracketed question mark, though the reader should assume that the Y and Z readings are probably identical.

[1]in *om*. F V   /   Sophisticam Z   [2]a Marsilio Ficino translata *om*. V
[4]Platonem Z   [5]intelligimus Z   [8-9]transmuntator Z   [12]ei *om*. V
[14]in *om*. Z   [16]ipse disponit *om*. H   /   magis Z   [25-26]multiplicem H Z
[26]Eleas Z   /   partem Z   [29]opificum Z   [29-30]in perfectum] imperfectum Z

Praefatio in Platonis Sophistam secundum Proculum a Marsilio Ficino Translata

Sophistam Plato vocat non hominem quendam solum sed etiam amorem, Plutonem, Iovem; et artem sophisticam praeclarissimam dicit. Ex quibus subintelligimus quod nobilius subiectum quam ap- 5 pareat hic dialogus respicit. Est enim intentio secundum magnum Iamblichum de sublunari opifice tractare. Nam est idolorum fictor, purificator animarum, a contrariis rationibus semper separans trans- mutator, et iuvenum divitum mercennarius venator. Dum animas suscipit plenas rationibus a superis venientes, mercedem ab illis 10 accipit, ipsam animalium fabricam, quae fit secundum mortalium rationem. Hic ei quod non est incumbit, quia quae sunt in materia gignit. Et quod revera falsum est diligit, id est, materiam. Simul autem in id quod verum revera est respicit. Est et multiceps, quo- niam sibi essentias vitasque multas vendicavit, per quas varietatem 15 generationis ipse disponit. Idem quoque magus est generatione, dum animas naturalibus rationibus mulcet et allicit adeo ut aegre a generatione amoveantur. Quinetiam et amor magus et natura maga a nonnullis dicitur propter reciprocos attractus atque illecebras, quae secundum naturam procedunt. Nunc igitur omnifariam sophistam 20 declarare vult. Etenim philosophus sophista est, quippe cum coeles- tem opificem et generationis opificem imitetur. Et distinctiva fa- cultas progressum rerum ab uno imitatur, et generationis opifex coelestem opificem, quare sophista est. Atqui et ipse homo sophista; quia magna imitatur, sophista dicitur. Et idcirco sophistam mul- 25 ticipitem appellavit. Eleates hospes repraesentat patrem opificum, supercoelestem et absolutum. Auditores autem opificis intelligen- tias. Ille quidem Iovis, hic naturae angelicae tanquam interpretator ac geometricus. Et quoniam opificium ab imperfecto incipiens in perfectum desinit, hospes ille primum cum Theodoro, deinde per 30 conversionem cum proprio Socrate versatur. Hactenus Proculi, dein- ceps Marsilii.

Marsilio Ficino's Introduction to the *Sophist*

While Plato treats in the *Sophist* of being, the concern of the philosopher, at the same time he treats of not-being, the lower concern
of the sophist. In Pythagoras and Plato God alone is *sophos*—that
is, wise—but the philosopher is God's true imitator while the sophist is the false and ambitious emulator of the philosopher. Plato
adduces six definitions of the sophist. However, one cannot have a
definition without division, for division takes the thing to be defined
and separates it from what do not belong to it, and distinguishes
its class through the differences. Finally, from the differences and
the class together the several species are compounded and defined.
Given all this, and since he is about to define the sophist, Plato first
postulates some extremely precise divisions. He warns us that nobody can discern at all the hidden nature of each thing unless he
has separated it entirely from a foreign quality. Consequently he
uses all his powers to introduce descriptions of being and of not-
being; and he subordinates being to the One, as he also does in the
Parmenides. He enumerates the five classes of being: essence, the
same, the other, rest, and motion. He teaches us that true essence
accords with incorporeals, but imaginary essence with corporeals.
Furthermore, he wholly detests those who deny incorporeals, and
also those who suppose that all things are only moved or are only
at rest. Again, he discusses knowledge and opinion, and true and
false speech, verb and noun, to the extent that it [speech?] seems
to bear on the argument about being itself. Finally, Plato discussed
the sophist along with the philosopher, and, since he had proved
that all the works of nature derive from a divine wisdom imparted
to the world, he concludes the book with a divine judgement [or
sentence], namely that natural things are the works of God. But
shadowy and deceptive things he says are the illusory tricks of
demons. In the same place Plato says that the sophist is hidden from
us since he is enveloped in the shadows of not-being or falsehood.
The philosopher too is equally hidden from us, although for a
different reason; for he is everywhere encompassed by the splendor
of authentic being which is the splendor of divine truth. Thus he
utterly overpowers the gaze of vulgar souls.

Argumentum Marsilii Ficini in *Sophistam*

Dum in *Sophista* de ente disseritur circa quod versatur philosophus,
tractatur interim de non ente ad quod sophista declinat. Apud Pytha-
goram et Platonem sophos id est sapiens solus est Deus, philosophus
autem verus imitator Dei, sophista ambitiosus et fallax philosophi   5
aemulator. Sex Plato sophistae definitiones adducit. Quoniam vero
definitio haberi absque divisione non potest, per quam ab ipsa re
definienda quae ipsius non sunt separentur, genusque ipsius per differentias dividatur, ex quibus tandem simul et genere componantur
species atque definiantur, idcirco Plato sophistam [1285] definiturus   10
exactissimas primum partitiones excogitat, admonens neminem omnino latentem rei cuiusque naturam discernere posse nisi eam penitus
ab aliena qualitate secreverit. Proinde entis atque non entis descrip-
tiones pro viribus affert atque ens, quemadmodum et in *Parmenide,*
subiicit uni. Entis quinque numerat genera: essentiam, idem et al-   15
terum, statumque et motum. Docet veram quidem essentiam rebus
incorporeis convenire, imaginariam vero corporeis. Eos praeterea
qui incorporea negant admodum detestatur, eos insuper qui vel
omnia moveri solum vel solum manere putant. Item de scientia
atque de opinione et oratione vera vel falsa, de verbo et nomine   20
disputat, quatenus ad entis ipsius disputationem pertinere videtur.
Demum postquam de sophista simul ac philosopho disputavit, divina
quadam librum concludit sententia, videlicet res naturales opera
esse Dei, siquidem omnia naturae opera a divina quadam sapientia
mundo infusa probaverat proficisci. Res autem umbratiles et fallaces   25
ait daemonicas esse praestigias. Ibidem et sophistam nobis occultum
esse inquit tanquam non entis, id est, falsi tenebris involutum, et
philosophum pariter occultum esse, quamvis alia ratione, quia videlicet entis ipsius, id est, divinae veritatis splendore undique cir-
cumfusus, vulgarium intuitum animorum prorsus exsuperet.   30

---

¹Marsilii Ficini Commentaria et Argumenta in Platonis *Sophistam*. Argumentum. Z; *Om.* L F V H
²Post *Theaetetum* de scientia, legendus est *Sophista* de ipso ente quod scientiae est obiectum. Dum vero
in *Sophista* de ente, etc. L Z Post *Theaetetum* de scientia, legendus est *Sophista* de ipso ente quod scientiae
est obiectum. Dum vero hic de ente, etc. F V H   ⁸-que *om.* Z   ¹¹petitiones Z   ¹⁴effert Z
¹⁷praeter ea Z   ¹⁸incorpora Z   ²¹ad entis] attentis L F V H
³⁰exuperet H

The Florentine Marsilio Ficino's Divisions and Summaries of the Chapters in the *Sophist*

Chapter 1: Introduction to the dialogue.

[216A1] Theodorus and Theaetetus lead Socrates to Melissus, the Eleatic, a Pythagorean philosopher. Philosophers as a class are divine, it is maintained, and this is unknown to the crowd. The question arises whether and how we may distinguish the philosopher, the sophist, and the statesman.

Chapter 2: The dialogue's arrangement.

[218B5] Melissus undertakes to deal with the true distinction between these three; but first he must define the sophist. He warns them that important and difficult matters must be investigated diligently by way of comparison with less important and easier ones.

Chapter 3: The first division of the arts.

[219A4] Since he had compared the sophist to a fisherman, particularly a fisherman with a hook, he now divides the arts, separating them as a class into the productive art and the acquisitive. The acquisitive he divides again into the art that acquires by way of exchange and the art that acquires by force. The latter in turn can be divided into the manifest art of fighting and the secret art of hunting.

Marsilii Ficini Florentini Distinctiones et Summae Capitum in Sophista

Introductio ad dialogum. Cap. I.

[216A1] Venimus o Socrates, etc.] Theodorus Theaetetusque ad Socratem ducunt Melissum Eleatem Pythagoricum philosophum. Philosophorum genus esse divinum asseritur et id quidem ignotum vulgo. Quaeritur praeterea utrum et quomodo philosophus et   5
sophista civilisque distinguantur.

Dispositio dialogi. Cap. II.

[218B5] Probe loqueris, etc.] Melissus recipit se tractaturum de vera illorum trium distinctione, sed in primis de ipsa definitione sophistae. Ammonet interea magna difficiliaque ex quadam mi-   10
norum faciliorumque comparatione diligenter investiganda.

Prima artium divisio. Cap. III.

[219A4] Age hinc, etc.] Cum comparavisset sophistam piscatori praesertim per hamum, artes iam dividit, ipsumque artium genus in artem efficientem et acquirentem. Acquirens dividitur in com-   15
mutationem et mancipationem. Mancipatio altera patens, scilicet certatoria, altera latens, scilicet venatoria.

Chapter 4: The second division of the arts.

[219D9] The hunting art is twofold: one kind captures inanimate things, another animate. The latter in turn can be subdivided into the kind that hunts after animals that graze and the kind that hunts after animals that move. The hunting of moving animals is twofold: there is either fowling or fishing. And one can fish either with nets or by striking at a fish. The latter method uses either a trident as it were or something similar or a hook.

Chapter 5: The third division.

[221C5] The sophist resembles a person who fishes with a hook. Again, hunting is either on land or on water; and hunting on land hunts after either wild animals or tame ones. Among the tame animals the sophist catches a man not by violence but by persuasion: he promises him virtue for a fee and ensnares rich youths with his promises.

Chapter 6: A description of the sophist.

[223C1] The sophist is a merchant who everywhere amasses a heap of arguments and teachings concerning laws and customs, with this aim: to exchange and sell them for a reward.

Chapter 7: A description of the sophist.

[224E6] The sophist is a greedy artisan who gives instruction in and deals with private quarrels for the sake of profit, and who professes the art of contradiction.

Secunda artium divisio. Cap. IIII.

[219D9] Venatoriam quoque, etc.] Venatoria est duplex: altera inanimata captat, altera animata. Quae rursus est gemina: altera venatur gressibilia, altera agilia. Agilium venatio duplex: aucupium et
piscatio. Piscatio vel retinaculis vel percussione capit. Quae per-
cutit, aut quasi tridente vel simili quodam utitur aut hamo. 5

Divisio tertia. Cap. V.

[221C5] Atqui secundum, etc.] Sophista similis est ei qui pisca-
tur hamo. Item venatio fit vel terra [53V] vel aqua; quae terra vel
agrestia venatur vel domestica. Sophista inter domestica hominem 10
captat non vi sed persuasione, dum virtutem mercede promittit,
iuvenesque divites eiusmodi pollicitationibus suis illaqueat.

Descriptio sophistae. Cap. VI.

[223C1] Praeterea hoc modo, etc.] Sophista est mercator quidam
qui disputationes disciplinasque morum eo consilio passim accumu- 15
lat, ut mercede quadam commutet atque vendat.

Sophistae descriptio. Cap. VII.

[224E6] Videamus iterum, etc.] Sophista est avarus quidam artifex
qui quaestus gratia privata litigia tractat et docet artemque contradictoriam profitetur. 20

²Veneratoriam Z   /   Veneratoria Z   ⁶quodum Z   ⁸ei] illi Z   ¹⁴haec Z
¹⁶quaedam Z   ¹⁹letigi Z

Chapter 8: The fourth division of the arts.

[226A6] The sophist is a various animal and is caught with difficulty. The art of division is twofold: one kind separates like from like, the other the worse from the better. The latter is therefore called purgation. But purgation is twofold: one kind purges the body, the other the soul. Again, that which purges the body purges either the inanimate or the living body. If it purges the living, it is called gymnastics and medicine and the art of bathing; if the inanimate, it is the art of the fuller and the like. But if it is the art that purges the soul, it is called the discipline of reason.

Chapter 9: Ignorance is like deformity, depravity is like disease.

[227C10] Just as evil in the body is twofold—deformity in the external limbs and illness in the humors—so there are two kinds of depravity in the soul. In the cognitive part dwells ignorance, a disgraceful condition like deformity; but in the affective part dwells wickedness like an illness. As with the body gymnastics is the remedy for deformity and medicine for disease, so with the soul instruction is the remedy for ignorance and judicial punishment for wickedness.

Chapter 10: Ignorance is twofold.

[229B1] Ignorance is twofold: one is the simple kind, the other double. The double kind is when someone thinks he knows what he does not know—this is called stupidity. To remedy the first kind we have instruction in the arts; to remedy the second, the discipline of refutation. This discipline is itself twofold: one kind draws on education and gentle admonition, the other on severer castigation and refutation. The latter is used against those who do not know that they do not know. The sophist resembles such a refuter, but we should beware of the comparison, for it is extremely deceptive.

Quarta artium divisio. Cap. VIII.

[226A6] Cernis verum, etc.] Sophista est animal varium difficileque comprehenditur. Ars discretoria duplex: una quidem simile secernit a simili, altera deterius a meliore. Haec igitur altera purgatio nominatur. Est autem duplex: una quidem purgat corpus, altera animam. Quae corpus rursus vel inanimatum vel animatum: si animatum, gymnastica et medicina balneatrixque vocatur; si inanimatum, fullonia similisque. Si animam, disciplina rationalis.

Ignorantia similis deformitati, pravitas morbo. Cap. IX.

[227C10] Egregie loqueris, etc.] Sicut in corpore malum est duplex, deformitas scilicet in membris externis morbusque in humoribus, sic in anima duae sunt species pravitatis: in parte quidem cognitiva est ignorantia, quae est turpitudo deformitati persimilis; in parte autem affectiva est im[1286]probitas quasi morbus quidam. Et sicut circa corpus adversus deformitatem est gymnastica, contra morbum medicina, ita circa animum, adversus ignorantiam est doctrina, adversus improbitatem iudicialis animadversio.

Ignorantia duplex. Cap. X.

[229B1] Doctrinam vero utrum, etc.] Ignorantia est gemina, altera quidem simplex, altera vero duplex, quando scilicet aliquis quae nescit scire se putat, quae nominatur inscitia. Illi quidem opponitur artium doctrina; huic autem redargutoria disciplina. Disciplina enim duplex: altera quidem educatio et admonitio lenis; altera severior castigatio atque redargutio, adversus eos scilicet qui nescire se nesciunt. Redargutori autem eiusmodi similis est sophista, sed a similitudine cavendum, nam maxime fallit.

3discretiora Z / simile *om.* Z 12*post* sic *add.* enim Z / cogitativa Z
17indicialis Z

Chapter 11: Six definitions of the sophist.

[231A8] The sophist is defined first as a mercenary hunter of rich youths; second, with regard to the learned studies of the mind, as a merchant; third, again with regard to such studies, as a shopkeeper; fourth, as a vendor of his own inventions concerning studies; fifth, as a disputant with regard to speeches and an ingenious litigant; and sixth, as an apparent purger of the soul who seems to root out the opinions that serve as an impediment to studies.

Chapter 12: The profession of the sophist.

[232A1] The sophist professes in the first place to exercise and to teach the art of contradiction. In this way he drags everything into contention.

Chapter 13: The sophist strives for opinion not knowledge.

[232E6] When the sophist strenuously contradicts in all matters and everywhere teaches, he seems indeed to know everything. But since he cannot know everything, he possesses an opinion, rather than knowledge, about everything.

Chapter 14: A description of the sophist.

[233D3] The sophist is a trickster and imitator who feigns in his speeches certain false images of all that is true. In this way he deceives the ears of the inexperienced in almost the same way that the accomplished painter or sculptor deceives the eyes of boys from afar when he imitates particular animals. But experienced men, like men who take a close look, detect the tricks of both.

Sex sophistae definitiones. Cap. XI.

[231A8] Lubricum porro, etc.] Prima sophistae definitio: venator iuvenum divitum mercenarius. Secunda: mercator quidam circa animi doctrinas. Tertia: circa easdem caupo. Quarta: venditor suorum circa doctrinas inventorum. Quinta: certator quidam circa   5
sermones, artificiosusque litigator. Sexta: purgator quidam apparet animae, dum videtur opiniones, quae doctrinis impedimento sint, extirpare.

Professio sophistae. Cap. XII.

[232A1] Numquid advertis, etc.] Sophista profitetur in primis artem   10
contradictoriam exercere atque docere, per quam omnia trahantur in controversiam.

Sophista opinione nititur non scientia. Cap. XIII.

[232E6] Tu vero, etc.] Sophista, cum in omnibus strenue contra-
dicat atque passim doceat, videtur quidem scire omnia. Cum vero   15
omnia scire non possit, opinionem habet circa omnia potius quam scientiam.

Descriptio sophistae. Cap. XIIII.

[233D3][54R] Ponamus ergo, etc.] Sophista est praestigiator quidam et imitator, qui omnium verorum fallaces imagines quasdam   20
sermonibus fingens ita ferme decipit imperitorum aures, sicut pictor aut sculptor summus animalia quaedam imitans eminus fallit oculos puerorum; periti vero, tanquam comminus inspicientes, fallacias utriusque deprehendunt.

---

¹Cap. viiiii Y   ²sophista Z   ⁸extirpatae Z   ¹⁴Tum Z   ²³communis Z

Chapter 15: The two kinds of imitation.

[235A10] There are two kinds of imitation. One kind looks at something that is true, and, committed to using the true as its exemplar, it fabricates likenesses, just as a painter and others do. The other kind has not yet gazed upon the true and yet strives to fabricate images of it. In the process, however, it produces phantasms that appear perhaps to resemble realities but are not true likenesses. We must put the sophist in the latter kind.

Chapter 16: Whether whatever we imagine is true.

[236D5] Whoever believes or says something seems to be believing or saying something that in a way exists, and therefore in a way to be saying something true. So the problem becomes whether we can rightly maintain that anyone may believe or say what is false and does not exist. This is especially because what appears to us and is as it were presented to our imagination appears too to possess some power and essence. But what is simply nothing, as Parmenides says, possesses no essence whatsoever.

Chapter 17: Something being, something one, and the absolute One.

[237B7] This term not-being cannot signify being; therefore it cannot signify something or some one thing. For the term "something" signifies something being and something one. Note that the three terms, something, and something being and something one, mean the same and are mutually interchangeable. Therefore something one is interchangeable with being. Yet it is not the absolute One. Therefore when they say that something signifies what is one, do not suppose that it is the absolute One, but rather one something, that is, one being. For one being is something one. I have dealt more carefully with these arguments and their corollaries in my commentaries on the *Parmenides*.

Imitationis species duae. Cap. XV.

[235A10] Deinceps cavendum, etc.] Duae sunt imitationis species. Altera quidem rem veram spectans atque hanc ipsam velut exemplar sibi proponens similitudines efficit, ut pictor atque similes. Altera vero rem ipsam veram nondum intuita conatur eius imagines fab-   5
ricare, machinatur vero phantasmata, quae apparent forte similia veris, neque sunt revera similia; hac in parte sophista ponendus.

Utrum quicquid imaginamur sit verum. Cap. XVI.

[236D5] Numquid ipsum, etc.] Qui opinatur vel loquitur aliquid videtur aliquod quodammodo ens opinari vel loqui; ergo et aliquod   10
quodammodo verum. Dubium est igitur, an recte dicatur aliquem opinari vel loqui falsum atque non ens; praesertim quia quod apparet nobis, et quasi imaginationi se obiicit, videtur vim aliquam essen-
tiamque habere, ipsum vero simpliciter nihilum (ut inquit Par-
menides) nullo modo ullam habet essentiam.   15

Ens aliquid, unum aliquid, simpliciter unum. Cap. XVII.

[237B7] Ita prorsus, etc.] Hoc nomen non ens non potest significare ens; ergo nec aliquid, nec aliquid unum. Hoc enim nomen aliquid significat ens aliquid et aliquid unum. Nota has tres dictiones, ali-
quid et ens aliquid et unum aliquid, idem significare invicemque   20
converti. Itaque unum aliquid converti cum ente; non tamen ipsum simpliciter unum. Ubi ergo dicitur hoc ipsum aliquid esse signum unius, ne intelligas ipsius simpliciter unius, sed alicuius unius, scilicet unius entis. Nam ens unum est aliquid unum. Sed de his atque sequentibus in commentariis in *Parmenidem* diligentius agimus.   25

---

¹⁰et *om.* Z   ¹⁴habere] bebere [?] Y   ²⁰et ens aliquid *om.* Z

Chapter 18: Being, not-being, and number. The ambiguous imagination of not-being.

[238A1] Absolute not-being should not be said to be. For what is called in a way being but in a way not-being ought to be called being with the same reason it is called not-being. But since the first number originates with the first being, and number itself principally pertains to essence, and since the one of essence and the many of essence are both in the class of number, it follows that neither one as a number nor many can accord with not-being, just as not-being does not accord with essence. Therefore we cannot correctly think or speak about not-being, since we are forced to go beyond reason and attach to it either one or many. Again, if you declare that not-being can be the subject of opinion or can be talked about, then you are admitting that it exists. But if you declare that it cannot be thought about or talked about, then you are similarly admitting that it exists. If we talk about this not-being itself, however, we will be attaching one fixed species to it. But this is ridiculous. When we say in truth that, if we can have an opinion about not-being, therefore it exists, we must understand that it exists in some way—in other words, that it exists only in the opinion but not therefore that it exists absolutely. For an opinion does not pretend that not-being exists, but makes the judgment that it does not exist. Finally, just as we cannot think about privation without the [complementary] condition of possession, so we cannot consider or speak about not-being without being.

Chapter 19: Speech about not-being is ambiguous.

[239B1] The sophist deals with shadows in speaking of not-being, and, wielding the power of phantastic art, he does not gaze upon things as they truly are, but fashions certain simulacra and appearances of realities. But it is extremely difficult to speak about these simulacra correctly and without contradiction. For to be and to be true are mutually convertible, and being seems to be entangled with not-being in marvellous ways. If we say therefore that a simulacrum

Ens, non ens, numerus, imaginatio non entis ambigua.
Cap. XVIII.

[238A1] Nondum, etc.] Neque ipsum simpliciter non ens debet dici
esse. Neque quod quodammodo quidem ens quodammodo vero non
ens dicitur dici debet ens eadem ratione qua non ens. Cum vero   5
simul cum primo ente primus numerus oriatur, maximeque ad essentiam numerus ipse pertineat, in genere vero numeri sit et eius unum
et multitudo eius, sequitur ut non enti non conveniat vel unum
numerale vel multitudo, sicut nec essentia competit. Non possumus
igitur de non ente recte cogitare vel loqui, siquidem cogimur ei   10
praeter rationem vel unum vel multitudinem applicare. Item sive
dixeris non ens esse opinabile vel dicibile, interea confiteberis esse.
Sive dixeris incogitabile et ineffabile esse, interim esse similiter
confiteberis. Sive dixerimus hoc ipsum non ens, unam ipsi certam
speciem assignabimus. Quod dictu ridiculum. Sed revera, quando   15
dicimus, si non ens est opinabile, ergo est, intelligere debemus
aliquo modo esse, scilicet in ipsa opinione dumtaxat sed non propterea simpliciter est, quoniam opinio non fingit non ens esse, sed
non esse iudicat. Denique sicut privationem non possumus absque
habitu cogitare, ita neque non ens absque ente considerare vel loqui.   20

Sermo de non ente ambiguus. Cap. XIX.

[239B1] De me igitur quis, etc.] Sophista circa non ens versatur in
tenebris, et arte quadam phantastica pollens non res quidem ipsas
veras inspicit, sed simulachra quaedam earum apparentia fingit.
De his autem difficillimum est recte et absque repugnantia loqui,   25
quoniam et ens atque verum invicem [54V] convertuntur, et ens
cum non ente miris modis videtur implicitum. Si ergo dixerimus
simulachrum simile quidem est vero et enti, [1287] neque tamen

---

⁴quodammodo¹] quedammodo [?] Y   ¹²decibile Z   ¹⁴ipsi] sibi Z   ¹⁵dicitur Z
²²quis *om.* Z   ²³pollenes Y   ²⁸quidam Z   /   1278 Z *perperam*

resembles the true and resembles being, and yet is not the true and does not have being, by this manner of speaking we will be compelled to utter opposites as it were. For when we say that it resembles the true but is something other than the true, then we declare in the meantime that it exists and therefore that it exists as something true—in other words, that it is a true image and truly an image. But when we say the simulacrum is not true, we admit too that it does not exist, since the true is interchangeable with what does exist and the false with what does not exist.

Chapter 20: Concerning not-being opinion is ambiguous.

[240C7] The sophist is a clever disseminator of false opinions. The person who has in mind to entertain such false opinions is the person who thinks either that what exists does not exist or that what does not exist exists. But it is doubtful whether anyone can form an opinion about what absolutely does not exist or what is utterly false, since in the opinion about such not-being is comprehended something that beforehand had moved the senses. Moreover, whatever is perceived as a new discovery perhaps is not entirely devoid of what exists and what is true. Finally—I do not know how exactly—we are always compelled to mix something of being with not-being. Otherwise it would not be lawful to think at all.

Chapter 21: How being is mixed with not-being.

[241B4] In the process of trying to define and condemn the sophist, Melissus falls into a number of doubts, and is compelled to examine the dictum of the divine Parmenides, his teacher. The meaning of this dictum he does not contradict; secretly rather he unfolds its terms. Parmenides forbade being to be mixed with not-being—that is, with pure nothing. He also forbade us to affirm anything with the same reason to exist as being and as not-being. Yet in Plato Parmenides himself, when treating of the One, affirms that something exists in one way and does not exist in another, although for a different reason. Melissus accepts this; for he is compelled to mix being with not-being when he confesses that false opinions and

est verum aut ens, cogemur ex modo loquendi quasi contraria dicere. Dum enim dicimus esse simile vero et esse aliud quiddam praeter illud, interim dicimus esse, ergo et esse aliquid verum, id est, imaginem veram atque vere imaginem esse. Dum vero dicimus non esse verum, confitemur quoque non esse, siquidem et verum cum ente et falsum cum non ente convertitur. 5

Opinio de non ente ambigua. Cap. XX.

[240C7] Qua ratione eius, etc.] Sophista est versutus falsarum opinionum disseminator. Falsa vero opinari putatur, qui vel ea quae sunt non esse vel quae non sunt esse putat. Ambigitur autem utrum possit 10 quispiam opinari omnino non ens poenitusque falsum, quippe cum in ipsa eius opinione comprehendatur aliquid quod antea sensus moverat, et praeterea novum quiddam concipiatur inventum quod forsan non prorsus ab ente cadit atque vero. Denique nescio quomodo semper cogimur nonnihil entis cum non ente miscere, alio- 15 quin excogitare non licet.

Quomodo ens cum non ente misceatur. Cap. XXI.

[241B4] Recte in memoriam, etc.] Melissus, dum sophistam definire et improbare contendit, in dubitationes plurimas incidit, cogiturque Parmenidis divini praeceptoris dictum examinare, cuius sensum qui- 20 dem non redarguit, sed clam verba declarat. Parmenides prohibuit ens cum non ente miscere, id est, cum puro nihilo. Prohibuit etiam affirmare aliquid eadem ratione ens atque non ens <esse>. Ipse tamen apud Platonem de uno disputans affirmat aliquid aliquo modo esse, aliquo modo non esse, ratione diversa. Id quidem Melissus 25 accipit, cogitur enim ita ens cum non ente miscere, siquidem confiteatur esse opiniones falsas atque phantasmata, quod quidem Parmenidis sui sententiae non repugnat.

13moveat Z   /   novum] unum Z   18detinire Z   23esse *supplevi*

phantasms exist. But this does not run counter to the opinion of his teacher, Parmenides.

Chapter 22: Opinions about being and the principles.

[242C4] The ancients lightly touched upon the subject of being and shadowed it forth with poetic fictions. Some of them, as perhaps Thales, postulated three prime entities: hot and cold at the extremities with wetness in between, wetness which sometimes harmonized them and sometimes did not. They did not place dryness in the order of the principles; for they considered dryness resulted from the absence of humor or from its condensation. The followers of Anaxagoras asserted there were four elements: two of them, hot and cold, as agents, the other two, dryness and wetness, as patients. Others of the ancients postulated only two of these principles. Heraclitus and Empedocles held the matter of the universe was one but its qualities were diverse. Because of these qualities, it was sometimes in harmony, sometimes in discord. But Heraclitus held that this world's condition almost always resembles a concord with a certain discord, although the condition does not remain entirely the same; for all things are perpetually in flux. Empedocles, however, held that the world's substance always remains the same, but that in one epoch all things are resolved into chaos because of the greatest discord, in another epoch that all are beautifully ordered because of the concord. Thus far the natural philosophers. The metaphysical philosophers, however, the Pythagoreans for instance, set these aside as not truly entities. Instead, they contemplated the first being as the one being that includes the rest. Finally, not-being naturally is unknown. Thus to that extent being too is almost equally unknown.

Chapter 23: On being and the One and the reason of being.

[243C10] Among the elements or classes described earlier, being is the first and most universal. Yet the first principle of things, therefore, which is not an element or a class, must not apparently be called being. For Plato locates the oppositions between the

Opiniones de ente atque principiis. Cap. XXII.

[242C4] Facili disputatione, etc.] Antiqui materiam de ente levi-
ter attigere, poeticisque figmentis adumbraverunt. Alii, ut forsan
Thales, tria entia prima posuerunt: calidum frigidumque extrema,
medium vero humidum, quod quandoque extrema conciliat quan- 5
doque minime. Siccum vero in ordine principii non locaverunt;
contingere enim putabant vel humoris privatione vel eiusdem con-
cretione. Anaxagorici autem elementa quatuor affirmabant: duo
quidem scilicet calorem et frigus ut agentia, duo vero siccitatem et
humorem ut patientia. Alii horum duo tantum. Heraclitus et Em- 10
pedocles unam universi materiam posuerunt qualitates vero diver-
sas, quibus aliquando consonet, aliquando dissonet. Sed Heraclitus
hunc mundi habitum una cum discordi quadam concordia ferme
semper esse consimilem, quamvis non prorsus eundem; omnia enim
iugiter fluitare. Empedocles autem eandem permanere substantiam, 15
sed alio quidem seculo propter summam discordiam in chaos omnia
solvi, alio propter concordiam exornari. Hactenus physici. Metaphysici vero, ut Pythagorici, haec quidem dimiserunt ut non vere
entia. Primum vero ens, ut unum caetera comprehendens, consider-
averunt. Denique non ens naturaliter est ignotum, ens quoque hac- 20
tenus ferme pariter est incognitum.

De ente et uno et ratione entis. Cap. XXIII.

[243C10] De multis quidem, etc.] Inter elementa vel genera superius
enarrata ens est amplissimum atque primum. Non tamen propterea
primum rerum principium, quod nec elementum nec genus est, 25
videtur ens appellandum; siquidem in primo ente oppositiones generum collocat, et differentias idearum, quae a primo, id est, ab ipso
uno, segregat in *Parmenide,* praesertim quia hic ens vel primum
cum non ente commiscet. Ipsum vero unum in *Parmenide* misceri

---

¹Opinione de entis Z   ⁴Thales *scripsi* tales Y Z (cf. Ficini *Opera Omnia,* pp. 1274, 1411)
⁶succum Z   ⁹duo] uno Z   ²²uno, rationis ente Z   ²⁴propter Z

classes and the differences between the Ideas in the first being. In the *Parmenides,* however, he dissociates these from what is first—that is, from the One. In this dialogue especially he mixes even the first being with not-being. But in the *Parmenides* he forbids us to mix the One itself with the not one. Therefore Plato adjudges the One to be simpler and higher than the first being.

Moreover, he supposes that they have already conceded that there is one reason of being in beings. Therefore he argues: You say that heat exists and cold exists. But what is this existence they share? If it is a third thing over and beyond them, then it follows that there are more than two classes. But if it is one of these two, heat say, then the reason of being will be the same as the reason of heating—in which case, being will not accord with cold. Similarly, if the reason of being is said to be the same as the reason of cold, then it will not accord with heat. Finally, if they say that both are being in that the reason of each is the reason of being, then, since this reason is everywhere one, heat and cold will not be two but one.

Chapter 24: Besides the one being there are many beings.

[244B6] Some of the ancients accepted the dictum of the Pythagoreans and principally of Parmenides, namely that all being is one, to mean that whatever of being exists at all is entirely one in number and without any multiplicity of being. Melissus argues against such a perverse interpretation as follows. Whether being and the one are entirely the same or utterly diverse, the two names—that is, being and the one—exist. But names are particular beings; therefore they are many beings. This is especially so because a name is different from the thing it signifies and both are beings. For, unless a name differed from the thing, it would follow that a name is the name of a name; that the name is unique and the name of itself; and that the thing it signifies does not exist unless somewhere it is named.

Chapter 25: On the one prime being and on the higher One.

[244D14] Now [Melissus] touches on the true sense of Parmenides. From the sensible sphere Parmenides devised the intelligible sphere

prohibet cum non uno. Unum ergo iudicat primo ente simplicius
atque superius.

Praeterea supponit quasi concessum ab illis unam esse rationem
entis in [55R] entibus. Itaque sic argumentatur: calorem dicitis esse
et frigus esse, quid igitur est hoc esse commune? Siquid tertium   5
praeter illa, sequitur ut plura genera sint quam duo. Sin alterum e
duobus, puta calor, iam ratio essendi atque calendi erit eadem.
Igitur frigori non competet esse. Similiter, si dicatur rationem entis
eandem esse atque frigoris rationem, calori non conveniet esse. Si
denique dixerint ambo sic ens esse ut utriusque ratio sit ipsa ratio   10
entis, siquidem haec ubique sit una, non duo iam erunt illa, sed
unum.

Entia plura praeter ens unum. Cap. XXIIII.

[244B6] Quid ad eos, etc.] Dictum illud Pythagoreorum praeci-
pueque Parmenidis, scilicet ens omne unum esse, quidam sic accep-   15
erunt ut quicquid usquam entis est sit penitus unum numero, absque
ulla entis multiplicitate. Contra perversam interpretationem eiusmodi Melissus argumentatur: sive ens et unum sit prorsus idem sive
diversum omnino, duo haec nomina sunt, scilicet ens et unum.
Nomina vero sunt entia quaedam; igitur sunt entia plura, praesertim   20
quia nomen est ab ipsa re diversum, et utraque sunt entia. Nisi enim
nomen sit ab ipsa re diversum, sequetur ut nomen sit nominis nomen, unicumque sit nomen suique ipsius nomen, resque ipsa non
sit nisi nominetur alicubi.

De primo ente uno, et de ipso superiore uno. Cap. XXV.   25

[244D14] Quid porro? etc.] Verum nunc Parmenidis sensum tangit.
Excogitavit ille ex hac sensibili sphaera sphaeram intelligibilem,

⁷erat Z   ⁸competit Z   ¹¹una] unum Z   ¹⁴Pythagoricum Z   ¹⁸et] ut Z
¹⁹duo haec *tr.* Z   ²⁵ipso *om.* Z

as the model of this world, and he called it the first and universal being. [In our commentary] on the *Parmenides,* we have talked about how it may be circular and multiple and similar to itself and equal, and what its center is or what its circumference. Melissus reasons thus: This intelligible being itself, although it is one in essence, is nevertheless multiple in essential powers and forms. Therefore above this one that is mingled with multiplicity and is the result of participation exists the absolutely One that participates in no multiplicity whatsoever. In this One there is no multiplicity of forms, no equality, no likeness, no power striving for action, no action demanding power. This is what Parmenides himself argues concerning the One. Therefore, although nothing is more equal [to itself] than the prime being, and nothing is greater or more powerful, nevertheless more eminent than that being is what we think of as the absolutely One.

Chapter 26: Being is totally the same [as itself]; but the One is higher.

[245B4] We must ascend from all individual particulars to the universal whole. But since any particular being is a whole and is composed at least of the finite, the infinite, and the rest that follow, then the first absolute being must needs be the absolutely and primarily whole. It is the origin indeed of the forms and is utterly omniform. Therefore, since it is omniform and equally omniform, it is certainly one by participation. Therefore it is not the absolutely One itself, because the absolutely One cannot be a whole, since a whole necessarily has parts and multiplicity, and these the absolutely One cannot have. Therefore, since the first being is a whole and is multiple and since it receives unity coming from above, the reason of being and the reason of being one must needs be different. We may conclude therefore that the prime being is many beings. Some people say that being itself, because it participates in the One, is utterly one and no longer the whole and the all. These people have already been refuted, yet Melissus continues the refutation as follows. I seek to know whether the whole and the all exists in the nature of things or not. If it does exist, but does so supposedly apart from being,

mundi huius exemplar, illudque appellavit ens primum atque omne. Quomodo vero ipsum circulare sit et multiplex simileque sibimet et aequale, et quid ibi centrum quidve circumferentia, diximus in *Parmenide*. Melissus ita ratiocinatur: hoc ipsum ens intelligibile, etsi unum est essentia, essentialibus tamen viribus atque formis est 5 multiplex. Igitur super hoc unum multitudini mixtum unumque participatione factum extat ipsum simpliciter unum nullius particeps multitudinis. Penes quod nec est multitudo formarum, nec aequalitas, nec similitudo, nex potentia nitens ad actionem, neque actio potentiam exigens; quemadmodum et Parmenides ipse de uno dis- 10 putat. Igitur etsi nihil est primo ente aequalius, nec maius, neque potentius, est tamen excelsius illud quod excogitamus simpliciter unum.

[1288] Ens et totum idem est, superius autem ipsum unum. Cap. XXVI. 15

[245B4] Utrum totum ipsum, etc.] Oportet super quaelibet particularia tota ascendere ad ipsum universale totum. Cum vero quodlibet ens sit aliquod totum, constans saltem ex finito et infinito caeterisque consequentibus, merito ipsum simpliciter ens primum est ipsum simpliciter primumque totum, origo quidem formarum, ac 20 penitus omniforme. Quoniam igitur est omniforme et pariter omniforme, nimirum est participatione unum. Non est ergo ipsum simpliciter unum, quoniam ipsum simpliciter unum non potest esse totum, siquidem totum necessario partes habet atque plura quae ipsum simpliciter unum habere non potest. Itaque cum ens primum 25 sit totum atque multiplcx patiaturquc unitatem desuper venientem, merito entis atque unius ratio est diversa. Unde concluditur ens primum esse entia multa. Siquis autem ipsum ens, ex eo quod participationem unius acceperit, dicat non amplius esse totum et universum sed penitus unum, etsi hoc iam est confutatum, tamen ita 30

---

then being itself will not have wholeness in itself (as we might say) and allness. Therefore it will have none of the ideal forms that are adjudged necessary to the prime being. Therefore, since it is wanting to itself—that is, wanting the condition necessary for itself—it follows that what was called being emerges now as not-being; or it follows at least that many utterly separate beings now exist (since on the one hand supposedly is being, on the other, completely separate, the whole). But if the whole and the all nowhere exist, similarly the being that is the same as the whole and the all will nowhere exist.

Not only had being—that is, eternal being—not been, however, but being could not even have been made. For whatever is made is made by an author, and has both its author's good and its own property (one that degenerates from that good). Therefore it is both multiple and something whole (especially because it would not have been made at any time unless it could have come to be). From this origin it unites power simultaneously with act and unites what follows. But it is said to have been made when it is perfected already as a whole. Therefore what has been made is necessarily something whole. Therefore, if we take the whole entirely away, something cannot come to be or be made. Therefore the eternal essence and a temporal being that is called generation will both cease, unless the whole exists and unless the absolutely One exists, by whose power whatever is is compounded as a whole and made one out of many. From thus being compounded it is born to be truly whole.

Moreover, unless the whole exists, no quantity whatsoever will exist either in dimensions or in numbers or in any degrees of power at all. But if the whole exists—that intelligible and omniform and creative universe—then the greatest possible multitude of essential reasons must needs flourish there; and from that multitude, as from a pregnant mother, the hosts of entities are everywhere born. Therefore being should not be posited as only one or two. For the first being is formally all things. Finally, since it pertains to essence to be both one and to be whole, but since the One itself cannot be whole, the One must needs be other than being and be simpler and higher.

Melissus ulterius instat. Quaero utrum ipsum totum et universum
extet in rerum natura necne? Si extet quidem, sed ut fingitur ab ente
seorsum, tunc ipsum ens non habebit in se totalitatem (ut ita diximus) atque universitatem. Igitur ideales formas nullas habebit, quae
primo enti necessariae iudicantur. Itaque cum seipso, id est, conditione sibi necessaria careat, sequetur ut quod ipsum ens dicebatur
iam non ens evadat, aut saltem ut plura sint entia prorsusque divulsa,
cum hic quidem ens ibi vero totum seorsum esse fingatur. Sin autem
ipsum totum et universum nusquam extet, nusquam similiter erit
ens ipsum quod idem est atque totum et universum.

Non solum vero non esset ens, scilicet aeternum, sed neque etiam
factum fuisse posset. Quicquid enim fit efficitur aliunde, habetque
et auctoris bonum et proprietatem suam inde degenerantem. Est
itaque multiplex ct totum quiddam, praesertim quia non esset aliquando factum nisi fieri potuisset. Ex qua quidem origine potentiam
simul cum actu coniungit et quae sequuntur. Factum vero iam esse
dicitur quando totum iam est absolutum. Itaque quod factum est
necessario est aliquod totum. Quapropter ipso toto sublato non potest fieri aliquid vel esse factum. Cessabit igitur aeterna simul essentia ac res quaelibet temporalis, quae dicitur generatio, nisi ipsum
totum extet, ac nisi extet ipsum simpliciter unum, cuius virtute quicquid est vel fit totum conficitur ex pluribus unum. Ex qua quidem
conflatione nascitur ut revera sit totum.

Praeterea nisi sit ipsum totum, non erit quantitas ulla, vel in di-
mensionibus, vel in numeris, vel in aliqui[55V]bus potentiae gradi-
bus. Atque si ipsum totum extat—universitas illa intelligibilis et
omniformis atque fecunda, merito et illic essentialium rationum
multitudo quamplurima viget, et ab ea velut praegnante entia passim
plurima pariuntur. Non debet igitur ens aut unum aut duo tantum
poni. Ipsum namque primum ens est formaliter omnia. Denique
cum ad essentiam pertineat ut sit unum atque totum, ipsum vero
unum nequeat esse totum, merito unum est aliud quam ens et simplicius atque superius.

²extet²] extat Z   ³⁻⁴in se . . . habebit *om post* habebit *per homoioteleuton* Z   ¹²fit *om.* Z
²¹extet¹] extat Z   ²⁹pariunt Z

Chapter 27: The people who have treated of being and those who have not.

[245E6] All the Pythagoreans indeed treated of true being itself—that is, of eternal substance—and they drew upon both true reason and figurative and poetic language. However, other philosophers treated of what is not true—that is, of what has been generated. Therefore the Pythagoreans did not declare falsehoods about being, but some of them did utter a few things rather obscurely. Wherefore, understand that here the great Parmenides—any Pythagorean indeed—is explained and resolved, not refuted. To be refuted are the natural philosophers, who supposed that the corporeal mass [of the world] alone is essence and who thought that nothing incorporeal at all exists. The Pythagoreans and others like them were the opponents of these natural philosophers. With a necessary reason they conclude that only what is incorporeal and is the proper object of the intellect exists as true being. They confirm this mainly in disputing about the Ideas, as is shown in our *Theology*. But they call the corporeal mass, which is divided endlessly into smallest bits and is dissolvable and continuously flowing, not essence but generation. Finally, we can accept the true reason of essence from them alone.

Chapter 28: The incorporeals alone are the true beings.

[246D4] Melissus argues thus against those who suppose that there only exists a corporeal mass. What is called animate and living body is animate and alive not because of the corporeal mass. Otherwise any body whatsoever would be living. Therefore body is animate and lives through some incorporeal nature, namely through the soul itself. Since the soul is everywhere the mover of the body and everywhere its mistress and therefore far more eminent than the body, deservedly it is adjudged to be an incorporeal substance. This is especially so for the rational soul. It is converted into itself as if it were existing through itself separable from the body, and it has been made capable of wisdom. But wisdom cannot be corporeal since it ascends to incorporeals. I have written at length on these issues in my *Theology*.

Qui vere de ente tractaverint, qui non. Cap. XXVII.

[245E6] Sermones quidem, etc.] Pythagorici quidem de ipso ente vero, id est, aeterna substantia, omnes ratione vera et quidam poetica figura tractabant. Alii autem philosophi de non vero, id est, de re generabili, tractaverunt. Pythagorici igitur de ente non falsa quidem locuti sunt, sed eorum nonnulli pauca quaedam et obscura dixere. Quapropter magnum Parmenidem et quemlibet Pythagoricum hic explicatum et absolutum intellige, non confutatum; physicos confutandos, qui videlicet solam corpoream molem esse essentiam putaverunt, rem nullam incorpoream cogitantes. Quorum qui adversarii Pythagorici similesque necessaria ratione concludunt solum quod est incorporeum propriumque intellectus obiectum verum ens existere, quod maxime de ideis disputando confirmant, ut in nostra *Theologia* patet. Rem vero corpoream, quae in minima sine fine dividitur solubilisque est et continue fluens, non essentiam sed generationem vocant. Rationem denique essentiae veram ab his solis accipere possumus.

Sola incorporea sunt entia vera. Cap. XXVIII.

[246D4] Praestaret illos, etc.] Contra illos qui solam molem corpoream esse putant ita Melissus argumentatur: Corpus quod animatum dicitur atque vivum non per ipsam corpoream molem animatum est et vivit, alioquin corpus quodlibet foret vivum; ergo per naturam aliquam incorpoream, per ipsam videlicet animam, quae, cum sit ubique motrix corporis et alicubi domina ideoque longe praestantior, merito substantia quaedam incorporea iudicatur. Praesertim rationalis anima, quae convertitur in seipsam, quasi per se existens a corpore separabilis, atque fit sapientiae capax. Sapientia vero corporea esse nequit siquidem ad incorporea surgit. Verum de his in *Theologia* nostra latissime.

¹tractaverit Z   ⁶et *om.* Z   ¹²solum quod] solumque Z   ¹⁴in¹] in *om.* Z
¹⁶denique] divinaeque qui Z   ¹⁹praestare Z   ²¹ipsum Z   ²⁶convertatur Z
²⁷sit Z   /   capacax Y

Furthermore, after they have been forced to postulate something incorporeal over and beyond the body—the life at least of the body and the qualities of the soul—and after they have been questioned about what is common both to this incorporeal something and to body by virtue of which both are said to exist, these natural philosophers will reply that what is common is being and essence. They will accept too that one and the same reason of being is present in both—that is, in such incorporeals and in bodies. But if these philosophers are again asked what is this reason of being and essence, they can respond nothing better for the moment perhaps than that it is the prime essence itself of acting in any way howsoever or the power of being acted upon. For to these philosophers this essence necessarily seems to be present both in single beings and in all beings howsoever.

Chapter 29: The true reason of being in eternal things.

[248A4] The Pythagoreans, who maintain that Ideas exist, and the Platonists likewise do not suppose that one reason of being is present equally in both eternal and transitory things. This is because they do not even refer to essence in transitory things but rather to generation, maintaining it to be incontrovertible that a distinction exists between the two. Therefore being does not proceed for them as far as the lowest things; but the One does so proceed. The One therefore is higher than being. But of this elsewhere. In short, being is a term that is predicated only equivocally of both an unmoving and a moving thing, just as the term man is used both of you and of your mirror image. The intellectual soul has communion with essence—that is, with eternal substance—through which communion she knows that essence. But this communion is not a power at all of mutually acting or of being acted upon. For essence is not moved by the soul who knows it; nor again is the soul strictly speaking moved by the essence. But the soul sometimes converts itself to the ideal reasons of that essence, reasons that are coeval with itself. By such conversion and illustration it knows. But there is no power in separated substances which is waiting to achieve a further act in time; rather, such substances always exist in act. Therefore

Isti praeterea, postquam coacti fuerint praeter corpus suspicari aliquid incorporeum, saltem vitam corporis et qualitates animae, in-
terrogati quidnam sit utrisque commune, per quod utraque dicuntur
esse, respondebunt ens scilicet et essentia; accipientque unam eandemque rationem entis ambobus inesse scilicet incorporeis eiusmodi   5
atque corporibus. Si ab istis iterum perquiratur, quaenam sit entis
vel essentiae ratio, nihil forte poterunt in praesentia melius respon-
dere quam essentiam esse primam ipsam agendi quomodolibet vel
patiendi potentiam. Haec enim necessario inesse videtur solis et
cunctis apud eos quomodolibet entibus.   10

Vera entis ratio in aeternis. Cap. XXIX.

[248A4] Ad specierum amicos, etc.] Pythagorici idearum assertores
similiter et Platonici non putant unam rationem entis inesse rebus
aeternis pariter atque fluentibus, quandoquidem nec essentiam quidem in his fluentibus nominant sed generationem, alterum extra   15
controversiam ab altero secernentes. Ideo ens apud illos non procedit
usque ad infima, unum vero procedit; unum igitur ente superius,
sed de hoc alibi. Ens summatim sic aequivoce de stabili et instabili
dicitur, sicut homo de te tuaque imagine speculari. Anima quidem
intellectualis communionem habet cum essentia, scilicet aeterna   20
substantia, per quam cognoscit eam. Sed haec communio non est
potentia ulla invicem agendi vel patiendi.[1289] Neque enim essentia illa movetur ab anima eam cognoscente; neque rursus anima proprie movetur ab illa. Sed anima nonnumquam ad rationes illius
essentiae ideales sibi congenitas se convertit; conversione quadam   25
et illustratione cognoscit. Omnino vero in substantiis separatis non
est potentia quaedam proclivis ad actum ulteriorem temporaliter
acquirendum, sed actu semper existunt. Idcirco definitionem illam
essentiae, quae per potentiam et agendi et patiendi dabatur, in illis
suscipere non debemus.   30

---

¹cocti Z   ⁹Hoc Z   ¹¹aeterno Z   /   xxxix Z   ¹⁵alteram Z   ¹⁸et *om.* Z
¹⁹speculaturi Z   ²²Neque] Atque Z (*sed* Neque *est signum paginae* Z)

we should not accept the natural philosophers' definition of essence as something involving the power of acting or of being acted upon as pertaining to such substances.

Chapter 30: In the reason of true being there is a vital motion and there is rest.

[248E6] Every true—that is, indivisible and eternal—essence has all the perfections necessary for the perfect essence. But these perfections are such that the essence may not only be but also live and understand. For life is the first perfection of essence. And understanding—that is, knowing—is the first perfection of life and the second perfection of essence. This is because essence naturally strives for life, and life proceeds to understanding and through understanding is reflected back into itself and into essence. Therefore every true essence has soul and motion—that is, potency and vital act. It has wisdom besides—that is, the power of understanding and of knowing. It cannot possess understanding except through the soul—that is, through the life that in a way precedes understanding. When we refer to true essence, we mean in the first place the first essence—that is, the prime intellect and the prime intelligible; then we mean any individual and unmoving substance whatsoever. Therefore all the perfections and properties that pertain to true essence exist primarily and in one way in the first essence, and secondarily and in another way in all subsequent to it. But we are currently talking mainly about the first essence. In it, since there is the idea and power of all soul, life, and understanding, accordingly there too formally is every potency for motion. For straight motion is assigned as it were to soul, circular motion to understanding. But understanding cannot be present to anything that is entirely unmoving—in other words, that is inert and ineffective and entirely unsuitable for life. But motion in the prime essence is understood not as piecemeal and imperfect, such as we find in bodies, but rather as full of life, effective, and in immediate progress from this to that. We have dealt with these issues in [our commentary on] the *Parmenides*. Not only does the reason and power of motion dwell in the prime essence, however, but so does the reason of unmoving

In ratione veri entis est vividus quidam motus atque status. Cap. XXX.

[248E6] Quid vero, etc.] Omnis vera, id est, indivisibilis aeternaque essentia habet perfectiones omnes ad perfectam essentiam necessarias. Hae vero sunt ut non solum sit sed vivat etiam et intelligat. Vita enim est prima essentiae perfectio. Intelligentia vero, id est, cognitio, prima quidem perfectio est vitae, secunda vero essentiae, siquidem essentia naturaliter contendit ad vitam, vita ad intelligentiam proficiscitur, per quam in se et essentiam reflectatur. Omnis igitur essentia vera animam et motum, id est, vigorem actumque vitalem habet; et insuper sapientiam, id est, intelligendi vel cognoscendi virtutem. Nec habere intelligentiam potest nisi per animam, id est, per vitam quodammodo praecedentem. Quando vero dicimus essentiam veram, primo quidem intelligimus [56R] essentiam primam, scilicet intellectum et intelligibile primum, deinde vero et quamlibet individuam stabilemque substantiam. Perfectiones igitur proprietatesque omnes ad veram essentiam pertinentes primo quidem et aliter sunt in essentia prima, secundo vero et aliter in sequentibus. Sed nunc de prima praecipue disputatur. In qua quidem cum sit idea virtusque omnis animae, vitae, intelligentiae, ibidem formaliter est omnis vigor ad motum. Motus enim quasi rectus tribuitur animae, sed intelligentiae circularis. Nulli autem rei prorsus immobili, id est, inerti et inefficaci et ad vitam prorsus ineptae, adesse potest intelligentia. Motus autem illic intelligitur non distractus et imperfectus, qualis est in corporibus, sed vividus et efficax subitusque processus ab hoc in illud, de quibus agimus in *Parmenide*. Non solum vero ratio visque motionis est ibi, sed etiam perseverantiae stabilis atque status, si modo idem ibi tenor essendi, vivendi, intelligendi viget. Non enim est seorsum ab identitate status. Omnis igitur intelligibilis intellectualisque substantia, quae sola dicitur essentia vera, excellentem quendam motum habet et statum. Praecipue

---

⁹et *om.* Z   ²⁶ab *scripsi* ad YZ   ²⁷ratio visque] rationisque Z   /   motonis Y
³¹motum] modum Z

persistence and of rest, if only because the same steady course of being, of living, and of understanding flourishes there. For rest is not apart from identity. Therefore every intelligible and intellectual substance that alone is called true essence has both a certain excellent motion and rest. But these exist preeminently in the first essence. Hence perhaps it might seem to someone that the reason of being consists in an excellent potency equally for motion and for rest.

Chapter 31: On the reason of being and of motion and of rest.

[249D9] The Pythagorean view, and at the same time the Platonic, is that while knowledge accords with higher things, for us there is commonly true opinion, and knowledge only for a very few. Therefore in Plato doubt is always simulated but doctrine dissimulated. Therefore successively Melissus everywhere teaches by doubting and little by little corrects and resolves what goes before in what follows. Hence, although in a way it had been truly said that the reason of being consisted in a potency for motion and for rest, yet he adjudges that we must not suppose that the reason of being is the same as the reason either of motion or of rest or of both together. For being is predicated of each separately and of both together. But neither can be predicated of the other or of both; nor can just one be predicated of both. Being therefore is other than and more simple and more universal than motion or rest. For motion and rest succeed to the reason of being as though they were later additions. Nor must we conclude that if being is not yet at rest it is therefore in motion; or that if it is not yet in motion it is therefore at rest. For such a consequence can have power in things that are lower than rest and motion; but it does not have power in the absolutely One that is higher than being or in absolute being that is higher than motion or rest. For both the One and being are not at rest nor in motion, just as rest itself is not at rest nor in motion, and motion itself is not in motion nor at rest. But of this more carefully in [our commentary on] the *Parmenides*. Therefore in its first degree being is in a way virtually devoid of opposites, just as a class is devoid of differences; in its second degree, however, it seems to admit oppositions.

vero haec sunt in prima. Hinc alicui forte videri poterit rationem
entis in excellenti quodam ad motum statumque vigore consistere.

De ratione entis et motus atque status. Cap. XXXI.

[249D9] Pape, etc.] Pythagorica simul et Platonica sententia est scientiam quidem superis convenire; nobis autem opinionem commu-   5
niter veram, paucissimis vero scientiam. Ideo semper apud Platonem
simulatur quidem dubitatio, doctrina vero dissimulatur. Deinceps
ergo Melissus passim dubitando docet, paulatimque consequentibus
antecedentia corrigit et absolvit. Quamobrem, etsi vere quodam-
modo dictum fuerat rationem entis in vigore quodam ad motum   10
statumque consistere, non tamen putandum iudicat rationem entis
eandem esse atque rationem aut motus aut status aut utriusque simul. Ens enim de utrisque et seorsum dicitur atque simul. Neutrum
autem vel de alterutro vel de utroque praedicari potest; nec etiam
de ambobus praedicatur alterutrum. Ens igitur est aliud et simplicius   15
et communius quam aut motus aut status. Rationi enim entis motus
et status quasi posteriores accedunt. Neque concludendum si ens
nondum stat ergo movetur, vel si nondum movetur ergo stat. Eiusmodi enim consequentia in rebus ipso statu motuque inferioribus
vim habere potest, sed in ipso simpliciter uno, quod est superius   20
ente, vel in ipso simpliciter ente, quod his superius est, vim non
habet. Nam et unum et ens ipsum neque stat neque movetur, sicut
nec status ipse stat vel movetur, neque motus ipse movetur aut stat.
Sed de his diligentius in *Parmenide*. Ens igitur in primo sui gradu
quodammodo est ab oppositis absolutum ferme, sicut genus a dif-   25
ferentiis; in secundo gradu oppositiones videtur admittere.

⁵superioris Z   ⁷dissimulator Z   ¹⁴alterutro *scripsi* alter vero Y altero vero Z
²⁶oppositionis Z

Chapter 32: What communion exists in the classes of being and what distinction.

[251A5] In order he signifies that all being is one and many. But since the One itself cannot be many, we must understand meanwhile that the One is more simple than and higher than being. But let us pursue what we have begun. In the *Parmenides* Plato held that unity itself is not multitude, nor the reverse. Similarly, identity is not otherness, rest is not motion, nor vice versa. Nor is any one of these opposite or different Ideas another [Idea]. Yet he maintains in the *Parmenides* that ideals have some sort of communion of participation with each other, and that whatever among us is singularly under one Idea at the same time participates in many Ideas; and finally, that what is one in substance is multiple in qualities.

It has been proved here in the *Sophist* that ideal beings too share in a certain mutual communion. For unless rest and motion themselves have some communication with essence itself, neither rest nor motion will exist as something and [the views of] all the schools will perish: the view that says that all beings are moved; the view that wants all being, since it is one, to remain at rest; the view that asserts the [existence of the] Ideas of all and thinks of them as at rest; and finally the view that believes that all things flow out of a certain one and flow back into the one—whether these things are infinite, as Democritus believed, or finite, as Anaxagoras and Empedocles believed, or whether they flow together in one age and flow away in another, or whether they always do both as it were. None of all this can happen without a certain mixing. Furthermore, were there no communion of things, all propositions would be dismissed. For, when we make an affirmation, we always join something with something; and when we make a denial, we are forced in a way to unite things. For when we say that fire is not water, we signify that each is something; whence they are united in having being, and likewise otherness, separation, and their own existence. For each has these conditions similarly. Plato mentions Eurycles [the ventriloquist], who, it is said, was vexed with an inner evil demon and was accustomed to arguing with himself and to warning himself and others of adversities.

Quae communio in generibus entis, quae distinctio.
Cap. XXXII.

[251A5] Dicamus plane, etc.] Deinceps significat omne ens unum
multaque esse. Cum vero ipsum unum non possit esse multa, interim
intelligitur ipsum unum esse simplicius et superius ente. Sed prosequamur inceptum. Tractatum est in *Parmenide* nec ipsam unitatem
esse multitudinem, neque contra. Similiter identitatem non esse alteritatem, statum non esse motum, neque vicissim. Nec ullam idearum oppositarum vel aliarum esse alteram. Communionem tamen
participationis aliquam idealia invicem illic habere; et quicquid
singulatim apud nos uni praecipue subest ideae simul partici-
pare multas. Denique quod unum est substantia esse multiplex
qualitatibus.
    Probandum est et hic entia etiam idealia mutuam quandam habere
communionem. Nisi enim ipse status atque ipse motus cum ipsa
essentia commertium aliquod habeat, neque status neque motus ens
aliquod erit peribuntque sectae omnes: tumque dicit entia omnia
moveri, tumque vult omne ens cum sit unum stare, tum etiam quae
asserit ideas omnium stabilesque putat, tum denique quae opinatur
ex uno quodam omnia effluere in unumque refluere—sive haec sint
infinita, ut apud Democritum, sive finita, ut apud Anaxagoram et
Empedoclem, sive alio seculo confluant alio diffluant, sive utrumque
quasi semper efficiant. Haec sine mixtione quadam fieri nequeunt.
Praeterea, si nulla sit communio rerum, sermones omnes tollentur
e medio. Sive enim affirmemus semper aliquid cum aliquo copula-
mus; sive negemus interim quodammodo coniungere cogimur. Dum
enim dicimus ignis non est aqua, significamus utrumque aliquid
esse; unde in ente conveniunt, item in alteritate, in separatione, in
existentia propria. Has enim conditiones similiter habet utrumque.
Commemoravit Euryclem, quem ferunt intimo [56V] vexatum dae-
monio sibimet adversari solitum, et adversa sibimet aliisque praedi-
cere. [1290]

¹¹subest] sunt est Y   ¹⁴entia *om.* Z   ¹⁷aliquid Z
¹⁸etiam] entium Z   ¹⁹stabilisque Z   ²²conflant Z   ²⁵semper] super Z
³⁰Euriclem Z   ³¹-que *om.* Z

Chapter 33: What communion and what distinction exists among the classes of being.

[252D2] We must not say that absolutely none of the classes of things are mingled in turn together, as we proved above; nor again that all the classes are equally mingled with all. The latter is proved as follows. If rest were mingled at all with motion or vice versa, either rest would be motion and the reverse, or rest would be moved and the reverse. Both are wrong. Therefore both are mingled with essence, but they are not confounded together. To know what classes accord with others or what classes do not accord, and to distinguish or to unite them correctly, this pertains to the highest knowledge, namely to dialectic which is the first philosophy (which they call metaphysics). The first philosopher is hidden from the eyes of the many because of the dazzling light of being itself. The sophist also is hidden but because of the shadows of not-being.

When individuals have been set aside and sensibles ignored, this dialectic distinguishes being itself—that is, the intelligible—into the ideal reasons of the classes and the species. First it deals immediately with the most special species and reduces them to the closest class. Thus it reduces the Ideas of man and of lion to the Idea itself of animal. Then it reduces the Ideas of animal and of plant to the Idea itself of animate body. Finally, by way of the appropriate intermediary [classes] it reduces them to the Idea of being, the Idea that is founded in the One itself and that is one in all intelligible beings; one, I say, by virtue of the most common, univocal reason. Nor does the fact that this reason is present in some beings first and in greater measure, but in others later and in less measure, prevent it from being univocal. For the reason of number is univocal in all numbers, although it is present earlier and later; and the reason of whiteness is univocal both in snow and in chalk, although it accords more with the one and less with the other. Finally, since being itself is the closest possible to the absolutely One itself and is also the first effect after the One's unity, there must needs be one reason of essence in all beings—that is, intelligible beings. With regard to such beings, however, sensibles are like mirror images with regard to bodies—that is, they are designated with the name of being but

Quae communio in generibus entis, quae distinctio.
Cap. XXXIII.

[252D2] Quid vero? Si, etc.] Neque dicendum est nulla prorsus
rerum genera invicem commisceri, ut est supra probatum, neque rursus omnia omnibus pariter commisceri. Quod ita probatur. Si mis-
cetur status omnino cum motu vel vicissim, aut status erit motus
atque contra, aut status movebitur atque contra. Utrumque falsum.
Miscentur igitur ambo cum essentia, sed invicem minime confun-
duntur. Scire autem quae genera quibus congruant vel non congruant, atque rite distinguere aut unire ad maximam scientiam pertinet:
ad dialecticam quae quidem est philosophia prima quam nominant
metaphysicam. Philosophus primus latet multorum oculos propter
exuberantem ipsius entis lucem. Sophista quoque latet propter non
entis tenebras.

Dialectica hic, individuis praetermissis sensibilibusque posthabi-
tis, distinguit ens ipsum, scilicet intelligibile, in ideales rationes
generum atque specierum; et primo quidem in praesentia species
tangit specialissimas, reducitque ad ipsum propinquum genus, ut
ideas hominis et leonis ad ipsam animalis ideam. Deinde ideas animalis et plantae ad ipsam animati corporis ideam. Denique per media competentia ad ipsam entis ideam et in ipso uno fundatam et
unam in cunctis intelligibilibus entibus; unam, inquam, ratione com-
munissima, sed univoca. Neque rationem univocam esse prohibet
quod aliis quidem entibus prius aut magis inest, aliis autem posterius
aut minus. Nam et ratio numeri in omnibus numeris univoca est,
quamvis prius adsit atque posterius; et albedinis ratio univoca est
in nive atque calce, etsi magis competit atque minus. Denique, cum
ens ipsum sit ipsi simpliciter uni quam proximum, atque etiam sit
primus post unitatem ipsius unius effectus, merito et una est in
cunctis entibus, scilicet intelligibilibus, essentiae ratio. Sensibilia

5

10

15

20

25

30

---

¹⁰aut] et Y   ¹¹nominat Z   ²⁰animatam Z   /   idearum Z
²¹et² *scripsi* tot Y *om.* Z   ²²⁻²³communissima] omunissima [?] Y   ²³rationem *scripsi* ratione Y Z
²⁸proximum] maximum Z   ²⁹unius] animas Z   /   affectus Z

in an equivocal or analogical condition. But Melissus says that the more universal Idea contains the less universal Ideas extrinsically, not because it actually exists somewhere apart from them, but because we think of the formal reason itself of the more universal Idea as existing apart from them as something absolutely absolute, although it is not in reality apart from them. Melissus means too that above the common nature innate in many sensibles there exists the nature which is its exemplar and maker and which is extrinsic to them all. Moreover, Melissus means that above the universal concept, which our reason fabricates after many singulars, there exists in the prime intellect the more universal Idea which has been postulated above and prior to the many less universal Ideas. For the power whereby our reason can think about what is more universal without less universal things derives exclusively from the fact that the more universal is more simple than and prior to less universal things, if not in our invention, then at least in nature and in the prime intellect. In the latter the formal reasons of things, in that they are intellectual, are thus intelligible; and in that they are intelligible, are thus natural too.

Chapter 34: Concerning the five classes of being and a comparison of them.

[254B7] The predications distributed into ten by Archytas the Pythagorean poet and celebrated by the Aristotelians are collected by Melissus into the five most universal classes known only to the Platonists: namely essence, motion, rest, the same, and the other (or identity and difference). These we have discussed in [our commentaries on] the *Philebus,* on the *Parmenides,* and on Plotinus. They are called the elements and classes of universal being: elements, because the prime being and any being whatsoever is produced from them; classes, because they are generally predicated of all things. Being seems to signify something as it were concrete, essence something abstract. Yet often one term is used for the other for the sake of style. In the *Philebus* Plato seems to produce essence from the following four elements as it were: from the One and the many, and from the limit and the infinite. What is there a compounded essence so to speak Melissus accepts here as the one and

vero, sicut speculares imagines ad corpora, ita se habent ad entia, aequivoca videlicet vel analogica conditione entis cognomine nuncupata. Inquit autem Melissus universaliorem ideam minus universales extrinsecus continere: non quia alicubi seorsum illa existat ab istis, sed quoniam ipsa formalis ideae universalioris ratio seorsum ab istis concipitur ut simpliciter absoluta, quamvis ista seorsum ab illa minime. Significat etiam supra naturam communem multis sensibilibus insitam extare naturam huius exemplarem et effectricem extra cuncta. Significat praeterea supra conceptum universalem, quem ratio nostra post multa singularia fabricat, extare penes intellectum primum universaliorem ideam supra multas minus universales ante istas excogitatam. Potentia enim, per quam quod est universalius potest absque minus universalibus rationabiliter cogitari, non aliunde pervenit nisi quia illud his et simplicius est et prius; et si non apud inventionem nostram, saltem apud naturam et intellectum primum—in quo rationes ipsae rerum formales, sicut intellectuales, ita intelligibiles sunt, sicut intelligibiles, ita etiam naturales.

5

10

15

De quinque generibus entis atque horum comparatione. Cap. XXXIIII.

20

[254B7] Postquam ergo, etc.] Quae ab Archita poeta Pythagorico in praedicamenta decem a Peripateticis celebrata distribuuntur, haec a Melisso in amplissima quinque genera solis nota Platonicis colliguntur: essentiam videlicet, motum, statum, idem, alterum (sive identitatem atque alteritatem) de quibus in *Philebo, Parmenide,* Plotino tractamus. Appellantur haec elementa universi entis atque genera: elementa quidem quoniam ens primum et quodlibet ens ex his conflatur; genera vero quoniam generatim de omnibus praedicantur. Ens quidem videtur aliquid quasi concretum significare, essentia

25

⁸insitum Z   /   extare] extra Z   ¹¹multis Z   ¹²ante *bis* Z   ¹⁴provenit Z
¹⁷ita¹] et Z

the first element so to speak of being. To this essence he adds four elements that correspond in a way to the first four. With the reason of the One and the limit are identity and rest; with the reason of the many and the infinite are difference and motion.

First, three elements are situated in true being, namely essence, motion, and rest. In addition to these three we must situate two more, identity and difference. For any one of the three is the same as itself and different from the others; but it is the same through identity and it is different through difference. Nobody doubts that any one of the three is the same as itself; but that they are mutually different must be proved as follows. Rest and motion are not mingled together, but each is mingled with essence; for both exist. Therefore rest and motion are mutually different and are other than essence. Likewise they are something other than difference or identity. In the first place this is because rest and motion are absolutes but the same and the other are relatives. Again, different things are called the same properly speaking only through identity, and other only through difference. But because of motion some things become alternatively the same in a way, and then other. For what is mobile is made so to speak the same as other moving things because of motion but different from things at rest. Similarly, because of rest what is at rest is made the same as things at rest but different from things in motion. But who is ignorant of the fact that not all things that are said to be the same or different are said to be such through rest and motion? Nonetheless, all things said to be the same must be called the same through identity; and again all things said to be different must be called different through difference. Furthermore, if motion and rest alike were identity, each would be entirely one and the same. Thus rest would move and motion would remain at rest. Finally, if either rest or motion were to cross over into difference, then through this difference each could immediately cross over into its contrary. Thus rest would cross over into motion and motion into rest, or at least rest would be moved and motion would be at rest.

But let us compare rest and motion with being. In the first place it is agreed that being is not the same as motion, since all things would be equally moved; nor is it the same as rest, otherwise all

vero abstractum; saepe tamen sermonis gratia aliud pro alio ponitur. Essentiam Plato in *Philebo* ex quatuor quasi elementis conflare videtur, ex uno scilicet et multitudine, item ex fine atque infinito. Essentiam illinc ita quasi compositam Melissus hic accipit quasi unum entis elementum atque primum. Huic addit quatuor elementa quodammodo respondentia primis: ratione quidem unius et termini identitatem atque statum, ratione vero multitudinis et infiniti alteritatem atque motum.

Tria primum posita sunt in ente vero, scilicet essentia, motus, status. Praeter haec ponenda sunt duo, scilicet identitas atque alteritas; quodlibet enim horum trium est sibi idem et ab aliis alterum: idem vero per identitatem, alterum quoque per alteritatem. Esse quidem quodlibet horum sibimet idem non dubitatur, esse vero haec invicem alia est ita probandum. Status et motus invicem non miscentur; cum essentia vero miscentur, [57R] ambo enim sunt. Igitur duo haec et alia inter se sunt et aliud quam essentia. Item duo haec aliud quiddam sunt quam alteritas vel identitas. Primo quidem quia status et motus absoluta sunt, idem vero et alterum relativa. Rursus per identitatem proprie alia dicuntur dumtaxat eadem, per alteritatem altera solum. Sed propter motum aliqua fiunt invicem quodammodo eadem, fiuntque quandoque altera. Nam mobile propter motum fit quasi mobilibus idem et alterum a stabilibus. Similiter propter statum stabile fit et stabilibus idem et mobilibus alterum. Sed quis ignoret non omnia quae dicuntur eadem vel altera per statum aut motum talia dici? Oportet tamen per identitatem omnia quae eadem dicuntur dici eadem, omnia rursus altera per alteritatem altera. Praeterea, si tam motus quam status sit identitas, erit utrumque penitus unum atque idem; ergo et status moveretur et motus staret. Denique, si vel status vel motus transcat in alteritatem, per hanc protinus alteritatem in suum contrarium pertransibit; ergo et status in motum et motus transibit in statum, aut saltem status quidem movebitur, motus autem stabit.

5

10

15

20

25

30

¹astractum Y   ³finito Z   ⁹sint Z   ¹¹aliis] his Z   ¹⁷alterius Z   /   identitatis Z
¹⁹⁻²⁰alternitatem alteram Z   ²⁶eadem] eandem Z

things would be equally at rest together; nor is it primarily and absolutely and formally both, lest perchance contraries would be entirely one. Therefore it must now be proved that being is other than sameness and difference; and first that it is different from sameness. For, were there one formal reason of being and of sameness, then, when we declare that motion and rest alike have being, we are declaring that they are entirely reciprocally the same; and this is false. Finally, it must be proved that being is different from difference. Were this not so, just as single things are said to be different among themselves only through difference, so all things would differ through essence and being and existence and would exist in a state of utter discord; and this is a shameful proposition. Again, being is common equally to absolutes and to relatives; but being different is always said with regard to another [i.e., relatively]. Finally, although otherness is different from the other four elements, yet all participate in otherness; for they are adjudged to be mutually other not through themselves but through this otherness.

Chapter 35: On the mutural comparison of the five classes of being.

[255E8] The ideal forms, whether they are classes or species, cannot be formally confused with each other. This is true not only for those that are opposite to each other but for any of them whatsoever. It is certain that motion is not rest, identity not difference; similarly that identity is not rest, difference not motion, man not ox; finally, that the reason of any one of the above mentioned is not the reason of being. But some are mingled together denominatively (i.e., predicatively), others not. Being indeed is mingled with all because it is predicated of all. The same is true for identity and difference, for single things are the same as themselves through identity and different from other things through otherness. But is identity mingled with otherness and vice versa denominatively (i.e., predicatively)? Yes indeed. For identity is different from the other classes through otherness—not, I repeat, formally and through itself, but through participation in otherness—and similarly otherness is the same as itself through identity. But the reason for motion is other than that

Sed comparemus haec duo cum ente. Primo [1291] quidem constat ens nec esse idem atque motum, omnia siquidem pariter mo-
verentur; nec esse idem atque statum, alioquin pariter omnia
conquiescerent; nec esse primo atque simpliciter et formaliter ambo,
ne forte contraria sint penitus unum. Probandum itaque nunc ens   5
esse aliud quam idem atque alterum; et primo esse identitate diversum. Nam si una sit ratio formalis entis atque identitatis, certe,
quando dicimus tam motum quam statum esse ens, dicimus ea invicem penitus idem; quod est falsum. Deinde probandum est ens ab
alteritate differre, alioquin, sicut per alteritatem singula dumtaxat   10
inter se altera nominantur, ita per essentiam et ens et esse cuncta
sine ulla concordia dissonarent; quod dictu nefas. Item ens quidem
commune est ad absoluta pariter atque relativa; alterum vero dicitur
semper ad alterum. Denique, etsi alteritas est aliud quam illa quatuor, omnia tamen alteritate participant; non enim per se sed per   15
hanc invicem altera iudicantur.

De mutua comparatione quinque generum entis. Cap. XXXV.

[255E8] Sic autem, etc.] Ideales formae, sive genera sint sive species, formaliter invicem confundi non possunt; idque commune est
non solum oppositis sed quibuslibet. Certum quidem est motum non   20
esse statum, identitatem non esse alteritatem; similiter identitatem
non esse statum, alteritatem non esse motum, hominem non esse
bovem; denique rationem cuiuslibet dictorum non esse rationem entis. Denominative autem vel praedicative quaedam invicem com-
miscentur, quaedam minime: ens sane omnibus, quod de omnibus   25
praedicatur; identitas quoque et alteritas omnibus, singula enim per
identitatem sibimet sunt eadem, per alteritatem ab aliis altera. Sed
numquid identitas per denominationem vel praedicationem misce-
tur alteritati atque vicissim? Certe. Nam et identitas per alteritatem
est ab aliis alterum—non, inquam, formaliter et per se, sed per   30
alteritatis participationem—et alteritas similiter per identitatem sibi

---

²motu Y   ⁶quam *scripsi* quasi Y Z   ¹²ens quidem *tr.* Z   ²⁴⁻²⁵comminiscentur Z
²⁵ens] eas Z   ²⁹et *om.* Z

for rest. For neither is rest made mobile through participation in motion, nor motion ever made stable through participation in rest. In fact, through the efficacy of action, motion more vehemently opposes rest than identity opposes otherness. Furthermore, the same and the different are called such relatively. But what are opposites relatively are usually easily mingled: for instance, what is the same for this person is at the same time different for that, and for others it is to the right rather than to the left. Rest and motion, however, are absolutes, so that they cannot be easily or formally or denominatively [i.e., predicatively] mingled.

Chapter 36: On otherness and how through otherness the mixture of being and not-being is achieved.

[256D11] The power of otherness itself when mingled in the ideal forms makes negation, and mixes not-being with being. Certainly, because motion is something other than rest, it is not therefore rest. For a like reason it is not identity, not otherness, and not being finally, since the reason of being is one thing, the reason of motion another. Yet it has being, since it participates in essence. Similarly through otherness any one whatsoever of the other classes and any one whatsoever of the Ideas is not the remainder, and it is not being itself. Therefore when they are called beings, they are also called not-beings. But with regard to any one of these [beings] being seems finite, because once or for a certain number of times it is this or that one [being], but numberless times it is not the remaining [beings] which are numberless. Finally, since the reason of being is one in itself and differs from the other reasons (which are innumerable) of all the ideal [beings], we are permitted, having already designated the reason itself of being, to say just once that this is being itself. We are also permitted to say numberless times that this is not being, because it can be said with regard to any one of the numberless [beings] that the reason of being is not this [being], and in turn that this [being] is not the reason of being. Therefore, not-being seems infinite in the first being, and hence we may confirm that the first being is not the absolutely first. In the absolutely first there can be no such discrepancy whatever nor as it were privation.

ipsi idem. Alia vero ratio est de motu atque statu; non enim vel
status per participationem motus fit mobilis, vel motus per participationem status fit aliquando stabilis. Motus enim per efficaciam
actionis vehementius repugnat statui quam identitas alteritati. Praeterea idem et alterum relative dicuntur; relative autem opposita
facile misceri solent, ut quod idem est huic, simul illi sit alterum,
et dextrum ad alios atque sinistrum. Status autem et motus sunt
absoluta, ut non facile vel formaliter vel denominative misceri
queant.

De alteritate, et quomodo per ipsam fit mixtio non entis cum ente. Cap. XXXVI.

[256D11] Sequitur itaque, etc.] Vis alteritatis ipsius idealibus formis
inserta negationem facit, atque non ens cum ente confundit. Profecto
quoniam motus alterum quiddam est quam status, idcirco non est
status; simili ratione nec est identitas, nec alteritas, denique neque
ens, siquidem altera est ratio entis, altera motus. Est tamen ens
quoniam essentiae particeps. Similiter unumquodque generum alio-
rum et quaelibet idearum per alteritatem nec est caetera, nec ens
ipsum. Itaque dum dicuntur entia, dicuntur quoque non entia. Videtur autem circa quodlibet eorum ens quidem finitum, quia semel
aut certo quodam numero est hoc vel illud, innumerabiliter autem
non est caetera, quae innumerabilia sunt. Denique, cum ratio entis
una quidem in se ipsa sit differatque a caeteris idealium omnium
rationibus quae innumerabiles sunt, semel licet dicere hoc est ens
ipsum, illa ipsa entis ratione designata; innumerabiliter etiam dicere
non est ens, quoniam circa unumquodque illorum innumerabilium
dici potest neque ratio entis est hoc, neque vicissim hoc est entis
ratio. Videtur ergo non ens infinitum in ente primo, ex quo con-
firmatur ens primum non esse ipsum simpliciter primum, in quo
nulla eiusmodi discrepantia vel quasi privatio esse potest. [57V]

⁵relative dicuntur *om. per homoioteleuton* Z   ²⁵ratio Z   /   innumerabilia Z
²⁶unum quoque Z   ²⁸quae [?] Y   ²⁹ipsae Y   ³⁰nulla *om.* Z

Chapter 37: On otherness and the mixture of not-being with being.

[257B1] Otherness itself seems to signify divisibility itself or the twoness of all difference and the origin of distinction. We must indeed arrive at this origin when it has been abstracted and freed from all particular diversities and differences. Otherness especially, because it is the origin of all distinction, even of formal distinction, certainly is both something and some being. But because it is other than absolute being itself and is everywhere the origin of negation and a certain privation and in a way of not-being, it must needs also be called not-being; and it is called, if one can say this, the essence or nature or power or origin of not-being sown in all beings. Otherness in the intelligible world is as it were a kind of matter. It is the cause there of any defect and difference, just as the matter in the sensible world, along simultaneously with dimension, is the cause of defect and disagreement everywhere and of distance. Indeed, this matter is the beginning not only of not being this or that, but of not-being absolutely. But otherness is the cause only of not being this or that. Through otherness this species, since it is other than that species or other species, deservedly this species is not that species and not that one and similarly not others through otherness. With logicians it is certain that, when we say that the large is not, we are dismissing absolute bigness itself; but when we say the not large, then we are able to introduce into the debate whatever is other than the large in any way. Similarly, if you say being is not, you are both dismissing being and signifying nothing, the contrary to being. But if you say not-being, you are able to indicate whatever can be postulated over and beyond the formal reason of being itself; nor is it contrary to being [like nothing]. If the beautiful through otherness is other than the not-beautiful and vice versa, otherness itself must needs be partly in the beautiful and partly in the not-beautiful opposed now to it; and these are similarly opposite beings and similarly the rest. In itself such a condition is opposite. But the otherness in all things is something, and its parts are everywhere something. For if otherness is something being, necessarily its parts are particular beings. But part of it is in the negative opposite, just

De alteritate et de mixtione non entis cum ente. Cap. XXXVII.

[257B1] Videamus et, etc.] Alteritas ipsa significare videtur divisi-
bilitatem ipsam sive duitatem differentiae omnis et distinctionis
originem, ad quam sane perveniendum est abstractam et ab omnibus
particularibus differentibus et differentiis absolutam. Haec utique   5
quoniam omnis distinctionis etiam formalis origo est, nimirum est
et aliquid atque aliquod ens. Quoniam vero et aliud est quam ipsum simpliciter ens, et ubique negationis privationisque cuiusdam
et quodammodo non essendi est origo, merito etiam non ens appellatur, diciturque, si dici potest, ipsa essentia vel natura vel vis vel   10
origo non entis entibus cunctis inserta. Haec in mundo intelligibili
quasi quaedam materia est ibique defectus alicuius ac differentiae
causa, sicut in mundo sensibili materia sua simul cum dimensione
causa est defectus et discrepantiae passim atque distantiae. Materia
quidem haec initium est non solum non essendi hoc aut illud, sed   15
etiam simpliciter non essendi. Alteritas autem illa causa solum est
non essendi hoc aut illud. Per illam enim species haec, cum aliud
sit quam ista vel aliae, merito species haec per alteritatem non est
ista vel illa similiterque nec aliae. Certum est apud logicos, cum
dicimus magnum non est, nos ipsum magnum simpliciter e medio   20
tollere; quando vero dicimus non magnum, in medium posse pro-
ducere quicquid est usquam aliud praeter ipsum magnum. Similiter si dixeris ens non est, et tollis ens et significas nihilum enti
contrarium. Sin dixeris non ens, designare potes quicquid praeter
formalem rationem entis ipsius excogitari potest, nec est enti con-   25
trarium. Si pulchrum per alteritatem est alterum quam non pulchrum
atque vicissim, merito alteritas ipsa partim est in pulchro partim est
in non pulchro illi iam opposito; suntque haec opposita similiter
entia, similiterque caetera. Eiusmodi inter se conditio est opposita.
In omnibus autem alteritas ipsa est aliquid, et partes eius ubique   30
aliquid. Si enim ipsa est aliquid ens, necessario partes eius sunt

---

²Videmus Z   ⁵absolatam Y   ⁷aliquod] aliquid Z   ¹⁵initia Z   /   aut] autem Z
¹⁶alteritas] alterius Z   ¹⁷aut] autem Z   ¹⁹similemque Z   ²⁰nos] vel Z
²⁷est² *om.* Z

as part is in the affirmative; for otherness is relative. Therefore it is something, some being, in not-being as in being. Therefore in not-being otherness does not oppose being as its contrary so to speak; rather, over and beyond the one being it introduces many beings.

Chapter 38: On otherness and the mixture of not-being with being.

[258C6] Although in anything otherness itself can be called the not-being mingled and mingling with being, yet in the negative opposite especially it is called the not-being mingled meanwhile with being. But this opinion seems at first glance to contradict Parmenides, who forbade us to join together beings with not-being. But in fact the opinion does not contradict Parmenides: it interprets him rather. It warns us that when Parmenides mentions not-being, we should understand him to mean not something that is not-being in any particular way, but to mean the absolutely nothing. Otherwise being and not-being can be united. But in what follows Melissus will say that such a distinction is trivial and easily found, meaning furthermore that we should not suppose that these trifles had been hidden from the great Parmenides. Consequently, when he says that being is other than individual classes or all the classes, you may understand that he means being as the reason thinks of it abstractly— that is, as essence. For being in the concrete is constituted as it were from all the classes.

Chapter 39: The communion and the distinction of the classes.

[259B8] In the intellect being can easily be mingled with not-being in the condition mentioned above, and there can easily be in turn among the classes the above-mentioned communion. Furthermore, it is important and necessary to affirm that otherness is not identity, nor, for the reason it is otherness, does it become in any way the same. Similarly identity is not otherness, nor, for the reason that it is identity, can it emerge as other except through otherness. Other-

entia quaedam. Est autem pars eius ita in opposito negativo sicut
in affirmativo; relativa enim est. Ita igitur est aliquid et aliquod ens
in [1292] non ente sicut in ente. Igitur in non ente non repugnat
enti quasi contraria, sed introducit ultra ens ipsum unum entia multa.

De alteritate et mixtura non entis cum ente. Cap. XXXVIII.

[258C6] Advertis ne? etc.] Etsi alteritas ipsa in quolibet dici potest
non ens cum ente confusum atque confundens, tamen in opposito
negativo praecipue non ens appellatur interim enti permixtum. Haec
autem opinio videtur quidem prima fronte Parmenidi contradicere
prohibenti coniungere entia cum non ente. Neque contradicit Parmenidi sed exponit, admonens videlicet nos ubi Parmenides dicit
non ens, ne intelligamus aliquid quoquomodo non ens, sed simpliciter nihilum, alioquin coniungi posse. Sed distinctionem eiusmodi
dicet in sequentibus leve quiddam esse facileque inventu, significans
interea non putandum exigua haec magnum Parmenidem latuisse.
Proinde ubi dicit ens alterum esse quam singula vel cuncta genera,
intelligas ratione abstracta, id est, essentiam. Nam ens concretum
quasi constat ex cunctis.

Communio et distinctio generum. Cap. XXXIX.

[259B8] Siquis contrariis, etc.] Facile quidem intellectu est ens cum
non ente conditione praedicta confundi, praedictamque communionem vicissim in generibus esse. Interea magnum est et necessarium
affirmare alteritatem ipsam nec esse ipsam identitatem, nec, qua
ratione alteritas est, fieri quoquomodo eandem; similiterque identitatem ipsam nec esse alteritatem, nec, qua ratione identitas est,
evadere posse alteram sed per alteritatem, quam etiam per identitatis
participationem fieri sibimet eandem (atque identitatem tamquam

ness even becomes the same as itself through participation in identity and identity is made other than the other classes only as the participant of otherness. The same reason applies for the rest of the preeminent classes and species.

Chapter 40: The communion and distinction of the classes.

[259D9] Unless some mutual communion of the classes and species existed, there would needs be no true conjunction for us of notions and of words. Thus the truth of understanding and of speech would cease. Perchance there would be no opinion at all or false speech, unless not-being were mixed in a way with being. Unless we were allowed to form an opinion about, or to speak of, things that do not exist, and thus to mingle these with things that do, we would not be allowed to form an opinion about, or to speak of, untruths; nor would there be any room at all for simulacra and phantasms. For a conjunction of being with not-being seems necessary for opinion and for false speech and for the appearance of phantasms.

Chapter 41: True and false speech.

[260C11] The sophist had said for a long time that all opinion and all speech are true, because he forever conceives of or expresses something and some being and therefore the true. Melissus objected to the contrary that in the being, however partial, of such opinion and speech some not-being is often mingled, whence falsehood can arise. Therefore he must deal with opinion and speech.

Chapter 42: True and false speech.

[262E3] All speech is speech about something. Again it is either true or false. True speech is what predicates of something things which exist and just as they exist. False speech predicates either those things which do not exist or otherwise than they exist.

alteritatis participem effici ab aliis alteram). Eadem est de caeteris praepositis generibus speciebusque ratio.

Communio et distinctio generum. Cap. XXXX.

[259D9] Caeterum o adolescens, etc.] Nisi aliqua generum spe- cierumque mutua sit communio, merito nec erit vera apud nos notionum verborumque coniunctio. Cessabit igitur intelligentiae orationisque veritas. Forte vero nec erit opinio ulla vel oratio falsa, nisi non ens cum ente quodammodo misceatur. Nisi enim liceat opinari vel loqui non entia, atque ita haec entibus admiscere, non dabitur opinari vel loqui falsa, [58R] neque locus usquam supererit simulachris atque phantasmati<bu>s. Nam et ad opinionem ora- tionemque falsam et ad phantasmatum apparitionem necessaria vi- detur quaedam entis cum non ente coniunctio.

5

10

De oratione vera et falsa. Cap. XXXXI.

[260C11] Sophistam utique, etc.] Sophista iamdiu dixerat omnem opinionem orationemque esse veram, quoniam semper concipit ex- primitve aliquid et aliquod ens, ergo verum. Contra Melissus obiecit in ipso aliquo ente opinionis et orationis eiusmodi saepe non ens aliquod admisceri, unde falsitas contingere potest. Ideo de opinione et oratione tractandum.

15

20

De oratione vera et falsa. Cap. XXXXII.

[262E3] Accipe et hoc, etc.] Omnis oratio est alicuius oratio. Item aut vera est aut falsa. Oratio vera est quae de aliquo praedicat ea quae sunt atque ita ut sunt; falsa vel ea quae non sunt vel aliter quam sint.

25

⁵mutua] multa Z   ⁷vel] nec Z   ¹¹⁻¹²rationemque Z   ¹³non *om.* Z

Chapter 43: Thought, opinion, phantasy.

[263D6] Thought is a certain activity of the discursive reason and interior conversation. The image of this is speech. Opinion is a conclusion of the process of thought conceived in the reason. Phantasy, finally, is a passion or appearance closely resembling this [opinion?], which occurs regarding things in the sense: first and always those in the inner sense, and also at times those in the external sense[s]. But phantastic passion or appearance is able either to precede opinion or to succeed it or to accompany it. It precedes it when it is incited by external objects or by corporeal passion. It succeeds it or accompanies it when it is the result of thought and opinion and is moved by them. Therefore, just as some speech is true, some false, and is affirmative and negative, so too is opinion.

Chapter 44: How the sophist feigns simulacra of what do not exist.

[264C4] The imaginary art is twofold. One kind is assimilative and it portrays something according to the model of something that actually exists. The other kind is phantastic and it feigns phantastic simulacra of what do not exist. The sophist is busy beguiling us with the phantastic kind. He is also a crafty merchant and shopkeeper.

Chapter 45: How the sophist feigns. Again on the works of God, of nature and of art.

[265A10] The sophist is a false maker of simulacra and an imitator. But there are two kinds of making faculty: the divine and the human. Mortal sublunar things, whether animate or inanimate, proceed from God the Maker—that is, from the power of the divine reason, art, and knowledge that is imparted to universal nature. However, by reason and by necessary persuasion we can demonstrate that they are made not by chance but by divine art. Whatever

De cogitatione, opinione, phantasia. Cap. XXXXIII.

[263D6] Quid autem, etc.] Cogitatio est quaedam agitatio rationis et interior collocutio: huius autem imago est oratio. Opinio vero est cogitationis conclusio quaedam in ratione concepta. Phantasia denique est passio vel apparitio quaedam ferme similis circa haec in 5 sensu contingens, primo quidem et semper in sensu intimo, quandoque etiam in externo. Potest autem phantastica passio vel apparitio praecedere opinionem vel sequi vel comitari. Praecedit quidem quando incitatur ab externis obiectis vel passione corporea. Sequitur autem vel comitatur quando a cogitatione opinioneque fit atque mo- 10 vetur. Sicut igitur est oratio quaedam vera quaedam falsa et affirmativa atque negativa, sic et opinio.

Quomodo sophista fingit simulachra non existentium. Cap. XXXXIIII.

[264C4] Imaginariam artem, etc.] Ars imaginaria est duplex: altera 15 quidem assimilativa quae ad rei alicuius existentis exemplar aliquid exprimit; altera vero phantastica simulachra fingens non existentium. In genere phantastico sophista versatur et fallit. Est etiam mercator quidam subdolus atque caupo.

Quomodo sophista fingat. Item de operibus Dei, naturae, artis. 20 Cap. XXXXV.

[265A10] Nunc vero, etc.] Sophista est effector quidam simulachrorum falsus et imitator. Effectricis autem facultatis duo sunt genera, divinum scilicet et humanum. Mortalia sub luna, sive animata sive inanimata, ab artifice Deo proficiscuntur, scilicet ab ipsa rationis et 25 artis scientiaeque divinae virtute infusa universae naturae; effici autem haec non casu sed arte divina potest et ratione et necessaria persuasione monstrari. Quaecumque igitur natura generari dicuntur

---

⁶⁻⁷quandoque] quamque Z   ²²Nunc F Hunc Y Z   ²³autem] aut Z   ²⁴⁻²⁵sive inanimata *om.* Z
²⁷autem] aut Z

are said to be generated by nature are thus made by divine art. The rest that proceed in imitation of them are made by human art.

Chapter 46: On the works of the divine and human art, on the demons, and on images and shadows.

[265E8] The making art is divided longitudinally when it is divided into divine and human. The divine is divided into the making of things and the making of images; the human is similarly divided when it descends from one thing to another and proceeds as it were in length. For the human faculty descends from the divine, and images depend in a way on things.

After Melissus had said that bodies and their images together with their shadows are divine works—that is, they have not been made merely through human art—he again takes up the topic and calls images and shadows demonic works. This is because, since the demons are followers of the gods, the likenesses of things, which are the followers of the prime divine works, must needs appear to be demonic contrivances as it were. Moreover, just as the nature of the demons is midway between higher and lower beings, so is light the medium between incorporeals and corporeals. In light there is a certain demonic power. In other words, light is the maker of images and of shadows, just as the demons too are accustomed to reveal certain wondrous sights to men not only when they are asleep or bemused but also when they are fully awake. Our imaginations also are possessed in a way of a demonic power. This is both because the demons excite the imaginations in ourselves by way of their own creative imaginations and tricks, and also because what imagines in us is in some respects a demon. The Platonic sect arranged the demons into three principal degrees. The first demons are wrapped only in fiery—that is, celestial—bodies; the second are wrapped in fiery bodies tempered as much as possible with air; the third are wrapped in bodies thickened from the quadruple vapor of the elements. Whenever you look within at our soul clothed as it were in spirit, perhaps you will suppose that you see a demon, a triple demon. For you will see too the celestial vehicle covered

arte divina fiunt; caetera vero ad horum imitationem procedentia
arte efficiuntur humana.

De operibus artis divinae atque humanae, et daemonibus, et imaginibus, atque umbris. Cap. XXXXVI.

[265E8] Cum vero, etc.] Ars effectrix dividitur per longitudinem, 5
ubi dividitur in divinam et humanam, et divina in effectionem rerum atque effectionem imaginum; humana quoque similiter, ubi
alterum ab altero descendit, et quasi procedit in longum. Nam et
humana facultas a divina descendit, et imagines a rebus quoquomodo dependent. 10
Postquam dixit corpora eorumque imagines simul et umbras esse
opera divina, id est, non per artem humanam dumtaxat effecta,
iterum repetens imagines atque umbras appellat opera daemonica,
quia, cum daemones pedissequi sint deorum, merito similitudines
rerum, quae pedissequae sunt primorum operum divinorum, quasi 15
daemonica machinamenta videntur. Praeterea, sicut natura daemonum inter superos atque inferos media est, ita lumen inter incorporea et cor[1293]porea medium. Et in lumine potestas quaedam
est daemonica, effectrix videlicet imaginum et umbrarum, quemadmodum et daemones solent mira quaedam visa non solum dormien- 20
tibus et abstractis sed etiam vigilantibus ostentare. Imaginamenta
quoque nostra quodammodo etiam daemonica virtute fiunt, non solum quia daemones efficacibus imaginationibus artificiisque suis
nobis imaginationes suscitant, verum etiam quoniam quod in nobis
imaginatur est quodammodo daemon. Daemonum tres praecipue 25
gradus Platonica secta disponit. [58V] Primi quidem igneis solum,
id est, coelestibus corporibus involvuntur; secundi igneis quibusdam
cum aëre quam plurimo temperatis; tertii corporibus quadruplici
elementorum vapore coactis. Siquando nostram animam introspex-
eris quasi vestitam spiritu, putabis forte daemonem te videre trinum- 30
que daemonem. Nam et vehiculum coeleste videbis igneo cuidam

12affecta Z   13daemoniaca Z   15sunt] suos Z   17-18incorporea et corporea *tr.* Z
18mediam Z   20colent Z   24quod *om.* Z   26ignei Z
28quatruplici Y   30vestitum Z

entirely with a fiery and an airy veil, and such a veil surrounded with spirit—with spirit, I say, compounded from the vapors of the four elements. You will know that the soul primarily and effectively exercises the imagination in the celestial vehicle and prepares all the sense through the whole vehicle; and through this vehicle as through a seal frequently it impresses images on the second veil; and through the second similarly it fashions the third. Finally, you will conclude that the images that are innermost in you, since they are made by this spiritual and demonic animal, proceed from a certain demonic contrivance.

Melissus says that shadows occur when darkness occurs (so to speak) in the fire—that is, when there is some opaque obstacle in the light, the light that proceeds ultimately from the celestial fire. The rays are in a way stopped by this object and burst out around it with some shadowy shape that has been immediately but invisibly stamped upon them. But, he maintains, more distinct images are made from a double light—that is, from the common light flowing externally around bodies and from the proper [or peculiar] light besides, namely from the nature, color, and shape of a face already surrounded with the common light. Each of these lights when it strikes a mirror surface creates an image there. Furthermore, you can achieve a manner of looking surpassing the one you commonly and habitually achieve. For, in addition to the fact that, at a straight glance, you customarily observe the mirror and the [your?] image simultaneously, you also descry simultaneously the things behind your back, when the [your?] visual ray, that is, has been reflected back directly from the mirror. But of this more opportunely in [my commentary on] the *Timaeus*.

Several have done away with such images and have argued that the eye is deceived when it supposes, while it gazes at the thing itself, that it sees an image. But, along with his followers, Plato wishes the images to be something. Otherwise no objects could appear in mirrors unimpaired. Therefore both here and in the *Timaeus* he maintains that images exist. Certainly here, when he says that idola are not the same as bodies, he means that they possess their own nature but do not have matter. He proves this most [conclusively] in the sixth book of the *Republic,* when he says that as

aërioque velamini prorsus infusum, eiusmodique velamen spiritu
circumfusum, spiritu, inquam, ex quatuor humorum vaporibus con-
stituto. Cognosces animam primo quidem efficaciterque imaginationem in coelesti vehiculo exercere, sensumque prorsus omnem per
totum vehiculum expedire; perque vehiculum hoc quasi per sigillum
secundo velamini imagines frequenter imprimere; per secundum
similiter tertium conformare. Postremo concludes imagines vobis
intimas, dum a spiritali hoc daemonicoque animali fiunt, machinatione quadam daemonica proficisci.

Inquit Melissus umbras fieri quando in igne fit (ut ita dicam) tene-
bra, id est, quando in lumine, quod tandem procedit ab igne coelesti,
opacum aliquod est obstaculum, cuius obiectu radii quodammodo
impediti circum inde prosiliunt tenebrosa quadam figura mox e conspectu signata. Expressiores autem imagines inquit fieri lumine
duplici, id est, ex communi extrinsecus corporibus circumfuso, atque insuper ex proprio, id est, indole, colore, figuraque faciei iam
lumine circumfusae. Utrumque lumen in corpus speculare concur-
rens imaginem ibi conficit. Interea praeter modum communiter solitum fit inspectio; praeter enim id quod more consueto speculum
recto quodam ictu et simul imaginem contueris, prospicis simul
quae a tergo tibi sunt, visuali videlicet radio ex speculo protinus
repercusso. Sed de hoc opportunius in *Timaeo*.

Nonnulli imagines eiusmodi sustulerunt, falli putantes oculum
putantem, dum rem ipsam intuetur, imaginem quandam se videre.
Plato vero cum suis imagines esse vult aliquid, non enim res integras
in speculis aliter apparere posse. Igitur et hic et in *Timaeo* existere
imagines asserit. Hic certe, dum inquit idola non esse eadem atque
corpora, significat naturam quidem suam habere, sed non habere
materiam. Quod plurimum in sexto de *Republica* comprobat, ubi
ait: sicut mathematicae formae ad divinas sese habent, sic ad corpora
imagines speculares; quasi actum suum modumque proprium habeant, sicut mathematica suum. Eandemque fuisse deinde Theophrasti
sententiam Iamblichus Pricianusque confirmant, ubi in librum eius

mathematical forms relate to divine forms, so do mirror images relate to bodies. The images have as it were their own act and mode,
just as the mathematicals have theirs. Iamblichus and Priscianus
[Lydus] confirm that Theophrastus's view was the same when they
comment on his book on the soul (we too have added an interpretation to this book). Proclus maintains the identical view in [com-
menting on] the sixth book of the *Republic*. Or rather, he strives to
assert that shadows have a power and nature as it were of their own
when he tells the story of the hyena that trod on the shadow of a
dog sitting above it and made the dog fall down from above and
then devoured it. Solinus also writes that a dog cannot bark when
it is within the shadow of a hyena. Proclus adds that magicians are
accustomed to affect things' images and shadows in marvellous
ways, and by means of these affected images and shadows similarly
to affect the things themselves. It is as if the images and shadows
had some nature of their own that reached to things and that through
this nature a certain mutual sympathy can be achieved. However,
although I do not venture to lay claim myself to these effects, I will
hazard the opinion nonetheless that such things could happen for
magicians, if, over and beyond the radial and spiritual images that
result only from light, one accepts the simulacra of Lucretius which
stream forth even when the light has been removed, and which drag
along with them the matter and the nature of bodies. Proclus seems
to have signified these simulacra, at least secretly. Our Platonic
Synesius in his book on dreams, however, apparently portrayed
them very openly. For he supposes that the sensible species in the
body is extended along with the matter in such a way that, when a
certain vaporous matter is exhaled through motions, the species
mingled with it may stream forth too. Hence therefore he supposes
the effect is such that, just as the species is called an *idos* in Greek,
so the efflux too from the special body may be called an *idolon,* as
if it were a specimen from the species or an attenuated species.
Given that it is fashioned from the entire body which has already
been shaped, the *idolon* is thence revealed, so they suppose, with
that shape; and this it preserves over a certain distance and for some
time. It seems the matter probably proceeds even farther than the
shape mingled with it. In turn, however, a certain immaterial species

de anima commentantur cui et nos interpretationes quoque nostras adiunximus. Asserit idem Proclus in libro de *Republica* sexto. Immo vero et umbras vim quandam et quasi naturam habere suam asseverare contendit, narrans hyenam calcantem canis in alto sedentis umbram illum ex alto praecipitare atque devorare. Scribit quoque 5
Solinus canem intra hyenae umbram latrare non posse. Adiungit Proclus solere magos miris modis afficere rerum imagines atque umbras, hisque affectis similiter res ipsas afficere, quasi imagines atque umbrae naturam aliquam habeant suam ad res attinentem, per quam mutua quaedam fieri compassio valeat. Ego vero etsi hos ef- 10
fectus asserere minus audeo, magis tamen opinari auderem posse contingere, si, praeter radiales spiritalesque imagines quae dumtaxat resultant ex lumine, Lucretiana illa simulachra ponantur quae etiam lumine sublato procedant, secumque materiam corporum trahant atque naturam. Haec utique Proclus clam significavisse videtur; Syne- 15
sius autem Platonicus noster in libro de somniis apertius expressisse. Vult enim in corpore sensibilem speciem esse cum materia simul extentam adeo ut, dum materia quaedam vaporalis per meatus exhalat, interim cum hac et species mixta procedat; hinc igitur effectum esse ut, sicut species ipsa Graece dicitur idos, sic et effluxus 20
e corpore speciali idolon appelletur, quasi ex specie specimen speciesve tenuis. Quae quidem cum exprimatur ex toto corpore figurato, illinc, ut putant, expromitur cum figura quam ad certum spatium tempusque conservet. Probabile vero videtur ulterius quidem materiam procedere quam figuram materiae mixtam; sed vicissim quoque 25
speciem quandam (ut ita dicam) immaterialem et spiritalem figurae modum longius procedere quam materiam, quemadmodum Peripatetici tradunt intentionem quandam odoris atque soni ultra materialem effluxum longissime propagari.

Proinde sicut radiales imagines alibi quidem quasi vanae sunt in 30
speculis autem instaurantur, ita eiusmodi simulachra, alibi quidem quasi divulsa, in spiritu animali atque phantastico, quasi suo quodam speculo, colligi reformarique putant; forte quemadmodum charac-

---

[16]somniis *scripsi* somnis Y Z   [18]permeatus Y   [20]εἶδος Z   [21]pecie Y
[23]exprimitur Z   [28–29]materiam Z

so to speak and spiritual mode of the shape probably proceeds still farther than the matter. Similarly, the Aristotelians hold that an intention of scent and of sound is propagated much farther than the material efflux.

Therefore, just as radial images, which are so to speak empty when elsewhere, are restored in mirrors, so such simulacra, which are so to speak torn apart from each other when elsewhere, are thought to be collected together and reformed in the animate and phantastic spirit as though in a mirror of their own. Perhaps the analogy might be with the characters traced out in the front of a closed book. Directly the book has been opened, they have disappeared, and directly it has been closed again, they have become immediately visible.

I set aside now how some things are affected by others by way of the efflux and conflux of the idola, and how imaginations may be moved through these idola by absent things almost as though they were approaching us, and how dreams occur. If the idola have any power at all, and to the extent that they endure as material effluxes, then it is likely that they affect the spirit naturally. But to the extent that they issue as spiritual effluxes, then it is likely that they affect the soul by way of knowledge, and are thus in harmony with the imagination in the same way as the radial images are in harmony with the eye.

Chapter 47: How the sophist feigns falsehoods.

[266D8] The phantastic class is divided into two: for some feign or imitate something by way of instruments as by way of specular bodies; others by way of their own person. As mimes they partially know what they are imitating, and as sophists partially not. Though they are ignorant both of things and of powers, the sophists use their opinion to feign things and to simulate powers.

Chapter 48: The description and distinction of the sophist.

[267E4] Some imitators are simple, such as artisans and mimes, but others are ironic. The sophist is an ironic imitator who possesses

teres in fronte clausi vo[59R]luminis designati aperto mox libro
disparuerunt, iterum clauso statim comparuerunt.

Mitto nunc quomodo per effluxum confluxumque idolorum alia
afficiantur ab aliis, et qua ratione imaginationes per haec ab absen-
tibus propemodum propinquantibus moveantur, insomniaque con- 5
tingant. Verisimile quidem est, siquid valeant, quatenus effluxus
materiales durant, afficere spiritum naturaliter; quatenus autem spir-
itales evadunt, afficere animum cognobiliter, atque ita cum imagina-
tione congruere, quemadmodum radiales imagines cum oculo con-
gruunt.[1294] 10

Quomodo sophista fingat falsa. Cap. XXXXVII.

[266D8] Reminiscamur, etc.] Genus phantasticum in duo dividitur:
alii enim fingunt imitanturve aliquid per instrumenta, ut per corpora
specularia; alii per suam personam. Atque hi partim cognoscunt
quod imitantur ut mimi; partim minime ut sophistae, qui, cum res 15
et virtutes ignorent, tamen pro opinione sua res ipsas fingunt vir-
tutesque simulant.

Descriptio distinctioque sophistae. Cap. XXXXVIII.

[267E4] Harum quidem, etc.] Imitatores alii quidem simplices sunt
ut artifices atque mimi, alii vero ironici. Sophista est imitator 20
ironicus multamque in se duplicitatem habet. Sed inter sophistas
alii sunt prorsus ignavi subitoque deprehenduntur, alii sunt versuti
plurimum et versatiles. Ironici praeterea vel publicas orationes ad
persuasionem componunt, vel privatim, artificiose, et ambitiose re-
darguunt. Primi quidem, quamvis appareant viri civiles, non sunt 25
tamen sed oratores, quos hic Plato clam tangit, in *Gorgia* vero
palam; secundi quoque, cum appareant sapientes, sunt sophistae.
Denique sophista est ignorans, phantasmatum fictor et praestigiator,
avarus ambitiosusque redargutor.

¹dissignati Z   ⁵⁻⁶contingat Z   ¹³alii] falsi Z   ¹⁵mimis Z   ¹⁹ali Z
²⁵et *add. post* quidem Z   ²⁸Denique sophista *tr.* Z   /   victor et praesignator Z

much duplicity in himself. But among sophists some are utterly cowardly and are suddenly apprehended; others are extremely clever and versatile. Moreover, the ironic sophists either compose public speeches for persuasion or in private refute craftily and ambitiously. The first kind, although they may appear to be good citizens, are nevertheless not so: they are orators. Plato refers to them secretly here, but openly in the *Gorgias*. The second kind also, although they may appear to be wise, are sophists. Finally, the sophist is ignorant. He is a feigner and manipulator of phantasms, and an avaricious and ambitious refuter.

Index Auctorum

[?] signifies a cross-listing for cases where Ficino is referring ambiguously either to a dialogue or more probably to his commentary upon it.

Ficino:

Commentaria in Parmenidem	229.25; 239.4; 247.26; 249.24[?]; 255.25[?]
Commentaria in Philebum	255.25[?]
Commentaria in Plotinum	255.26
Commentaria in Timaeum	273.22[?]

Theologia (Platonica)   243.14, 29

Plato:

Gorgias	277.26
Parmenides	219.14; 235.28, 29; 249.24[?]; 251.6; 255.25[?]
Philebus	255.25[?]; 257.2
Respublica VI	273.29
Sophista	219.2, app.
Theaetetus	219. app.
Timaeus	273.22[?]; 273.26

Proclus:

In Rempublicam VI	275.2

Synesius:

De Insomniis	275.15–16

Theophrastus (in Priscianus Lydus; see chap. 5, n. 19 above):

De Anima	273.33 ff.

Index Nominum

Appendix 1: Ficino's Greek Text of the *Sophist* Scholion

The following is based upon the edition of the scholion by William Chase Greene in his *Scholia Platonica,* American Philological Association Monograph 8 (Haverford, Pa., 1938), p. 40, but with the substitution of the "T" variants as found in the Laurenziana's MS. 85.9, f. 78r (I am indebted here to Professor James Hankins). This manuscript was Ficino's Plato exemplar and belongs to the group derived from the Marciana's Venetus Append. Class. 4, cod. 1 (see pp. 92ff. above). For Ficino's Latin rendering, and for an English version of it, see pp. 217 and 90–91 above. For an English rendering of the Greek, see John Dillon, *Iamblichi Chalcidensis in Platonis Dialogos Commentariorum Fragmenta* (Leiden, 1973), p. 91. The substituted variants are: 1. a lacuna of two words after Πλάτων and the omission of καὶ τὸν ⟨Ἔρωτα⟩; 4. ὁ before σκοπὸς omitted; 5. καὶ before εἰδωλοποιὸς omitted and κάθαρσις (sic) for the correct καθαρτὴς; 7. λόγων for ἀλόγων; and 24. συγγίγνεται.

ΣΟΦΙΣΤΗΣ.

ὅτι σοφιστὴν καλεῖ ὁ Πλάτων   καὶ τὸν Ἄιδην καὶ τὸν Δία, καὶ παγκάλην λέγει εἶναι τὴν σοφιστικὴν τέχνην· ὅθεν ὑπονοοῦμεν ὅτι γλαφυρωτέρου σκοποῦ ἔχεται ὁ διάλογος. ἔστι γὰρ κατὰ τὸν μέγαν Ἰάμβλιχον σκοπὸς νῦν περὶ τοῦ ὑπὸ σελήνην δημιουργοῦ. οὗτος γὰρ εἰδωλοποιὸς καὶ κάθαρσις ψυχῶν, ἐναντίων λόγων ἀεὶ χωρίζων, μεταβλητικός, καὶ νέων πλουσίων ἔμμισθος θηρευτής, ψυχὰς ὑποδεχόμενος πλήρεις λόγων ἄνωθεν ἰούσας, καὶ μισθὸν λαμβάνων παρ' αὐτῶν τὴν ζωοποιΐαν τὴν κατὰ λόγον τῶν θνητῶν. οὗτος ἐνδέδεται τῷ μὴ ὄντι, τὰ ἔνυλα δημιουργῶν, καὶ τὸ ὡς ἀληθῶς ψεῦδος ἀσπαζόμενος, τὴν ὕλην· βλέπει δὲ εἰς τὸ ὄντως ὄν. οὗτός ἐστιν ὁ πολυκέφαλος, πολλὰς οὐσίας καὶ ζωὰς προβεβλημένος, δι' ὧν κατασκευάζει τὴν ποικιλίαν τῆς γενέσεως. ὁ δ' αὐτὸς καὶ γόης, ὡς θέλγων τὰς ψυχὰς τοῖς φυσικοῖς λόγοις, ὡς δυσαποσπάστως ἔχειν ἀπὸ τῆς γενέσεως. καὶ γὰρ ὁ ἔρως γόης, καὶ ἡ φύσις ὑπό τινων μάγος κέκληται διὰ τὰς συμπαθείας καὶ ἀντιπαθείας τῶν φύσει. νῦν οὖν τὸν παντοδαπὸν σοφιστὴν βούλεται διδάσκειν. καὶ γὰρ καὶ ὁ φιλόσοφος σοφιστὴς ὡς μιμούμενος τόν τε οὐράνιον δημιουργὸν καὶ τὸν γενεσιουργόν. καὶ ἡ διαιρετικὴ μιμεῖται τὴν ἀπὸ τοῦ ἑνὸς τῶν ὄντων πρόοδον, καὶ ὁ γενεσιουργὸς τὸν οὐράνιον δημιουργόν· διὸ καὶ σοφιστής.

καὶ αὐτὸς δὲ ὁ σοφιστὴς ἄνθρωπος ὢν διὰ τὸ τὰ μεγάλα μιμεῖσθαι σοφιστὴς καλεῖται· ὅθεν καὶ τὸν σοφιστὴν πολυκέφαλον εἴρηκεν. ὁ δὲ ζένος εἰς τύπον τοῦ πατρὸς τῶν δημιουργῶν νοείσθω ὑπερουράνιος καὶ ἐξῃρημένος, οἱ δὲ ἀκροαταὶ εἰς τὰς δημιουργικὰς νοήσεις, ὁ μὲν εἰς τὴν τοῦ Διός, ὁ δὲ εἰς τὴν ἀγγελικὴν ὡς Ἑρμαϊκὸς καὶ γεωμετρικός. καὶ ἐπεὶ ἡ δημιουργία ἐκ τοῦ ἀτελοῦς εἰς τὸ τέλειον, διὰ τοῦτο πρῶτον ὁ ξένος τῷ Θεοδώρῳ συγγίγνεται, εἶτα δι' ἐπιστροφῆς τῷ διίῳ Σωκράτει.

Appendix 2: A Guide to Ficino's Chapter Divisions of the *Sophist*

The following is a guide to Ficino's chapter divisions of the *Sophist*. It is keyed to his Latin translation as it appeared in the Florence 148[4] edition of his great work, *Platonis Opera Omnia,* many copies of which survive. The edition was printed in two Gothic types, the first kind being used for the first of five parts and the second kind for the remainder and the introduction. Of folio size, it is made up of many gatherings ranging from four to ten folios, each gathering being marked by a quire signature. Since the same signature appears more than once, however, the binders had trouble ascertaining the sequence and thus copies vary, though the dialogues are always to be found on the same signatures if one can locate the signatures in the sequence. It is important for the scholar to know, therefore, that I have used UCLA's copy of the first part (with the shelf mark A1.P69o).

Neither the pages nor the folios are numbered, and one has to rely, therefore, on signatures. Most of the gatherings for the first part consist of eight folios, and this is true of the N and O gatherings containing the *Sophist* translation, though signatures 5, 6, 7, and 8 are, predictably, not so designated. The full page has two columns (I have designated them A and B) of forty-six lines each, and the running titles are intermittently wrong. For a full description of the edition and a determination of its date, see Paul Oskar Kristeller, "The First Printed Edition of Plato's Works and the Date of Its Publication (1484)," in *Science and History: Studies in Honor of Edward Rosen,* ed. Erna Hilfstein, Pawel Czartoryski, and Frank D. Grande, Studia Copernicana, vol. 16 (Wroclaw, 1978), pp. 25–35.

The dialogue itself, which is preceded by the *Ion* and succeeded by the *Statesman,* appears between signatures N3v. col. B, line 1 (henceforth formatted as N3v.B1) and O7v.A. Ficino divided it up into forty-eight *summae* or chapters when he established summae for the 1496 *Commentaria* edition, keying each summa to the 1484 Latin translation by way of incipits. These summae subsequently appeared in the three editions of Ficino's *Opera Omnia* published in Basel in 1561 and 1576 and in Paris in 1641. My references to the line-numbering of the Greek text are to the Oxford edition by J. Burnet (1900 ff.), 1:357–442.

INCIPIT	*TEXT*	*CHAPTER*	*SIGNATURE*
Venimus o Socrates	216A1	I	N3v.B1
Probe loqueris	218B5	II	N4r.B1
Age hinc	219A4	III	N4r.B30
Venatoriam quoque	219D9	IIII	N4v.A17–18
At qui secundum	221C5	V	N4v.B33
Praeterea hoc modo	223C1	VI	N5r.B13
Videamus iterum	224E6	VII	N5v.A26
Cernis verum	226A6	VIII	N5v.B23–24
Egregie loqueris	227C10	IX	N6r.A4–3up
Doctrinam vero utrum	229B1	X	N6v.A12
Lubricum porro	231A8	XI	N6v.B5up
Nunquid advertis	232A1	XII	N7r.A31–32
Tu vero	232E6	XIII	N7r.B26
Ponamus ergo	233D3	XIIII	N7v.A8
Deinceps cavendum	235A10	XV	N7v.B23
Nunquid ipsum	236D5	XVI	N8r.A10up
Ita prorsus	237B7	XVII	N8r.B14–15
Non dum	238A1	XVIII	N8r.B3up
De me igitur quis	239B1	XIX	N8v.B3–4
Qua ratione eius	240C7	XX	O1r.A11–12
Recte in memoriam	241B4	XXI	O1r.A4up
Facili disputatione	242C4	XXII	O1v.A6
De multis quidem	243C10	XXIII	O1v.B5
Quid ad eos	244B6	XXIIII	O1v.B12up
Quid porro?	244D14	XXV	O2r.A9
Utrum totum ipsum	245B4	XXVI	O2r.A28–29
Sermones quidem	245E6	XXVII	O2r.B13
Praestaret illos	246D4	XXVIII	O2v.A2
Ad specierum amicos	248A4	XXIX	O2v.B11
Quid vero	248E6	XXX	O3r.A8
Pape	249D9	XXXI	O3r.B1
Dicamus plane	251A5	XXXII	O3v.A9–10
Quid vero? Si	252D2	XXXIII	O3v.B11up
Postquam ergo	254B7	XXXIIII	O4r.B20
Sic autem	255E8	XXXV	O4v.A5up
Sequitur itaque	256D11	XXXVI	O4v.B12–11up
Videamus et	257B1	XXXVII	O5r.A8
Advertis ne?	258C6	XXXVIII	O5r.B21
Siquis contrariis	259B8	XXXIX	O5v.A10
Caeterum o adolescens	259D9	XL	O5v.A30
Sophistam utique	260C11	XLI	O5v.B14–15

Accipe et hoc	262E3	XLII	O6r.B16
Quid autem	263D6	XLIII	O6v.A6
Imaginariam artem	264C4	XLIIII	O6v.A9up
Nunc vero	265A10	XLV	O6v.B18
Cum vero	265E8	XLVI	O7r.A9
Reminiscamur	266D8	XLVII	O7r.A4–3up
Harum quidem	267E4	XLVIII	O7r.B3–2up

Bibliography of Works Cited

Ackrill, John L. "*Symplokê Eidôn.*" *Bulletin of the Institute of Classical Studies in the University of London* 2 (1955), 31–35. Reprinted in *Studies in Plato's Metaphysics* (see under Reginald E. Allen in this Bibliography), pp. 199–206; also in *Plato I* (see under Vlastos in this Bibliography), pp. 201–209.

Albinus (Alcinous). See under Hermann.

Alexandre, Charles, ed. *Gemistus Plethon: Traité des lois.* Paris, 1858.

Allen, Michael J. B. "The Absent Angel in Ficino's Philosophy." *Journal of the History of Ideas* 36 (1975), 219–240.

―――. "Cosmogony and Love: The Role of Phaedrus in Ficino's *Symposium* Commentary." *Journal of Medieval and Renaissance Studies* 10.2 (1980), 131–153.

―――. "Ficino's Lecture on the Good?" *Renaissance Quarterly* 30 (1977), 160–171.

―――. "Ficino's Theory of the Five Substances and the Neoplatonists' *Parmenides.*" *Journal of Medieval and Renaissance Studies* 12.1 (1982), 19–44.

―――. "Marsile Ficin, Hermès et le *Corpus Hermeticum.*" In *Présence d'Hermès Trismégiste,* edited by Antoine Faivre, pp. 110–119. Paris, 1988.

―――. "Marsilio Ficino on Plato, the Neoplatonists and the Christian Doctrine of the Trinity." *Renaissance Quarterly* 37 (1984), 555–584.

―――. "Marsilio Ficino on Plato's Pythagorean Eye." *Modern Language Notes* 97 (1982), 171–182.

―――. "Marsilio Ficino's Interpretation of Plato's *Timaeus* and Its Myth of the Demiurge." In *Supplementum Festivum* (see under Hankins in this Bibliography), pp. 399–439.

―――. *The Platonism of Marsilio Ficino: A Study of His "Phaedrus" Commentary, Its Sources and Genesis.* Berkeley, Los Angeles, London, 1984.

―――. "The Second Ficino-Pico Controversy: Parmenidean Poetry, Eristic and the One." In *Marsilio Ficino e il ritorno di Platone: Studi e documenti* (see under Garfagnini in this Bibliography), pp. 417–455.

―――. "Summoning Plotinus: Ficino, Smoke, and the Strangled Chickens." Forthcoming.

―――. "Two Commentaries on the Phaedrus: Ficino's Indebtedness to Hermias." *Journal of the Warburg and Courtauld Institutes* 43 (1980), 110–129.

―――, ed. and trans. *Marsilio Ficino and the Phaedran Charioteer.* Berkeley, Los Angeles, London, 1981.

————, ed. and trans. *Marsilio Ficino: The Philebus Commentary*. Berkeley, Los Angeles, London, 1975. Reprint, 1979 (with corrections).

Allen, Reginald E. "Participation and Predication in Plato's Middle Dialogues." *Philosophical Review* 69 (1960), 147–164. Reprinted in *Studies in Plato's Metaphysics* (see under Reginald E. Allen in this Bibliography), pp. 43–60.

————, ed. *Studies in Plato's Metaphysics*. London and New York, 1965.

Allen, Thomas William, ed. *Plato: Codex Oxoniensis Clarkianus 39 Phototypice Editus*. Leiden, 1898–1899.

Aristotle. See under Barnes.

Armstrong, Arthur Hilary. *Plotinus: Enneads*. 7 vols. Loeb Classical Library. Cambridge, Mass. and London, 1966–1988.

Baltes, Matthias. *Die Weltentstehung des platonischen Timaios nach den antiken Interpreten*. 2 vols. Philosophia Antiqua, vols. 30 and 35. Leiden, 1976–1978.

Barnes, Jonathan, ed. *The Complete Works of Aristotle: The Revised Oxford Translation*. 2 vols. Princeton, 1984.

Baron, Hans, ed. *Leonardo Bruni Aretino: Humanistisch-philosophische Schriften*. Leipzig and Berlin, 1928.

Beierwaltes, Werner. *Marsilio Ficinos Theorie des Schönen im Kontext des Platonismus*. Sitzungsberichte der Heidelberger Akademie der Wissenschaften: Philosophisch-historische Klasse, Jahrgang 30, no. 11. Heidelberg, 1980.

Benardete, Seth. *The Being of the Beautiful: Plato's "Theaetetus," "Sophist" and "Statesman," Translated with Commentary*. Chicago, 1984.

————, "Plato's *Sophist* 223b1–7." *Phronesis* 5 (1960), 129–139.

Bianchi, Massimo. See under Fattori.

Bluck, Richard S. *Plato's "Sophist": A Commentary*. Edited by Gordon C. Neal. Manchester, Eng., 1975.

Blumenthal, H. J. "Soul, World-Soul, and Individual Soul in Plotinus." In *Le néoplatonisme: Colloque international du Centre national de la recherche scientifique, Royaumont, 9–13 juin 1969*, pp. 55–66. Paris, 1971.

Bregman, Jay. *Synesius of Cyrene, Philosopher-Bishop*. Berkeley, Los Angeles, London, 1982.

Brown, Virginia, ed. See under Cranz.

Burnet, John, ed. *Platonis Opera*. Oxford, 1900 ff.

Bywater, I., ed. *Prisciani Lydi Quae Extant: Metaphrasis in Theophrastum et Solutionum ad Chosroem Liber*. In *Supplementum Aristotelicum*, vol. 1, part 2. Berlin, 1886.

Cairns, Huntington. See under Hamilton.

Charrue, Jean-Michel. *Plotin: Lecteur de Platon*. Paris, 1978.

Chastel, André. *Art et humanisme à Florence au temps de Laurent le Magnifique*. Paris, 1961.

————. *Marsile Ficin et l'art*. Geneva and Lille, 1954. Reprint, Geneva, 1975.

Collins, Ardis B. *The Secular Is Sacred: Platonism and Thomism in Marsilio Ficino's "Platonic Theology."* International Archives of the History of Ideas, no. 69. The Hague, 1974.

Copenhaver, Brian P. "Hermes Trismegistus, Proclus and the Question of a Philosophy of Magic in the Renaissance." In *Hermeticism and the Renaissance: Intellectual History and the Occult in Early Modern Europe,* edited by Ingrid Merkel and Allen G. Debus, pp. 79–110. London and Toronto, 1988.

———. "Iamblichus, Synesius and the *Chaldaean Oracles* in Marsilio Ficino's *De Vita Libri Tres:* Hermetic Magic or Neoplatonic Magic." In *Supplementum Festivum* (see under Hankins in this Bibliography), pp. 441–455.

———. "Renaissance Magic and Neoplatonic Philosophy: *Ennead* 4.3–5 in Ficino's *De Vita Coelitus Comparanda.*" In *Marsilio Ficino e il ritorno di Platone: Studi e documenti* (see under Garfagnini in this Bibliography), pp. 351–369.

———. "Scholastic Philosophy and Renaissance Magic in the *De Vita* of Marsilio Ficino." *Renaissance Quarterly* 37 (1984), 523–554.

Cornford, Francis Macdonald. *Plato's Theory of Knowledge: The "Theaetetus" and the "Sophist" of Plato Translated with an Introduction and Running Commentary.* London, 1935.

Corsi, Giovanni. *Vita Marsilii Ficini.* In *Marsile Ficin (1433–1499)* (see under Marcel in this Bibliography), pp. 680–689.

Couliano, Ioan Petru. *Eros et magie à la Renaissance, 1484.* Paris, 1984. Translated by Margaret Cook under the title *Eros and Magic in the Renaissance,* with a foreword by Mircea Eliade. Chicago, 1987.

Cousin, Victor, ed. *Procli Philosophi Platonici Opera Inedita.* Paris, 1864. Reprint, Frankfurt am Main, 1962.

Cranz, F. Edward, Paul Oskar Kristeller, and Virginia Brown, eds. *Catalogus Translationum et Commentariorum: Mediaeval and Renaissance Latin Translations and Commentaries: Annotated Lists and Guides.* 6 vols. to date. Washington, D.C., 1960–.

Craven, W. G. *Giovanni Pico della Mirandola, Symbol of His Age: Modern Interpretations of a Renaissance Philosopher.* Geneva, 1981.

Culianu, Ioan Petru. See under Couliano.

Curtius, Ernst Robert. *European Literature and the Latin Middle Ages.* Translated by Willard R. Trask. New York, 1953. Reprint, New York and Evanston, Ill., 1963.

Des Places, Edouard, ed. and tr. *Numenius: Fragments.* Budé series. Paris, 1973.

Detel, Wolfgang. *Platons Beschreibung des falschen Satzes in Theätet und Sophistes.* Hypomnemata: Untersuchungen zur Antike und ihrem Nachleben, Heft 36. Göttingen, 1972.

Devereux, James A. "The Textual History of Ficino's De Amore." *Renaissance Quarterly* 28 (1975), 173–182.

Diehl, Ernst, ed. *Procli Diadochi in Platonis Timaeum Commentaria.* 3 vols. Leipzig, 1903–1906. Reprint, Amsterdam, 1965.

Diès, Auguste. *La définition de l'être et la nature des idées dans le "Sophiste" de Platon.* Paris, 1909.

Diller, A. "Notes on the History of Some Manuscripts of Plato." In his *Studies in*

Greek Manuscript Tradition. Amsterdam, 1983.
Dillon, John M. *The Middle Platonists, 80 B.C. to A.D. 220.* London and Ithaca, N.Y., 1977.
———, ed. and trans. *Iamblichi Chalcidensis in Platonis Dialogos Commentariorum Fragmenta.* Leiden, 1973.
See also under Morrow.
Dodds, Eric Robertson. *Pagan and Christian in an Age of Anxiety.* Cambridge, 1965.
———, ed. and trans. *Proclus: The Elements of Theology.* Oxford, 1933. 2d ed., 1963.
Dupréel, Eugene. *Les sophistes: Protagoras, Gorgias, Prodicus, Hippias.* Neuchâtel, 1948 (1949).
Fattori, Marta, and Massimo Bianchi, eds. *Spiritus: IVo Colloquio Internazionale del Lessico Intellettuale Europeo (Roma, 7–9 gennaio 1983).* Rome, 1984.
Festugière, André-Jean, trans. *Proclus: Commentaire sur la République.* 3 vols. Paris, 1970.
———, trans. *Proclus: Commentaire sur le Timée.* 5 vols. Paris, 1966–1969. See also under Nock.
Ficino, Marsilio. *Commentaria in Platonem.* Florence, 1496.
———. *Opera Omnia.* Basel, 1576. Reprint, Turin, 1959, 1983.
———. *Platonis Opera Omnia.* Florence, 1484. 2d ed., Venice, 1491.
———. *Plotini Enneades.* Florence, 1492.
See also under Allen, Kristeller, La Porta, Niccoli, Marcel, Ottaviano, Rensi; also under Jayne, Members.
Field, Arthur. "John Argyropoulos and the 'Secret Teachings' of Plato." In *Supplementum Festivum* (see under Hankins in this Bibliography), pp. 299–326.
Finamore, John F. *Iamblichus and the Theory of the Vehicle of the Soul.* American Classical Studies, vol. 14. Chico, Calif., 1985.
Fitzgerald, A. *The Essays and Hymns of Synesius of Cyrene.* 2 vols. Oxford, 1930.
Frede, Michael. *Prädikation und Existenzaussage: Platons Gebrauch von "ist" und "ist nicht" im Sophistes.* Hypomnemata: Untersuchungen zur Antike und ihrem Nachleben, Heft 18. Göttingen, 1967.
Garfagnini, Gian Carlo, ed. *Marsilio Ficino e il ritorno di Platone: Studi e documenti.* 2 vols. Florence, 1986.
Garin, Eugenio. *La cultura filosofica del Rinascimento italiano.* Florence, 1961.
———. *Giovanni Pico della Mirandola: Vita e dottrina.* Florence, 1937.
———. "Per la storia della cultura filosofica del Rinascimento." *Rivista critica di storia della filosofia* 12 (1957), 3–21.
———. "Ricerche sulle traduzioni di Platone nella prima metà del sec. XV." In *Medioevo e Rinascimento: Studi in onore di Bruno Nardi* 1:339–374. Florence, 1955.
———. *Rinascite e rivoluzioni: Movimenti culturali dal XIV al XVII secolo.* Bari, 1975.

————, ed. and trans. *Giovanni Pico della Mirandola: De Hominis Dignitate, De Ente et Uno, e scritti vari.* Florence, 1942.

Gentile, Sebastiano. "Note sui manoscritti greci di Platone utilizzati da Marsilio Ficino." In *Scritti in onore di Eugenio Garin,* pp. 51–84. Pisa, 1987.

————. "Per la storia del testo del 'Commentarium in Convivium' di Marsilio Ficino." *Rinascimento,* 2d ser., 21 (1981), 3–27.

Gentile, Sebastiano, Sandra Niccoli, and Paolo Viti, eds. *Marsilio Ficino e il ritorno di Platone: Mostra di manoscritti, stampe e documenti (17 maggio—16 giugno 1984).* Florence, 1984.

Gersh, Stephen. *From Iamblichus to Eriugena: An Investigation of the Prehistory and Evolution of the Pseudo-Dionysian Tradition.* Leiden, 1978.

————. *Kinêsis akinêtos: A Study of Spiritual Motion in the Philosophy of Proclus.* Philosophia Antiqua, vol. 26. Leiden, 1973.

————. *Middle Platonism and Neoplatonism: The Latin Tradition.* 2 vols. Notre Dame, Ind., 1986.

Gilbert, Neal Ward. *Renaissance Concepts of Method.* New York, 1960. Reprint, 1963.

Giusta, M. *"Albinou Epitomê o Alkinoou Didaskalikos?"* Atti della Accademia delle Scienze di Torino, Classe di scienze morali, storiche e filologiche 95 (1960–1961), 167–194.

Gouk, Penelope. See under Walker.

Greene, William (Guilielmus) Chase, ed. *Scholia Platonica.* American Philological Association Monograph 8. Haverford, Pa., 1938. Reprint, Chico, Calif., 1981.

Guthrie, W. K. C. *A History of Greek Philosophy.* 6 vols. Cambridge, 1962–1981.

Hadot, Pierre. "Etre, vie, pensée chez Plotin et avant Plotin." In *Les sources de Plotin,* pp. 107–157. Entretiens Hardt, vol. 5. Geneva, 1960.

————. *Plotin ou la simplicité du regard.* Paris, 1963.

————. *Porphyre et Victorinus.* 2 vols. Paris, 1968.

Hallyn, Fernand. "Copernic et le platonisme ficinien." In *L'invention au XVIe siècle,* pp. 135–151. Bordeaux, 1987.

————. *La structure poétique du monde: Copernic, Kepler.* Paris, 1987.

Hamilton, Edith, and Huntington Cairns, eds. *The Collected Dialogues of Plato Including the Letters.* Princeton, 1961.

Hamm, V. M., trans. *Pico della Mirandola: Of Being and Unity.* Milwaukee, 1943.

Hankins, James. "Latin Translations of Plato in the Renaissance." Ph.D. diss., Columbia University, 1984.

————. "Some Remarks on the History and Character of Ficino's Translation of Plato." In *Marsilio Ficino e il ritorno di Platone: Studi e documenti* (see under Garfagnini in this Bibliography), pp. 287–297.

Hankins, James, John Monfasani, and Frederick Purnell, Jr., eds. *Supplementum Festivum: Studies in Honor of Paul Oskar Kristeller.* Binghamton, N.Y., 1987.

Heitzman, Marian. "L'agostinismo avicennizzante e il punto di partenza della filosofia di Marsilio Ficino." *Giornale critico della filosofia italiana* 16 (1935), 295–322, 460–480; 17 (1936), 1–11.

Helleman-Elgersma, W. *Soul-Sisters: A Commentary on Enneads IV.3 [27].1–8 of Plotinus*. Amsterdam, 1980.

Henry, Paul, and Hans-Rudolf Schwyzer, eds. *Plotini Opera*. 6 vols. Paris and Brussels, 1951.

Hermann, Karl Friedrich, ed. *Platonis Opera*. 6 vols. Leipzig, 1852–1856. Reprint, 1887–1902, 1921–1936. Vol. 6 contains Albinus's *Eisagoge* and *Didaskalikos* on pp. 145–189.

Iamblichus. See under Dillon and Larsen.

Inge, William Ralph. *The Philosophy of Plotinus*. 2 vols. 2d ed. London, 1923.

Jaeger, Werner. *Paideia: The Ideals of Greek Culture*. Translated by Gilbert Highet (from the 2d German ed.). 2d ed. Oxford, 1945.

Jayne, Sears R., trans. *Marsilio Ficino: Commentary on Plato's Symposium on Love*. Dallas, Tex., 1985.

Joukovsky, Françoise. *Le regard intérieur: Thèmes plotiniens chez quelques écrivains de la Renaissance française*. Paris, 1982.

———. "Plotin dans les éditions et les commentaires de Porphyre, Jamblique et Proclus à la Renaissance." *Bibliothèque d'humanisme et Renaissance* 42 (1980), 387–400.

Jowett, Benjamin, trans. *The Dialogues of Plato Translated into English with Analyses and Introductions*. 4th ed. Edited by D. J. Allan and H. E. Dale. 4 vols. Oxford, 1953.

Kerferd, G. *The Sophistic Movement*. Cambridge, 1981.

Ketchum, R. "Participation and Predication in the *Sophist* 251–260." *Phronesis* 23 (1978), 42–62.

Kissling, Robert Christian. "The *ochêma-pneuma* of the Neo-Platonists and the *De Insomniis* of Synesius of Cyrene." *American Journal of Philology* 43 (1922), 318–330.

Klein, Jacob. *Plato's Trilogy: Theaetetus, the Sophist and the Statesman*. Chicago, 1977.

Klein, Robert. "L'imagination comme vêtement de l'âme chez Marsile Ficin et Giordano Bruno." *Revue de métaphysique et de morale* 61 (1956), 18–39.

Klibansky, Raymond. *The Continuity of the Platonic Tradition during the Middle Ages*. Munich, 1981.

———. "Plato's Parmenides in the Middle Ages and the Renaissance." *Mediaeval and Renaissance Studies* 1 (1943), 281–330.

Kristeller, Paul Oskar. "Ficino and Pomponazzi on Man." *Journal of the History of Ideas* 5 (1944), 227–239.

———. "The First Printed Edition of Plato's Works and the Date of Its Publication (1484)." In *Science and History: Studies in Honor of Edward Rosen*, edited by Erna Hilfstein, Pawel Czartoryski, and Frank D. Grande, pp. 25–35. Wroclaw, 1978.

————. *Marsilio Ficino and His Work after Five Hundred Years.* Quaderni di Rinascimento, no. 7. Florence, 1987. Also in *Marsilio Ficino e il ritorno di Platone: Studi e documenti* (see under Garfagnini in this Bibliography), pp. 15–196.

————. "Marsilio Ficino as a Beginning Student of Plato." *Scriptorium* 20 (1966), 41–54.

————. "The Modern System of the Arts." *Journal of the History of Ideas* 12 (1951), 496–527. Reprinted in *Renaissance Thought and the Arts* (see under Kristeller in this Bibliography), pp. 163–227.

————. *The Philosophy of Marsilio Ficino.* New York, 1943. Reprint, Gloucester, Mass., 1964. *Die Philosophie des Marsilio Ficino.* Frankfurt am Main, 1972. *Il pensiero filosofico di Marsilio Ficino.* Florence, 1953. Rev. ed. with updated bibliography, 1988.

————. "Proclus as a Reader of Plato and Plotinus, and His Influence in the Middle Ages and in the Renaissance." In *Proclus: Lecteur et interprète des anciens,* pp. 191–211. Colloques internationaux du C.N.R.S. Paris, 1987.

————. *Renaissance Concepts of Man and Other Essays.* New York, 1972.

————. *Renaissance Thought and Its Sources.* Edited by Michael Mooney. New York, 1979.

————. *Renaissance Thought and the Arts.* Princeton, 1980.

————. "Some Original Letters and Autograph Manuscripts of Marsilio Ficino." In *Studi di bibliografia e di storia in onore di Tammaro De Marinis* 3:5–33. Verona, 1964.

————. *Studies in Renaissance Thought and Letters.* 2 vols. Rome, 1956–1985.

————. *Supplementum Ficinianum.* 2 vols. Florence, 1937. Reprint, 1973.

————. *Le thomisme et la pensée italienne de la Renaissance.* Montreal, 1967. See also under Cranz.

Kroll, Wilhelm (Guilelmus), ed. *Procli Diadochi in Platonis Rem Publicam Commentarii.* 2 vols. Leipzig, 1899–1901.

La Porta, G. *Marsilio Ficino: L'essenza dell'amore.* Rome, 1982.

Larsen, Bent Dalsgaard. *Jamblique de Chalcis: Exégète et philosophe.* Plus supplement, *Testimonia et Fragmenta Exegetica.* Aarhus, 1972.

Lee, Edward N. "Plato on Negation and Not-Being in the *Sophist.*" *Philosophical Review* 81 (1972), 267–304.

Lindberg, David C. *Studies in the History of Medieval Optics.* London, 1983.

————. *Theories of Vision from al-Kindi to Kepler.* Chicago, 1976.

MacKenna, Stephen, trans. *Plotinus: The Enneads.* 3d ed. Revised by B. S. Page. London, 1962.

Malcolm, J. "Plato's Analysis of *to on* and *to mê on* in the *Sophist.*" *Phronesis* 12 (1967), 130–146.

Manasse, E. M. *Platons "Sophistes" und "Politikos": Das Problem der Wahrheit.* Berlin, 1937.

Mansfield, J. "Bad World and Demiurge: A 'Gnostic' Motif from Parmenides and

Empedocles to Lucretius and Philo." In *Studies in Gnosticism and Hellenistic Religions,* edited by R. van den Broek and M. J. Vermaseren, pp. 261–314. Leiden, 1981.

Marcel, Raymond. *Marsile Ficin (1433–1499).* Paris, 1958.

———, ed. and trans. *Marsile Ficin: Commentaire sur le Banquet de Platon.* Paris, 1956.

———, ed. and trans. *Marsile Ficin: Théologie platonicienne de l'immortalité des âmes.* 3 vols. Paris, 1964–1970.

Marten, Rainer. *Der Logos der Dialektik: Eine Theorie zu Platons Sophistes.* Berlin, 1965.

Members of the Language Department of the School of Economic Science, London, trans. *The Letters of Marsilio Ficino.* 4 vols. to date. London, 1975–.

Mettauer, T. *De Platonis Scholiorum Fontibus.* Zurich, 1880.

Milham, Mary Ella. "C. Julius Solinus." In *Catalogus Translationum et Commentariorum* (see under Cranz in this Bibliography), 6:73–85.

Moerbeke, William of. See under Steel.

Mohler, Ludwig. *Kardinal Bessarion als Theologe, Humanist und Staatsmann.* 3 vols. Paderborn, 1923–1942. Reprint, 1967.

Mommsen, Theodore, ed. *Caius Julius Solinus: Collectanea Rerum Memorabilium.* Berlin, 1864. Rev. ed., 1895. 2d rev. ed., 1958.

Monfasani, John. "For the History of Marsilio Ficino's Translation of Plato: The Revision Mistakenly Attributed to Ambrogio Flandino, Simon Grynaeus' Revision of 1532, and the Anonymous Revision of 1556/67." *Rinascimento,* 2d ser., 27 (1987), 293–299.

———. "Pseudo-Dionysius the Areopagite in Mid-Quattrocento Rome." In *Supplementum Festivum* (see under Hankins in this Bibliography), pp. 189–219. See also under Hankins.

Moraux, Paul. "Quinta Essentia." In Pauly-Wissowa-Kroll, *Realencyclopädie der classischen Altertumswissenschaft* 24.1 (1963), 1171–1263, esp. 1251–1256.

Moravcsik, Julius M. E. "Being and Meaning in the *Sophist.*" *Acta Philosophica Fennica* 14 (1962), 23–78.

———. "*Symplokê Eidôn* and the Genesis of *Logos.*" *Archiv für Geschichte der Philosophie* 42 (1960), 117–129.

Morrow, Glenn R., and John M. Dillon, trans. *Proclus' Commentary on Plato's Parmenides.* Princeton, 1987.

Napoli, Giovanni di. "L'essere e l'uno in Pico della Mirandola." *Rivista di filosofia neo-scolastica* 46 (1954), 356–389.

———. "L'essere e l'uno in Pico della Mirandola." In *Il pensiero italiano del Rinascimento e il tempo nostro: Atti del V Convegno internazionale del Centro di Studi Umanistici, 8–13 agosto 1968,* edited by Giovannangiola Tarugi, pp. 117–129. Florence, 1970.

———. *Giovanni Pico della Mirandola e la problematica dottrinale del suo tempo.* Rome, 1965.

Neal, Gordon C. See under Bluck.

Nebel, G. "Terminologische Untersuchungen zu *ousia* und *on* bei Plotin." *Hermes* 65 (1930), 422–445.

Niccoli, Sandra, ed. *Marsilio Ficino: El libro dell'amore.* Istituto Nazionale di Studi sul Rinascimento: Studi e Testi, no. 16. Florence, 1987. See also under Gentile.

Nock, Arthur Darby, and A.-J. Festugière, eds. and trans. *Corpus Hermeticum.* 4 vols. Paris, 1945–1954.

Numenius. See under Des Places.

Olympiodorus. See under Westerink.

Orpheus. See under Quandt.

Ottaviano, G. *Marsilio Ficino: Sopra lo amore.* Milan, 1973.

Owen, G. E. L. "Plato on Not-Being." In *Plato I* (see under Vlastos in this Bibliography), pp. 223–267.

Philip, J. A. "The Platonic Corpus." *Phoenix* 24 (1970), 296–308.

Pico della Mirandola, Giovanni. See under Garin; also under Hamm, C. G. Wallis.

Plato. See under Burnet, Hermann; also under Cornford, Ficino, Hamilton, Jowett.

Plotinus. See under Armstrong, Ficino, Mackenna.

Pollet, G. See under Sleeman.

Portus, Aemilius, ed. and trans. *Procli Successoris Platonici in Platonis Theologiam Libri Sex.* Hamburg, 1618. Reprint, Frankfurt am Main, 1960.

Proclus. See under Diehl, Dodds, Kroll, Portus, Saffrey, Westerink; also under Festugière, Steel.

Purnell, Frederick, Jr. "The Theme of Philosophic Concord and the Sources of Ficino's Platonism." In *Marsilio Ficino e il ritorno di Platone: Studi e documenti* (see under Garfagnini in this Bibliography), pp. 397–415. See also under Hankins.

Putscher, M. *Pneuma, Spiritus, Geist.* Wiesbaden, 1973.

Quandt, Guilelmus, ed. *Orphei Hymni.* Berlin, 1955.

Ray, A. Chadwick. *For Images: An Interpretation of Plato's "Sophist."* Lanham, Md., 1984.

Rensi, Giuseppe, ed. *Sopra lo Amore ovvero Convito di Platone.* Lanciano, 1914.

Rijk, Lambertus Marie de. *Plato's "Sophist": A Philosophical Commentary.* Amsterdam and New York, 1986.

Rist, J. M. "Mysticism and Transcendence in Later Neoplatonism." *Hermes* 92 (1964), 213–225.

Romilly, Jacqueline de. *Magic and Rhetoric in Ancient Greece.* Cambridge, Mass., 1975.

Rosen, Stanley. *Plato's "Sophist": The Drama of Original and Image.* New Haven, Conn., 1983.

Runciman, W. G. *Plato's Later Epistemology.* Cambridge, 1962.

Russell, Donald Andrew. *Plutarch.* London, 1973.

Saffrey, H. D., and L. G. Westerink, eds. and trans. *Proclus: Théologie platonicienne.* 5 vols. to date. Paris, 1968–.

Sayre, Kenneth M. *Plato's Analytic Method.* Chicago and London, 1969.

————. *Plato's Late Ontology: A Riddle Resolved.* Princeton, 1983.

Schmitt, Charles B. "Priscianus Lydus." In *Catalogus Translationum et Commentariorum* (see under Cranz in this Bibliography), 3:75–82.

Schwyzer, Hans-Rudolf. See under Henry.

Seligman, Paul. *Being and Not-Being: An Introduction to Plato's "Sophist."* The Hague, 1974.

Sicherl, Martin. "Neuentdeckte Handschriften von Marsilio Ficino und Johannes Reuchlin." *Scriptorium* 16 (1962), 50–61.

Sleeman, J. H., and G. Pollet. *Lexicon Plotinianum.* Leiden and Louvain, 1980.

Steel, Carlos, ed. *Proclus: Commentaire sur le Parménide de Platon, traduction de Guillaume de Moerbeke.* 2 vols. Louvain and Leiden, 1982–1985.

Tarán, Leonardo. *Academica: Plato, Philip of Opus, and the Pseudo-Platonic Epinomis.* Memoirs of the American Philosophical Society, vol. 107. Philadelphia, 1975.

Taylor, A. E. *Plato: The Man and His Work.* London, 1926.

Teloh, Henry. *The Development of Plato's Metaphysics.* University Park, Pa., 1981.

Terzaghi, Nicolaus, ed. *Synesii Cyrenensis Opuscula.* Rome, 1944.

Torre, Arnaldo della. *Storia dell'Accademia Platonica di Firenze.* Florence, 1902.

Trinkaus, Charles. *In Our Image and Likeness: Humanity and Divinity in Italian Humanist Thought.* 2 vols. London, 1970.

————. "Marsilio Ficino and the Ideal of Human Autonomy." In *Marsilio Ficino e il ritorno di Platone: Studi e documenti* (see under Garfagnini in this Bibliography), pp. 197–210. Also in *Ficino and Renaissance Neoplatonism*, edited by Konrad Eisenbichler and Olga Zorzi Pugliese, pp. 141–153. University of Toronto Italian Studies, vol. 1. Ottawa, 1986.

————. *The Scope of Renaissance Humanism.* Ann Arbor, 1983.

Verbeke, G. "Guillaume de Moerbeke traducteur de Proclus." *Revue philosophique de Louvain* 51 (1953), 349–373.

Viti, Paolo. See under Gentile.

Vlastos, Gregory. "An Ambiguity in the *Sophist*." In his *Platonic Studies,* pp. 270–322. Princeton, 1973. Rev. ed., 1981.

————, ed. *Plato I: Metaphysics and Epistemology.* Garden City, N.Y., 1970.

Walker, D. P. *The Ancient Theology: Studies in Christian Platonism from the Fifteenth to the Eighteenth Century.* London, 1972.

————. "The Astral Body in Renaissance Medicine." *Journal of the Warburg and Courtauld Institutes* 21 (1958), 119–133.

————. *Music, Spirit and Language in the Renaissance.* Edited by Penelope Gouk. London, 1984.

————. *Spiritual and Demonic Magic: from Ficino to Campanella.* London, 1958. Reprint, Notre Dame, Ind., 1975.

Wallis, C. G., P. J. W. Miller, and D. Carmichael, trans. *Pico della Mirandola: On the Dignity of Man, On Being and the One, Heptaplus.* Indianapolis and New York, 1965.

Wallis, R. T. *Neoplatonism*. London, 1972.

Warden, John, ed. *Orpheus: The Metamorphoses of a Myth*. Toronto, Buffalo, London, 1982.

Weiss, Roberto. "New Light on Humanism in England during the Fifteenth Century." *Journal of the Warburg and Courtauld Institutes* 14 (1951), 21–33.

Westerink, Leendert Gerrit, ed. and trans. *Anonymous Prolegomena to Platonic Philosophy*. Amsterdam, 1962.

————, ed. *The Greek Commentaries on Plato's Phaedo*. 2 vols. Amsterdam and New York, 1976–1977.

————, ed. *Olympiodorus: Commentary on the First Alcibiades of Plato*. Amsterdam, 1956.

————, ed. *Proclus Diadochus: Commentary on the First Alcibiades of Plato*. Amsterdam, 1954.

See also under Saffrey.

Whittaker, J. "Lost and Found: Some Manuscripts of the *Didaskalikos* of Alcinous (Albinus)." *Symbolae Osloenses* 49 (1973), 127–139.

Wind, Edgar. *Pagan Mysteries in the Renaissance*. Rev. ed. New York, 1968.

Wolters, Albert M. "The First Draft of Ficino's Translation of Plotinus." In *Marsilio Ficino e il ritorno di Platone: Studi e documenti* (see under Garfagnini in this Bibliography), pp. 305–329.

Zadro, Attilio. *Ricerche sul linguaggio e sulla logica del "Sofista."* Proagônes: Collezioni di studi e teste, edited by Carlo Diano, Studi, vol. 5. Padua, 1961.

Zanier, Giancarlo. *La medicina astrologica e la sua teoria: Marsilio Ficino e i suoi critici contemporanei*. Rome, 1977.

Index to Introduction and Part I

Activation theory, 121–122
Aelian, 189 n. 24, 191 n. 28
Aesthetics, 167
Aether: Aristotelian concept of, 158, 178–179; as fiery air/pure fire, 158, 172, 173, 177, 178; as fifth element, 178 n. 11; Platonic concept of, 178–179
Aethereal: demons, 174, 175–176 n. 10; vehicle of soul, 201, 202–203
Aglaophamus, 80
Ahriman, 98
Air: airy, 172, 173; demons inhabit, 163–164, 172, 173–174, 177–178; as element, 178; enters ear, 163; fiery, 158, 172, 173, 177, 178; light associated with, 172; as medium of transfer of sound, 163, 172; misty, 172, 173; shaped by vocal arts, 163
Airy: air, 172, 173; demons, 174, 175–176 n. 10, 177–178; men, 181; veil/vehicle of soul, 178, 179, 180, 201
Alberti, Leon Battista, 134
Albertus Magnus, 124 n. 7
Albinus (Alcinous), 17, 39, 40, 120 n. 4
Alcibiades, 26
Alcibiades I, 85, 87, 88
Alexander of Aphrodisias, 36
Alexandrian circle, 83, 84
Ammonius, 83, 97
Anaxagoras, 74, 126
Angels: arts of, 136, 138, 139, 141, 142, 146–147; demons equated with, 164; as individuals, 138 n. 29; intelligence of, 140, 141; as mediators, 138; powers of, 128; preside over celestial nature, 150; as species, 138 n. 29, 139

Animals: arts of, 135–136, 142, 143, 148–149; souls of, 135–136
Apelles, 149
Apology, 5, 27, 88
Apuleius of Madaura, 27, 79
Aquinas, Thomas, 37, 60, 67, 124 n. 7, 138 n. 29, 155 n. 62
Archimedes, 149, 154
Architecture, 156; as art, 139, 162; of churches, 133, 134; form in, 132–134; personal, 133
Archytas of Tarentum, 78, 79, 80, 149
Arethas, 91
Argyropoulos, John, 22–23 n. 22, 207 n. 6
Aristophanes, 26, 27
Aristophanes of Byzantium, 15 n. 8
Aristotelians, 2, 184, 196; as sophists, 22–23 n. 22. *See also* Pico della Mirandola, Giovanni
Aristotle: on aether, 158, 178–179; on arts, 137; on being, 19, 38, 46 n. 65, 54, 72, 78; on form and matter, 157, 169 n. 2; on God's actuality, 46 n. 65; on hyena, 189 n. 24, 191; on intelligible realm, 54, 71 n. 30; intentions of, 196, 197, 203; *Metaphysics* of, 38; on mirror imagery, 189–190; on nature of soul, 187–188 n. 19; on not-being, 72; on One, 38, 72; *Physics* of, 169 n. 2; Plato reconciled/contrasted with, 36–37, 38, 39–40, 47, 54, 71–72, 157, 187–188 n. 19; on pure intelligence, 160; as sophist, 207 n. 6
Arithmetic, 153
Arts, 132; actual/practicing, 137, 138–139; of angels, 136, 138, 139, 141, 142, 146–147; of animals, 135–

Division/divisibility, 61 n. 27, 70, 84
Dog, and hyena, 189, 190, 191
Dreams, 169, 170, 171, 194, 199. *See also* Images; Shadows
Dryness, 76

Ear, 163, 172, 176
Earth, 178, 201, 202
Ecstasy, 141, 153
Effluxes, 195–196, 197, 199–200
Egyptians, 149, 159, 173
Eleatics, 20, 74, 77, 78, 79, 80, 81. *See also* Melissus; Pythagoreans
Eleatic Stranger, 13, 77; on arts, 170–171; auditors of, 12, 45, 113; on being, 44–45, 53, 56, 62, 74–75, 206; on change and motion, 56; as Demiurge, 112, 114; described, 73; on essence and existence, 62; on external images, 182; Ficino identifies as Melissus, 11, 12 n. 3, 66, 73, 115, 168, 182, 206; on Ideas, 44; on imitation, 117; on not-being, 74–75, 168, 206; on One, 44; as Parmenidean, 11, 73; Parmenides attacked by, 168, 206; on phantastic realm, 175; on sophist, 108; *Sophist* scholion on, 112, 113, 114
Elements, 99, 151, 178, 179. *See also* Air; Earth; Fire; Water
Elizabethans, 191 n. 27
Empedocles, 76–77, 185, 193
Enneads of Plotinus, 50, 53, 70, 99, 100, 120 n. 4, 127; Ficino influenced by, 2, 19, 24, 31, 49, 51, 81–82, 200
Epicureans, 157, 197
Epinomis, 126, 178–179
Essence: abstract, 60; as being, 19, 60, 61, 62, 66, 67; distinct from being and existence, 60, 62; of Ideas, 66–67; imaginary, 19, 21; of incorporeals, 19, 67; infinite bestows, 61; -life-understanding, 57; from One, 62
Eurytus, 79, 80
Euthydemus, 103 n. 59
Exercise/fitness, 162
Existence, 60, 61, 62, 66–67. *See also* Being

Eye, 117–118, 172

Faculties, 135, 136, 173–174, 177, 204. *See also* Soul
Fate, 204
Festugière, A.-J., 101, 103
Ficini, Ficino, 32–33 n. 34
Ficino, Marsilio: anthropocentrism of, 132–134, 142, 148; Aquinas influenced, 67, 138 n. 29, 155 n. 62; *Argumentum in Platonicam Theologiam* of, 146; on astrology, 160; on astronomy, 153–154, 159; Augustine influenced, 128 n. 12, 130, 146; Averroes influenced, 150; on beauty, 128 n. 12, 130; Bruni influenced, 13–14; Calcidius as source for, 186 n. 18; as Christian Platonist, 2, 4, 21, 34, 37, 65–66, 99, 120 n. 4, 126–127, 152; *Commentaria in Platonem* of, 1, 4, 32–34, 50–51 (*see also* individual commentaries by name of dialogue); *De Amore* of (see *Symposium* commentary); *De Vita* of, 163; on demons' skill, 3; on Eleatic Stranger as Melissus, 11, 12 n. 3, 66, 73, 115, 168, 182, 206; on Florentine architects, 132–134, 156–157; *Iamblichi de Mysteriis et Alia* of, 194; Iamblichus influenced, 102; influence/impact of, 33, 128 n. 12, 148, 162, 167, 207 n. 6, 210; on life of contemplation, 156; Lucretius influenced, 192–193; Neoplatonists influenced, 83; *Opera Omnia* of, 16–17, 85, 90, 194; optimism of, 153 n. 57; Orphic lyre of, 164; pessimism of, 153 n. 57; v. Pico, 2, 35–48, 64, 71–72, 82; *Platonic Theology* of, 3, 4, 31, 32, 79, 80, 96, 127–166, 201–202; *Platonis Opera Omnia* of, 14, 15; Plotinus influenced, 2, 3, 4, 19, 24, 31, 49, 51–53, 59, 81–82, 83, 200; Proclus influenced, 18, 49, 83, 89–91, 94, 96, 100, 115, 168–169, 188–189, 190, 193, 209; on St. Paul, 33, 173; Scholastics influenced, 67; *Sophist* scholion attributed to Proclus

167. *See also* Icastes/icastic art; Phantastes/phantastic art

Images: Aristotle on, 189–190; as demon's realm, 3, 21–22, 170, 171–172, 175, 177, 191; external, 182; God's, 128, 156, 164; ideal, 122; idola as, 199, 203; idolum mediates, 201, 202; imagination processes, 185, 200; inverted, 186; and lesser demiurges, 170; light affects/produces, 182–183, 185, 192; magicians use, 185, 191; material, 185, 197; mirror/specular, 164, 183, 185–186, 187, 189–190, 192, 197, 198; origin of, 197; radial, 185–186, 192, 193, 197, 198; and sensation, 181, 182; from sensible species, 196–197; shape of, 182; and simulacra, 189, 201; sophist creates, 108; in *Sophist,* 3, 21; of soul, 100; as species, 190; spiritual, 185, 192, 193, 197; in sublunar realm, 199; as substantive, 190; things of, affected by, 191; as transitory, 199

Imagination, 3, 168; celestial vehicle and, 180, 181; demonic, 175–176, 177, 181–182; distorted, 180–181; in dreams, 176, 199; Freudians on, 204; as good or bad, 181, 182; images act on/are processed by, 185, 200; independent of sensation, 181, 182; move through idola, 199; and phantasy, 124, 198; Romanticism on, 204; shadows perceived via, 175; and universal sense, 180

Imitation, 29, 124; art as, 117, 118, 119–120, 122, 146, 147, 149, 150–151, 153, 155, 156, 166; Eleatic Stranger on, 117; v. emulation, 18; of form, 131, 132, 170; by Homer, 30; of Idea, 118, 119–120, 122; of intelligible world, 118–119, 168, 169, 170; ironic, 125, 205; by man, of God, 18, 119, 128, 147, 149, 150–151, 152, 153, 154, 155, 156, 166; partial not-being in, 118; by philosopher, 18, 164; pyramid/hierarchy of, 170; shadows and dreams as, 170; by

sophist, 111, 112, 114, 116, 205; by sublunar demiurge, 111, 114, 170

Incorporeals, 19, 67

Indivisible and divisible, 61 n. 27

Infinite, 34, 49, 50, 61, 62, 63–64

Instrumentality, 146, 150, 159, 160, 185, 198

Intellect, prime, 38, 65, 67, 68. *See also* Mind

Intelligence, 109, 140, 141, 160

Intelligible realm/world: Aristotle on, 54, 71 n. 30; being of, 54, 58, 65, 66, 77, 78; creation of, 118–119, 126; forms of, 130, 131–132, 170–171, 172, 174; imitation of, 118–119, 168, 169, 170; v. sensible world, 68, 70, 132; sophist looks up to, 109

Intentions, 196, 197, 200, 203

Ion, 140

Ion, 16, 17, 140

Jove/Jupiter: as aspect of Cronus, 102, 105, 106; as aspect of Mind, 105, 112; as demiurge, 105, 113, 114, 115; great and greatest, 107; Socrates represents, 113, 114; as sophist, 108, 111, 115, 206. *See also* Zeus

Julian, 97 n. 39, 174–175 n. 9

Jupiter (planet), 106

Justinian, 187–188 n. 19

Klein, Robert, 124 n. 7

Knowing, v. seeing, 117–118, 203

Knowledge, 78, 124

Kristeller, Paul O., 15, 31 n. 31, 76, 154 n. 59, 157; on soul's idolum, 200, 201–202

Landino, Cristoforo, 14, 139

Language, 126, 155

Larsen, Bent Dalsgaard, 92, 95

Lascaris, Janus, 93, 188

Laws, 13, 20 n. 18, 88, 97, 104 n. 61, 179

Letters, 126, 130, 179

Life, 56, 57, 58–59, 147

Light: above sound, 174; air associated

matter/as matter, 69, 70, 77, 169; in
Mind, 72; in One/of One, 19, 71,
72, 169; otherness as, 69, 70; Parmenides on, 175; partial, 118; in
phantastic art, 127; Pico on, 42–43,
44; Plotinus on, 69, 169 n. 2; relative, 70; in sensible realm, 70; in
shadow world, 125, 175; sophist on,
116, 125; *Sophist* on, 74–75, 84,
168, 206, 208; as univocal, 69, 78.
See also Being
Nous. *See* Mind, Plotinus's concept of
Numbers, 190 n. 26
Numenius, 98 n. 42

Oceanus, 99
Olympiodorus, 83, 87, 88, 89, 94
Olympius, 26, 27
One: as absolute, 168–169, 170; Aristotle on, 38, 72; as attribute of being,
42, 50; and being, 19, 35, 36, 37–48,
60, 68; before being, 169; being is,
38, 41–42, 45, 72, 77; being is not,
66; being is subordinate to, 2, 38,
39, 41, 45–46, 50, 59, 61, 64, 65,
67, 71, 72, 78, 82, 169; Christian
theology on, 38; and difference, 70;
Eleatics on, 78; essence from, 62;
father as, 112; and Good, 116; Idea
as, 49; as immanent, 169, 170; beyond knowledge, 78; limit and infinite from, 49, 62; and many, 56,
62, 63, 64; matter in, 70, 169; and
Mind, 56; motion and, 70; Neoplatonists on, 2, 45–46, 169; not-being
of, 19, 71, 72, 169; Parmenides on,
77; as *Parmenides* theme, 35, 36,
39, 41, 49, 56, 64, 67, 82, 86, 208;
Philebus on, 49, 61, 64; Pico on, 2,
35, 36, 41–42, 82; Plotinus on, 56,
70, 169; power of, 68; procession
from, 70, 112; Proclus on, 68, 168–
169; Pythagoreans on, 78; *Sophist*
on, 19, 41, 42, 44, 45, 50, 64, 82;
transcendence of, 71, 169; beyond
understanding, 78
Ontology, 35, 44, 55, 73. *See also*
Being

Optics, 174, 175, 184
Oratory, 153, 162
Orpheus, 80
Otherness, 69, 70. *See also* Not-being

Painting, 162; Ficino's influence on,
128 n. 12; icastic and phantastic,
117–118, 121–123, 125
Pannonius, Johannes, 22–23 n. 22, 51
n. 3
Panurge, 116
Parmenideans, 11, 19–20, 73, 79–80.
See also Melissus
Parmenides, 81, 115; on Being, 45, 46,
77, 80; Eleatic Stranger attacks, 168,
206; monism of, 44; on not-being,
175, 206; on One, 77; Plato influenced by, 11, 75, 79; poetic devices
of, 75–76; as Pythagorean, 73–74,
77, 79; on rest and flux, 13; Socrates
on, 11–12
Parmenides, 4, 16, 54, 210; arts of
demonstration and resolution in, 207,
208; on Being, 35, 36, 41, 64, 82;
as dialectic, 40, 46, 74; hypotheses
in, 55–56, 86, 168–170; Ideas in, 13,
49, 55; on many, 64, 71; Mind in,
55–56; monism of, 21; One as theme
of, 35, 36, 39, 41, 49, 56, 64, 67,
82, 86, 208; *Philebus* linked to, 49,
64; Pico on, 35, 36, 39–40, 44, 46,
47; Plotinus on, 55–56, 59, 86;
Plutarch on, 86; Proclus on, 18, 32,
39, 49, 55–56, 70–71, 170; *Sophist*
linked to, 13, 19, 33, 44, 49, 55–56,
59, 64, 73, 74, 85, 96, 209; *States-*
man linked to, 74; in teaching cycle,
39–40, 85–86, 88; *Timaeus* linked to,
86, 96
Parmenides commentary, 18, 31, 32,
33, 35, 47, 49, 51, 67, 73, 74, 75–
76, 94, 168–170, 189, 206
Paul of Middelburg, 134
Perception, 121–122, 132
Phaedo, 28–29, 55, 58, 87, 88, 126–
127
Phaedrus, 4, 10, 20, 27, 63, 139, 208,

Designer:	U.C. Press Staff
Compositor:	Prestige Typography
Text:	11/13 Times Roman
Display:	Times Roman
Printer:	Braun-Brumfield, Inc.
Binder:	Braun-Brumfield, Inc.